Debts without Redem
Cultural differences in First Wor

Aris Gaaff

Debts without Redemption

Cultural differences in First World War finance

Uitgeverij Aspekt

Debts without Redemption
Cultural differences in First World War finance
© 2017 Aris Gaaff
© 2017 Aspekt Publishers
Aspekt Publishers | Amersfoortsestraat 27
3769 AD Soesterberg | The Netherlands
info@uitgeverijaspekt.nl | www.uitgeverijaspekt.nl
Coverdesign: Mark Heuveling
Cover image: munitions factory, Chilwell, UK, 1917.
Lay-out: Paul Timmerman

ISBN: 978-94-6338-189-5
NUR: 680

This book is an enlarged and updated version of the original Dutch issue published by Aspekt
Publishers in the summer of 2014, titled *Vier jaar vechten op krediet* (Four years of fighting on
credit), ISBN 978-94-6153-212-1

Contents

Preface   9

1   War financing   13

Episode I – 1870-1914 Financial war plans and financial mobilisation
2   French reparations   29
3   *La Circulaire bleue*   35
4   *Finanzielle Kriegsbereitschaft?*   43
5   The City   53

Episode II – 1914-1919 Spending, creating and circulating money
6   War expenditure: beyond comprehension   65
7   Sources for funding: a menu with limited choices   77
8   Taxes: an inconvenient option for politicians   99
9   Domestic war loans: a patriotic mortgage on the future   117
10   Borrowing abroad: loyal allies or business relationships?   165
11   Monetary financing: the central bank as an ATM machine   187

Episode III – 1920-2015 The debts question: a century of small payments and large cancellations
12   Back to normalcy: mission impossible   203
13   The Financial Armistice of 1931   239
14   Clearing domestic debris   253
15   Two Wars later   273

Epilogue   283

Annex. What is the meaning of a sum of money of 1914-'18 a century later?   297
Glossary   303
Notes   309

Literature 355
    Some remarks on sources 355
    References 361

Index 379

'The problem of paying for the war was not tackled until after the war'

Paul Einzig, 1935[a]

---

a   Paul Einzig (1897-1973), economic and political writer, published many books on international finance. The quote is from *World Finance 1914-1935*, **Einzig** (1935), p. 51.

Preface

Innumerable books have been written about the First World War. In many publications on the subject, the number of casualties can be found. Although estimates may vary, a number of 9 to 10 million killed on the battlefield seems generally accepted, to which half as many civilians can be added. Apart from them, at least as many were wounded, for a lifetime disabled physically or mentally, drowned, deprived of their possessions or driven out of their country.

A question less generally answered, is how much the war has cost in *monetary* terms. In the majority of publications it remains unaddressed. Even in the flood of commemorative treatises, new or re-edited, appearing on the occasion of the centenary of the Great War, the issue of paying for the war receives little attention, let alone the question of how, by whom and when. This is strange, as money in all its vulgarity forms an easy, visible and measurable indicator for the way society functions. In extreme situations, among which wars certainly are the most obvious ones, this is even more pronounced. The question of financing the Great War has fascinated me ever since I realised, some 35 years ago, that the well-known German reparations were only a link in a worldwide chain of debts that had been built up over four years of fighting. The question of how these debts arose and how they were (not) settled is at least as intriguing as the question who started the war and who was to blame.

For military historians and generals alike, financing a war is a non-issue. John Keegan, for example, in his standard work on the Great War, spends not a single word on the hundreds of billions that have been spent during the war (in currency values of 1914-'18, of course).[1] Barbara Tuchman, in her otherwise very detailed account of August 1914, gives no more than a glimpse of the financial panic in the weeks before the war.[2] The shelf of works on the financial aspects of the war is very, very modest in comparison to the total bookcase, or rather: the library of works on the

First World War. And an overview over the complete period, starting from 1870 up to 2015 was still lacking.

Indeed, every history has its own pre-history and its aftermath. The war itself lasted just over four years, from August 1914 to the Armistice on 11 November 1918. War preparations, however, started long before the outbreak, not only in the military domain, but also in the field of finance. In this book, I obviously place the period 1914 in a central position, but the developments in Europe in the decades 1870-1914 form an indispensable background for understanding war finance itself. During that period the minds, prejudice and reflexes were formed of those who were to lead the financial war. And the story of war financing certainly did not end in 1918, although the populations in the various countries might have expected so. The war had generated unprecedented debts that would dominate and spoil for decades domestic and international relations. Politicians were forced to deal with the impossible mission of cleaning up the mess of four years of practically unlimited spending – to some extent a familiar phenomenon in the light of the 2008 financial crisis and its present aftermath.

Dealing with a time span of 150 years implies that certain details – and sometimes more than details – can only be touched upon, but not worked out. In some instances, I chose one or two countries as case studies to describe and explain a characteristic phenomenon. In other areas, I focused on the differences between countries. Although the basic principles are equal for every country financing a war, governments have dealt with it in their own way, driven by tradition, culture and personal choices. Textbooks on economic and financial theories generally make no distinction between countries and nations, as if it does not matter. In the First World War, governments did make their own – and not seldom different – choices. It is an open question whether they were free to do so, but it is evident that they did. It was one of the challenges in writing this book to make these differences visible and comprehensible.

Emphasis in this book is on the four major western players: Germany, France, Britain and the United States. The list of references contains sufficient suggestions for further reading. In line with this self-restriction,

I have sought to present only some characteristic graphs and avoided annexes filled with figures and tables.[a] These details can all be found in the – admittedly – fragmented literature and the reader is invited to form her or his own judgement. For there are many lessons to be learned, even if the action took place a century ago. Indeed, the fundamental choices that were made remain the same: how does a society distribute, in war and in peace, burdens and benefits among individuals, groups and generations.

One final word might be said about the structure of this book. Behind the 'cold' statistics in pounds, dollars, *marks* or *francs*, there are always people; people who implemented the clean and technical mechanisms of lending, borrowing, taxation and servicing debts. This immense army of bank employees, collecting clerks, cashiers, tax officials and as least as many volunteers remains practically unknown to us. Their stories have been recorded much, much less than those of the *tommies*, *poilus* or *Frontschweine* in the trenches. Probably, these stories will be less spectacular, but certainly no less instructive. We know little of it, and we will have to content ourselves with the likewise scarce material about the financial generals, those colourful guardians of the treasury and governors of central banks who led the financial war. I have inserted short biographical sketches of some of the major players. What we see, are not men in military dress, but respectable middle-aged citizens in tailored suits; their most powerful piece of artillery was often simply the banknote printing press. We should, however realise that even their names, at that time as well-known as Alan Greenspan, Ben Bernanke, Mario Draghi or Christine Lagarde, have been almost forgotten and that first-hand information is not abundant. Unfortunately for historians, bankers seldom write their memoirs.[b]

---

a   The notes, the annex with some economic terminology, and the list of references give (much) more detail. *Footnotes* (such as this one) present short commentaries or contextual information, intended for easy reading. The numbered *endnotes* contain detailed references to the literature, accounts of calculations and remarks of a methodological nature.

b   A notable exception is the governor of the *Banque de France* Émile Moreau in his rather unreserved narrative of a short but crucial period in French and international finance, published in abridged form as early as in 1937 and posthumously in a detailed volume of over 600 pages in 1954 (English translation: 1991).

I wish to thank the employees of the *Banque de France*, the Bank of England and the Imperial War Museums for their help and suggestions in the preparation of this book. Furthermore, the research would not have been impossible but certainly physically much heavier without the digital services of the Federal Reserve Bank of St. Louis, the UK Parliament, the *Bayerische Staatsbibliothek*, The Economist and the National Library of the Netherlands.

Above all, I wish to thank those people who have given me, without any personal interest, useful comments, text corrections and suggestions. In alphabetical order, I mention Patrick Dassen, Jeroen Euwe, Jane Harrold, Ed Jansen, Roel Jongeneel, Hein Klemann, Henk van der Linden, Barend Linders, Arnaud Manas, Marie-Luise Rau, Geert Woltjer and last, but not least, my wife Elly Verzaal. Of course, all remaining inaccuracies are mine.

1

War financing

*'Economic sacrifices demanded of the people by war cannot be
reduced or shuffled off on to future generations by any financial policy'*
The Economist[a]

A war is waged with men, material and strategy, not with coins, banknotes and portfolios of securities.[1] This may be true, but equally correct
one might say that without sufficient financial means a war will not last
and will not lead to victory. Soldiers need to be fed and transported, ammunition needs to be produced, wounded need to be looked after, etc.;
this is all impossible without money. War and money are inseparable and
history is full of examples. Mercenary troops have dominated European
battlefields for centuries. The Bank of England owes its foundation to
a group of businessmen who were prepared to rescue King William III
with a credit in the Nine Years' War.[2] Money really is 'the sinews of war'.
The First World War is no exception. The only difference is scale. The
intensity and industrial technology gave rise to unprecedented expenditure that required enormous financing mechanisms imposed on all parties involved.

A financing problem for governments

The governments of all belligerent countries faced the same problem and
their solutions were to a certain degree the same. Expenditure had to be
funded in order to pay the armies on the battlefield, to buy guns and
battleships, to provide medical care and to pay widows and orphans. No
country could pay this from normal, peacetime government revenues.
While expenditure increased explosively, revenues lagged far behind;
payments could not wait. All countries had budget deficits from the first
day of the war; and if they had a deficit before the war it only increased.
The subject of this book is the way in which countries tackled this

---

a   The Economist 30 September 1939, p. 590.

problem, with emphasis on Britain, France, Germany and the United States.

During the war the problem of financing was a problem for finance ministers and central bank presidents. It hardly reached the general public, with the obvious exception of the large war loans that were issued with an appeal to patriotism (Chapter 9). Not only was the man in the street ignorant, parliaments were not well informed either. Indeed in Europe they had excluded themselves from the beginning, with the notable exception of the British parliament. The German *Reichstag* had effectively transferred financial war management to the (non-elected) *Bundesrat* on 4 August 1914; on the same day the French *Assemblée Nationale* and the *Sénat* had passed its power in an analogous way to the Council of Ministers and the Council of State, both institutions without a mandate from elections. In Austria the situation was even worse: parliament had ceased its meetings as early as March 1914 (in contrast to the Hungarian parliament) and the Russian Duma had already been a symbolic company before the war. On the European continent financial war management had been effectively disposed of any serious democratic legitimacy. It was at the mercy of a restricted inner circle of middle-aged men led by examples from the past and by prejudice – and by the demands of the military commanders, of course.

Before the war there had been heated discussions on armament programmes and their financial consequences. Notably in Britain and Germany, military commanders had to employ all their power of moral persuasion to raise sufficient financial backing for their plans of extending the army and the navy. Compared with the expenditure during the war however, these pre-war budgets were peanuts although contemporaries perceived it differently. They had been impressed by the magic of unprecedented *nominal* amounts. It is true that German military expenditure jumped ahead between 1901 and 1913 from less than 900 million *marks* to over 1,600 million *marks* while the French military budget rose from 1.1 billion *francs* to 1.9 billion *francs*.[3] What was overlooked was the enormous expansion of the economy during these years. In terms of the national economy, as measured by **GDP**,[a] the growth was much

---

a   Gross Domestic Product. Some financial or economic expressions that appear regularly in this book have been listed in a glossary at the end (page 303). The first time that an entry appears in the text, it is marked **boldface**. A definition of 'money' can also be found in the glossary.

less spectacular: from 2.7% to 2.9% in Germany and from 3.2% to 3.8% in France.[4] In the decades before the war, military expenditure claimed a relatively modest share of the national economy, despite large-scale armaments programmes.[5]

However, at the moment that the war had started, all normal mechanisms of assessment were abandoned.[6] In normal times, a proposal to spend 40% of the national economy to just one objective would have been regarded as complete madness; during the war it became the most natural thing in the world (Chapter 6). If money played a role in decisions at all, it was a secondary one. With an appeal to the Emperor, the King, the country, *la patrie*, any argument of reason could be suppressed; a practical and temporarily valid argument was that the war would be short and financial shortages soon resolved.

War expenditure and war costs

This books deals with the way the war was financed, not with the purpose of the expenditure such as ammunition, food, clothing and transport. In short: the central theme is revenue, not expenditure. Expenditure is taken more or less as an external factor, dictated by strategy, innovation and progress on the battlefield. In fact, that is just what it was for the finance ministers in war cabinets, although they sometimes uttered doubts when resources were wasted. Therefore the main subjects are: tax measures (Chapter 8), domestic war loans (Chapter 9), borrowing abroad (Chapter 10) and monetary financing, the so-called printing press (Chapter 11). In doing so, we incidentally get an impression of the expenditure and of the differences in financing mechanisms in the belligerent countries. As an overview, Chapter 7 analyses the most important financing mechanisms and their advantages and disadvantages.

Although expenditure itself is given, it is good to have a look at the gigantic amount of money that was spent on the war; this will be done in Chapter 6, both for the whole war and for individual countries. This expenditure is expressed in a sum of money; they express the *money* costs of the war. Expenditure implies sums of money actually paid in a transaction. There is always a counterpart for whom expenditure (by the government) is a source of income: a soldier, an arms supplier, shipyard, a food trader, a railway company or an investor who receives interest on his war bond.

It is essential to distinguish *expenditure* from *costs*. War costs refer to a much broader concept, a concept that is hard to express in monetary terms – and even then only partially.[a] War costs represent the wealth that has been lost by waging war instead of living on peacefully.[7] A part of these costs is material; this part consists of the production that otherwise would have been realised and the consumption that would otherwise have been enjoyed. Using economic theory and a lot of assumptions about historical development in the absence of war, something could be said about this part, albeit not without effort.[8] An other part of the war costs however is immaterial: loss of lives, disability, starvation, deprivation, refugees, all misery that is in fact the largest expense of the war, although it cannot be reasonably expressed in money and even not in numbers. They remain out of sight when we are talking about expenditure. We have to rely on literature, works of art, music, and narratives of combatants and their homefolks instead of economy or finance to catch a glimpse of these real war costs.[9]

Financing, economy and the role of the nation state

Although finance is the central theme in the following chapters, it is worthwhile to spend a few words on economic backgrounds. In everyday life the concepts 'finance' and 'economy' are easily interchanged. Finance is restricted to money in all its forms, from coins to long-term loans, from capital to tax revenue. Economy deals with production and consumption, satisfaction of human needs for goods and services and the use of scarce resources. Much can be said – and in fact has been said – about the economic aspects of warfare. Many publications on the subject have chosen for a more economic than a financial perspective.[b] Economic aspects of the First World War deal with subjects such as production of military equipment, dependence on external resources, the significance of domestic agriculture for food production, mining and steel industry, transport, employment, imports and exports, hoarding,

---

a   In publications on 'war costs' the word 'costs' is often misleading. They mostly deal with *money* costs, that is: expenditure. For example **Bogart** (1920), *Direct and indirect Costs of the Great World War*, concentrates on expenditure, but also mentions some other 'costs'. On the other hand, **Clark** (1931), *The Costs of the World War to the American People* analyses a wider concept of costs; a critical discussion can be found in **Broadberry & Harrison** (2005), a modern and accessible overview from the economic viewpoint, in particular p. 22 ff. and p. 333. See also the section 'Some remarks on sources', page 355.

b   Exceptions can be found in the older literature, written shortly after the war and the more recent work of **Strachan** (2004) which all make a rather strict financial delimitation.

etc. Research and development and medical findings during the war can also be placed in the economic domain to some extent.

At a sufficiently high level of abstraction, the economic picture is fairly simple. When the war broke out, a new actor with a large demand entered the market: the national state, represented by the government. Its purpose was to reshape social and economic processes such as to maximise the military effectiveness at the battlefield, while at the same time continuing indispensable civil tasks despite the withdrawal of a substantial labour force. To achieve this, the government could employ economic, financial and other means and quite often they were combined. Among economic measures were forced mobilisation of labour by conscription, nationalising vital industries or placing them under government control, food rationing, encouraging women to work in industry and fixing non-market prices.[10] Financial instruments for example were higher taxation (Chapter 8), restrictions on ownership and on free trade of foreign currency and gold (Chapters 3 and 11), issuing loans and intentionally keeping interest rates low (Chapter 11). Apart from that, the government could – and did – use moral suasion to change the process of production and consumption into the direction of its own benefit (Chapter 9). And finally the government could apply what may be called support policies by imposing restrictions on the press; this blocked free exchange of information, a crucial element in the economic process.[a] Evidently, the government could not change fundamental economic laws. It could however change the rules of the game by special legislation to its own benefit. And it could circumvent rules that other market parties had to obey.

One should realise, that the use of financial instruments by the government tacitly assumes the existence of a liberal economic system, where the government is just one of many actors in the market, albeit a special one. A different reality was inconceivable in the world of 1914. All nations had started the war from the fundamentals of a nineteenth century liberal economic principle of free markets and free trade, where the government purchases its goods and services to wage the war. Of all belligerent countries, this system had the strongest tradition in Britain,

---

a   Apart, of course, from military censorship for strategic reasons. A clear illustration of an indirect intervention in the economic process was the prohibition of the publication of stock prices and exchange rates in Germany, issued 25 February 1915, **RT** 315, nr. 43 p. 87.

where – at least at the beginning of the war, before conscription – the government had to buy military force on the labour market.[11]

Although governments used all kinds of instruments to control the economic system, not a single country assumed the shape of a totalitarian regime during the First World War. In such a system the national state claims *all* production factors (labour, capital, land) by force and hence money becomes symbolic. In 1916 Germany started to move into that direction with the so-called *Hindenburg programme* – not by accident named after the highest military commander. It was not implemented to the extreme.[a] In Germany in 1917 and 1918 liberal and capitalist ideas were (still) too strong to reshape society in such a way as to allow for an economy directed towards total war.

Economic sources for war financing
In the end, a country has only two legal sources to provide for the material costs of the war: the current, annual national income and its national wealth or national capital.[12] These are the only sources that are immediately available. The future has not yet materialised and any appeal to it must take place through these two sources. In addition to these legal sources, there are indeed a few illegal sources such as requisitions in occupied territories, confiscations of ships and blocking bank accounts of citizens from hostile countries, and finally: reparations. Apart from reparations, all these sources are called upon *during* the war, although it may not always be realised by the population or even by the authorities.[13] A new tax, for example, instantly influences national income because it diverts the options for consumption by the population (and this, of course, is exactly what the government is trying to achieve). In the same way, subscription to a domestic war loan has an impact on the subscriber's consumption opportunities or his or her capital, depending on whether it was paid from current expenditure or from savings; again, this impact is effected *instantly*, not sometime after the war. The

---

a   The programme comprised, among other measures, general conscription for men between 17 and 60 years old, increase of arms production and improvement of (transport) infrastructure, **Hardach** (1987), p. 181 ff., **Roesler** (1967), p. 98. The objective was to nationalise the economy and make it subordinate to warfare. According to **Von Mises** (1974), p. 77, rigorous implementation would have meant that Germany had become a totalitarian state. The lobbying in the preparation of the programme and the role of the military-industrial complex are described for example in **Armeson** (1964) and in more detail in **Feldman** (1966).

only thing that happens in this case is a transfer of wealth between individuals and groups in society. Financing the war by means of loans merely shifts wealth from the subscribers to the government, which they assume to recover after the war in the form of interest and principal payments from the government. The total wealth however does not change by loans as such.

What did change wealth was the way in which the economic value was employed. Practically without exception this has been destructively and not intended to create wealth *during* the war.[a] The only way to yield return on the investments was by a final victory. If this was not realised, or in the case that a claim on the defeated party did not materialise, all investments would prove to be unproductive and the invested capital and labour lost and wealth destroyed instead of created. This would in fact be the outcome for all participating countries after the First World War. The *distribution* of this loss among the population depended in the first place on political choices. It was however not independent of the way of financing the war: as the example of war loans shows, financing instruments determined expectations among the population about wealth distribution after the war (Chapter 7 and Chapter 12).

From an analytical and methodological point of view it is useful to distinguish these economic sources. They constitute the 'real' economic background against which monetary flows act.[14] These flows of money, the subject of this book, represent the government's revenue to pay the bill of the war. The amounts and the nature of these flows, in other words, express the ways by which governments have mobilised the economic sources of their countries to cover their expenditure: to finance the war.[15] Money makes the use of economic resources tangible (see also the box on page 20). Finance therefore was closer to the perception of those who were to decide about these resources, and that is precisely what makes it interesting. After the war, even some basic economic truths would completely get out of sight and the discussion would be confined to money.[b (next page)]

---

a   That is, apart from a few adventurers and arms manufacturers who derived real benefits from the war on its own. For the population as a whole, it is hard to maintain that wealth increased by exploding shells on a distant battlefield thereby destructing productive labour force or disabling them for lifetime. A war is not a fireworks show.

How to use financial instruments to exploit economic sources

There were several ways to use the two economic sources national income and national wealth. The most direct way was through the current national income as it was determined by production and consumption. Both were not invariable; in fact they could be re-adjusted by the carrot and the stick to enhance the share of war production. A financial instrument to this end was the introduction of extra taxes on luxury goods, or on war profits, or simply on all private consumer goods (Chapter 8). New levies on imported products, in particular products that were not indispensable for the war industry, made resources available for the purchase of goods that were necessary for the war industry or to secure foreign loans (Chapter 7 and 9).[16]

Using accumulated national wealth brought about more difficulties; not all forms of capital could be liquidated easily or even completely, but in view of the total amount of national wealth it was worthwhile for governments to seize as much as they could. Stocks of goods could be used, which in fact meant an acceleration of their consumption. But most capital was fixed in a form that was not directly accessible for use in warfare. It might be true that German national wealth ('Volksvermögen') had been estimated before the war at an amount of 350 billion marks, but 80% of it consisted of fixed assets such as land, buildings, industrial plants, infrastructure etc.[17] The most simple way to use up these fixed assets was by refraining from regular replacement investments, a slow but effective way to decrease the value of the invested capital. Wealth in the form of bank deposits could easily be mobilised by means of war loans (Chapter 9) or by devaluating it by printing new paper money with insufficient gold backing (Chapters 11 and 14).

Personal property, such as gold and other valuables, and foreign securities could easily be seized and mobilised by the government, both by law and with heavy moral and social pressure. Restrictions on the possession of these assets and programmes to surrender these forms of capital

---

b   To mention just two post-war examples: Britain and France demanded that Germany paid reparations but did not want the country to realise the export surplus to pay these reparations; The United States imposed import barriers, but at the same time demanded that France and Britain repaid their loans in dollars.

were an almost universal part of a government's repertoire to mobilise wealth. An example was the massive purchase by the British government of foreign securities from citizens (Chapter 10). By transferring them to the United States, it not only diminished national wealth but also future national income: British citizens would no longer receive dividends on the American railway bonds they had sold during the war. Borrowing abroad caused a similar effect: it created negative wealth. At the moment itself it was only a paper loss of wealth. (For the country that lent the money, the loss of wealth was real and immediate, for example by reduced consumption. Ultimately, foreign borrowing was a shift of the loss of wealth to the creditor country until the loan would be repaid. After the war it would be a real loss when interest and principal payments had to be made. In contrast to servicing domestic loans, this would become a substantial financial and economic burden. The distribution of this burden among the population needed to be determined, a difficult task that explains the persistent – and largely successful – attempts to get out of it (Chapter 12).

Restrictions...

It is impossible to analyse all aspects of financing of the First World War *and* its inseparable aftermath in one book, probably not even in three volumes. The most important geographical restriction here, is that Eastern Front and neutral countries are largely disregarded, apart from an occasional remark about the curious Russian tax system and Dutch commercial loans to Germany. On the side of the western allies, the analysis certainly does not do justice to the ingenious British war savings programme, the issue of local money in occupied Belgium and northern France and – partially imposed by lack of data – to the subscriptions to war loans by social classes.

The **Gold Standard**, important as it was in both domestic and international monetary systems, is only present in the background. In the period before the war, the Latin monetary union was an important political and monetary institution, for which the reader is referred to the literature, both in its historical and current significance.[18] The German hyperinflation of 1922/'23 is addressed only in the context of (domestic) war debts. Despite these restrictions, there remain sufficient storylines and details. One of the most prominent lines is the difference between countries that will appear in many – and sometimes unexpected – places.

...and perspective

As opposed to limitations, there are extensions as well. So far, emphasis in this chapter has been on finance and economy *during* the war period proper: 1914-1918. Finance however by its nature has longer-term implications. The history of financing the Great War spans almost one and a half centuries, from 1870 to 2015 with a continuously changing focus. It is not difficult to divide this long period in three large episodes: before the war, during the war and after the war, with short transitory periods in between as shown in illustration 1.1. The remaining chapters of this book have been structured along these lines.

Phases in the military/political development of the First World War and its financial counterpart (Illustration 1.1)

	period	military and political events	financial facts and measures
Episode I	until August 1914	war plans	preparation of crisis measures; building 'war chest'
chapters 2-5	August 1914	mobilisation	restriction on gold imports and exports; suspending convertibility; rapid issue of paper money
Episode II chapters 6-11	August 1914 – November 1918	hostilities	financing war expenditure
Episode III	November 1918 – circa 1920/'21	armistice; demobilisation; peace treaty	specification of reparations; continuous borrowing; preliminary agreements on inter-ally debts
chapters 12-15	after 1921 – 2015	aftermath (reconstruction, political turmoil, war invalids, ...)	aftermath (currency depreciation, new debts, devaluation, cancellation of debts, ...)

Episode I. The first period is the one of war preparation. While the military commanders prepared the next war – with the previous one in mind – French and German forwardly looking financial policy makers anticipated the conflict and took measures in order to be prepared. The preparations differed by country, depending on the sense of urgency and the balance of power among financial institutions within the country. Many years, even decades before the war broke out, secret measures were taken: law texts were written, secret agreements signed and banknotes printed, just in case. When tensions rose in July 1914, financial mobilisation measures could be implemented as easily as military mobilisation measures. The financial preparations ran synchronously with the railway timetables to transport the soldiers to the front. This period, including the mobilisation, is covered in Episode I of this book, that is: Chapters 2-5.

Episode II, comprising Chapters 6-11, addresses actual war financing in all its variety. These chapters analyse the mechanisms to provide the money to pay for the inconceivable expenditure. Again, emphasis is on the three large western European belligerents: Germany, France and the British Empire, and of course, on the United States as a universal lender, both before and after it entered the war in April 1917.

Other European parties involved in the conflict are missing in this list and this is not because they are not interesting. Austria-Hungary for example would be a beautiful historic case study of essentially two countries with different economies and a common currency; they issued separate war loans. Their warfare and preparation probably showed as much improvisation on the financial side as it did in military aspects, whereas the aftermath was distributed over numerous successor states. The tsarist and later revolutionary Russia mainly played the role of a questionable debtor both before, during and after the war. Italy is interesting too, because it promised to take the side of the allies only after negotiating a bonus package including a substantial loan. And finally, the enormous contributions of the overseas countries of the British Commonwealth (apart from those on the battlefield) remain out of sight together with their financial relations with the European homeland.

The Armistice of 11 November 1918 marked the end of hostilities in the trenches but in the financial arena it was only the beginning. What followed was a period of tough negotiations between the victors about peace conditions, including the financial consequences of the peace, to paraphrase Keynes. It lasted two and a half years until 1921 before it became clear what these consequences entailed, although even then they were not generally recognised. This marks the transition to Episode III.

Episode III describes and analyses the most important milestones in the traumatic aftermath (Chapters 12-15). This is the period of never-ending negotiations and conferences meant to clean up the mess of four years unlimited borrowing and creating money. Since the issues of war debts and reparations are completely entangled, they have been taken together in one long chapter (Chapter 12). Only after the Second World War a sustainable solution could be formulated, but even then it lasted almost half a century and a Cold War to be fully implemented. The financial closure of the accounts (and even that only partially) took place some years after the last veteran had passed away.[a]

These three parts are written from different perspectives:
In Episode I, we look forwards from the relatively comfortable position at the end of the nineteenth century where the financial planners were preparing an uncertain future with the knowledge they had at that time.

In Episode II, we are in the midst of the turmoil of financial warfare. Loans and tax measures are flying around as heavy or light missiles to have their devastating effect or just to blow over. The reader for whom this is too intense an experience can find refuge behind the frontline in the short biographies of the 'money marshals'. Or, he or she may desert from the battlefield and stealthily flee to Episode III and look in agreeable spas for the company of diplomats who determinedly tried to continue the battle with other means for some decades.

The epilogue offers the reader – armoured with a good deal of hindsight – the possibility to perceive what is still relevant today and what has become history.

Converting currency

Some publications systematically convert amounts of money to one single currency, for example American dollars. This facilitates a comparison, but it does not do justice to diverging developments of currencies, both internationally and in domestic use over time. In many instances in this book sums of money are denoted in their original currency with indications of that amount in dollars or pounds to make comparisons easier. French francs are called 'francs' and German marks 'marks', both in italics. 'Frank' is the Belgian frank/franc. The 'gold mark' was the

---

a   In fact, one of the most recent developments, the redemption of the large British 3.5% War Loan, took place in March 2015 between the first and second Dutch editions of this book.

value of the German currency before the war (in the Gold Standard era); the expression was often used after the war to distinguish it from the inflating mark; from 1924-1948 German currency was officially called 'reichsmark'.

Just to get a first and global impression of the value, it helps to know that 1 pound Sterling (£) was worth 5 American dollars ($) and that 1 dollar was roughly 4 marks or 5 francs. These are the pre-war exchange values based on gold parity; some of them, notably the Stirling-dollar ratio was rather stable during the war. By multiplication, £ 1 corresponded to 25 francs, which makes the Stirling values appear smaller in comparison to francs. For example, a French loan in London of £ 50 million corresponded to 1.25 billion francs. In the Annex not only pre-war exchange rates are presented but also those of 1919 and 1929 as an illustration of various devaluations (page 299).

A rule of thumb for conversion of exchange rates at the beginning of the war:

£ 1 <--> 25 francs <--> 20 marks <--> $ 5 <--> 25 frank

Episode I

1870-1914

Financial war plans and financial mobilisation

2

French reparations

'gaz à tous les étages'[a]

The legacy of the Franco-Prussian War

If there exists one history of the First World War that starts with the Franco-Prussian War of 1870-1871, it is the history of finance. 'France pays His Majesty the German Emperor the sum of 5 billion *francs*'. Thus, it was stated bluntly in Article 2 of the provisional peace treaty of February 1871, signed by the German Chancellor Otto von Bismarck and the acting French Head of state Adolphe Thiers.[1] In contrast to the Treaty of Versailles, signed almost half a century later, there is no mention of responsibility for causing the war. In 1871 it was still the most natural thing in the world that a defeated country had to pay, whoever had started the conflict. Even the word 'reparation' is not used in the provisional treaty – in fact a more formalised armistice; the expression used is 'contribution', suggesting that it covers only part of the costs. The final Treaty of Frankfurt (May 1871) reads more or less as a technical elaboration of conditions France had to meet than as an agreement between two sovereign countries. France is given a period of barely three years to comply, the deadline being 2 March 1874.[2] And France had little choice because German troops had invaded far into France (Paris was occupied, Le Mans just captured) and their withdrawal was subject to the payments.

An amount of 5 billion *francs* was by no means insignificant. It represented roughly 25% of French GDP at that time.[3] It also equalled 2.5 times the annual tax revenue, which meant that if France had to pay it

---

a   'Gas on all floors'. The blue enamelled signs with this text on the frontage of Parisian apartment buildings indicated that in the late nineteenth century modern comfort had reached the highest (and most modest) floors. Outside Paris, they are notably found in Strasbourg, be it in the German language: *Gas in allen Étagen*. Although Strasbourg, capital of Alsace, was part of the German Empire from 1870-1918, the signs indicate that culturally it remained French – at least to some extent.

from taxation within the required three years, more than 80% of the tax revenue would have been dedicated to reparation payments, which was virtually impossible.[4] It was clear that France had to resort to other means of funding. Payment in French *francs* notes was no option, since this had been explicitly excluded in the treaty. Germany wanted to avoid being paid less in case of a devaluation of the *franc*. There was one exception: France was allowed to pay one first instalment of 125 million *francs* in notes of the *Banque de France*, provided that they were delivered within 25 days. Bismarck apparently had sufficient confidence in the *Banque*.[a] After all, it was only 2.5% of the total amount and quick delivery was worth the risk as it provided a practical way of paying purchases by the occupying forces.

How France settled the reparations bill

For the remaining 4.875 billion *francs*, France had three options to pay: (1) in gold or silver in bullion, (2) in Prussian bank notes or bank notes issued in neighbouring countries with sound currencies,[5] or (3) in international **bills of exchange** drawn in one of these currencies. Although they appealed to the imagination, payments in gold or silver were less than 10% of the total 5 billion *francs*.[6] Stories that it was as though gold was poured into Germany in railway wagons did not conform to the real state of affairs.

In reality, France used predominantly payments by means of bills of exchange to meet its reparations obligation.[7] The French government bought those bills from citizens, private companies, banks or other institutions and transferred them directly or through banks to Germany or neighbouring countries. In these markets, they were sold and the French government received *marks* or other eligible currency to pay the reparations. To understand this procedure, one might compare it to a foreign government buying travellers cheques in dollars or in pounds that travellers had bought and stored in their drawers for future use.[b] International trade in the nineteenth century (and a long time

---

a   Bismarck was not the only one to acknowledge the value of the *billet* of the *Banque*. At the same time the Paris Communists – politically exactly Bismarck's opposites – appealed to the *Banque* just as easily, **Ahamed** (2010), p. 246.

b   As always, the comparison is not rigourous. In contrast to travellers cheques, bills of exchange had a well-determined expiration date. Purchase by the French government had to be made before that date.

afterwards) depended heavily on the use of these bills, which were traded at financial markets in London, and to a much lesser extent, in Paris and Berlin.[8] Thus, the French government (or its intermediates) acted as a purchasing party in these markets. It was a relatively easy task, because there were many outstanding German debts, particularly in London. They were both commercial debts and short-term public loans that the German government had contracted to finance the war.[9] The whole operation amounted to France buying out German international debt; it took place almost completely on paper, apart from the relatively modest physical gold transfers.

France financed these transactions by a parallel activity: the issue of public loans. Apart from a private loan of 1.5 billion *francs* at the *Banque de France*, the government launched two large public loans of 2 and 3 billion *francs*, respectively. Within one year, the French government possessed sufficient means to perform the said transactions in the financial markets. The loans were an overwhelming success.[10] The first one raised the sum of 2 billion *francs* within one day, the second one, in July 1872, was 12 times oversubscribed (this, by the way, reflected the smooth operation of the international financial markets in the second half of the nineteenth century). There was a broad syndicate of banks involved and the subscribers were certainly not restricted to French citizens. Many wealthy Europeans or institutions were attracted to invest in French national debt; after all, the **effective yield** was 6% and the bonds were considered safe. No less than one third of all subscriptions came from Germany and even funds of German invalids were believed to have invested in these French bonds.[11] In contrast to the war loans of 1914-'18, it was not necessary for the government to appeal to patriotic feelings, although undoubtedly some Frenchmen might have sold their foreign securities to buy the new bonds.[12] It was the financial return that dominated. Again, by the way, it can be noticed that the financial markets were highly internationally interwoven and open in the late nineteenth century Europe.

The loans – and the simultaneous transactions in the financial markets – allowed France to pay off its reparations bill half a year before the deadline of 2 March 1874. No doubt, at first sight this was a remarkable performance and a boost of French national pride. This may have contributed to the fact that they were easily forgotten and not collectively remembered – at least outside France! – in contrast to the traumatic German reparations imposed by the Treaty of Versailles. Thanks to the loans, the financial burden of the debt was spread out over a long period. The reparation debt of the government of France to the government of Germany had been effectively transformed into the prevalent public debt of a state to private bondholders. Within three years, French reparations had been depoliticised and commercialised.

The consequences of the reparations for France and for Germany

Of course, the obligation to pay had not disappeared economically or financially. France had merely exchanged the short-term debt to the German Empire into a long-term debt to French and foreign private bondholders.[13] In acting so, France literally had drawn a bill on the future. Indeed, the loans required a long-lasting heavy burden on the budget in the form of interest payments. They added to the already enormous public debt of France before the Franco-Prussian War, estimated at 60%-65% of the national economy. The French economy itself flourished, but the growth rate of the debt surpassed it easily. During the years 1870-1874 the rate of the debt in terms of annual GDP would rise to 78% and five years later even to 100%. Around 1900 it peaked at 140%.[14] Modern rating agencies would not have hesitated to condemn late 19th century France to junk status.

France's already relatively high national debt increased rapidly after the Franco-Prussian War (Illustration 2.1)

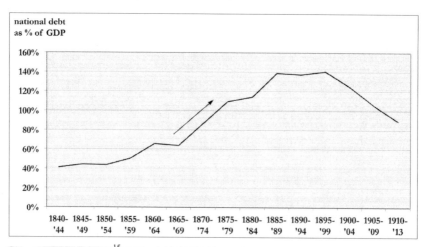

Source: CEPII, Bonney.[15]

Despite the debt burden imposed on France by Germany, the decades from 1875 to 1905 were not poisoned by financial animosity and bitter debates over reparations, as would be the case after the First World War. In France, worries had been averted – at least for the time being. The country entered a period of robust economic growth, development of international trade, technological innovation and a strong belief in progress; the Eiffel Tower, erected for the World Fair of 1889, is still the visible reminder. It is not a coincidence that this period of prosperity, roughly from 1880 to 1914 and peaking around 1900, is often referred to with its French name: *la belle époque*, literally: the beautiful era. Above all, it is the French memory of the past that gave it its rosy name only after the First World War. At the time itself, it was certainly not all beautiful for everyone, as can be read in Hector Malot's *Nobody's Boy* (French original: *Sans famille*, without family). Reality was that the last decades of the 19th century were years of unbridled liberalism, capitalism and colonialism. The simple fact that 9.5 million people emigrated from North and Western Europe to the United States in the period 1874-1914 shows that not everyone shared in general prosperity and progress.[16]

Whereas France did not suffer visibly after the Franco-Prussian War, on the other side of the Rhine, in Germany, the war left different traces. A single impulse of 20% of the economy cannot remain without consequences.[17] Although there were investments in the real economy, for instance in new railways with effects in supply industries (coal, iron, steel), the flow of 'free' money entailed what it always does: inflation and speculation.[18] Within two years, from August 1870 to November 1872, the Berlin stock exchange index rose by 100%, a boom that is partially attributed to positive expectations about reparations.[19] Undoubtedly these expectations contributed, but at least initially the fact that the French government acted as a purchasing party in the financial markets might have boosted prices as well. In 1873 the German stock exchange crashed and it would decline further for another four years. The Germans got the wind up and the positive connotation of the *Gründerzeit* (Founder Epoch) became mixed with the depression years 1870 and '80, decades in which victorious Germany did not perform economically better than defeated France. Anyhow, Bismarck is said to have declared in despair that at the next victory over France, Germany would insist on paying reparations instead of receiving them.[20] Although

Germany in fact lost the following war, in this respect he would not have been disappointed.

Assessment

French reparations after the war of 1870/'71 seemed to have done more harm to Germany than to France. In France, resentment about the lost territory of Alsace and Lorraine dominated, and reparations played no significant role, although they were not forgotten. After the First World War, in 1919, they would appear again in the French press, inflated by accrued interest to an amount of 60 billion *francs*.[21]

France itself would enter the Great War with by far the largest national debt of all countries involved in the conflict, apart from Italy. The annual burden on the budget – mainly interest payments – was twice as large as in Britain, with a population that was 10% smaller.[22] This large debt found its origin largely in the Franco-Prussian War of 1870/'71 and its reparations bill.

3

La Circulaire bleue

'When war broke out, the Banque was ready for it'
Georges Robineau, 1923[a]

A financial fortress of national defence

In the years preceding the Great War, France lived in the optimistic supposition that it was financially strong, at least stronger than Germany. These feelings of self-assurance were based on its large investments abroad, expanding colonial empire and massive gold reserve.[b] This strong position was felt a prerequisite for victory in a future military conflict.[1]

Some day this war would come. Although reparations of 1870-'71 did not dominate the political debate, the traumatic and tangible loss of Alsace-Lorraine was well alive and called for revenge. Reconquering these territories formed a tacitly accepted motive for being prepared for a new war. The military commanders developed one plan after the other to defend the country, *la patrie*, against attacks from the east; at the eve of the First World War, the current plan was Plan XVII. Meanwhile, the *Banque de France* constructed what they would call later 'one of the most powerful lines of national defence'.[2] The core of it was the systematically strengthened gold reserve, that would make France prepared for 'any eventuality', the code word for revenge for 1870.[3] By doing so, the *Banque* tacitly made the necessary preparations for the next war.

---

a   Robineau (1860-1927) was Governor of the *Banque de France*; the words were spoken at the funeral of his predecessor Georges Pallain.

b   French investments abroad had not always been successful, as the fiasco of the Panama Canal had shown. Investments in Russian railways, more strategic than commercial, were lost after the Russian revolution; see note a on page 142.

At first sight, this may seem strange because the *Banque* was a private company.[a] In contrast to the Bank of England, however, its ties with government were strong. The French government appointed the governor and his deputies. The *Banque* possessed a large network of subsidiaries and branch offices all over the country, but the management was strongly centralised from Paris within walking distance from the government offices and the presidential palace. The man who held the position of governor both in the preparation and during the war, from 1897 until his retirement in 1920, was George Pallain (see box, page 37). He took measures in four different areas to guarantee that the government could rely on the availability of sufficient financial means in case of war.[4]

French financial war preparations

The first and systematically continued action was the expansion of gold reserves. When Pallain took office on Christmas Eve, 24 December 1897, he found in the vaults of the *Banque* an amount of gold worth 1.9 billion *francs*. Within 16 years, he saw it almost doubled it to 3.5 billion *francs* early 1914.[5] This made the French central bank the second largest holder of gold, surpassed only by the Russians, who had their own gold mines.[6] Even the Bank of England, with its 'considerable' gold reserves (page 57) possessed only £ 40 million, equivalent to roughly 1 billion *francs* whereas the British economy was considerably larger than the French.[7] In particular if compared to Germany, France was far ahead in its gold reserves, and this lead was permanent (illustration 3.1).

---

a   The private character of the *Banque* was expressed, for example, by the obligation of the (government appointed) governor to buy a considerable amount of shares in the *Banque*, emphasising that he should participate in the venture capital of the company, **Vignat** (2001), p. 14, **Ahamed** (2010), p. 244. This is in striking contrast to modern central bank managers, who are being paid as employees, incurring no personal financial risk at all.

The Banque de France systematically built up her gold reserve; it was permanently far ahead of the German Reichsbank in a kind of financial arms race (Illustration 3.1)

gold reserve	France	Germany
million £, 1901	94	32
million £, 1913	135	51
£ per capita, 1901	2.42	0.56
£ per capita, 1913	3.40	0.76
as % of GDP, 1901	7.2%	2.0%
as % of GDP, 1913	6.9%	1.9%

Source: calculated on the basis of data from Petit, Zilch, Ritschl & Spoerer, CEPII, HISTAT.[8]

The second preparatory action of Pallain consisted of a set of arrangements with the French government about the latter's urgent credit needs in case of war or even during military mobilisation. It culminated in the formal agreement between the *Banque* and the then Finance Minister Louis-Lucien Klotz, dated 11-11-'11 (!). In two agreements (*'conventions'*) they laid down, that in the case of a general mobilisation the *Banque* would advance the Treasury (on request) a sum of at most 2.9 billion *francs*.[9] This was by all standards a huge amount for a private institution, about 6% of the French GDP of that time.[10 a] These conventions would be kept secret for more than 2½ years, until they were eventually legalised on 5 August 1914, immediately after the outbreak of the war.[11]

Georges Pallain (1847-1923), governor of the Banque de France from December 1897 until August 1920.[12]

Pallain was the man holding the office of governor longer than anyone since the establishment of the Banque by Napoléon Bonaparte in 1800 and he was to be the longest presiding governor ever. When he entered the Banque, he could boast at a splendid career in French public finance. He had been a private secretary to Finance Minster Léon Say (a grandson

---

a   Translated into present-day values according to GDP, this would correspond to a commitment of the FED to lend the US government $ 1,100 billion (US) or of the Bank of England to lend £ 110 billion to the UK government, respectively.

 *of the famous economist Jean-Baptiste Say) and a State Counsellor Extraordinary in the Department of Foreign Affairs. Until he left for the Banque, he had been the Director-general of Customs, a responsible post in view of the financial interest of import duties for the French government.*

At least as important as his professional posts, however, was his involvement in the foundation of the French Third Republic in 1870/'71.[13] In these days he had cooperated with men like Adolphe Thiers and Léon Gambetta, the memory of whom is kept alive in every self-respecting French city in the names of squares and avenues. To be short, he possessed the perfect network to apply for the higher positions in the French administrative system. And finally, the fact that he was married to a sister of the wife of Finance Minister Georges Cochery, will undoubtedly not have had a negative effect on his career.[14] Nevertheless, Georges Pallain was at least a man of virtues as of relations. Among all personalities in high finance in Europe, he was undoubtedly the one with the most impressive erudition.[a] He was, for example, executor of the will of Victor Hugo, he had published the letters of the famous French politician Talleyrand and he lobbied for a statue of the revolutionary hero Mirabeau in the city of Montargis (100 km south of Paris).

In his function of what we would now call CEO of the Banque de France, Pallain moved in the highest circles of France. The Board consisted of twelve 'regents', recruited mostly by heritage from the 200 most influential families of the country. The company that Pallain presided over counted such impressive names as Baron de Rothschild or Wendel. They possessed the formal and de facto power in the Banque, in which they had invested their capital and prestige. However, as Vignat rightly remarks, Pallain was not a man of power, but a man of influence. It was Pallain, not one of the regents, who proposed to raise the discount rate

a   Apart from the somewhat excentric Montagu Norman, governor of the *Bank of England* in the period 1920-1944, **Ahamed** (2010).

from 4.5% to 6% in the Saturday morning session of 1ˢᵗ August 1914. He had been informed that the bank rate in London had been raised to an exceptional 10%. The regents could do nothing but agree.[15] Public statements of Pallain are almost as scarce as personal expressions, in line with attitudes of central bankers at that time who preferred actions rather than words. One of the rare occasions where Pallain has given his views on banking affairs – and even then in relatively neutral terms – was an interview with US Senator Nelson Aldrich.[16]

Apart from his financial expertise and enthusiasm for the history of France, Pallain is remembered by the staff of the Banque for his human interest in his employees, regardless their position. The director of the subsidiary in Lille, for example, mentions the emotions he felt when Pallain had sent an inspector specially from Paris to bring his personal greetings at the occasion of the liberation of the city and the resumption of banking activities in the region.[17] It is said that the only enemies he made in his long career, were smugglers. As a director of Customs, he had introduced the then innovative X-rays to detect contraband.[18]

After the war, Pallain took some voluntary positions, such as honorary treasurer of the War Blind Relief Fund. He had also been for many years the mayor of the village of Gondreville, where the main street still bears his name, one of the few, perhaps the only one in France. Pallain died in 1923. Not long afterwards, a monument in his honour was erected in the nearby city of Montargis, facing the statue of Mirabeau. The structure was topped with a bronze bust, but during the Second World War the French Vichy regime had it removed to recast into guns. Since then the monument appears somewhat lost against the enormous façade of the local Peugeot garage.

The credits promised to the government by the *Banque* would be sufficient to cover at least the costs of mobilisation. The agreements were known only in an extremely restricted circle and they could properly be called a state secret.[a] For commander-in-chief Joseph Joffre

---

a   Curiously enough, there are three agreements dated 11 November 1911: the two secret *'conventions'* concerning the advances of the *Banque* in the case of mobilisation and a third, completely harmless agreement about an interest-free loan of (only) 20 million *francs*. The latter had been disclosed quickly, approved by the French parliament and included in   →

it was reassuring to know that the subject received serious attention, although probably even he was not aware of the details and assumed that the Treasury and not the *Banque* was responsible for the money.[19]

Signing agreements was only the beginning of the preparations. At least as important were practical matters to anticipate mobilisation, which was the third action of Pallain. In those days, and certainly in France, payments were largely made in cash, and currency circulation depended on the availability of coins and notes in small denominations. The latter were the responsibility of the *Banque*; indeed it had built a stock of banknotes to ensure continuity in trade in case of mobilisation and to make the necessary payments for transport of men and equipment. As early as December 1908, the *Banque* had made a reservation in its 1909 budget to print a surplus of *5-franc* notes and distribute and stock them in the branch offices in the provinces.[20] This happened almost six years before the war broke out and even well before the Balkan Wars. Indeed, it was prepared for any eventuality.

The final practical preparation that Pallain made consisted of the so-called Blue Circular (*Circulaire Bleue*). This document, illustrating the hierarchical structure of the *Banque*, was a secret instruction to the directors of the branches all over the country. It had been sent many years before the war and contained in astonishing detail the actions the directors had to take (or to omit) in the case when the government decreed a general mobilisation.[21] It reminded the regional directors that the *Banque* was a private enterprise and not a state institution. As such its own possessions as well as customers' securities in the vaults were immune to seizure by foreign occupation powers, according to the 1907 Hague Conventions of War on Land. Indeed, during the invasion in 1914, directors appealed to this clause when German commanders entered the *Banque's* buildings; at such moments, the Circular appeared not as secret as pretended, as the Germans were well

the Act of 29 December 1911. A century later, it is impossible to answer the intriguing question whether it was for practical reasons that MM. Pallain and Klotz signed three documents on this chilly Saturday in Paris, or that the published one (the *convention*, singular) was a cover for the secret ones (the *conventions*, plural). Pallain has left no autobiography; Klotz, then finance minister, lets the question pass in his memoirs, published 13 years afterwards, **Klotz** (1924), pp. 16-17.

aware of it.[22] Nevertheless, in most cases the Germans could whistle for any valuables, because most of the gold reserves, securities and

The Blue Circular: 'act with calmness, alertness, initiative and determination; ...and cease issuing gold immediately!' [a] *(Illustration 3.2)*

BANQUE DE FRANCE

Secrétariat Général

SECRET

Le Gouverneur de la Banque de France

a MM. les Directeurs des Succursales et
les Chefs des Bureaux Auxiliaires

La mobilisation générale impose à la Banque et à son personnel des devoirs immenses et périlleux.

L'heure est venue pour vous et pour ceux qui restent vos collaborateurs de justifier notre confiance en dominant cette épreuve redoutable par le calme, la vigilance, l'initiative et la fermeté.

La nécessité où nous sommes de sauvegarder avant tout et quand même le crédit du billet de Banque commande des règles d'extrême prudence, quelque pénibles qu'elles puissent être pour les intérêts privés.

Nous avons tenu à ce que, dès le premier jour, vous trouviez ici quelques indications à cet égard pour vous en inspirer sans délai.

Nous les compléterons selon les circonstances.

Vous les prendrez pour guide et vous en observerez au moins l'esprit, si l'urgence ou l'interruption des communications vous obligent à prendre sur l'heure certaines déterminations avec le seul avis, plus précieux que jamais, de votre Conseil d'administration.

1° Encaisse

Vous cesserez immédiatement et en principe toute remise d'or et ne vous départiriez de cette règle qu'en présence de nécessité absolue, que nous ne prévoyons pas, mais que, s'il vous en était justifié, vous auriez le devoir de contrôler en toute rigueur par tous les moyens en votre pouvoir.

Tout défaut de vigilance à cet égard engagerait gravement votre responsabilité.

En cas d'insuffisance de vos réserves d'écus et de billets, vous prendrez toute initiative pour assurer votre réapprovisionnement auprès des Succursales voisines, dans le cas où vous seriez privé de communications avec la Banque Centrale.

Vous devez avoir dans votre serre des paquets cachetés déposés par la Banque Centrale et dont le nombre est régulièrement vérifié par

---

a   © *Banque de France*. This is a copy of the only surviving document, dug up in a survey in the 1950s in the branch office (*succursale*) of the *Banque* in the city of Moulins. Nowadays it is in the *Banque's* central archives in Paris. The author's special thanks go to the staff of the *Banque* for their assistance in making available this and other documents.

banknotes had been rescued.[23] The Circular itself survived in one copy, a print of which is given in illustration 3.2.

Apart from formalities, the most important instruction was the immediate cessation to issue gold. Starting with the mobilisation, **convertibility** of the *Banque's* notes, **legal tender** in France, into gold was terminated immediately. This measure meant no less than France suspending the Gold Standard. It immunised the *Banque's* gold reserve against domestic hoarding and foreign speculation. Suspending convertibility by means of an instruction in a circular was a measure taken autonomously by the *Banque*. Formally it even violated the *Banque's* privilege, but it cannot have been written without the government's informal consent. The action of the *Banque* was legalised formally only afterwards in the Act of 4 August 1914.

Assessment

The conclusion is inevitable that if one institution in France was preparing financially for the war, it was the *Banque de France*. Many years later, in 1923 at Pallain's funeral, it was no exaggeration when the words were spoken in aptly formulated French: *Quand la guerre éclata, la Banque était prête*.[24] Unfortunately, however, France was prepared for a local conflict *à la* 1870, not for the World War 1914-1918 that would last for more than four years at an unprecedented scale and intensity.[25]

4

Finanzielle Kriegsbereitschaft?

> *'The notes should already have been printed and stocked
> in peacetime'*
> Jacob Riesser, 1913[a]

In Germany, just as in France, the frame of reference for a future war was the Franco-Prussian War of 1870/'71. The lesson learned, was that there should be sufficient cash at mobilisation. The government realised that a shortage of coins and notes should not be a restraining factor at the moment that soldiers would leave their barracks and travel by trains to the front en masse.

In preparing for a next war, every country used its own strengths and tradition and so did Germany. In contrast to France, the German central bank, the *Reichsbank* (Imperial Bank), lacked the history and the prestige (and to a certain extent also the gold reserve) of the *Banque de France*. After all, it had been established as late as 1876, a few years after German unification.[1] It would play its role in the financial war preparations, but not as dominant as the *Banque*, which was a pivot institute in the French monetary system. Germany mainly prepared for the war financially by three measures. In the first place it cherished a war chest. In the second place there were energetic scientific and public discussions about the most desirable way to finance a war. But above all, an army of bureaucrats with a background in law prepared a multitude of legislative measures, ready to pull them from the drawer and implement them punctually when war broke out.

---

a   *'Die Scheine hätten aber schon im Frieden angefertigt werden und bereit liegen sollen'*, the influential banker **Riesser** (1913), note p. 146, reflecting on the slow progress in the war of 1870/'71.

The German war chest

In order to have an initial fund in the next war, the German government had earmarked a small part of the revenue from the previous war. A fraction of 3% of the French reparations was kept in Berlin in the Julius Tower, in the form of gold coins. It was a sum of 120 million *marks* ($ 30 million, £ 6 million, at that time), an amount that would afterwards be sufficient for two days warfare, on the average in the First World War (illustration 6.3, page 74). Although nobody at that time could foresee the expenses that a coming war would require, it must have been evident that a war chest of this magnitude was absolutely insufficient. It was more to reassure the German mind than of any practical value. For a period of forty years it was not used in an economically productive way, not even passively to back the issue of bank notes, but it was impeccably administrated. In 1913, when the war was felt forthcoming, the government doubled it by adding an equal amount of silver, making it only a little less inadequate.[2] The (original) war chest was just enough for one day of mobilisation expenses, even before a shot was fired.[3]

Scientific discussions

At the end of the 19th century, and for decodes to come, Germany excelled in theoretical and applied science.[a] It is no surprise therefore that a discussion about financing a war was held primarily in a scientifically inspired public debate.[4] One of the main issues was whether the principal source for war financing should be taxation or borrowing (illustration 4.1). The question was presented as if those options were mutually exclusive; we shall deal with this in more detail in Chapter 7.[5] In practical and political decision making in parliament, however, the question appeared of little importance. If politicians dealt with it all, they confined themselves to short-term answers: how to cover the immediate need for money during mobilisation; this task was easily entrusted to the *Reichsbank*.[6] And for the rest, the German government assumed that for the long run there would be no finance problem at all, since the war would be short, would be won, and the defeated enemy would

---

a   As an illustration, from the first award of the Nobel Prize in 1901 until the First World War, no less than 17 German scientists won the prize, over 1.3 on the average each year and more than half of them was in physics or chemistry (http://www.nobelprize.org/nobel_prizes/lists/all/); from 1900 to 1920 almost 60% of all innovations in chemistry worldwide came from Germany, **Andraos** (2000-2012).

bear the burden. As a consequence, almost all computations would largely underestimate future war expenses.

Examples of the scientific discussion in Germany about war financing before the Great War (Illustration 4.1)

Die finanzielle Mobilmachung der deutschen Wehrkraft. Von Dr. Joseph Ritter von Renauld, Edler von Kellenbach, Oberst a. D.	FINANZIELLE KRIEGSBEREITSCHAFT UND KRIEGFÜHRUNG VON Dr. J. RIESSER GEHEIMER JUSTIZRAT UND ORDENTL. HONORAR-PROFESSOR AN DER UNIVERSITÄT BERLIN
1901	1909/1913

Kriegssteuer oder Kriegsanleihe?

Von

Heinrich Dietzel

1912

* Renauld: Financial mobilisation of German defence; Riesser: Financial war preparedness and warfare; Dietzel: War tax or war loan. Source: author's collection.

Cash

One practical measure, taken by the *Reichsbank* and the German government together, was to guarantee the availability of cash. This programme had already started in 1909, when the notes of the *Reichsbank* were formally declared legal tender.[7] Sooner or later this would have been done anyway with (Germany lagged far behind other countries in declaring bank notes legal tender), but at that moment it was a practical measure in war finance preparation. Indeed, when it becomes urgent, notably during mobilisation, bank notes are far more easily to produce than coins, be it in gold, silver or otherwise.[8] Once the bank notes had been declared legal tender, the whole German monetary and credit system could easily be switched to a paper system by suspending convertibility. This was exactly one of the implications of the bundle of War Acts that were unanimously adopted by the German Parliament, the *Reichstag* on 4 August 1914.[a]

Legislative preparations

Apart from the suspension of convertibility, the package of War Acts contained regulations on ample credit facilities of the government. Although they were presented to parliament as if they were a quick response to the state of war, the proposals were the result of many years of careful preparations. There was no such thing as improvisation in these matters and it characterises the German financial war preparation process: every action, every change, every new relationship should be *gesetztreu*.[9] The word itself is basically untranslatable, having meanings between 'compliant', 'respectful' and 'law-abiding', and expresses a notion with almost religious connotations.

It is easy to have recourse to vague notions such as national character, customs and traditions or culture to explain why the idea of a statutory basis lived strongly in Germany. Probably it is a more convincing explanation to look at the education and professional background of those who had shaped the country in financial matters as a Secretary of the Treasury (*'Staatssekretär'*, see *Note on names*, page 47). Without exception, all those 12 men who had successively served the German Empire in this office from 1880 until the First World War had followed an education in law. The vast majority of these counts, barons – and, indeed some commoners – had graduated in pure law. Often, they had been working in professional legal functions, for example as a judge. The president of the *Reichsbank* himself, Rudolf Havenstein was a jurist, as well as his two

---

a   In most historical descriptions, these Acts are narrowed down to the one concerning war credits. In fact, the *Reichstag* voted unanimously on 17 legislative proposals, 9 of which regulated in detail the whole German war finance. It will be difficult to find a similar occasion in history where so many far-reaching laws were adopted without any discussion in so short a time: in less than half an hour, between 5:21 p.m. and 5:50 p.m. on 4 August 1914, **RT** 306, pp. 8-11 and **Roesler** (1967), pp. 36-48. At about the same time, the French parliament voted on 18 proposals, 4 of which had a financial character. (Incidentally, 4 August 1914 was a heavy day for parliaments everywhere; at that same day, the US Congress for example passed a bill to extend the limits on the issue of emergency currency, **Silber** (2007), p. 73).

predecessors.[a] No wonder that financial war preparation in Germany was addressed primarily as a problem of law and orderly administration.

A note on names of officials

Names of public offices, in particular historical ones, cannot be translated one-to-one in current English or American terminology. The function of *Staatssekretär im Reichsschatzamt*, literally Secretary of State in the Imperial Treasury, was the man who was primarily responsible for financial aspects of warfare in the entire German Empire, but formally he was not a Finance minster, simply because the German Empire had no ministers (the Germans States, such as Prussia or Bavaria had). The British function of *Chancellor of the Exchequer* comprised, apart from finance, economic aspects as well, etc.

I have used the generic functional name 'minister' for these politicians in France and Germany, and the appropriate names Chancellor (of the Exchequer) or Secretary (of the Treasury) in Britain and the United States, respectively.

The same holds for names of financial instruments such as the German *Darlehenskassenscheine* and French *bons de la défense nationale* and institutions: *Reichstag* and *Reichsbank* for the German parliament and national bank, etc. In this book original names have been used as much as possible, recognisable in *italics*.

Pawnshop notes

Legally watertight, but financially and economically highly questionable was the construction of the so-called *Darlehenskassen*, loan banks. These institutions were a kind of state-owned pawnshops where citizens and companies could deposit goods and securities in exchange for a special

---

a   A minority had an academic education in Law & Political Science (*Rechts- und Staatswissenschaften*) and therefore some background of public administration and macroeconomics. Economy as an academic discipline was in any case a field in development. The only one who could call himself a financial specialist was Finance Minister Karl Helfferich (Chapter 7) who held a PhD in political science, but only after a study of law, **Williamson** (1971), p. 16. The real financial and economic specialists were more likely to be found in the northern German trading cities among bankers, industrialists and even agriculture than in the civil service.

type of bank notes, the *Darlehenskassenscheine*. On 4 August 1914, these notes would be introduced legally, but they had been prepared long before.[10] As early as in 1891, still under Chancellor Leo von Caprivi, they had been discussed in the Prussian government as an important instrument in financing a future war.[11]

Darlehenskassenschein, a source of paper money. The note bears the date 5 August 1914, one day after the German Parliament voted on the Act introducing the notes, an indication of a thorough preparation (Illustration 4.2)

Source: collection Hugo Meyer.

Indeed, the notes issued by the *Darlehenskassen* did not appear out of the blue. They had been successfully used by Prussia in the wars of 1848, 1866 and 1870/'71 to provide for liquidity quickly and smoothly.[12] The notes were *not* legal tender for normal payments, but only for government authorities at all levels, from national to local.[13] Notably, they could be used by the public to pay taxes. In practice, however, citizens did use them as a means of payment for any transactions. After all, at the end of the chain of transactions there was someone who had to pay national or local taxes and hence the notes represented value. In particular the smaller denominations of 1, 2 and 5 *mark* were used frequently parallel to the official *Reichsbank* notes. Banker Jakob Riesser, advocating a quick financial mobilisation, had insisted in 1913 that they should be printed in advance (page 43, note a). Actually, at that moment they had already been printed and stocked, just as at the other side of the Rhine the 5 and 20 *franc* notes were waiting for the mobilisation in the vaults of the *Banque de France*.[14]

Creation of money by the Darlehenskassen and the relationship with the Reichsbank

Two mechanisms made the *Darlehenskassenscheine* a source of inflation, a mild one and a severe one. The mild one originated in the possibility, explicitly stated in the Act on the *Darlehenskassen*, to pledge bonds issued by communities and German States. They were not accepted at face value, but at a discount. Nevertheless, this implied an uncontrolled multiplication of money in circulation, because actual and future debts of lower authorities could be used to automatically create new money at the national level.

A more serious danger was found in the relationship with the *Reichsbank*. The *Darlehenskassen* had been authorised by the national government to issue money and so did the *Reichsbank*, which raises the question as to the relationship between both. Strictly speaking, they were separate institutions. In reality the *Darlehenskassen* were shaped almost completely by the *Reichsbank*. Its branches were in cities where the *Reichsbank* had branches; the *Reichsbank* staff worked for the *Darlehenskassen* (and they were paid in full by the government). In fact it was only the text of the laws that kept them distinct.[a]

The idea of establishing the *Darlehenskassen* was to enlarge the *Reichsbank's* own possibilities to grant credit.[15] Every loan given by the *Darlehenskassen* was not recorded as a liability on the balance sheet of the *Reichsbank*, which enabled the latter to give more credit to other borrowers, read: the German government. But this was only a beginning, since the *Reichsbank* was not only spared passively; its possibili-

---

a   A subtle distinction between both institutions concerned the credit rating of borrowers. Whereas in the *Reichsbank* this was a matter of its own staff, in the boards of the *Darlehenskassen* local personalities with authority in financial matters were envisaged to perform this task. Although everything had been prepared in detail, the appointment of those local representatives had not taken place before the war. The risk of leaking, in particular abroad, was considered too high. Such a detailed financial preparation of war would not give a peaceful impression, **Zilch** (1987), p. 123.

ties were enlarged actively. The *Reichsbank* had always been obliged to back the notes it issued for one third by gold. The laws of 4 August 1914 also permitted the *Reichsbank* to use all *Darlehenskassenscheine* that it received to back the issue of bank notes. They were in fact legally equalled to gold. By this legal trick, the *Reichsbank* could completely *gesetztreu* uphold the fiction of high and comforting 'gold' backing rates. Thus it avoided abandoning the gold backing obligation, which would have been humiliating both domestically and abroad, while at the same time it could issue as much paper money as it liked, the only limit being the legal ceiling on the amount of *Darlehenskassen* in circulation. This stock of *Darlehenskassen* had initially been restricted to 1.5 billion *marks*, but this ceiling could easily be increased without the consent of parliament or even the *Reichsbank*, which of course happened again and again.[16] Through this system, German financial authorities had accomplished legally and indisputably what medieval alchemists never had been succeeded to do: making gold from paper.[17]

In spite of all legal aplomb, it remained remarkably vague who was ultimately responsible for the debt contracted at the *Darlehenskassen*, that is to say: who backed the notes. Formally, the German Chancellor was responsible for the central management of the *Darlehenskassen* in Berlin and hence for the production and the distribution of the notes. But what about their *value*? The bills bore the signature of the rather unknown president of the National Debts Administration (*Reichsschuldenverwaltung*), not the signature of the finance minister or the president of the *Reichsbank* (illustration 4.2)![18]

Few people bothered about such details. Hardly any deputy in the *Reichstag* must have realised the far-reaching consequences of the laws they adopted on 4 August 1914. They certainly had other things on their minds than to grasp the meaning of texts such as 'in the sense of §§ 9, 17 and 44 of the Bank Act of 14 March 1875, *Darlehenskassenscheine* shall be equated to *Reichskassenscheine*'.[19] [a] Of course, the legal people who had been working on texts like these for years knew perfectly well what it meant – that is to say, in the legal sense, not economically. And maybe

---

a   The *Reichskassenscheine* (Imperial (Treasury) notes) were notes issued by the government in amounts completely negligible compared to the gold stock, but just as the latter they counted fully as backing for the issue of *Reichsbank* notes.

it would have all come well in the end, if the war had been short, if the whole construction could have been demolished timely and if Germany had received reparations rather than imposed upon it.

Assessment

With its War Acts, including the *Darlehenskassen*, German authorities had constructed a legally perfect system to issue unlimited amounts of money. Germany had made financial warfare an essential part of total warfare, going far beyond other countries. All necessary provisions had been prepared in detail in the years preceding the war and on 4 August 1914 they were attested by parliament unanimously and without discussion. The whole system was based on legal fiction and lacked a sound economic and even financial foundation. It was significant that the large package of carefully prepared measures that were supposed to finance the war contained not a single tax proposal.

5

The City

*'[For Britain] politics and warfare are the continuation
of business by other means'*
Karl Helfferich, 1915[a]

World power

Britain's financial preparation for a war on the continent was practically negligible. The British Empire was a world power, in fact *the* world power. All developments on the European continent, however threatening they might be, always took place against the background of Britain's global interests: the Indian subcontinent, African colonies, Russian ambitions in Asia, the emerging power of the United States in Latin America, to mention a few.[1] With a cynical undertone, one might say that Britain as a world power was in fact in a permanent state of war – or war preparation – and its politics were shaped accordingly. Domestically, issues such as Irish Home Rule and women's suffrage were considered far more important on the political agenda than a potential war on the continent.[2]

British hegemony was inseparably connected with its financial dominance in all fields of international trade, ranging from commercial credits to shipping insurance, commodity markets and futures. London, or rather 'the City', was the undisputed financial centre of the world. Banks all over the world kept a sharp eye on the interest rates that were set in London.[b] According to one estimate, 60% of world trade was financed through banks in London.[3] Obviously, Britain was under no circum-

---

a   Helfferich was Finance Minster of Germany (see note on names of public offices on page 47). In his budget speech on 15 March 1915, he declared that 'the well-known words of Clausewitz "War is he continuation of politics by other means" should be translated into English as: politics and war are the continuation of business by other means', **RT** 306, p. 37 ('Die Politik und der Krieg sind die Fortsetzung des Geschäfts mit anderen Mitteln').

b   See, for example, the bank rate policy of the *Banque de France* in the text box on George Pallain, page 37. Recent commotion about the Libor rate shows that little has changed in the past century.

stances willing to give up this position in favour of any European competitor or ally. Admittedly, there was the *Entente Cordiale* with France, agreed in 1904. It had been a breakthrough in the relations between the two countries since the Napoleonic wars, but it was confined to issues of a global and strategic character. It contained no reference or hint to economic and financial cooperation or coordination in Europe, not even in the secret clauses.[4] Along with 'Britannia, rule the waves!' went: Britannia rules the money.

British preoccupation with the Empire did not mean that it failed to notice war preparations on the continent by France and Germany or that it did not act at all. In the best of political traditions, a committee was formed and memoranda were written. The most important political body entrusted with preparations for a possible war in Europe was the *Committee of Imperial Defence* (CID), operational since 1902. It was a rather powerless institution, mainly concerned with the problem of coordinating individual government departments and the armed forces in case of war; British commercial and trade interests were an important issue for the committee.[5] Until 1911, financial war preparation was barely looked after by the CID and even later only as a minor issue.

In 1911, a sub-committee was formed, led by the 5th Earl of Desart (hence: the Desart Committee). Its task was to elaborate the question how trade was to be managed in wartime, regardless of who would be the enemy. The only recommendation the committee could produce was that the Gold Standard should be maintained in all circumstances. Sterling should remain as good as gold. In order to keep its position as a banker of the world and the world leader in commercial affairs, it was essential that confidence be defended to the utmost, implying unlimited convertibility of the national currency, or rather the Bank of England's currency.[a]

The Bank of England

In contrast to its colleague central banks on the continent, the Bank of

---

a   The British attitude has been concisely expressed during the war by the then Chancellor of the Exchequer Reginald McKenna, speaking in Parliament: 'if we are to emerge from this War not merely victors in the battlefield, as we shall, but with our financial position unimpaired, we must make great sacrifices now', 15 June 1915, **HC**, 583; see also **Horn** (2002), p. 37, author's underling.

England initially took no special precautions in the months before the war.[6] Just as the British government, it acted according to circumstances, while carefully keeping a sharp eye on the interests of the financial sector. In July 1914, between the attack in Sarajevo and the mobilisation on the continent, panic broke out in the European financial markets and it was clear that sooner or later Britain would be involved. It was usual for commercial banks in London to have large short-term debt positions balanced by at least equally large claims.[7] By a sudden breakdown of commerce, these banks would be brought into a position where they could not meet their obligations, igniting a chain of failures. At that moment, the Bank of England threw in its full weight to support commercial banks. It is one of those rare moments in history where a central bank acted as a lender of last resort (instead of threatening to do so), obviously not without consultation with the government.

Within three days, the Bank raised its **discount rate** at an unprecedented speed from 3% on 29 July 1914 to 10% on 1st August. Although the measure itself had hardly any material effect, together with the adherence to convertibility of Sterling, it was a signal for the financial markets that matters were taken seriously. Within a week, the financial markets calmed down, partly due to some additional visible measures, such as a prolonged bank holiday and the provision of surveillance of enemy (German) banks to prevent smuggling gold and securities out of the country. The cool-headed action of the Governor of the Bank, Walter Cunliffe, gave him a reputation that none of his predecessors had ever known (see box, page 56).

During the following years however, the Bank of England's freedom of action would be reduced, despite Britain's liberal principles of free trade and private enterprise, the Gold Standard, and even the prestige of Cunliffe. It might have remained somewhat wider than in France, Germany, Italy and Russia, but nevertheless: reduced. More and more it became the Treasury that held the reins of financial management. The government listened carefully to the bankers – in the City as well as in the country as a whole – but the ultimate responsible body was the government. The official discount rate (bank rate) practically lost its significance as a beacon in the financial world (Chapter 11, page 197), just as the jump to 10% on 1st August 1914 had been only of a symbolic meaning.[8]

Walter Cunliffe (1855-1920), Governor of the Bank of England, 1913-1918 [9]

In the eventful days of late July and August 1914, Cunliffe played a crucial role. His decisive actions did not go unnoticed. Still in the same year, King George V rewarded him with a hereditary peerage as Baron Cunliffe of Headley.[10] Within a few years he was among the first to be appointed Knight Grand Cross of the British Empire (GBE).[11]

Cunliffe was a man of calibre and he made no secret about it. Born and bred in a wealthy banking family, educated at Harrow and Cambridge, he was destined to play an important role in the City. After having founded a bank with his brothers, he became one of the directors of the Bank of England in 1895 and its deputy governor in 1911. The Bank of England had a rotating presidency. Every two years, the acting deputy governor, recruited from the 'old boys network' of bankers, was appointed governor for two years, after which he had to return to the position of an ordinary member of the board, meanwhile running his own banking business.[12] For Cunliffe things went differently, when he was called to this high office in 1913. Without any dispute his term was extended year after year, making him the first governor to lead the Bank for more than three consecutive years since it had been founded in 1694. He would, however, not serve out the last term.

Cunliffe ruled the Bank like a sovereign, making decisions without consulting anyone, including his fellow directors. During the days of crisis, in 1914, he was beyond doubt the right man in the right place. In the four years of war, however, he did not really appreciate that the balance of power in the financial world shifted, even in Britain. His self-willed actions proved fatal in the summer of 1917. On his own authority, he cabled the Canadian government in Ottawa, where

Britain held a gold deposit, with the directive to ignore instructions of the UK Treasury about gold transactions. It was true that the Bank was responsible for the exchange rate, and indeed, the Bank was formally independent of the government, but this action meant no less than arrogating the authority of a sovereign state. This was too much for the British government; Chancellor Bonar Law almost exploded and even the good relationship with Prime Minster Lloyd George could not save the baron. Cunliffe's position could not be maintained.[13] As a kind of compensation he was appointed president of a committee of economic experts.

After the Armistice, Cunliffe was a member of the British delegation at the Paris Peace Conference in preparation of the Treaty of Versailles. In that capacity, he proposed German reparations that went far beyond any sort of reality: eight times German GDP. This would have implied that 40% of the German economy would have to be paid just for interest payments on reparations.[14]

Just as in the case of his French colleague Georges Pallain, the life of Walter Cunliffe is still waiting for a reliable biography. From the scattered available sources he emerges as a strong-willed personality, who could make enemies more easily than friends in the business environment. There is a story about a governor of the Bank of England talking about its gold reserves that is probably correctly attributed to Cunliffe. He is said to have answered a question about the amount of gold held by the bank, by declaring that it was 'very, very considerable'. As that answer was not quite satisfactory and the governor was asked to be a bit more specific, he replied that he was 'very, very reluctant' to add something to his previous statement.[15]

Cunliffe died in 1920 on his estate Headley Court, the mansion south of London, being built on his commission. Headley Court became a rehabilitation centre for Royal Air Force aircrew in 1949 after the Second World War; it became the tri-service rehabilitation centre during the 1980s.

Photo courtesy of the Bank of England; ©The Governor and Company of the Bank of England.

Assessment and conclusion of Episode I

Financial preparations of the war were limited to cover the costs of mobilisation and the first few weeks or months of a future war. Although they differed by country, they had in common that they all anticipated a short war. During the mobilisation and the outbreak of the war, the visible measures ran in parallel with the military mobilisation, as can be seen from illustration 5.1. Sometimes they even ran ahead of the military mobilisation *de facto* (Germany and France), being legalised only afterwards.

Financial and military mobilisation measures (Illustration 5.1)

	convertibility suspended	gold export prohibited	military mobilisation
Germany	4 August 1914; *de facto* 31 July 1914	4 August 1914	1 August 1914
France	5 August 1914; *de facto* 1st August 1914	3 July 1915; previously: restricted	1 August 1914
Britain	not formally; *de facto* restricted	not formally; *de facto* restricted	4 August 1914*
United States		restricted from 6 October 1917	6 April 1917*

* State of war.

Source: Brown, Hardach, Harris, Kirkaldy, Strachan.[16]

On the European continent, the visible financial mobilisation had been preceded by years of preparations in secret. The difference between financial and military war plans was, that in the latter case it was evident who developed the plans, even though they were secret: the military commanders. In the financial domain, it was not always possible to identify one player. The initiative was highly subject to national tradition and internal lines of power. For that reason alone, financial war preparations largely differed by country.

France focused on the vast amount of gold in the vaults of the *Banque de France*, with its personal relationships with French politics, undisputed reputation from right to left, financial involvement of the highest and mightiest families in the country and its branches all over the country, but firmly controlled from its headquarters in Paris. Actually, for the financial side of the mobilisation the government relied completely on the *Banque*, a private organisation, although it could influence the *Banque's* policy by the appointment of the governor. Indeed, the *Banque* acquitted itself very well of this task. Advances to the government had been prepared many years before the war broke out, bank notes were printed and distributed for the case of emergency and local directors and cashiers had received detailed instructions. In the first weeks of the war gold and securities were evacuated and during the rest of the war the *Banque* would behave irreproachably as was becoming of a patriotic institution.[17] The gold reserves (of the *Banque*, not of the state) were regarded as a power by itself, emanating stability and confidence, both domestically and abroad.[18]

The French blind spot was the apparent wealth, visible in its capital Paris and (with varying success) invested in foreign countries, such as Russian railways and the Panama and Suez Canals. Meanwhile, an enormous national debt had been built up, partly as a consequence of the reparations of the Franco-Prussian War, but also due to domestic infrastructure investments. This debt could develop into a constraint when it came to securing new international credit in the approaching war.

Germany, on the other hand, relied – apart from its industrial innovative capacity – on the force of legal power as might be expected in an environment where legal people with a narrow vision on economy and finance dominated the bureaucracy. Scientific debates on how to finance a war offered politicians sufficient variety to pick out what best fitted their actual priorities. They designed a rigid system of domestic loans with the possibility of virtually unlimited – but fully legalised – creation of money with the fiction that paper was as good as gold. The country finally cherished its war chest, left over from the previous war with France; compared to its symbolic value its real significance was negligible.

It was the German state, or rather the Prussian bureaucracy, that took the initiative in preparing financially for the war. The preparation was thorough, but heavily biased towards borrowing and creation of money by monetary financing. It was based on the assumption of a short war that would be paid by the defeated enemy. Behind the scenes, the government authorities, in close cooperation with the *Reichsbank*, had prepared the legal basis for a swift and unlimited supply of money. Awkward time consuming measures, such as tax increases were completely lacking. The enthusiastic *Reichstag* meeting of 4 August 1914 marks the end of this period of silent preparation. From that moment on, the whole machinery could be put into action. It would take almost the full period of the war before the population realised that the entire construction was based on undue confidence in the financial authorities.

British financial war preparation rested on two pillars. The first and foremost was its well-developed professional and flexible financial sector, necessary for its international trade position. At the top of the pyramid of the (mostly) sound and solid banks stood the Bank of England, guardian of Sterling, the *de facto* international currency that was as good as gold. Apart from solidity, a second characteristic of the banking sector was the ability to adapt to the continuously changing circumstances the Empire and the world were faced with. This gave the government, the business sector and the population confidence not to be afraid of a possible war on the continent. Indeed, they had seen wars coming along on the continent so many times before and they even offered interesting opportunities to make some money. Of paramount concern was that British financial dominance should not be affected, not only during the war, but also – and this was as least as important – after the war, when things would have to return to business as usual as soon as possible. Furthermore, the government could always rely on the second pillar, the loyalty of the taxpayer. When it came down to war, over the past centuries the British taxpayer had always been willing to make the necessary sacrifices, as the Crimean War and the Boer War had shown only recently. In contrast to almost any other country, Britain had a well-developed income tax system as a flexible and respected instrument with simple buttons to adapt government revenue to the demands of warfare. This had all been sufficient to fight any war – and to make money from it – so far.

Common to all European financial preparations was the expectation of a short war. A short war implied that usual financial instruments would be sufficient, because they would not really cause a significant intervention in the liberal economic system. A short war would also mean that it would be easy to return to the familiar pre-war circumstances of 1913, the seemingly endless period of the *belle époque*. Both the length of the war and its unprecedented scale would disprove these suppositions.

Meanwhile, at the other side of the Atlantic, there were no financial war preparations, at least not officially. The United States found itself in a kind of 'splendid isolation'. The Democratic President Woodrow Wilson had been elected in 1912 and re-elected in 1916 on a platform of neutrality. However, once the war in Europe had started, bankers with probably more Republican sympathies made financial arrangements with Britain and France that would inevitably drag the United States into the war, if only it lasted long enough. It did.

Episode II

1914-1919

Spending, creating and circulating money

6

War expenditure: beyond comprehension

'To be told that we are spending at the rate of 3 millions sterling
a day means very little to the ordinary man.
It is better to tell him that we are spending £ 2,000 a minute,
or that £ 100 saved and lent to the Government will last three seconds.'
John Simon, 1915[a]

What is war expenditure?

Financing a war deals primarily with the question of how the money was raised, for example by means of taxes or loans. This is the subject of the next chapters and the main issue of this book. In that perspective, expenditure itself is something that is given, as a kind of external condition beyond discussion. But before entering that analysis, it is useful to have a look at the amount of this expenditure: the money costs of the war. This is not as easy as it appears. In any case, it is far more difficult than determining the number of casualties, which amounts ultimately to counting.[b] Of course, one might argue about including military deaths caused by Spanish flu, or civil casualties by starvation, but in the end it is just counting bodies, a rather unambiguous notion.

There are four aspects that matter in the expression of war expenditure in one number – or one number by country: what do we mean by it (defining)? which data do we use (measuring)? how to obtain this data (sources)? and, finally, what does this all mean (interpretation)? These questions together imply qualification. Just giving a number like $ 200

---

a   John Allsebrook Simon (1873-1954), then Home Secretary of the United Kingdom in a speech on 5 July 1915, quoted in **The Economist** 10 July 1915, p. 51. £ 100 represented one year's salary for a British worker those days, and an amount of money he was never able to save in his whole lifetime. Just evaporated within 3 seconds... And this was only 1915, spending would increase considerably in the years to come.

b   This supposes that reliable records were kept, an activity that was probably done with greater accuracy on the Western front than on other battlefields.

billion without any context is only part of the answer to the question of war expenses – and it might easily be misunderstood.

Defining war expenditure

The first thing to note is that we are talking about war *expenditure*, not war *costs* (in line with Chapter 1, pages 15, 16). The value of lost human lives is undoubtedly a war cost, but not war expenditure or *money cost*. Expenditure is the money that has really been paid, though not necessarily in the form of banknotes or coins. In the case of the First World War, it includes payments that belligerent and neutral states have made, regardless to whom, when and in which capacity, or, as Germans say 'for war's cause' (*aus Anlaß des Krieges*). But what does that comprise?

Payments for shells shot on the battlefield are counted as war expenditure, without any discussion. War pensions paid to widows or veterans can be considered as war expenditure, even if they are still being paid decades after the end of the war. But the costs of scrapping unused dreadnoughts transferred by a peace treaty and demolished in a neutral country? Even without a war, these costs would have to be made eventually. Strictly reasoning along these lines, however, would imply that all payments for national defence, even if they were made in peace-time, could be regarded as war expenditure; it just remains to identify the war they have to be attributed to, in this case: which part of national defence expenses must be counted as expenditure for the Great War of 1914-1918.[a]

It is evident, that a comprehensive definition of war expenditure is difficult to make; moreover, if there is one, it immediately raises the question of the availability of data to comply with this definition. Therefore, a more pragmatic approach for determining war expenditure starts with available data and amends these by adding or subtracting other data or correcting for obvious errors. In the end, three large categories of war expenditure can then be distinguished: purely military expenditure,

---

[a] A special problem is the attribution of civil servant's salaries. As soon as a country has shifted from a peace economy to a war economy, a distinction between government effort for military and civil tasks becomes vague. If this is true for the national government, the more it holds for local and regional authorities seeing their social and relief budgets explode as a consequence of the massacres at distant battlefields.

additional civil expenditure (including post-war expenditure such as hospitals and rehabilitation centres) and capital costs like interest on war loans. Apart from that, loans granted to allies are expenditure during the war (for the lending country), but could be compensated by redemption in later years.

What was the money spent on?

Source of the photo: *U.S. Naval Historical Center*/Wikipedia.

HMS Dreadnought (1906-1923), construction costs £ 1.8 million.[1] *Between 1906 and the end of the war, Britain built almost 50 of these ships with increasing power and costs. Germany completed 26 battleships, France 18, Austria-Hungary 7, the United States 16 (starting 1910), Russia 13, Japan 12 and Italy 10. Together with the naval plans of smaller countries, in the decade before the First World War some 160 cruisers and battleships were constructed. At a conservatively estimated price of the Dreadnought herself, this all amounts to an investment in the order of $ 100 billion, translated into current value. Some younger ships, such as the Hood (1918-1941) were technologically more advanced and hence considerably more expensive. Maintenance, operational and scrapping costs are – as usual – disregarded in such calculations.*

Not only capital was needed for the construction of such ships, samples of advanced technology as they may be called, but also a lot of time. The average lead-time from laying the keel until the ship was operational was about 2.5 years. British shipyards were a bit faster while German shipbuilders took three months longer, on the average. The German Finance Minister Helfferich (see box on page 81) was absolutely right in 1915 when he withstood pressure from the military commanders to laying down a new battleship: before the ship would be operational the war should be over, at least in the view of the very same commanders. It happened to be the only case that he resisted the wishes of the army and navy leaders, as he confessed afterwards.[2]

Whereas expenditure for battle ships was largely confined to the pre-war period, during the war the money was spent on food, ammunition and clothing (illustration 10.3, page 183). One third ($ 3.2 billion) of the purchases made by Britain, France, Italy and Russia in the United States was spent on cereals and other foodstuffs, both for men and horses.[3] One quarter of the purchases was for weapons and ammunition, varying from revolvers to shells and another quarter was for clothing and textiles, mainly cotton. This kind of military expenditure, domestically and abroad, was responsible for three quarters of all war-related expenditure made during the war (included in these figures are payments to families of the soldiers fighting in at the front; according to a French estimation, they were about 10% of all military expenditure).[4] The remainder of the expenditure on the war (and during the war) was mainly for financial purposes such as loans to allies and interest on war loans.[5]

Measuring war expenditure

War expenditure can be measured in several ways.[6] The simplest method is adding all war credits voted by parliaments that enabled governments to start or to continue the war. By doing so, one disregards the actual destination of these financial means, for example the question whether the credits were spent in full or exclusively for military purposes. This is a rather crude method, but it could be sufficient for a first estimate. A variation of this method looks at increasing state debts; in attributing these to war, one gets a picture of annual expenditure.

A more refined method starts from all state expenditure, taken from realised budgets (accounts, not estimations). This data however comprise not only war expenditure, but also payments for education, police, justice, governance and a lot of other government tasks.[a] By subtracting the amounts realised in peacetime, for example 1911-1913, from the corresponding values during the war (and adjusting for inflation!), one obtains an estimate of the additional government expenditure attributed to the war. This method assumes that the normal, non-war expenditure remains constant, which need not be true. Even econometric estimations of a trend cannot fully remove this limitation. Furthermore, long-run expenditure, such as pensions and interest payments on war loans remain out of the picture. Despite these drawbacks, this method has been widely applied.[7]

A third method, scrutinising budgets and government accounts employing a comprehensive definition would be the best, but in practice it is difficult to maintain. In the first place, it would be naïve to assume that governments are transparent in publishing their military spending, especially in wartime, as it is strategic information for the (potential) enemy. But also domestically, detailed data could be hidden, just to avoid uncomfortable questions or even political unrest. In Germany, for example, the government presented an annual 'normal' budget (*ordentlicher Haushalt*), to be discussed and voted by the *Reichstag*. This distracted attention of the members of parliament and the population from the 'extraordinary budget' (*außerordentlicher Haushalt*), where all war-related expenditure was included. This part of the budget was not a subject of parliamentary discussion; the only action expected from parliament was to approve huge credits to feed this extraordinary budget, while shouting 'bravo!'[8] It is generally assumed that expenditure that ought to be accounted for on the normal budget was actually shifted to the extraordinary budget.[9] This is just one example to show that a bottom-up construction of war expenditure is tricky.

---

a   A centruy ago, these other government expenses were much smaller than they are today; expressed as a fraction of GDP, government budgets were less than 10%, whereas nowadays they can easily reach 45% or more in Europe or just over 20% in the United States (**Eurostat** Table gov_10a_main and **USBUD** 2016, Historical Tables, Table 1.2).

One important measurement problem is comparing sums of money between countries and years. This is in strict contrast to counting casualties. In the latter case, a well-known British lieutenant fallen in the retreat from Mons in August 1914 is simply added to an anonymous infantryman from the Austrian-Hungarian army at the battle of Vittorio Veneto in October 1918. In fact, it would be unethical to do it otherwise. The numerical values of a British pound Sterling and an Austrian *krone* of theses dates however cannot simply be added, although in some way they both count. Obviously, budgets and statistical records of the countries involved did not anticipate such problems for historians. All expenditure mentioned was presented in *marks*, pounds, *francs*, *kronen*, or whatever currency in the value of that time. All sources reporting war expenditure were obliged to recalculate the original data and they did so with varying degrees of reliability and justification.[10]

Sources

Most sources on war expenditure quote other sources, to arrive eventually at original and official data, such as Annual Reports, declarations of responsible treasurers, central bank governors, etc. In publications dating from immediately after the war, these original sources are often given as a reference, whereas in later years the original sources appear to be consulted less and less. In this chain of citations, all kinds of assumptions could be made, for example about the period (calendar year or fiscal year, until the Armistice or December 1918 or including 1919, etc.), about exchange rates, price indices, etc.[a] It would be a useful research project by itself to construct a genealogy of sources.

An estimation of the total sum spent on the war

A frequently mentioned sum for the total money costs of the First World War is $ 200 billion.[11] In the light of the preceding remarks, however, the $-sign is questionable and the amount suggests more accuracy than can be justified. The older estimates are based on data for individual countries, converted to dollars at pre-war (gold parity) values, disregarding inflation (which varied considerably by country) and disregarding developments in exchange rates. From a US perspective based on dollars, it amounts to current prices of the years 1914-1918, simply

---

a   See the note 'Some remarks on sources' in the literature section (in particular pp. 357, 358) and methodological details in various endnotes.

added; for other countries it is a rough indication.[12] More meaningful is an amount that takes into account price and exchange rates. In that case, a sum of roughly **$ 80 billion** appears, where the $-sign stands for the 1913 value of the dollar.[13]

It should be noted that all such calculations are based on state expenditure during the war and a short time after the war, covering a period of five or six years, depending on the country. Long lasting payments for medical care and rehabilitation, veterans' and widows' pensions, reconstruction of damaged areas, etc. are only partially included or not at all.[14] In this regard, such amounts *underestimate* the real expenditure, even in monetary terms (let alone in non monetary, economic or human and social terms).

There are several ways to express the total money costs of the First World War. In 1913 prices, the sum was roughly $ 80 billion (Illustration 6.1)

	expenditure on the First world War in $ billions (rounded)	
	uncorrected for inflation; 'current prices'	in prices of 1913
Allies (Entente)	145	60
Germany *etc.* (Centrals)	70	20
Neutrals*	< 2	< 1
Total	**215**	**80**

* Expenditure of neutral countries – the Netherlands, Scandinavian countries and Switzerland – mainly for mobilisation is fully negligible in comparison with those of belligerent countries. **Bogart** (1920), p. 298 estimates a total sum of $ 1,6 billion in current prices, which would amount to roughly $ 650 million in 1913 dollars. According to the same estimation, 40% of it could be attributed to the Netherlands. Although these amounts are small as a fraction of the total war expenditure, for small neutral countries themselves they were by no means negligible, although it remains true that a lot of money could be saved by not spending it.

Source: see text and notes.

Interpretation...

But what does it mean, a sum of 80 billion 1913 dollars, apart from the fact that it sounds like a lot of money? One way to get an impression is relating the amount to the size of the economies of the countries involved, commonly expressed in GDP (see also the Annex, page 297). Then there appear large differences between countries. For Germany and France, the annual war-related expenses during the most intense years (1916-1918) were about 40%-50% of one year's GDP.[15] In Britain, the order of magnitude appears somewhat lower, 30%-40%, although there are also estimates leading to values above 40%.[16]

The United States was involved for a shorter period but intensely, though at a distance. In the years 1917 and 1918 war expenditure represented roughly 15% of the American economy. Estimations for Italy and Austria-Hungary lead to indicative annual values of 20% and 25% of their GDP, respectively.[17] For Russia, participating in the war until September 1917, annual expenditure was in the order of 25% of GDP as well.[a]

These rates provide some indication about the impact of the war on the economy and finance of a country. By relating expenditure to GDP, the effect of inflation is neutralised, which makes it comparable to present-day values. If the United States would spend presently (say 2015) as much on war relative to its economy as it did in 1917-1918, this would have been $ 2,700 billion; the actual value of 2015 was $ 600 billion. The financial and economic burden of the First World War during that war was almost 4.5 times as high as present-day American defence expenditure. For Britain, the figures are even more dramatic. Taking a moderate 35% of GDP spending on war, as it may have been the case during the First World War, this would amount to £ 660 billion in 2015/'16. The actual defence budget in 2015/'16 was £ 45 billion, which implies a factor of almost 15 between then and now.[18] In financial terms, for Britain it was the Great War indeed[b] and these figures show that other and less wealthy countries could really go bankrupt on it.

... and a breakdown by country
All those figures are indicative, because they are calculated on the basis of incomplete data and many assumptions, however hard researchers tried

---

a   The example of Russia, by the way, shows the ambiguity of estimates of the total costs, since all expenditure after September 1917 is disregarded, although state expenditure after that date was undoubtedly war-related to some extent, although it is virtually impossible to determine this share.

b   See also illustration 14.1 on page 254.

to get them as accurate as possible. In virtually all calculations long-term obligations such as pensions remain out of sight; they are indeed much smaller than the enormous flows of money during the war. In any case, they were not important for the immediate task of financing the war, as will be analysed in the next chapters. In the end, they would be financed in a more 'normal' way, just as the arms race before the war had been financed largely from normal budgets. Formally, however, they should be taken into account if one wishes to calculate the total money costs of the war.[19]

The United States and Britain paid almost half of the total money cost of the war, as measured in 1913 dollars [in brackets $ amounts per capita] (Illustration 6.2)

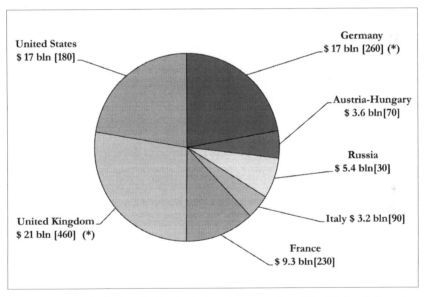

* For Britain, only the British Isles (including the present Republic of Ireland). For other Commonwealth countries taken together, the amount is roughly $ 2 billion. On the scale presented here, contributions of other belligerent countries such as Bulgaria or the Ottoman Empire are negligible. Data for Germany include expenditure made by the federal states. Source: see text and notes.[20]

A complication in calculating expenditure by country is given by the loans, mainly between the Entente allies. A country that had lent money to an ally took a larger amount to finance, over and above its own needs. It was the United States, but also Britain and to a lesser extent France that advanced enormous sums of money to its allies.[a] For receiving (borrowing) countries, these loans were resources for their current expenditure *during* the war and a cause of expenses *after* the war in the form of interest and redemption payments. If all loans had been paid back neatly after the war, they would not have been counted as war expenditure for the initial lender. History shows however, that few of the loans have indeed been paid back (Chapter 13). With hindsight we may therefore properly assign these loans as war expenditure of the *lending* (creditor) country. This gives a more realistic picture of the eventual financial burden. As a result, the American and British war expenditure is larger than it would have been expected on the basis of their operational war effort alone. For example, loans to allies are responsible for almost 30% of the American war expenditure as presented in illustration 6.2; for Britain, the corresponding share is 25% (in the total sums in figure 6.1. these loans have evidently been counted just once).

Pre-war estimations

Before the First World War broke out, estimations had been made of the costs, as attempts to image the unimaginable. Those calculations were made on the basis of key figures about daily costs for soldiers, ammu-

Only a few pre-war estimations approximated the real expenditure (Illustration 6.3)

German war expenditure, as estimated in 1901*	compared to		conclusion
	in millions of pre-war *marks*		
daily: 62	war chest:	120	1 day of war ≈ 50% war chest
monthly: 1,845	government budget:	1,856	1 month of war ≈ annual budget 1899
annually: 22,000	national economy (GDP):	33,600	1 year of war ≈ 65% GDP
	national wealth:	240,000	1 year of war ≈ 1/11 national wealth

* For Germany (including federal states), the realised expenditure over the five fiscal years 1914/'15-1918/'19 would be on the average 30,000 million marks; corrected for inflation, this would be about 14,000 million pre-war *marks*.

Source: Von Renauld;[b] Ritschl & Spoerer; Helfferich.[21]

---

a   Formally, the US was not an 'ally' of the Entente powers but their 'associate'.
b   Joseph *Ritter* von Renauld (1847-1913), author of the publication, served as an officer in the Bavarian army, retired with the rank of colonel, received his PhD in economics and became a professor at the Bavarian Agricultural University.

nition, etc. They served a different purpose than to evaluate the costs of the war in retrospect. These computations resulted in amounts that were exorbitant for the contemporary public, in such a way as to evoke deterrence – or, on the other side of the political spectrum, to encourage politicians to really take care of raising the money.[22]

In retrospect, practically all of these calculations fell short if compared with the real war expenditure. One of the highest estimations that came close to the real value was considered so extreme, that the author distanced himself from his calculations because he thought them out of proportion.[23] But even this estimation was below the realised value if expressed in current *marks*; only if it is corrected afterwards for inflation, it overshoots the actual value, although not by an absurd amount, see illustration 6.3, page 74.[a]

Conclusion

The amounts of money paid for the First World War were unprecedented. Calculations of the total sum (\$ 80 billion in 1913 dollars) always have the character of estimates, dependent on assumptions and available sources. Attempts to increase the robustness of the amounts contribute relatively little to comprehension of the almost unimaginable sums.

For the countries involved, in some cases the war absorbed 40% or more of the national economy. Even without formally switching to a war economy, war expenditure completely distorted government budgets. Britain and the United States were deeply involved in a financial way as they had to pay not only their own war efforts but also finance their allies. In the first years of the war it was notably Britain that acted as a banker for less well off countries; during the war, the United States would take over this role.

---

a   Special mention might be made of the Polish banker Jan Bloch. In his book *The Future of War*, first published in 1898, he presented a sum of \$ 35 billion as the total expenditure of a future war with five countries involved (Germany, Austria-Hungary, Italy, France and Russia). If these are taken as 1913-dollar values (not unreasonable in a period of low inflation and under the Gold Standard), this is remarkably close to the value of \$ 38.5 billion of illustration 6.2 for these countries. Although the total sum is roughly correct, Bloch highly *under*estimated the value for Germany while *over*estimating the amount for other countries, notably Russia, **Bloch** (1899), p. 144.

7

Sources for funding: a menu with limited choices

'If we had to fight against a Triple League; if England would block
our ports, if the French would be at this side of the Rhine and the
Russians at this side of the Vistula, then financing by loans could fail;
but in that case covering expenditure by taxation would fail as well;
[and] paper money should remedy the situation'.
Heinrich Dietzel, 1912[a]

Finance mechanisms

Government expenditure increased spectacularly during the war. Every government faced the problem of how to cover the budget gap that resulted from the disparity between revenue and expenditure. There were four important options to choose from: taxation, domestic war loans, creating money by the central bank and foreign loans.[1] Apart from these main sources, there were a few additional and relatively minor methods, such as relying on a war chest and selling surplus army goods after the war. And finally, a successful army could force occupied countries to contribute financially by imposing taxes and by more or less organised forms of looting.

After the war, governments could call effectively on two other mechanisms. In the first place, there was the option of not paying back war loans – either domestically or abroad or both – or paying back in devalued currency; this in fact still shifted the burden to taxpayers. The other method was imposing reparations, obviously an option only available for victors. Every belligerent (and neutral) country found its own way of

---

a   **Dietzel** (1912), p. 63: *'Gewiß [...] – sollte Deutschland einmal zu fechten haben gegen einen Dreibund; blockierte England unsere Häfen, stünden die Franzosen diesseits des Rheins, die Russen diesseits der Weichsel, dann wäre denkbar, daß Anleihedeckung versagte. Aber dann würde auch Steuerdeckung versagen – würde die Erhebung der Abgaben unter so starken Hemmungen, mit so gewaltigen Ausfällen vor sich gehen, daß, statt oder mindestens neben dem beweglichen Faktor Einkommens- oder Vermögenssteuer, der noch beweglichere Faktor Papiergeld würde aushelfen müssen.'*

using these different sources. They acted according to their specific possibilities, traditions and – of course – expectations about progress, duration and outcome of the war.

The four most important financial flows will be analysed in the next chapters 8-11; they have been depicted in illustration 7.1. In this illustration they are linked to the funding parties: the population, both as taxpayers and as subscribers to war loans, the central bank and foreign 'investors'. Like all models, the illustration is a simplified scheme of reality for several reasons. In the first place, only actors immediately related to the national state have been included; the banking sector, for example, has been omitted as well as tax levied on industry, in particular war industry. In the foreign block, the distinction between private lenders (foreign bankers) and governments, a difference that would be crucial in the conditions of the loans, had been disregarded in the scheme (see Chapters 10 and 12).

A second simplification is that the illustration suggests that the population can be split into two separate groups: on the one hand taxpayers and on the other hand citizens who used their savings to buy war loans. In reality both groups of course coincided at least partially. Subscribers on war loans undoubtedly paid taxes as well, in view of their income and wealth. In that sense, the border was not sharp; it was sharp in the distinction between the finance mechanisms: paying taxes was mandatory, subscription to war loans was voluntary (at least formally).

And finally, there is one crucial aspect of finance that is impossible to express in an illustration: time. Money created by short-term loans or printing banknotes entered the economy *immediately*, either as paper money or on bank accounts, only to flow back (partially) to the government with a certain *time delay*, after it had been in the economic process of production and consumption and finally collected by taxes or war loans. Also, private money invested in the war by means of war loans was immediately available, while taxes were always levied and collected afterwards, in particular income tax and capital and property tax. In the meantime, the total amount of money had grown, as had individual flows. If the arrows had to represent the *volume* of financial flows, they should not only have different size, but also be changing continuously

The principal war financing mechanisms in a simplified picture (Illustration 7.1)

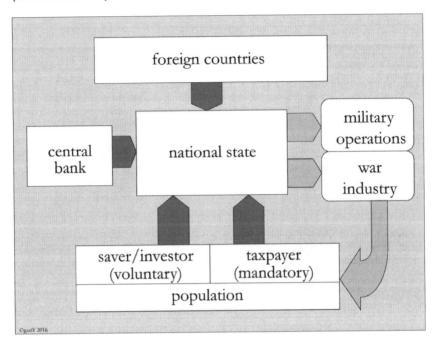

in size – and differ by country.[a] Nevertheless illustration 7.1, simplified as it may be, expresses the main funding methods for war finance. In the rest of this chapter we shall discuss their pros and cons. Chapters 8-11 describe in more detail the way in which Britain, France, Germany and the United States employed these various methods as well as the amounts of money involved.

Taxation
On the revenue side of the budget, a government ultimately has only one sustainable source of money: taxes.[2] Taxation of citizens and companies can assume many forms: direct taxation on income, profit, capital, and indirect taxes on consumer goods such as VAT, or import duties and stamp duties. If the state runs companies, such as railways and postal services, profits made by these enterprises and paid to the treasury are also a form of taxation. The same holds for state monopolies; at the time

---

a   In this sense, the illustration is static, not dynamic; at the end of the war, proportions of financial flows differed largely from those at the beginning of the war.

of the First World War, this was for example the case in Russia for alcohol and in Italy on life insurances.[a]

Taxes, however, are more than annual revenue for the government. They form the collateral to borrow, because for a lender the steady flow of income guarantees interest and redemption payments. This, in fact is the theory, or as you like, the fiction that governments maintain. A steady flow of tax revenue determines a country's credibility, at least in international financial markets. In the First World War, taxation played a minor role in financing (Chapter 8); only in Britain and the United States did it contribute more than a negligible share. Far more important were (war) loans and monetary financing by the central bank.

Domestic loans

The most obvious other way of financing is borrowing.[b] In Germany, Finance Minister Karl Helfferich (see box on page 81) even called loans the most important source of finance when he presented his first war budget in the *Reichstag* in March 1915.[3] For Helfferich, taxation was the least important source. His opinion was based on a 'normal' budget – that is, without military expenditure! – that was formally balanced and therefore no new taxation would be required.[4] A further argument was that war was waged for the future of the nation, so that future generations would benefit from it, which justified the use of loans. And finally he declared, with enthusiastic supporting exclamations of the *Reichstag* members, that after the war the bill would be presented to the defeated enemies. This latter fact of course was a political viewpoint for which a finance minister of a belligerent country could not be blamed – although after the war Helfferich would be furious when the victorious enemies applied this same principle to Germany itself. It should be noted however, that these ideas were not confined to Germany, although in that

---

a   In pre-war Russia, no less than a quarter of all tax revenue was produced by excise duties on alcohol, together with a government monopoly on liquor. At the moment of mobilisation alcohol consumption was prohibited by ukase and the state liquor stores were closed. This of course had little effect on alcohol consumption, but all the more on the government's revenue from excise duties, which fell by a quarter. Evidently financial war preparation had been badly coordinated in Russia, **Hardach** (1987), pp. 166-167. For this and other examples of ineffective taxation in other countries, see **Strachan** (2004), pp. 88-90, 94, 102.

b   A more direct way of collecting money, but with less revenue and not repeatable, was to press the population to surrender gold (as coins or in any other form) or comparable valuables in exchange for paper money. This amounts to a one-time liquidation of assets; in Germany, for example, see **RT** 315, nr. 26, p. 7.

country they were more openly communicated. In France there was no less a tendency to shift the burden to a defeated enemy or to future generations.[5] And just as in Germany, the result was more borrowing and less taxation.

The German Financial High Commanders, part 1: Quartermaster Helfferich[6]

Karl Theodor Helfferich (1872-1924) was finance minister of the German Empire (formally Staatssekretär des Reichsschatzamtes, *see note on page 47) from 1ˢᵗ February 1915 until 22 May 1916. In a*

period where crucial decisions were made about war finance, he was one of the two men that commanded the German financial army, together with the president of the Reichsbank, Rudolf Havenstein (page 129). The duo might be rightfully called the German Supreme Financial Command (Oberste Finanzleitung)*, analogous to the military Supreme Command* (Oberste Heeresleitung)*.*[a]

Karl Helfferich was the eldest of seven children. His parents owned a small textile mill in Neustadt, in the Palatinate region, then part of the kingdom of Bavaria. Young Karl was the cleverest boy at school and he would remain so in whatever high circles he was to move. After studying law in Munich, he received his PhD in economics in Strasbourg (at that time a German city) with a thesis on the German-Austrian monetary union of 1857. Finally he acquired his full academic Habilitation degree in Berlin. In the meantime he published papers on all matters related to money

---

a   During the larger part of the war, the military Supreme Command consisted of General field marshal Paul von Hindenburg and Quartermaster general Erich Ludendorff. It is questionable whether Havenstein can be compared with Hindenburg; the comparison between Helfferich and Ludendorff is probably more realistic and has been put forward by Benedikt Kautsky (the son of the socialist Karl), **Kautsky** (1931), p. 19.

and policy, culminating in what was to become the standard treatise Money (Das Geld) in 1903, reprinted many times.[7] The book Germany's Wealth (Deutschlands Volkswohlstand), published 10 years later, has been for a long time the first and only reliable source on the size of the German economy in an international perspective. The aim of this publication was straightforward: to supply scientific evidence for Germany's position as an economic and financial world power at the occasion of the 25th anniversary of William II as German Emperor.

Through his research and his publications he soon came into contact with the financial elite of Wilhelminian Germany, where his intelligence and ambition did not go unnoticed. As a young man in his thirties he was made responsible for one of the subsidiaries of the prestigious Deutsche Bank (not to be confused with the Reichsbank) responsible for financing the construction of the famous Baghdad railway; he then lived in Istanbul for some time. When he became a director of the Deutsche Bank in 1908, it was evident that he was now himself a member of the country's financial elite. In 1915 Helfferich was the man destined to lead Germany's war finance when he succeeded the weak and bureaucratically minded Herman Kühn as finance minister of the German Empire. He was the first man in this office with experience in the banking world. Before that, he had been a personal advisor to the German Emperor on the optimal way to exploit occupied Belgium: maximising production under German supervision. In passing he estimated the amount of reparations required from Belgium and France, once they were defeated.[8] The prospect of such future capital flows will not have gone without influencing his view on the way Germany should finance the war.

Already as a boy, Helfferich had shown an overwhelming ambition. He sought bitter discussions rather than avoiding them; although in most cases the strength of his analyses would have been sufficient for winning debates, he kept it as personal as possible. Even though he was a politician, banker and financial expert, he essentially remained straight-thinking in narrow-minded legal terms. He preferred to charge his political enemies, such as Matthias Erzberger in court. It is characteristic for his way of thinking that he wanted the government of the later Weimar Republic condemned for treason instead of accepting a democratically elected majority.[9]

During the war, this was still the future. Shortly after having presented his second war budget, he was called in May 1916 by Chancellor Theobald von Bethmann Hollweg to the high office of Deputy Chancellor and Home Secretary. In this function he became in fact the third highest in rank in the Germans State hierarchy, after the Emperor and the Chancellor himself – except for the military of course, who held the real power. Karl Helfferich's career is a splendid example of the emancipation of a liberal middle class in an economically expanding Germany in the last quarter of the 19th century.[10] In his way of thinking, he would always remain a man of Wilhelminian Germany, even after the war. A revealing detail is his choice of the godfathers of his only son, born 1922: the then former field marshal Hindenburg and no one less than the exiled Emperor Wilhelm II himself.[11]

Borrowing abroad

In the collective memory of borrowing for the war, most attention is given to the large domestic war loans, often issued with spectacular campaigns. After the war, the memories of the raising campaigns with their appeal to patriotism were not easily forgotten and the propaganda posters and even the bonds themselves are collector's items today. There were, however, two other types of loans that were at least as important, notably those from abroad. The first type was aimed at private investors at the international financial markets in neutral and allied countries; the second type consisted of loans from the governments of allied powers. There were large differences between these two types of loans, both in conditions (Chapter 10) and in the way in which they were paid back (Chapters 12 and 13).

In the case of loans negotiated on international financial markets, the creditors were private investors, banks and individuals, who were essentially looking for profitable or reliable investments. They lowered the risk by imposing strict conditions in the form of collateral (a gold deposit would be perfect) and a premium on interest. When a country nevertheless failed, they had few possibilities to force a country to pay. Legal procedures could be long, tedious and expensive without guarantee of success.[12] In fact the only sanction private creditors to countries could exercise, was the potential loss of credit standing of a country in default, which would make it more difficult to generate new credits or refinance current credits. All things considered, for governments seeking money abroad, credits on the international capital markets were relatively expensive.

Borrowings from allied governments, on the other hand, were not charged with such commercial burdens. They merely created a debt from one country against the other and they always had political tenor. Motives to lend could range from pure ideology to enlightened self-interest. Examples of the first kind were used when a country wanted to help their 'brethren' or to buy political or strategic influence; support for its own industry could be a motive of the second kind, as was the case with American loans to allies (Chapter 10). This latter type of loan was not without obligations; one obvious restriction was that the money could only be used for purchases in the creditor country. Anyhow, both the negotiations on the loan and its repayment – after the war – were subject to political discussions. This political element could be positive or negative. The financial costs were relatively low, credits could be ample and collateral was not hard to negotiate. Britain, France, Italy and other allied countries easily received enormous sums of money from the United States, once it had entered the war. The downside was the dependence on political developments, both in the creditor and the receiving country. When the political tide changed in the creditor country – as it did in the US around 1920 when President Harding succeeded Wilson – conditions about repayments could be strengthened, in particular when they had been recorded vaguely. The same holds of course for the debtor country, where a regime change could evoke completely different views on repayment of the once highly appreciated financial support (Chapter 12).

An assessment of taxes and loans
In the long run, the only way to finance a war is either from taxation among the population, or from abroad by imposing reparations or by receiving grants. But as Keynes remarked, in the long run we are all dead.[13] The real question was how to find the funds for a war *during* the war, moreover, a war that was supposed to be short but that threatened to take more time. Both taxes and loans have their own practical and strategic pros and cons, that have been put forward before and during

the war, not only by politicians like Helfferich and his colleagues in belligerent countries, but by a series of economists and historians as well.[14] In Europe, these discussions mainly took place during the years of investments in armaments before the war and occasionally during the war; in the United States heated debates arose at the moment when involvement in the European war became a realistic prospect, in 1916 and in particular in the spring of 1917.[15] The main arguments can be traced back to three elements: speed, burden-sharing and credit status.

The argument of speed

Speed works in favour of loans. Mobilisation of financial means by borrowing can be realised far more quickly for a government than by collecting taxes. In a short war, this can be decisive, just as a rapid and smooth mobilisation of troops could make the difference between victory and defeat. Since the nineteenth century, both governments and the wealthier part of the public were familiar with government bonds, such as the British Consols or gilts, French *perpétuelles*, Russian state bonds, etc. They were long-term loans, often even **perpetuals**, and they found their way to institutions such as banks and insurance companies but also to individuals. If necessary, the central bank facilitated the issue to the public. This instrument of finance was available for governments virtually at the moment that the war was declared, provided that the public and institutions were able and prepared to bring in their money. The factor of speed held *in extremis* for short-term loans or advances from the central bank itself.

Taxes, on the other hand lacked this speed and flexibility for two reasons: in preparation and in collection. Every new tax – or an increase in existing taxes – needed parliamentary discussion and approval.[a] Such a discussion was always highly political because it concerned a redistribution of wealth among the population and therefore it could consume much time, while the war went on and the military needed money *now*. For example in Germany, there had been a long-lasting discussion about a national income tax, which had ended finally in 1913 in a one-time levy (*Wehrbeitrag*) for owners of large property and capital and high in-

---

a With the exception of countries where parliamentary power was weak, such as in Austria where parliament did not meet, or Russia where the tradition of ukase was stronger than that of the Duma. In those cases the inevitable political discussion took place behind closed doors in the government's bosom.

come. As soon as the war had begun in August 1914, almost everyone avoided challenging the precarious equilibrium between national government and federal states and between right and left. The party truce (*Burgfrieden*) was a welcome excuse for many years of postponement of new tax proposals (Chapter 8). In France the excuse for postponement was the occupation of the northern region. In Britain taxes were at hand to use them as an instrument for war finance, but even there it was not easy to find a balance between underlying and presumably real conflicts of interest between Conservatives, Liberals and the rising Labour party.[16] In the US, where democracy and open discussions in Congress flourished, there was heavy lobbying from interest groups, both on the types and rates of taxes and on the principle.[a]

Apart from party political arguments, in every country there was initially the general and positive feeling that the war would be short, which could be undermined by starting a discussion about taxes. And finally, the population might be afraid that taxes would last once the war was over and direct necessity had disappeared. With hindsight, this was a serious concern, since new taxes on income have never been abolished and turnover taxes, high excise duties on alcohol, tobacco and 'luxury' goods were only partially decreased after the war.

The second disadvantage of taxation appeared once they had been adopted: collecting. Indirect taxes on consumption such as on tobacco, sugar and alcohol could still be collected relatively easy, as they were paid to and administered by shopkeepers and companies. But direct taxes on income, turnover and property, required information from individuals and were governed by declarations and time periods such as fiscal years. In Germany and in France, where eventually in 1916 taxation was taken up seriously, it would have an effect on next year's budget only. In fact for France, the largest tax revenues arrived only *after* the war.

All these awkward political discussions and slow revenues were avoided by issuing loans. As soon as parliament had voted for credits, its role was over. The rest was just a matter of technical details in which the govern-

---

a   For example, it will be no surprise that bankers lobbied for less taxation and more borrowing, because the later instrument obviously better suited their business model; see **Gilbert** (1970), p. 89 ff. and pp. 105 ff. for some lobbying activities.

ment had more or less *carte blanche*. Of course an attentive parliament – notably the British Parliament had several debates – could discuss interest rates and tax profits for subscribers, but the largest obstacle had been cleared quietly and the government had assured an undisturbed flow of revenue. Earlier experience, albeit in peacetime, learned that issues of government bonds were often oversubscribed, which implied that the money would indeed flow in. Financial planning by loans was far more assured than by taxes, at least in the short term.

Sharing the burden

Apart from practical considerations of speed, there were more fundamental aspects in a government's decision between taxation and borrowing. A subject that received considerable attention in the German literature before the war was the argument that taxes could be unfair because they did not take personal circumstances into account, or at least not sufficiently. In the case of loans, the argument was that money that could best be missed would become available first. In a natural way, wealthy people would contribute more than the poor and without state coercion.[17] And, of course, it could be done without introducing the kind of highly progressive tax rates necessary to obtain sufficient revenue. In economic terms, allocation of resources would be more efficient, because the best available capital would be used first.[18] Finally, taxes offered many possibilities for evasion.[19]

Although these arguments might be true to some extent, they are not convincing in favour of loans and against taxes. Indeed, after the war loans would have been repaid – with interest – from taxes and then the arguments about personal circumstances and evasion would still hold.[a] Only in the case – tacitly assumed by the proponents – of shifting the burden to the defeated enemy, would such arguments make sense. Without this assumption, they had the character of a plea against taxes in general rather than just for the purpose of financing the war by loans.

---

a   It depended on the type of loan to what extent loans would have to be redeemed. The French perpetual loans were never to be repaid in full, they only bore interest. But even fixed-date loans could be refinanced at maturity by new loans. In Britain and the US it was common practice to provide for interest and redemption payments by means of a **sinking fund**, filled annually from the regular budget. In the French and German tradition such funds were absent.

A more serious point was redistribution of wealth. In economic terms, taxation implied a visible distribution of wealth among the population or at least a visible *re*distribution. Every tax proposal called into question the social *status quo* and this was precisely what a government in wartime wanted to avoid; concealed conflicts of interest between social groups became overt, because it was visible who had to make sacrifices and to what extent. On the other hand, refraining from tax measures also implied redistribution effects, but only in the long run. Subscribers to war loans received revenue on their investment, to be paid by the government. Or, to reframe it in ideological terms: the taxpayer had to pay for the war profits of the capitalists who had invested in government bonds (where it should be noted that taxpayers and subscribers could overlap to some extent). Thus, social unrest avoided by refraining from taxation would be fuelled by loans that were profitable for people who already seemed to benefit from the war (or actually got profit from the war). Although it was not war profit in the usual sense, people's sentiments would not necessarily be less. By means of loans social unrest in the short term was exchanged for potential or real unrest in the long term.[20] And indeed this term could be very long, since payments for interest and redemption on long-term war bonds would pose a burden on the population for many decades to come. Few people realised that financing the war by borrowing logically implied that taxes would not decrease when the war was over, or at least they did not mention it.[21] Helfferich must have been aware of it when he said that the war was waged for the future. Undoubtedly in his view it would not be the next generation of *Germans* that had to pay back the loans.

Credit standing

To use the instrument of loans effectively, a country needed an adequate credit rating. Foreign investors in particular would not line up when a government with a financial junk status would call for a loan. In any case, they would require a higher risk premium in the form of a higher interest rate, collateral or a reduced loan term. But even domestic subscribers to loans would be reluctant if they suspected that their money was not in safe hands. Taxes and loans had an opposite effect on a country's credit ranking. Taxes worked in a positive direction, because investors knew that the government had solid, trustworthy and sustainable collateral and a source for future repayments and interest. Loans, on the other hand, undermined the credit rating. In particular large and successive loans would rightly give the impression of decreasing repayment capacity leading to increased borrowing, still higher rates of interest and ultimately even default.

The actual importance of the credit standing of a country for borrowing depended on the significance attributed to this notion in the first place; at this point there were large differences between countries, based partially on tradition but also on expectations about the effort to obtain domestic and especially foreign loans. The largest differences were between Britain and Germany. For Britain with the tradition of a trading country, a superior credit rating was all-important. It issued the minimum number (three) of large war loans of all large belligerent countries and it paid them back, the last one in 2015. Admittedly, the British government deployed a large arsenal of other kinds of loans (Chapter 9), but always with its finger on the pulse – or rather its hand on the tap – and in close cooperation with the financial sector.

Germany, on the other hand had always been confronted with a lower credit rating than Britain or France.[22] It expected to call on foreign creditors very modestly during the war (Chapter 10). The issue of no less than 9 large domestic war loans, at fixed intervals and without seriously increasing attractiveness, clearly shows that credit ratings were not considered a serious issue in Germany. Helfferich's preference for loans instead of taxes was not a difficult one. Germany relied on its military power and its advanced industry for its victory and as the basis for its credit standing. If at some moment domestic credit rating counted at all, it was behind the scenes and not an issue for the general public buying war bonds.[23]

One important argument *against* loans has not yet been mentioned, because it played no role at all during the First World War. War loans on which the public was supposed to subscribe were public – as the name implies. Success or failure of the loan was visible for everyone, both at home and abroad. Although the censor could try to boast a success and obscure failures, the number of subscriptions and the amount raised acted as indicators for the war sentiment in a country.[24] In a direct way, because the loans appealed to patriotic feelings; the number of subscribers was a measure for the part of the population convinced by these arguments. In an indirect way it was also a barometer of the sentiment in the country as it was a measure for subscribers who were led by the more material argument of return on investment. Indeed, the opportunity to get a profitable yield depended strongly on the expectations about a quick and decisive military victory, as demonstrated by Lloyd George's words that 'success means credit; financiers never hesitate to lend to a prosperous concern'.[25] For a government, war loans were the overt measure for public support. Finance ministers from all belligerent countries boasted in their parliamentary speeches on their results, preferably comparing it with the enemy who was supposed to exert much more effort to raise money.[26] In fact war loans were the only visible measure of war sentiment or war commitment in the absence of general elections that had been postponed in all belligerent countries; simple and clear: 'a national loan is a referendum'.[a] It was a message heard loud and clear by the enemy. This was exactly the reason why the Nazi regime did not issue war loans, both before and during the Second World War. Although the need for money was no less, financing took place 'silently'.[b]

Massive subscriptions to war loans meant massive popular support; to the boys in the trenches: you too, subscribe, please! (Illustration 7.2)

Die fünfte Kriegsanleihe
Ein Flugblatt der Kriegszeitung der IV. Armee
Von R. Bruhn Lt. d. R. (Marinekorps)

Kameraden!

Das Deutsche Reich fordert in der Zeit vom 4. September bis zum 4. Oktober zur Zeichnung auf die fünfte deutsche Kriegsanleihe auf. Was heisst das für uns?

Unsere Heimat, der wir nun schon über 2 Jahre fern sind, um sie zu schützen, stellt an das deutsche Volk daheim und an die deutschen Soldaten an der Front, in Feindesland, zum fünften Male eine schicksalsschwere Vertrauensfrage, von deren Beantwortung die Behauptung des Sieges und die Gestaltung eines Friedens abhängig ist, welcher Deutschlands Existenz und Zukunft sichern muss.

Unsere bisherigen **Kriegsanleihen** sind in ihren Ergebnissen gewaltige **Kundgebungen des deutschen Volkes**, seines unerschütterlichen Willens zum Durchhalten und zum Siege geworden. Sie sind besonders durch die **Millionen der kleinen Zeichner** zu wahren Volksanleihen geworden. Eine Volksanleihe aber ist **eine Volksabstimmung**.

Source: *Kriegszeitung der IV. Armee*, August / September 1917, collection Jos Kleinhans.

---

a   '*eine Volksanleihe [...] ist eine Volksabstimmung*', see illustration 7.2.
b   **Aly & Chase** (2007), pp. 294, 298; this 'silent' way of financing amounted – apart from expropriating Jewish property – to a highly opaque way of accumulating debts, for example by a forced conversion of savings into government 'securities' and issuing bills of exchange by a government controlled fake company, the 'Metallurgic Research Corporation Ltd.' (*Metallurgische Forschungsgesellschaft GmbH*), the so-called *Mefo*-bills.

Monetary financing

Printing fresh banknotes offered a fast and easy way for governments to provide for money during mobilisation and the first few weeks of the war. In France and Germany, this had been prepared long before the war. It would not be confined, however, to the beginning of the war; on the contrary, it would develop into a practise with increasing popularity, in particular on the European continent, sometimes referred to as 'running the printing presses'.

The usual mechanism was that the central bank bought government securities in the form of short-term debt obligations, placed these on its balance sheet and issued new bank notes as legal tender.[a] The short-term government obligations, often called treasury bills, had a typical life of three months. By means of the new money, the government increased its purchasing power, allowing it to buy the goods it needed for the war (the out-arrows in illustration 7.1). The government used this workaround, because the central bank had the privilege and the monopoly[27] on issuing bank notes as legal tender.[b] This increase in the form of paper bank notes would never have been possible had these notes been convertible into gold at the counters of the central bank since physical gold reserves clearly cannot be increased by administrative policy measures. Suspending the convertibility of bank notes therefore was a necessary and logical simultaneous measure (Chapter 11 and illustration 5.1, page 58).

The great advantage of short-term treasury bills was that they could be produced almost instantaneously when needed; they provided the government practically at the same moment with extra money, without tiresome discussions about taxes or the bargaining about conditions for public war loans. On the negative side, there were two less pleasant properties. The first one, the short term of the obligations, was a minor worry; indeed, at maturity they could easily be rolled over into new bills and added to new short-term government paper.[28] By this procedure, the government accumulated an increasing floating (short-term) debt at the

---

a   This technique is sometimes cryptically referred to as **discounting** treasury bills (or exchequer bills). The central bank could resell (part of) the bills to other banks.

b   New paper money could also be issued directly by the government, as was the case to some extent in Britain during the war or in the United States before the FED was operational, but the financial and economic effect is evidently the same, **Pigou** (1941), p. 10.

central bank, in particular the German and French governments (and their respective allies on the continent). The money in circulation was a visible indicator of this floating debt. The implicit idea was, that these short-term debts would be repaid from large long-term war loans issued to the public from time to time. Instead of continually increasing, the burden would be spread out over many years, in any case to the period after the war. During the war, however, the pattern was that redemption of this short-term debt became less and less normal practice. It is illustrative to see the increase of Germany's floating debt being increasingly less reduced by the revenue from large war loans, illustration 7.3. This pattern was visible in all belligerent countries, although less pronounced.

The second and most important negative effect of new money in circulation was that it would inevitably lead to a rise of prices and fuel inflation.[a] The extra money in circulation was not accompanied by a comparable increase in goods and services. On the contrary, consumer's products became scarce, as industrial production had shifted to war industry. More money among the population and less to buy led to an increase in prices; higher prices evoked wage demands and these were indeed paid because the war went on and needed new material; thus an inflationary spiral grew.[29] The idea of a larger purchasing power by having more money in the pocket was an illusion.

For a long time, this inflationary impact of monetary financing remained hidden during the First World War for three reasons. In the first place, governments set fixed maximum prices for daily consumer products such as bread. This concealed the general increase in prices and for a long time inflation assumed the character of suppressed inflation.[30] Suppressed inflation was accompanied by the development of black markets. Apart from fixing prices, governments could blame general scarcity for a rise of prices; in Germany, the British blockade was an easy excuse. Increase in price level was presented – and seen by the population – as an inevitable consequence of the war as such and not of the way it was financed. The

---

a   Monetary financing did not necessary imply more banknotes in the wallet. It could just as well assume the form of larger bank deposits. The crucial point is an increase in the available amount of money in the economy, expressed in *marks*, dollars, *francs*, pounds or whatever currency. We leave aside discussions among economists whether 'inflation' merely reflects the increase of the amount of money or – and primarily – the rise in price level and the effect on exchange rates.

In 1916 German war finance went out of control. Short-term debts (depicted in the illustration) increased rapidly and the semi-annual war loans were less and less sufficient to reduce it (Illustration 7.3)

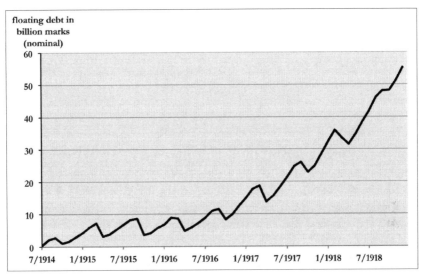

Source: calculated from Holtfrerich.[31]

link with monetary financing was not made, particularly not in France and Germany; in the latter case the financial authorities even explicitly denied the relation (Chapter 11, page 195). In Britain, the conservative London *Economist* did not tire of reminding the government and the public in the strongest terms of the danger of inflation. It must be said that here the Treasury itself was more alert than in France or Germany – not to mention Austria-Hungary or Russia.[32]

A third factor concealing inflation (or, rather its danger) was that the population was not familiar with the phenomenon as such.[33] This may appear strange to modern eyes, but it must be realised that the second half of the nineteenth century was a period of price stability or even sometimes deflation, notwithstanding regular financial crises. The Gold Standard guaranteed stability. When suddenly during the war prices rose by 20% or more every year, this was considered an exceptional situation that would end as soon as the war was over.

A consequence of inflation was that the **real interest rate** – the **nominal** interest rate minus inflation – soon became negative, implying that borrowing money was in fact more profitable than lending. Nevertheless hoarding and a flight into durable goods and real property remained limited during the war. Even in Germany the population maintained its confidence in the *mark*, undoubtedly supported by the censor and propaganda. Only in Austria-Hungary the *krone* lost confidence during the war and there was a flight into material assets (*Sachwerte*) such as real estate.[34]

Inflation works as a creeping tax on capital. The simple example given by Keynes presents a country with an economy worth $ 36 million in goods and services at some moment; in the economy circulates an amount of 9 million of bank notes, thus each representing a value of $ 4.[35] If the government decides to print an additional 3 million of these same banknotes, the total value of the economy remains the unchanged $ 36 million, but now represented by 12 million of notes. Their value has been reduced to $ 3, that is by 25%. All people with bank notes have contributed an invisible one-time levy of 25%.[a] This was a tax, moreover, that was difficult to evade, for which the government could hardly be blamed, a tax that could be collected without any effort and that could even be imposed abroad.[b]

Not every country relied on the printing press to the same extent (Chapter 11), but no government escaped from it. The obvious way to avoid the inflationary effects was skimming additional money among the population by means of taxes and war loans. The former evidently was only effective when taxes were levied substantially which was not the case on the European continent. The latter method, issuing war loans,

---

a   Formally, the banknotes issued are counterbalanced in the central bank's accounts by the government securities; the latter could be redeemed with simultaneous withdrawal of the bank notes. In practice, however, this requires an almost superhuman willpower (apart from favourable economic circumstances) that can be produced very difficultly or only marginally. After all, if issuing new paper money were equivalent to imposing an invisible tax on capital, withdrawal of notes would be equivalent to a silent tax refund on capital, a strange phenomenon indeed. Hence, for issued banknotes it holds: once issued means issued forever.

b   Foreigners with capital or securities denoted in currency of the inflating country were taxed in exactly the same way as inhabitants. It has been estimated that by this mechanism Germany has passed on a bill of 15 billions of (gold) *marks* to other countries during the hyperinflation of 1923, **Holtfrerich** (1977), p. 285.

could only be effective if the money was really committed for a longer period and ceased to be in circulation as money. Practically all systems however had all sorts of 'leaks' by which money in subscriptions to war loans re-entered circulation.[36]

Looting, confiscation and reparations

Taxes, loans and the printing press cover the major part of war financing, but there are some additional options. During the war Germany employed the classic practice of imposing heavy levies on the population in occupied territories. Part of the costs of the army could be covered without burdening their own population. This is a financing method that is often overlooked, but not so in the occupied regions.[37] For the costs of the German occupation army, Belgium received a bill of 2.4 billion *franks*, roughly 2 billion *marks*.[38] This amount had to be paid by the provinces at a rate of 40 million *franks* each month in 1915, increasing to 60 million *franks*/month in 1917.[39] This was only the money, to which must be added the confiscated goods, intermediate products and raw material that were expropriated by the German occupation authorities. The total amount of it has been estimated at 2.5 billion *marks*, of which only one third has been actually paid. The larger part was not paid at all or with a worthless slip of paper.[40] For France, the total amount that had been paid by the population of the occupied territories in the form of levies, fines and contributions was of the same order: 2.5 billion *francs* or 2 billion *marks*.[41] Based on this estimated data, roughly 2.5% of the German war finance had been paid by the occupied population on the western front.[42]

Demanding contributions from occupied territories was not illegal. In the Articles 49 and 52 of the Hague Conventions on war on land (1907), an occupying power was permitted to levy this kind of taxation on the population and to demand services, but exclusively for the maintenance of the troops.[43] From this viewpoint, taxation for billeted troops was to some extent a legal way of war finance by which part of the burden could be shifted abroad. It is not difficult to see that the border between legal and illegal is vague. It became illegal if the taxes were used not for an occupation army behind the frontline but for troops actually fighting on the front against the forces of the occupied country's own armies, as was the case in Belgium and France. Confiscations from citizens and companies were also controversial. At best the owner got a receipt with the promise that he would be compensated later.[a]

It was not even necessary to actually occupy a country to extract wealth from it to finance the war. Assets held abroad by citizens from enemy countries, such as securities and commercial vessels could easily be confiscated.[44] In the first days of the war, Britain 'wangled' three war ships that were under construction in British shipyards on behalf of the Ottoman Empire and Chile. Obviously the total value of it, £ 7.5 million in 1911 values, was completely negligible to the British war finances; it was rather a kind of bonus.[45]

Whereas taxes and confiscations were taking place during the war, reparations are by definition financing mechanisms to be used *after* the war. In 1915 Helfferich had anticipated reparations – to be paid *to* Germany – when he justified loans instead of taxes. In his own words, Germany 'cannot and shall not refrain from [...] having our enemies to pay for the material damage'.[46] The *Reichstag* loved it: 'applause and approval'. In August 1915 he went even further with the famous words 'The instigators of this war have earned this lead weight of billions; may *they* drag it down through the decades, not *we*.'[b] Here too, the German parliament supported this policy by shouting 'quite right' and 'very well'. After the war Germany was not to receive reparations but to pay them. For the allied countries, the received payments were a belated source of war finance. Although Germany did not pay any way near the amount it was supposed to do (Chapter 12), the reparations actually received by the allies, estimated at 12.5 (gold) *marks* were not completely negligible; they accounted for 5% of their war expenditure.[47]

---

a   Anyhow, this administrative process was an improvement as compared to the usual practice until (and including) the Napoleonic wars, where looting took place in a disorderly manner. Although the French sharply condemned legalised looting by Germany in the First World War, **Lewandowski** (1923), these same methods had actually been applied by French troops under Napoleon a century before without the legitimating veneer of the Hague Conventions.

b   'Das Bleigewicht der Milliarden haben die Anstifter dieses Krieges verdient; sie mögen es durch die Jahrzehnte schleppen, nicht wir', **RT** 306, p. 224; translation derived from **Williamson** (1971), p. 131.

Miscellaneous

A final form of war financing, also only applicable after the war, was selling surplus army and navy equipment. Although many of the materials used during the war were practically worthless outside the battlefield (submarines, long distance guns, gas shells), there were objects or parts that could be traded on the market for civil commodities. Clothing, food stocks, vehicles, horses, electrical and optical equipment, metal, etc. were wanted; after the war they were bought by individuals through dump stores (see the text box on page 205). The price could be below the original production costs due to excess of supply and limited practicality; nevertheless, the dump store route formed a temporary but small source of revenue for the governments of belligerent countries.

Summary and reflection

The repertoire of financing instruments comprised taxation, domestic war loans, commercial and government loans abroad, monetary financing, revenues from occupied territories and reparations. Borderlines between the various instruments were not always clear. Monetary financing, for example, worked out as a levy on capital through inflation. Short-term government credits that had been redeemed strictly before the war, gradually shifted to monetary financing during the war.

In practice during the First World War every country used *all* instruments, but with a different mix. The general principle was that the government borrowed most of the money in some way or other, and that taxation played a supplementary role; in Britain and the United States taxes were levied and increased from the beginning, in continental European countries this did not happen substantially before 1916. Short-term treasury bills bought by the central bank were supposed to be redeemed by the revenue from large-scale war loans extending over several decades. The financial obligations of these loans would lay an enormous burden on government's budges for a long time after the war unless revolution, other domestic social unrest or inflation would end them prematurely.

Before the First World War, there had been heated discussions about the question whether taxes or loans should be used to finance a coming war. Participants in these discussions presented the issue as mutually exclusive options with a real choice. This however was a false contrast. A war as large as the First World War simply could not be financed exclusively – and not even to a substantial amount – from taxes.[48] It would (and will) always be necessary to borrow, if only under the pressure of military developments. The question to what extent the resulting burden should be distributed among various groups of the population – both actually and in the future – ultimately comes down to a matter of politics, not of economics or finance.

8

Taxes: an inconvenient option for politicians

'when war comes, [governments] are both unwilling and unable to increase their revenue in proportion to the increase of their expense. They are unwilling, for fear of offending the people, who by so great and so sudden an increase of taxes, would soon be disgusted with the war.'
Adam Smith, 1776[a]

According to classical liberal doctrine roughly one third of war expenditure should be covered by taxes.[1] And liberalism was the predominant ideology in practically every western country before the First World War. Nevertheless, only in Britain and the United States, countries where this tradition was strongest, war expenditure would be covered by more than 20% by taxes. Thus, in Europe, the United Kingdom with a tax coverage of 20-26% was the big exception and outside Europe, the US attained 23%.[2] Initially the Americans had aimed at 33% (or even 50%) but this soon proved impossible, despite the short participation in the war;[3] it was not so much its own war expenditure, but in particular the large loans to their allies that forced the United States to have recourse more to loans than to use taxation.[4] Continental European countries started with some forms of taxation only during the war, reluctantly and with meagre result. It was just too little and too late, see illustration 8.1.

Great Britain
The United Kingdom had a tradition of paying for wars by taxes. In most of the wars that the country had fought before 1914, taxes had contributed an average of 40% to cover war expenditure; the remainder being

---

a   The full quotation reads: *'The ordinary expense of the greater part of modern governments in time of peace being equal or nearly equal to their ordinary revenue, when war comes, they are both unwilling and unable to increase their revenue in proportion to the increase of their expense. They are unwilling, for fear of offending the people, who by so great and so sudden an increase of taxes, would soon be disgusted with the war'*, Adam Smith (1723-1790), **Smith** (1976 [1776]), p. 919; **Kang & Rockoff** (2006), p. 7.

The major part of war expenditure in the First World War was financed with loans, not from taxes (Illustration 8.1)

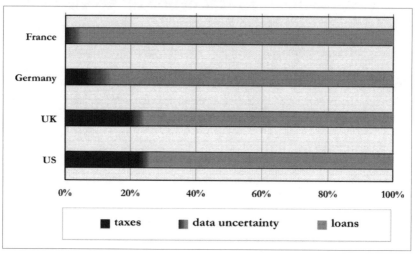

Source: Balderston, Strachan, Ferguson, Bogart, Knauss.[5]

paid by loans that were repaid in the decades after the war.[6] Indeed, at the eve of the First World War Britain had the best developed tax system of all belligerent countries, not only because of liberal principles, but also by its imperial interests. Wars were always fought overseas and over the seas of the world the Royal Navy was invincible.[a] And the population had to fork out to deploy the forces over there – or to provide Britain's allies with necessary means. The British tax system was perfectly suited to adapt to continuing changing circumstances of war and peace.

Compared with other countries, British per capita expenditure for warfare was the highest of all. Nevertheless, the contribution was rather modest if the size of the Empire was taken into account and the (extra) tax was considered as an insurance premium for its global commercial interests.[7] The complete arms programme before the war had been financed from taxes, including the construction of large battleships in the *Dreadnought* programme.[8] Despite all these material preparations for a possible war, Britain entered the First World War with a budget surplus.[9]

---

a   This has been expressed aptly by the words 'Orders came for sailing somewhere over there' in the British version of the war song Lili Marlene.

The strength of the British tax system was its income tax, an instrument that was practically absent in all other European countries, at least at the national level. Income tax (together with property tax) accounted for almost one quarter of total government revenue.[10] It had been introduced in 1799 during the Napoleonic wars and it had been largely maintained, albeit with rates depending on the intensity of war efforts, such as the ones fought in colonial wars.[11] On 1st July 1914, one month before the war broke out, the income rate tax had been determined at 6.25%, or, in the then used terminology, 1 s. 3 d. (1/3) to the £.

In line with the tradition, Chancellor of the Exchequer David Lloyd George announced that taxes would be raised when he presented a supplementary budget in 1914. Since 1908 Lloyd George had played the part of Chancellor in the Asquith cabinet, although in the words of Keynes he had 'not the faintest idea of the meaning of money'.[12] One might argue about that, but it is evident that his achievements in the field of social welfare were more sustainable than in war finance. In today's language he would certainly have declared not to be a number freak. Anyhow, in 1915 after a rearrangement of cabinet posts, he could enjoy himself at the spending department of Munitions without bothering about the bill that he could pass to his successor, about whom we shall come to soon.

By the first increase in income tax, the rate was doubled to 12.5%.[13] Eventually in the 1918/'19 budget (a British fiscal year covered the period from 1st April to 31 March of the next year), the rate would be as high as 30% (6 s. to the £), far exceeding anything of the like in continental Europe. Income tax was one of the two pillars of direct taxation in Britain, the other being the war profits tax. Both were applied with increasing intensity. Apart from that, indirect taxes on consumer's goods and luxury goods were levied and raised. The effect was that the total tax pressure that had started at 6.7% of GDP before the war ended at 15.3% in 1919.[14 a]

---

a   Despite this doubling, the tax rate was low by present-day standards. In 2012 *total* tax rates in Britain were 28.8% and even 35.4% if social security contributions are taken into account; the implicit tax rate on labour was 25.2% (European Union averages were 27.7% and 39.4% of GDP, respectively and the implicit rate on labour 36.1%), **Eurostat** (2014), pp. 174, 175, 256.

It was Lloyd George's successor Reginald McKenna who would take up the task of developing taxation as a solid financing instrument in the First World War. There could hardly have been found any other person since the time of Gladstone in whose hands the liberal ideas were more secure (see textbox, below). McKenna supervised the Treasury for a relative short period, until December 1916. He nevertheless made his presence felt in the British tax system for decades. He immediately used the fact that the income tax system itself was not called into question and that the system provided two simple buttons to increase tax revenue for the government: the tax rate and the income threshold.

Reginald McKenna, Chancellor of the Exchequer from 25 May 1915 until 10 December 1916.[15]

When McKenna became responsible for British war financing, he had a rich ministerial career behind him, including First Lord of the Admiralty (1908-1911). In this position he enforced – against much resistance – the ambitious fleet reform programme of building eight Dreadnoughts, which enabled his successor Winston Churchill to rely

on still the mightiest navy in the world when the war broke out. As a Home Secretary (1911-1915) he introduced the controversial 'Cat and Mouse Act'. By this law, imprisoned suffragettes on hunger strike could be released if their health situation deteriorated, just to be re-arrested as soon as they were recovered.

Despite McKenna's presence at the heart of British governmental power for a quarter of a century, followed by just as long a position as the chairman of the board of the largest bank of Britain, he has been a somewhat neglected personality, at least in the biographical sense. For almost 60 years the only source of information has been the lively literary 'memoir' by his nephew, the author Stephen McKenna. Only recently the first volume of a biography by Martin Farr has appeared, based on personal documents.[16]

Reginald McKenna emerges as a clever man of integrity with a tendency of nerdism. It is a typical story that he traded on the stock exchange not to make money but to demonstrate his superior insight into price developments.[17] *His interest in matters of finance can be understood by the financial loss that his father had suffered when the then famous bank Overend, Gurney & Company failed during the credit crisis of 1866. The bank was 'too big to fall' but the Bank of England refused to rescue it (it goes without saying that the nowadays popular policy of saving banks by the government at the costs of the taxpayer was out of the question in the liberal climate of the nineteenth century). The McKenna family had to live for years on very modest means and a good sense of the value of money became a central theme in the life and thinking of the later finance minister.*[18] *Presumably this experience from his childhood has also influenced his relationship with the governor of the Bank of England, which was not smooth, to say the least. If necessary he crossed swords with governor Cunliffe, to make clear who had the last word in financial matters in Britain during the war: not the Bank but the Treasury.*[19] *McKenna promoted the Treasury more clearly than Lloyd George had ever done, very much welcomed by its ambitious and capable staff, among whom a young John Maynard Keynes.*[20]

A larger contrast between McKenna and Lloyd George was hardly imaginable. Indeed, they were members of the same liberal (later coalition) cabinet and they both represented a Welsh constituency, but here the similarities end. Lloyd George was the politician of the two, the man who played the game of power eagerly and unscrupulously; the man who could sketch compelling visions of the future, who was fully committed to the welfare state and had been a very successful lawyer. McKenna had also been working in law practice, but the heart of his education in Cambridge's Trinity College had been mathematics to which he had been devoted. He preferred 'logic and hard facts to rhetoric and emotion'.[21] *Or, as a cabinet minister once said very to the point: 'Lloyd George [...] saw everything in pictures, while McKenna reduced everything to figures'.*[22] *Lloyd George described him as 'a mas-*

ter of finance in blinkers'.[23] For every observer it was evident that they could not share the same room for long. In fact, their relationship was a smouldering peat moor fire within the Asquith cabinet.

Illustrative is the attitude of both gentlemen towards women. Whereas Lloyd George was legendary as a womanizer, in McKenna's life only two women played a role: his mother Emma, who lived in France, and Pamela Jekyll, whom he married only after the former had died.[24] The marriage, Reginald aged 44 and Pamela just 19, reinforced the ties within the inner circles of the liberal establishment in London. Pamela was not merely the upper middle class daughter of Colonel Herbert Jekyll; her cousin Katharine Frances Horner was the daughter-in-law of Prime Minister Herbert Henry Asquith himself.[25] It had been Asquith who had brought his protégée and McKenna together.[26]

Although, Britain had an income tax, this did not imply that everyone was taxed for it. In fact, until 1914 roughly 85% of the voters were exempt from income tax.[a] Only the well-to-do paid income tax, despite the general rise in prosperity from the end of the 19th century.[27] Therefore McKenna implemented essentially two other measures. He lowered the income threshold from £ 160 to £ 130 per annum, thus immediately doubling the number of contributors.[b] Furthermore he increased the existing supertax (or 'surtax') on high incomes; those who earned more than £ 2,500 per year[c] would have to pay more income tax at a rate that could be as high as 17.5% for an income over £ 10,000.[28] In fact, only the really wealthy people, 0.6% of the electorate had to pay this amount.[29] In the field of indirect taxes, McKenna introduced a new tax on luxury goods; these 'McKenna duties' would survive with some interruptions

---

a   The 8 million voters represented less than 20% of the total population.
b   Inflation also contributed to broadening the tax base because it automatically increased the number of income earners above the threshold. This by the way also introduced new problems in the implementation. Labour unions were resolutely against deductions on paid salaries as advances to income tax (general practice today). In some cases taxation by employers even led to tax strikes, **Daunton** (2002), p. 48. War casualties formed a more cynical way by which the tax base was extended for inheritance taxes – at least those from the more wealthy classes; compensation measures were put in place to avoid distressing situations and a substantial rise in inheritance tax did not take place in any belligerent country, **Strachan** (2004), 64-65.
c   Just to get an impression, an annual income of £ 2,500 in 1915 had the 'economic status value' of roughly £ 1 million in 2016, **Officer & Williamson** (2014).

into the 1950s. None of these measures attracted serious resistance, in view of the circumstances. *The Economist* welcomed his approach and was relieved to conclude that in tax matters McKenna did what Lloyd George should have done instead of his 'lax tradition of spend as you please'.[30]

The really new element in McKenna's tax proposals, however, was not in the field of income tax, but the introduction of the excess profits duty. It had not long gone unnoticed that quite a few companies or individuals made a lot of profit from the war. Public support for taxation of these profits was high, as would be the rates. Initially the tax rate was 50% on profits above comparable results in pre-war years.[31] In the first year of introduction, the revenue for the government was modest, but in the budget year 1916/'17 the Treasury received £ 140 million, almost £ 55 above estimations. Meanwhile, the rate had been increased to 60%.[32] At that moment, the excess profits duty supplied 27% of all tax revenues, an amount that would even increase to 36% in 1918/'19, almost equal to the revenue from income tax.[33] This proved the value of an effectively imposed tax on profits generated by public contracts to industry. At the same time the tax somewhat pruned the amount of money in circulation, slowing down inflation.

With a total revenue of £ 650 million during the war, the excess profits duty was a serious cornerstone of British war finance.[34] It would find followers in many other countries. Despite this success, there were some circumstances that prevented this happy choice from producing even more.[35] A general problem with new taxes is to define practical criteria for the tax base: no one will be against it until the moment comes when it has to be decided what it may cover. In the first place there were industries that had made large profits in the arms race in the years before the war. In that case they could easily go on making high profits, as there was no *excess* profit during the war. Most war related industries were less affected than one might expect. Also, ammunitions factories remained beneath the firing line, because the government could directly intervene in their management and set limits to profits by wage measures. The shipping industry was practically exempt since the Admiralty had chartered tonnage. And finally agriculture was levied less than could be expected from increased production and profit. Tax assessments were based on declarations of the farmers themselves, who kept hardly any accounts of their commercial results. A serious and to some extent unfair draw-back of the excess profits duty was that it did not discriminate between the source of profit. Profit from increased productivity was treated on the same footing as speculation profits. And, to conclude this series of objections, companies could just pass the additional burden to their customers. This invoked inflation, but it also made the direct tax on profit a hidden indirect tax. Nevertheless, McKenna's excess profits duty meant a substantial contribution.

McKenna's successor in the Treasury, the Tory Andrew Bonar Law, did not essentially change the lines of his liberal predecessor, although a slight shifting in political accents could be seen. The rate at which income taxes increased was slowed down, while indirect taxes were doubled. These indirect taxes – apart from those on luxury goods – laid a heavier burden on the working class, for example the excise duties on beer and tobacco. The overall effect was that the government had to appeal to loans more intensely.[36]

The conclusion must be that British income tax formed the reliable backbone of the country's war finance, with a total contribution of almost 40% of the total *tax* revenue, averaged over the whole war.[37] In other European belligerent countries this did not exceed a few per cents. Apart from that, there was the excess profits duty, accounting for almost 30% of tax revenue. It was fully justified to observe the 'exceptional loyalty and discipline of the British taxpayer'.[38] This is not altered in any way by the fact that less than a quarter of British war expenditure had been financed by taxes. The expenditure itself was simply too large to bear, even for the British Empire.

Germany

The German fiscal landscape was completely different from Britain's. Germany was, although economically strong, far from being a world power; moreover it had existed for only 40 years as a united country under one emperor. The German fiscal system dated from the pre-empire period and it was not particularly tailored for war financing, strange its as may seem in the perspective of its military tradition and reputation. The background is the *so-called* German unification; it existed as an idea but in practice it still had to grow and it was certainly not completed at the outbreak of the First World War. The German Empire, the *Reich*, had a responsibility in three fields: foreign policy, the army and the navy. In the last years before the war, the army and navy absorbed 60% of all the *Reich's* expenditure; the revenue at the national level was inadequate for this task.

The most important financial sources for the German Empire were customs duties and indirect taxes. The latter comprised levies on consumer goods such as food products, tobacco and beverages. Excise duties on spirits brought in 230 million *marks* in 1914, sugar 215 million *marks*, beer excise 180 million *marks* and stamp duties another 180 million *marks*.[39] These four indirect taxes together made up almost one third of all the *Reich's* revenues. Needless to say that the German war machine could not be kept running on the population's consumption of sugar, beer and liquor.

The German problem was that there were indeed other sources for direct taxation; these however were the exclusive rights of the states that constituted the German *Reich*. These states, such as Prussia, Bavaria, Saxony and a lot of smaller ones were to a large extent autonomous within the framework of the German Empire that acted more like a federation than as a unitary state like France.[a] Pre-war attempts to change these relationships and to give the federal government greater financial room for manoeuvre had been just as numerous as unsuccessful. During the first two years of the war this situation remained frozen, as were the military positions on the western front.[b]

The cause of this paralysis was a double opposition: between left and right and between the *Reich* and the states. On the political left side, the emerging social democrats united in the SPD faced the liberals and conservatives. The social democrats had won the 1912 general elections and they were by far the largest party in parliament, but with 28% of the seats miles away from a majority.[40] If it came to war, a policy they had always rejected, in their view the costs should be borne by taxes because this would be an instrument for a fairer sharing of the burden. One of

---

a   The individual states were called *Bundesstaaten* (also called *Länder*), both in official documents (**RGBl.**, 1875) and in common language (**Helfferich**, 1914). This notion itself expresses *voluntary* cooperation of otherwise autonomous political and geographical entities.
b   The pre-war armament program had been financed by a special one-time contribution, the '*Wehrbeitrag*' (defence contribution).

their political demands was a shift from indirect taxes on consumer goods – the products that laid a heavier burden on low-income groups – towards direct taxes on property, income and profit.[41] At the same time, the social democrats had always been opposed to armament (unless it concerned a people's army), which was precisely the cause of higher expenditure. At the other side of the political spectrum stood the representatives of the various conservative parties who completely rejected new national taxes on property and income, but who were in full support of the war that required new government revenues. The traditional left-right opposition thus led to the remarkable result that liberals and conservatives preferred an increase of the national debt, while socialists advocated higher taxes to reduce this national debt (or at least to prevent it from increasing).

Apart from the right-left contrast, there was the clash between the *Reich* and the states, partly working along the same lines. The conservatives wanted a strong German Empire with all the consequences of an outward directed military power. Domestically however, they were not prepared to give up the privileges of the individual states, among which levying income tax was one of the strongest.[42] Although the states were obliged to pay a part of their revenues to the *Reich*, this contribution (the so-called *Matrikularbeiträge*) formed only a negligible 2% of the national government's revenue and it was even diminishing. Both oppositions implied a deadlock for war financing by taxes in Germany; this was more or less officially agreed in the party truce (*Burgfrieden*) of the first week of August 1914, when the Emperor had declared that from then onward he recognized no parties, only Germans.[43] As a consequence the War Acts, voted by the *Reichstag* on 4 August 1914 contained no mention whatsoever of taxation.

Arguments that the war would be short and would be won were sufficient to refrain from a serious reform of the tax system to adapt it to the war situation. Until 1916 practically nothing happened. After all, it appeared unnecessary to rush into new taxation. Finance Minister Helfferich himself had declared that the normal budget was balanced and that the defeated enemy would pay; so why bother? Only after the war Helfferich called it an 'open question' whether taxes should have been raised earlier and stronger, at least to reduce short-term debts and the danger of inflation.[44] This somewhat superficial remark in fact recognised the inadequate German fiscal policy, although it was undoubtedly intended to blame his successors more than himself.

Only in mid 1916 did things begin to change.[45] In the first place excessive war profits became visible in Germany too; something had to be done. New taxes – and specifically at the national level – were supposed be the answer, although this argument was more socially inspired than economically or financially based. It was a financial argument that the revenues from war loans lagged behind as compared to what was necessary. And finally the main classical sources of taxation, duties on consumer products and import duties, became thinner and thinner as the population became impoverished and the British blockade remained effective. Revenue from indirect taxes had fallen from 1,700 million *marks* in 1913 to 1,100 million *marks* in 1915, even uncorrected for inflation.[46] Import duties, responsible for 30% of the government's revenue before the war, crumbled to less than 2% in 1918.

At the same time, interest payments on war loans consumed an increasing part of the budget. The budget heading 'interest' continued to grow. In 1915 it took 72% of the normal budget, in 1916 it was 85% and in 1917 it would rise to over 90%, mainly due to disappointing tax revenues.[47] These interest payments (during the first years there were redemption payments, but they stopped) were real expenditure for the government, presented on the normal budget that needed the *Reichstag's* approval. When the budget approached the moment that all revenue would be absorbed by interest payments, the government could no longer avoid additional measures if it wanted to present a credible budget. Loans and monetary financing obviously would not resolve this problem and an increase of tax revenues remained the only way out.

As could be expected in the German political situation, an increase in tax revenue did not necessarily imply the introduction of *new* taxes. The first measure was an increase in rates of existing taxes and a broadening of the tax base by extending it to other products. This postponed the discussion for some time. What the government did do was the introduction of a wealth accumulation tax and – analogous to the British excess profits duty – a war profits tax, although they would only be effective in 1917. By their character these taxes affected as little as possible the precarious balance between the Reich and the individual states. They did not have the shape of national taxes on income (or profit) as such, a horrible idea for the conservatives, but only on *increase* of income. By using the correct words, the government justified the new taxes legally. To make it clear that the wealth accumulation tax was not an ordinary capital tax it was called a one-time 'extraordinary war levy' (*außerordentliche Kriegsabgabe*).[48] It was only after the war that national income taxes would be introduced in Germany (Chapter 14, page 259).

France

France had been traditionally a country of indirect taxes *par excellence* and this did not change significantly until 1916, in the midst of the war.[49] The French tax system, modern as it had been made during the Revolution, was out-dated at the beginning of the 20th century. A leading principle was the freedom of the individual citizen, a freedom that the national government had to respect without reservation.[50] It was generally considered as inappropriate if the government made inquiries about the financial status of its citizens.[a]

The consequence of this principle was that direct taxation was limited to publicly visible objects such as real estate and even then in the form of taxes on items that could be observed from outside like windows and doors. Besides, all kinds of interest groups had successfully lobbied to be spared, for example the mighty farmers' organisations and liberal professions. French government bonds ('*rentes*') were exempt from taxes that held for other securities; yields on National defence obligations (Chapter 9) were free from tax as well.[51] Due to these measures equal income situations were treated unequally in tax matters. Such situations did not particularly contribute to a high standard of tax ethics and large revenues from income, wealth and corporate taxes.[52]

Indeed, there had been attempts to introduce income tax in France. This had led to little more than a promise for an introduction, in a politi-

---

a   It was not without reason that article 2 of the Declaration of the rights of man and of the citizen, proclaimed in the revolutionary year 1789, mentioned four natural and imprescriptible rights: liberty, property, safety and resistance against oppression! (« *Ces droits sont la liberté, la propriété, la sûreté et la résistance à l'oppression.* », *Déclaration Française des Droits de l'Homme et du Citoyen*, 26 August 1789, art. 2). We note in passing that in the second Declaration, proclaimed 4 years later (17 June 1793) during the Terror period, the 'right of resistance against oppression' had been replaced by the more harmless 'equality'.

cal compromise in connection with the 3-year conscription period in 1913.[53] The introduction was foreseen for 1915, with a very modest tax rate of 2%, less than a third of the pre-war British rate. Once the war had begun, the government easily found fresh arguments in the war situation to postpone it to 1916. And indeed, for politicians there were some arguments at hand to avoid discussions about the modernisation of the tax system. The northern part of the country, a centre of industrial production, was occupied by German troops. Valuable labour force, among which capable tax administrators, had been called to arms. After all, the Western front was situated 50 miles from Paris, where the artillery could be heard – or at least the proximity be felt.

Moreover, the liberal-conservative Finance Minister Alexandre Ribot had always been a pronounced opponent of income tax. In 1916, however, even he had to admit that something had to be done when it became clear – as it did in Germany – that at least interest payments on war loans had to be paid from the regular budget to maintain some kind of credibility.[54] Otherwise, extra loans would have to be issued in order to pay the interest of previous ones, which indeed became inevitable at the end of the war.[55] The belated introduction of income tax, the inadequate rate, the uninterested implementation, and to some extent the occupation of the prosperous northern region, they all resulted in a meagre 1% contribution of income tax to French war financing.[56]

War profits were observed, but not immediately addressed. Members of parliament became critical about profitable defence contracts that some skilful suppliers had negotiated.[57] However, Ribot wanted to avoid scandals and to maintain social stability at all cost.[58] Again in 1916 it could no longer be denied that a few people could build fortunes at the expense of the nation. The British excess profits duty became an example for France as well, but it took a long time to generate revenue. Despite the high rates of 50%, later even 80%, the revenue of the war profits tax contributed hardly 1% of the French war expenditure, in fact even less than income tax.[59] It was only *after* the war that the money would pour in, thanks to tightened legislation.[60] The largest revenue came in 1921, more than two years after the end of the war: 3.3 billion *francs*, twice as much as during the whole war (corrected for inflation).[61]

United States

The US tax system had in common with that of continental European countries that it was under development. Before 1914, the system leaned heavily on customs and excise duties, both accounting for roughly 45% of the total receipts of the federal government ($ 724 million), the remainder being produced by a special excise tax on corporations and other miscellaneous sources such as a duty on playing cards.[62] Almost one third of the government's income was generated by the production and consumption of alcohol, technically distinguished as distilled spirits and fermented liquors. In this respect, the system resembled more the continental European (in particular German) scheme of customs duties and indirect taxes than the British tax system with its relatively large share of income tax. The First World War would change this situation drastically and with remarkable speed, although not without heated discussions in Congress.

Although there had been a temporary income tax in the United States during the Civil War, an attempt to introduce such a tax in peacetime in 1894 failed when the Supreme Court decided (by a majority of one) that it was unconstitutional.[63] After an amendment to the Constitution had been made, the Act of 3 October 1913 established a new and comprehensive income tax for individuals and corporations. The revenue in its first 10 months in the fiscal year 1913/'14 was $ 28 million for the individual income tax and $ 32 million for the corporations income tax, making a total share of 8% of the government revenue.[64] It was a modest starting if compared to Britain, where the share of income (plus property) tax was three times as high already before the war; if compared to continental European countries however, it was at a level that France and Germany would never reach during the war.[65] In the period of American neutrality, until April 1917, income tax steadily developed into the most important contributor to government revenue; in 1915[a] it contributed 11% of the total revenue, in 1916 it was 16% and in the fiscal year when the United States entered the war, this had again doubled to 32%.[66] Amounts not only grew as a percentage of total revenue, but also in absolute value: in 1917 revenue from income tax had increased to $ 275 million. In the last full fiscal year of the war, 1917/'18, income tax together with the

---

a   That is, fiscal year 1914/'15, starting 1st July 1914, ending 30 June 1915.

excess profits tax introduced in 1917, was responsible for $ 2.8 billion or 68% of total government revenue.[67]

Evidently such increases would not have taken place without the shadow of the war in Europe or actual war from April 1917. Admittedly, the shift from tariffs to income tax was an important policy objective of the new Wilson administration, but the relationship to war financing had not been made explicitly or even informally.[68] It turned out to be a good choice. As soon as the war started in 1914, income form customs duties fell considerably due to a severe reduction of imports. One third of the pre-war revenue from customs duties had been lost by 1915.[69] Even without additional expenditure, new sources had to be found. As early as in October 1914, low-hanging fruit was mobilised in the Emergency Revenue Act that increased indirect taxes on consumers' goods; this soon proved insufficient.[70] Although the United States government strictly adhered to its policy of neutrality, Secretary of the Treasury William Gibbs McAdoo foresaw that in the near future higher expenditure for 'national defense and preparedness' would require additional revenue and he stated that this should be accomplished by higher taxation instead of financing by issuing government bonds.[71] Although it would always be a political decision, economically there was a great potential for increased taxation: the 'resources and wealth of the country [were] so great and are increasing so rapidly that the needs of the government [... could] readily be met';[72] indeed, the share of government revenue in the national economy in 1915 was (only) 1.8%, as compared to 8.3% for Britain in the last pre-war year;[73] at the end of the war, in 1918 and 1919 the US government would have tripled it to (over) 6% thanks to a series of tax increasing measures.[a]

The first step was already taken in the autumn of 1916, during the period of neutrality. McAdoo deployed the classical instruments of increasing revenue from income tax and indirect taxes and introduced a new estate tax and a special tax for munitions manufacturers, the industry obviously gaining the largest benefits from the war in Europe.[74] Income tax rates were raised and tax exemption amounts were lowered; the result was an increase in revenue from $ 80 million in 1915 to $ 125 million in 1916.

---

a   At the moment (2015 / 2016), this share for the US is ten times as high as before the First
     World War: 18%, **USMB** (2015), Historical Tables, table 1.2 (Fiscal Year 2016).

When war became real in April 1917, McAdoo immediately asked Congress to provide for additional means, and taxation was to play a dominant role in his plans.[75] At that moment the US was confronted with the same dilemmas – and partially forced into the same solutions – that the European countries had encountered many years earlier, including heavy deliberations both in academia and in parliament.[76] Whereas the first war loan was issued on 15 May 1917, only ten weeks after the declaration of war, it took half a year before the War Revenue Act on increased taxes was passed (3 October 1917), at a moment when even the second war loan was already sold to the public.[77] Again, income tax exemptions were lowered and rates increased, including a raise in income-dependent surtaxes that made taxation more steeply progressive; an excess profits tax and heavier indirect taxes completed the scheme. The highest personal income rate became 67% (for those privileged people earning over $ 2 million in 1917).[78] Nevertheless, ever increasing expenditure made higher taxes necessary, because the Wilson administration, represented by Secretary of the Treasury McAdoo, wanted to avoid the broad way that leads to destruction by heavy borrowing and monetary financing.[79]

The whole summer of 1918 was devoted to political discussions on new and higher taxes; in particular excess profit taxes were under attack. Finally the senators were overtaken by the Armistice, after having postponed the discussions until after the November elections, six days earlier. On the one hand, the end of the war made further drastic increases less urgent, and on the other hand the provisions of the previous measures of October 1917 were out-dated. The result was, that in February 1919 income tax rates were raised again, with a highest combined rate of normal and surtax of no less than 77%.[80] At that moment, practically every good, service or any economic activity in the US was subject to taxation (except parts of the war loans! see pages 158, 159).[a] The country indeed had beaten all other belligerent countries – including Britain – in financing war expenditure by taxes, even if that share was less than 25%.

---

a   Taxation included such diverse items as umbrellas, kimonos, petticoats and shooting galleries, **Bogart** (1920), p. 180, **ARTS** 1940, pp. 506, 518.

Summary and conclusion

Of all European countries, in 1914 only Britain had a tax system and a tradition that were equipped for financing a war. Its income tax, accompanied by a war profits tax, was a flexible and undisputed instrument to increase government revenue. In particular Chancellor of the Exchequer McKenna made it the backbone of the tax component of British war finance, apart from the usual and relatively easy increase in indirect taxes. The United States soon took tax measures that would contribute in a significant way to war financing as well. It lacked the British tradition, but it was able to speed up taxation during the period of neutrality when the country experienced 'a period of unparalleled prosperity,'[81] partially boosted by the war itself, as this wealth was the other side of the coin formed by the large purchases of war material by European countries. Taxes could easily be increased 'without appreciable burdens upon the American people.'[82] Within three years, Secretary of the Treasury McAdoo had completely transformed the American tax system from a customs-based revenue scheme into an income-based system.

Despite their flexible tax systems, traditional in Britain and brand new in the United States, and despite their sound budget policy and determined treasurers, both countries could not avoid that the contribution of taxes in financing war expenditure was at most 25%. This is a remarkable contrast with both their allies and enemies. In other (European) countries, the share of tax revenue in war financing was almost negligible before 1916. If new taxes were introduced, it was for social reasons and partially for financial reasons: excessive war profits were socially unacceptable and interest on war loans began to consume a substantial part of the budget. In 1916 however, it was too late for Germany and in particular for France, for new taxes to contribute seriously to war financing, notwithstanding the circumstance that the war would go on for another two years.

Taxes introduced during the war would only play a serious role after the war in most countries. Furthermore, it became evident that those taxes that had often been presented as temporary were not to disappear or to be reduced to a pre-war level. Indeed, debts that had been made during the war had to be paid off; but there were also enormous social problems, initially caused by masses of demobilised men. And finally, the role of the national state in social issues had been changed markedly during the war and a substantially larger part of the economy flowed through the government's budgets than had ever done in the liberal period before 1914 – at least in Europe. These developments, however, are beyond the scope of this book.

Domestic war Loans: a patriotic mortgage on the future

*'The system of raising funds necessary for wars by loan
practises wholesale, systematic, and continual deception upon the people.'*
William Ewart Gladstone, 1854.[a]

Issuing large domestic war loans was the instrument *par excellence* to mobilise the home front, and moral suasion was a decisive element of it. While the boys in the trenches gave their lives for their country, the least good citizens could do was supporting them with all their wealth. And they did so on an overwhelming scale. In all belligerent countries together the population subscribed for over $ 45 billion (roughly £ 9 billion, all in 1913 values) to these loans.[1] This was a substantial contribution to war financing.[2]

The propaganda for war loans is a story of interest in its own right and indeed this story has been written, although a modern comprehensive study covering all belligerent countries and their peculiarities would be welcome.[3] All the stops of patriotism were pulled out and products with great lyrical and visual impression have been produced, posters that have reached a certain status in the history of art. But let us confine ourselves to the prosaic financial aspects.

Success (and failure) factors for a war loan

War loans as such did not differ principally from regular government loans in peacetime. A government that issued such a loan asked for money and it had to offer conditions sufficiently attractive for investors

---

a   Quoted by David Marshall Mason in British Parliament, 21 June 1915, **HC**, 987. William Ewart Gladstone (1809-1899) is supposed to have stated this on 8 May 1854 as Chancellor of the Exchequer in a debate on financing the Crimean War. Although these words cannot be found in this exact phrasing in the (digitised) Hansard Parliamentary Records of that particular day, they have been quoted frequently, for example by **Morley** (1903), p. 516, and **Low & Sanders** (1907), p. 104. They certainly express Gladstone's view, although even he realised that waging a war without borrowing would be extremely difficult.

*Posters for war loans: patriotism, moral pressure and investment
(Illustration 9.1)*

Source: *Library of Congress.*

to entrust their money for some time to this actor. These investors were individuals with money free to invest or institutions such as insurance companies, commercial banks, pension funds, savings banks, trust funds and dedicated investment companies. In normal circumstances, 'financial markets' determined the conditions for loans; during the war, moral suasion based on patriotism helped to persuade investors, although financial return on investments always remained a factor. And there the governments had a variety of options.

Interest rate

The first and most obvious factor was the interest rate. A high interest rate stimulated subscriptions; it would provide the government with ample money but at the same time with decades of high interest payments, for long after the war. The crucial factor was the market interest rate, which in its turn was determined by the investor's alternatives. These alternatives could be limited, for example because stock exchanges were closed – in Germany and for some time in France – or if there were limitations on issuing new shares by private companies – as was the case in Britain. In such cases it was in fact the government itself that controlled the financial market and therefore the interest rate. But even then the outcome could be uncertain when the government failed to judge market sentiment. In order to play it safe, governments appeared to prefer an interest rate at the top of the range to be sure that the loan became a success, which in its turn led to criticism from those politicians and economists that detested high national debts.

There were other arguments against high interest rates than a heavy burden on future budgets of large national debts. A political argument was that a high interest rate on war loans was a clear signal to the enemy (and to investors in neutral countries) that the government had trouble raising money and therefore its war status might be worsening on all fronts. Domestically, high interest rates on war loans provoked the social criticism that a new class of war profiteers was created (apart from the arms industry): capitalists who could invest in profitable war loans, just because they possessed the money to subscribe.[4] All together, sufficient arguments for a government to use the interest rate instrument prudently and to 'camouflage' the terms of war loans by means of other indicators not generally known to the public at large.[5]

Issue price
At least as important for an investor was the price at which the loan was issued. It was always specified prominently in announcements of war loans. The issue price was important for several reasons. In the first place it increased the interest rate: if a bond with a face value of 100 was issued at say 95, an investor paid £ 95 for an asset worth £ 100; an interest rate of 4% of £ 100 became effectively an interest rate of 4.2% (100/95 * 4%). Moreover, at maturity the government redeemed the loan at the full price of £ 100; at that moment the saved £ 5 could be cashed. The real value of these bonuses depended evidently on the development of the actual interest rate and of inflation, but by all means, 95 was better than 100. It all implied a higher – but less visible – effective yield than the nominal interest rate and to some extent it could be estimated. And finally there was the speculative effect: a price below par (lower than 100) implied that it might rise and the investor could make profit, and the more so if the issue price was lower. Of course it all depended on inflation and – in case of foreign loans – on exchange rate development, but in principle the government offered additional profit for the subscriber.

The issue price of war loans revealed large cultural differences between countries. French investors appreciated a somewhat lower interest rate

119

if it was compensated by a substantially lower issue price. Apparently for them the prospect of profit from rising prices was more important than the initially lower coupon (interest) payment.[6] British investors on the other hand were of a different opinion. In particular in war circumstances, they preferred an immediate 4% to a 3.5% interest rate combined with a profit at redemption.[7] Germans were keen on stability: in their view an issue price close to 100 was a signal of soundness. German politicians in the *Reichstag* were highly excited in December 1915 about the French way of issuing loans at low prices; the minutes noted: large fun (*'große Heiterkeit'*).[8] In Berlin, this way of issuing loans expressed French weakness, not only financially, but evidently also in a military sense. In fact these preferences were all prejudiced: so many countries, so many customs. If issue price and interest rate are appropriately tuned, there is no real financial difference in yield between a loan at low interest rate together with a low issue price or a high interest rate and issue at par.[9]

Financial authorities simply had to comply with the tradition in their countries and the subscribers had little choice. For them there were two great uncertain factors: expectations about inflation and the risk of not getting their money back after the war. Inflation would erode their capital, but this was not considered a serious point in the first years of the war when the rise in price level was moderate and the war was supposed to be short. The risk of not getting their money back was evidently assessed very low by the population: the war would be won if one believed the government and the military commanders. The real choice between high interest rates and low issue prices was open to investors in neutral countries. This choice was even offered, as shown by the textbox below.

Cultural differences in war loan conditions

In contrast to inhabitants of belligerent countries, who were bound by patriotism, investors in neutral countries could make real choices between investments in war loans based primarily on a profit perspective. A remarkable example of this choice was offered to investors in neutral Holland towards the end of the war. In the liberal newspaper Algemeen Handelsblad *of 19 October 1918 two*

Cultural differences in war loan conditions (Illustration 9.2)

Neunte Deutsche Kriegsanleihe.

5 % Deutsche Reichsanleihe.

Zeichnungspreis: 98 Mark.

Das Reich darf die Schuldverschreibungen frue-
hestens zum 1. Oktober 1924 kuendigen und kann
daher auch ihren Zinsfuss vorher nicht herabsetzen.
Sollte das Reich nach diesem Zeitpunkt eine Ermae-
sigung des Zinsfusses beabsichtigen, so muss es die
Schuldverschreibungen kuendigen und den Inhabern
die Rueckzahlung zum vollen Nennwert anb ieten

4¹/₂ % Deutsche Reichsschatzanweisungen.

Zeichnungspreis: 98 Mark,

auslosbar mit 110 % bis 120 %.

Fuer Einzelheiten wende man sich an seinen
Bankier.   (53350)
            Zeichnungsschluss : **Mittwoch, den**
23. Oktober 1918, mittags 1 Uhr.

Source: KB / Algemeen Handelsblad.[10]

announcements were published next to each other – on purpose or accidentally, illustration 9.2.

In the left announcement, the Germans offered a 5% loan priced 98 and a term of at least 6 years. Next to it, the French government promised the Dutch investor 25 years of 4% interest on bonds that could be bought at an issue price as low as 70.8 (and therefore a potential speculative value of 30%). If all other conditions had been equal, it would not have been difficult to choose for the French proposal. But the investor had to take into account more considerations before he would put his strong guilders into one of the belligerent countries' war finance, such as the expected victor, alternative investment options and, very importantly, the exchange rate risk. The bonds had to paid in Dutch guilders because both the Germans and French needed international currency to pay for their purchases of food (Germans) and military equipment (French). All interest payments and redemptions would be made in marks and francs, however, and the investor bore the risk of fluctuating exchange rates. Confidence in a return to pre-war exchange rates had long been untouched, but in the autumn of 1918 when the offers were made, doubt might have spread, although few could have foreseen at that moment the post-war inflation in France and the hyperinflation in Germany (Chapter 14).[11]

The clause 'auslosbar' in the German loan conditions meant that the bonds could be drawn for redemption prior to maturity; the bondholder then received 110% or 120% of the face value, depending on the moment of drawing. Incidentally, the advertisement shows that even in October 1918, three weeks before the Armistice, the risk premium for long-term bonds was only ½% point compared to the simultaneously issued Treasury Notes; in fact both the conditions for the bonds and the notes were far from a realistic market price. A second observation is that the Germans advertised in Dutch newspapers in the German language, whereas the French chose for Dutch, probably reflecting a target group policy.

The amount of the loan

The amount of the loan was less an issue for the subscriber than it was for the government. It was a signal for the country's need for money and the government had two options: a fixed amount or open subscriptions. A fixed amount entailed the risk of undersubscription. This meant loss of face for the finance minister but it was also a signal that the country lacked financial means to continue the war or that war sentiment among the population was waning. Moreover, it would make new loans more difficult unless the government would offer still higher interest rates. And in the case that the fixed amount was exactly met, the government could rightly assume that larger revenues could have been realised under the same (interest) conditions. New loans would have to be issued earlier than necessary, which would again be a signal of high financial needs, etc.[12][a] Anyhow, McKenna – in contrast to Lloyd George in the previous loan – had sufficient reasons to leave it to the financial markets to determine a feasible amount: 'for that reason we put in no amount'.[13] In Germany too, amounts were not fixed with the intention to raise as much money as possible and to prevent fake (over)subscriptions.[14] The

---

[a] This is a subtle play with information in the economy: the government had better insight into its need for money than the financial markets; a fixed amount for a loan would reveal this advantage of information and weaken its position; investors on the other hand had more accurate information about the available (potential) capital in the market which they had to unhide only partially in subscriptions. Stakes were very high indeed as was illustrated by the fact that the conditions of the first British war loan were still in discussion on the evening before the budget speech in parliament, **Wormell** (2000), p. 73. For an original analysis and many examples of economic concepts in military history such as asymmetric information or diminishing marginal returns, the interested reader is referred to **Brauer &** **Van Tuyll** (2008).

United States on the other hand systematically issued loans with a fixed amount. The amounts were used as targets that had to be met and for which sacrifices had to be made; they were also supposed to stimulate competition between states, cities and social groups to contribute as much as possible. France applied a mixed policy, depending on circumstances, as we shall see below.

Term to maturity
The fourth important factor for a loan was its time span. For the government a long-term loan had the advantage that the financial burden could be spread over many years; in the meantime it could make reservations for its redemption at the end by means of a **sinking fund**. For the creditors, however, it was a risk: they could not use their money for other purposes for a long time and the price might fluctuate. This was a discouraging effect for long-term loans.[a] Therefore the time between subscription and maturity – although it was not often realised – was a crucial element for the willingness to subscribe, for the government's future obligations and for the effective yield of the investor. Here too, there were large cultural differences between countries. German war loans for example had no other condition than they would *not* be redeemed *before* a certain date, mostly in 1924; for the early loans this implied a life of at least 10 years, for subsequent loans it became proportionally shorter. It remained unclear what would happen after that date.

Such a policy would have been unthinkable in Britain. The financial markets would have greeted the government with howls of derision if it issued a loan without a fixed date. The first loans had a maturity date in the period 1925-1928, while for the later loans this went as far as the mid-1940s, which amounted to a life of 30 years. Some loans were double-dated: the government had the right of redemption at an earlier date under certain conditions (page 256); in retrospect this proved a skilful policy, as we shall see in Chapter 14. US war loans were – with one exception – double-dated with a redemption date varying from 4 to 15 years and a final repayment (expiration) date varying from 5 to 30 years. France continued its traditional policy of perpetual loans:

---

a   On the other hand, long-term loans could be attractive if the interest rate was sufficiently high and the investor's objective was a guaranteed revenue for a long period; see page 227 for the Dawes loan of 1924.

the government did not commit itself to paying back the principal at a fixed date; it reserved the right however – but not the obligation – to do so after some time, for example after 25 years, depending on market conditions. Illustration 9.2 gives some insight into these differences.

Other incentives

Interest rate, issue price, amount and term to maturity were the most important financial factors to persuade investors to subscribe to war loans, but there were additional features. During the war all countries went through a learning process in which they became increasingly smarter to address target groups. Three such incentives were actions to involve lower income classes, tax incentives and **conversion** options. The first one offered the possibility to decrease the smallest amount to subscribe through special savings programmes enabling lower income classes to contribute with low-valued stamps to collect on a savings card. This enlarged the contributing groups from the usual class of well-to-do subscribers on government bonds to the masses. The effect on revenue however should not be overestimated; the lion's share had to come from large subscribers: small denominations are simply too small to add up to large amounts, even if there are millions of them.

Tax reduction was an incentive to persuade higher income classes to subscribe to war loans. It was particularly appealing for the target group with large private wealth and high income, as these were the only direct taxpayers before the war. In the United States for example – where at some moments in time income tax rates were as high as 70% – tax reduction on interest and principal invested in war loans could be highly profitable for those who could afford it. In all western countries, governments offered tax exemptions for war loans, with the exception of Germany where national taxes were insignificant (page 107 ff.). For a government it was a delicate balance between revenue from tax or from loans. It can be no surprise that the British government sometimes let the markets decide; it offered the choice to the potential subscriber: either a loan free of tax or a loan subject to income tax but bearing a higher interest rate (page 148). An argument for tax exemption that might appeal to investors was that the loan was so to speak tax increase proof; bond prices would not fall – probably even rise – in case of tax increases.[15] The political choice for tax exemption was, of course, that it implied transfer of wealth to bondholders.

Finally there was a variety of smaller marketing tools to attract subscribers. Germany offered a discount if the payments for subscription were made early on a special account; in the last years of the war it issued bonds that could be drawn for redemption with a premium for the lucky bondholder. France at one point started to make interest payments in advance. The British government offered a range of profitable options to convert one loan into the other and the possibility to pay inheritance tax with war loans. In short, governments became more and more clever raising money by skilfully adapting the conditions. The most important strategy to promote loans, however, was not of a financial, but of a moral nature.

Moral pressure

All large war loans – with the remarkable exception of the first British war loan of November 1914 – appealed to the public not only as investors but in the first place as patriots. Governments applied with all creative means carrot and stick alike to persuade potential subscribers. Subscription to a war loan would evoke good feelings of bringing offers at the home front for the boys in the trenches. Extra pressure came from subscriptions from soldiers who not only risked their lives but sacrificed their money as well (illustration 7.2). Strong and appealing images such as 'silver bullets' intensified the relationship between finance and fighting. In Britain the idea of 'feeding the guns' was sometimes taken literally when the receipts of the subscriptions could be stamped in the barrel of a gun posted during special events. Competitions between regions and towns were set up to increase the revenue and to strengthen a local community's cohesion and patriotic feelings: publication of lists of revenues per capita or by region, a bonus for the city with the highest revenue or – in the US case with fixed amount loans – an allocation of amounts to be raised by region.[a] Celebrities were invited to show their support and serve as public examples (see illustration 9.6, page 160), etc.[16]

---

a   Institutions operating countrywide were sometimes obliged to compete with itself: after the Royal Bank of Scotland had bought £ 200,000 war bonds in the Edinburgh Tank Week, it could not escape buying another £ 100,000 the next week in a similar event in Glasgow, a city that would successfully beat the Scottish capital, http://www.rbsremembers.com/banking-in-wartime/supporting-the-nation/tank-banks.html.

The other side of the coin was that dodgers were depicted as unpatriotic, as a deserter or simply as a donkey. In pamphlet-like publications, the German *Reichsbank* frequently mentioned less informed people, citizens that were not familiar with financial matters, people who had not grasped the idea of war bonds. One publication blatantly mentions 'less informed circles among the population and in the countryside'.[17] The message was clear: intelligent people subscribe to war loans and escaping from subscription is not only a matter of unpatriotic behaviour but also of poor mental development.

It remains the question whether this bombardment of propaganda really contributed to raise money. There are indications that large American investors were led merely by financial return on their investment and that patriotism was relatively unimportant in their decisions.[18] On the other hand, it is not unlikely that social pressure indeed played a role. Available statistical data about subscriptions and their breakdown to denominations have a limited value, however. It would be far more interesting to know which arguments really were decisive for the Bordeaux solicitor, the Freiburg watchmaker or the Glasgow shipyard worker to contribute their money – the latter one most probably in the form of a savings card at the post office. What was the atmosphere in discussions between savers and the local bank employee? Which arguments were used in the family circle? Lacking empirical evidence in the form of oral financial history, we can only conclude that governments regarded their increasingly subtler efforts worthwhile. Anyhow, the large campaigns were welcome and tangible events to mobilise the people, to rouse national unity, to forget internal controversies and to show the enemy that war sentiments were alive.

German war loans: a thorough and predictable scheme

Germany issued more war loans than any other country;[19] the loans were spread regularly over time and the conditions changed only slightly over four years of war. The interest rate, for example, remained 5% from 1914 to the autumn of 1918, regardless of changing external circumstances. Thanks to this solid series, they provide us with a good insight into the ups and downs of the war, better than the British, French of American war loans do. Therefore they deserve to be described in some more detail than the loans of the other countries.

With their clockwork precision at six months' intervals, the nine war loans were considered the backbone of the German Empire's war finance. Starting in September 1914 the German population and investors alike could rely on an issue in March and September of every year, although of course nobody could foresee that it would have to continue for four years. When the final account was made up, 96 billion *marks* had been invested (without considering inflation, but including 12 billion *marks* of public short-term loans).[20]

Undoubtedly, the first loan had been prepared thoroughly before the war by the *Reichsbank* and the Finance Department. It was issued at the moment that Germany was about to be defeated at the battle of the Marne.[21] A large newspaper campaign was launched at 9 September 1914. In 2,800 papers all over the country the government addressed the nation, supported by editorials 'to appeal in the strongest possible terms to patriotism' as the government had requested.[22] In the years to follow, these practices would be normal, but for September 1914 standards it was a skilfully orchestrated marketing operation.

This **first** war loan – in fact the first of all public war loans in the First World War – was an enormous success, although this could not have been guaranteed in advance. No government had recent experience with such a large public loan in wartime. Both the expected amount and an appropriate interest rate were a shot in the dark in military terminology. Some months after the loan Deputy Chancellor Clemens Delbrück declared that the financial authorities had little more than 'conjectures' about the right conditions and the outcome.[23] And he was certainly right, because prospects for German public loans were not favourable as measured by the prices of current government bonds: before the war German 3% government bonds quoted 82 against 96 for Belgian bonds, for example.[24] Investors' behaviour was unpredictable, although the government assumed that sufficient capital was waiting for a meaningful destination.[25] This was a correct assumption: whereas the authorities expected to raise some 2 billion *marks*, the real proceeds were almost 4.5 billion *marks*. Several reasons contributed to this success.

In the first place, the interest rate was attractive: 5% as compared to at most 4% for usual government bonds. In the second place, there were in fact two loans, servicing different target groups. On the one hand institutional investors who wanted to deposit large amounts of money for a limited period of time. They could subscribe to a fixed-amount loan of 1 billion *marks* in treasury bills for an average period of 5 years. And on the other hand there was the loan for the public at large with no maximum amount and a term of at least 10 years. This appeared to be a clever move because the loans were linked: the conditions stipulated that all oversubscriptions to the treasury bills could automatically be transferred to the long-term bonds. This eliminated speculators with the intention to buy treasury bills just to sell them at a higher price. The government would benefit from all the money subscribed. At the same time there was no danger of a disappointing result because there was no fixed amount for the large public loan (the limit for the treasury bills was relatively low and investors had few other options since the stock exchange was closed).

The effective yield was even slightly higher than 5% since the issue price was 97.5.[a] The real value of this bonus, to be received at redemption date, evidently depended on the time between subscription and redemption – and on inflation, but few people would care about that in September 1914. For the war loan proper, after 10 years the interest rate would fall to 4% to come in line with other government bonds. At that time, 1924, the war would be over; as we now know, all bonds would then be virtually worthless, but the subscribers could not have guessed so in September 1914 and probably neither any of the financial authorities would have believed it.

Probably even more important than a small interest bonus was the possibility to withdraw money from savings accounts and deposits without a period of notice or a penalty, provided that the money was used for subscription to the war loan. This will have persuaded many small savers to transfer their money from low-interest accounts, the more so since the subscription period was restricted to 10 days, although payments could be made in instalments within a few months.

---

a   For subscribers who committed themselves to not selling the bonds within six months, there was even a small extra bonus of 0.2%; to obtain this, they had to register the bonds instead of buying them as bearer bonds. The government offered this option, since it would save printing costs and because it was supposed to prevent speculation, **Lotz** (192), p. 36. This seemingly harmless registration option would cause the German government a lot of trouble after the war, as will become clear in Chapter 14.

All these measures, however, were of a material nature. Far more important was the mobilisation of enthusiasm and patriotism that accompanied the first war loan in Germany. All previous government loans had been issued by bank consortia; this time, the government applied directly to the population. Banks, public savings banks and insurance brokers were mobilised by the government to act as intermediaries for the public under the supervision of the *Reichsbank*. Subscription itself was possible at some 500 branches (sub-offices) of the *Reichsbank*. It was considered as an important indicator for the success of the loan that almost one out of five subscriptions, a total of 230,000, had been made for amounts of 100 of 200 *marks*. These were the real small savers and others who had contributed through schools, clubs and social organisations. Evidently broad sections of German society had responded to the appeal. It is true that all these small amounts taken together contributed less than 1% of the total of 4.5 billion *marks*, but it was a real breakthrough as compared to previous government loans that had been supported only by institutional investors and the well-to-do. The class of (government) bondholders had been expanded explosively and patriotism had undoubtedly contributed to this effect, presumably more than a slightly higher interest rate on a savings account.

The German Financial High Commanders, part 2: Yield Marshal Havenstein[26]

Rudolf Emil Albert Havenstein (1857-1923) had good reasons to claim the success of the first and the following German war loans. Havenstein, born in East Prussia and educated in Law, was president of the Reichsbank from 1908 until 1923 and his organisational power was admired in the press domestically as well as abroad.[27] *In no time he collected titles and military decorations by the dozen; the latter perfectly echoed his pet name allegedly given by the Kaiser himself: my Yield Marshal.*[a] *Havenstein had already followed*

---

a   The original pun in German was Feldmarschall/'Geldmarschall' (litterally: Money Marshal) *a splendid career as a model Prussian civil servant before he was called to the high office of president of the Reichsbank, where he could bear the title of Real Privy Counsellor ('wirklicher Geheimer Rat'). He had been a judge in several places in his home region, he had been employed at the Finance Department in Berlin and finally he had been president of the Prussian National Bank.*

Havenstein was definitely a man of the old school with corresponding standards and values. This, however, did not prevent him from initiating monetary innovations. One of his most prominent achievements was making the Reichsbank notes legal tender in 1909, which placed the relatively young Reichsbank on the same footing as its sister institutions in France and Britain. Meanwhile, he secured the support of German industry. He was a welcome guest at the Krupp family in Essen, a fact that has undoubtedly contributed to the confidence he enjoyed from the highest leaders in Berlin.[28] Behind the scene Havenstein used his experience to work thoroughly towards a system of legislation that would prepare Germany financially for the war. Making the Reichsbank notes legal tender was just one of the measures. In the first days of August 1914 a complete system of draft laws and organisational measures was ready to ensure that a lack of money would not in any way hamper the war machine.[29] During the war he was the driving force behind the war loans and the ever-increasing short-term debts of the government.

Although Havenstein shares the absence of a comprehensive biography with his colleagues Pallain and Cunliffe, some characteristic features of his personality are known from other sources. Central themes are duty and high moral standards. The influential Hamburg banker Max Warburg wrote about Havenstein that 'obedience and subordination to the presumed superior authority [...] had become so much part of his flesh and blood that, even where it would have been possible, he did not know how to maintain the independence of the Reichsbank.'[30] When food rationing became increasingly sharper during the war, he refused to resort to the black market, although he was in a better position than anyone else to do so; he even shared his scarce food ration stamps with less privileged compatriots.[31]

... to be continued on page 262.

The next few German war loans showed a pronounced upward trend. The **second** loan, issued March 1915, exceeded the first by 100%. The proceeds of the loan were 9 billion *marks*. No less than 1 million of the subscriptions were for 500 *marks* or less, which made it a real people's loan; apparently savings accounts had been made use of since 500 *marks* was still almost half a year's salary for unskilled labour.[32] The subscriptions facilities had been extended and social organisations were engaged; teachers and clergymen were supposed to promote the loan in sparsely populated regions.[33] There was a leaflet in simple language (*'in allgemein verständlicher Weise'*) with all kinds of information about the loan. Moral pressure was intensified. In parliament, Finance Minister Helfferich declared that Germany not only knew general conscription, but also a general duty to save and to pay for loans. Dodging was seen as desertion and the *Reichstag* approved it, although it was not formally declared a capital offence.[34] The loan was a success despite the somewhat lower conditions as compared to the first loan. The financial authorities had gained insight into market conditions. Although publications of bond prices was formally forbidden, they knew that the first loan was traded above the issue price of 97.5, so the second loan was issued at 98.5, raising without effort the amount for the government by 90 million *marks*.

The upward line continued unabated with the **third** German war loan. It brought the German government 12 billion *marks* at an issue price that had even been increased to 99, which implied that investors could forget a substantial rise in price.[35] Even more than the previous loans, it was a people's loan: 70% of all 2.75 million subscriptions were for amounts up to 1,000 *marks*. This success might have been caused by the now perfectly running propaganda machine, but probably even more by the military success at the Eastern front. Just a few weeks earlier Brest-Litovsk had fallen and German troops entered Warsaw, events that were not only important from a military and strategic point of view, but above all it was appealing symbolically; it meant prospects for a victory.

German war loans: results reflecting military fortunes

The relationship between military successes and financial war support was not a new phenomenon. Battles that were won and relentless advances raised expectations for victory and a spirit to make a new loan a success, while at the same time earlier loans gained attractiveness. As the

British major Hamilton-Grace[a] had written 'Practically the ebb and flow of victory can be read from the quotations on the Stock Exchange'.[36] Not only highlights are visible, but setbacks as well. The war year 1916 was tough, not only for Germany but for its enemies as well. Successes, if any, were obtained at a disproportional price: Somme, Verdun. Both German war loans of that year, the **fourth** and the **fifth**, generated disappointingly less than the third loan (illustration 9.3). It was a bad omen that the fifth loan did not compensate for the disappointing fourth. In fact 1916 meant a turning point in the war loans, as it was in other aspects. The purpose of the large loans had always been to refinance the short-term government debts at the central bank and to turn them into longer-term treasury bills and long-term bonds. This policy had worked well during the first years of the war; in the spring of 1916 it had been realised by the narrowest margin and at the end of 1916 it became impossible.[37] The four remaining loans of 1917 and 1918 contributed less and less to absorbing the short-term debt.

Nevertheless, the **sixth** loan in March 1917 was celebrated as a success, because the revenue of 13 billion *marks* surpassed all previous loans. Undoubtedly prospects of a favourable turn of the war after the February Revolution in Russia and the unrestricted submarine warfare had contributed to this relative success.[38] In the course of the year 1917 however, prospects for Germany worsened. A new enemy, the United States, was sending its first troops to Europe and in Germany itself the effects of monetary financing became visible; wholesale prices rose at an unprecedented rate in the summer of 1917.[39] The financial authorities intensified their efforts probably because they were afraid of a setback.

German war loans: the endgame
German expats were directly entreated to subscribe to the forthcoming **seventh** loan in eye-catching advertisements in newspapers in neutral countries.[40] Havenstein himself addressed a large meeting of captains of industry in Frankfurt to ensure their support, the sound recording of which has been preserved as one of the first recorded speeches to

---

a   Hamilton-Grace published his book about war finance five years before he was killed in 1915 in active service in a motor accident near the front in Hazebrouck, France, **Harrow** (1918).

Revenues from German war loans reflect ups and downs at the military theatres; the trend is upwards if measured in marks, but corrected for inflation the trend is unmistakably downwards from September 1915 (Illustration 9.3)

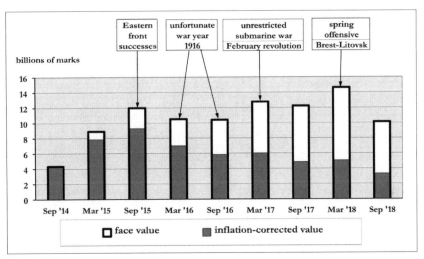

Source: calculated from Roesler and inflation data.[41]

promote a war loan with patriotic arguments.[42] [a] All these efforts did not pay off. The proceeds of the seventh loan did not surpass the third loan two years earlier, and half of the amount came from subscriptions of over 100,000 *marks*. This was a signal that only banks, institutional investors and the very rich were still able to contribute. Havenstein's appeal to this segment of investors had been successful, but the large German middle class had dropped out.

One last time, in the spring of 1918, German prospects for a successful end of the war revived and with it came the unprecedented revenue of the **eighth** war loan. The military operations of the *Kaiserschlacht* (or operation *Michael*) in the west and the Treaty of Brest-Litovsk in the east were encouraging signals and they were used in the propaganda for the new loan. It was suggested that it could be the last loan of the war.[43] For investors with more material motives, the government had a novelty as

---

a   The speech is a masterpiece of intellectual German; it quotes a romantic poet (Emanuel Geibel) reflecting on the Franco-Prussian War and it contains a sentence of over 80 words, a horror for any modern public relations officer.

well. After the war surplus army and navy material would be for sale and holders of war bonds were promised that it could be bought with war loan bonds.[44] Furthermore, the government tried to increase the attraction of this route by 2% by offering that on such an occasion it would pay the nominal value of the bond that had been issued at 98. This 2% profit was pure fantasy – of downright deception – since in March 1918 inflation in Germany had reached a rate of at least 0.75% *per month*.[45] This 2% profit would be made only if the war came to an end (and the dump store transactions settled) within two or three months. With hindsight this was clearly wrong. From the perspective of the German population in the spring of 1918, this was not necessarily unrealistic in view of the optimistic presentation of the military commanders about the successes on the western front.

The only thing that can be said about the **ninth** and last German war loan is, that it was a failure in every respect despite all official statements.[46] That brings us to the real revenue of these nine loans. Official statistics invariably presented the revenue in nominal amounts, that is: in current *marks*. Presented in this way, the amounts showed an upward trend from September 1914 up to March 1918, with ups and downs as described above. A March 1918 *mark* however was quite different from a September 1914 *mark*. If the amounts of the war loans are corrected for the ever-declining purchasing power of the *mark*, the picture changes dramatically, as shown in illustration 9.3. Starting in September 1915, the real revenue of German war loans shows an unmistakably downward trend. No success on the battlefield had ever reversed this trend.

Meanwhile the national debt had grown by almost 100 billion *marks*, largely as a consequence of these loans. Furthermore, the annual interest payments alone had increased to 5 billion *marks* or two thirds of the ordinary budget. This was obviously not a stable situation for Germany's financial future. It was a small comfort that its enemies seemed not much better off.

French war loans: short-term borrowing

If compared to the repeating rifle of the German war loans, the French method of domestic borrowing looked more like a pragmatic use of shotguns combined with heavy artillery. Until 1917 Finance Minister Alexandre Ribot deployed a variety of instruments to secure the government's need for money. It was only after 1916 that a more systematic pattern of war loans became apparent; this was due to fundamental and to practical considerations.

The fundamental background was that French leaders were absolutely convinced that the war would be short and that the advances of the *Banque de France* would be sufficient to bridge the period until the victory. The government also used the argument that the financial system of the country was disrupted: the northern region was a battlefield, or even occupied. And finally on 9 August 1914 the government had issued by decree a **moratorium** blocking all bank accounts, not particularly a favourable circumstance to issue a large war loan on the private capital market. In fact the government relied initially completely on the *Banque*, whereas soon loans in Britain and the US supplemented domestic borrowing (these external loans are the subject of the next chapter).

The more practical obstacle was that the French government had issued a large loan less than a month before the war broke out, nine days after the assassination of the Archduke in Sarajevo, to be precise. The conditions of that loan could have been suited for the pre-war period but they were absolutely unfit for the war: 3.5% interest and redeemable in 25 years.[47] During the first days of August 1914 the discount rate had risen spectacularly to 6%, which made this old loan extremely unattractive. Investors might rightly expect that the government would soon appeal to the market with better conditions. The market was reluctant. Although the loan of 800 million *francs* was largely oversubscribed at the moment of issue (mainly by banks), in the first week of August only 40% of that sum had actually been deposited and it was highly improbable that the remainder would ever be paid.[48]

In August 1914 therefore a new large loan for war financing was impossible in France. When Alexander Ribot succeeded Joseph Noulens as the new finance minister on 26 August he knew what to do. In the first place he had to manoeuvre out of sight the 3.5% loan that had been issued at the most impractical moment before a new loan could be launched. But moreover, as he realised that the advances of the *Banque de France* would not be sufficient if the war happened to drag on and he disliked taxes, other methods were necessary. These methods were designed to appeal to the small savers and investors.

The first of these instruments were the *Bons de la défense nationale*, literally: treasury bills for national defence. The phenomenon of these bills as such was not new. In fact these bills for three, six or twelve months were used by banks, large industrial enterprises and railway companies as a safe and profitable deposit for temporary cash surpluses. They were hardly known to the general public before Ribot gave them the flavour of patriotism by linking the neutral notion of 'bills' to the emotional 'national defence'.[49] This latter expression had automatically roused enthusiasm in France ever since the days of the Revolution. The *bons* were given certain privileges that normal bills lacked.[50] The interest rate was considerably higher than the old July loan offered: initially even 5%, later 4% for 3-month bills and 4.5% for 6-month bills. Just like in Germany, a dense network including post offices was established to sell the *bons*; brokers received bonuses to sell as many of them to the public. In order to collect the maximum amount of money the previous legal maximum on the issue of treasury bills was substantially extended.[51]

For the government the *bons* had two sides. On the one hand, they were extremely flexible – in contrast to large war loans. They could be issued when necessary, both in frequency and in amount. And they could be adapted to market circumstances by offering various terms and interest rates, although in practice the interest rate remained rather stable. On the other hand, this short-dated paper posed a potential problem when the government would be unable to refinance the bills at maturity date. The government committed itself to offer continuously competing conditions without on the other hand increasing interest rates in an unrealistic way, a general problem with successive loans. Transferability of the *bons* was a second risk, not for the government but for the economy. At the macro economic level their presence meant that the monetary base increased beyond the regular mechanism of banknotes.[52] They could even be used as collateral for other loans. In this respect the French *bons* had the same effect as the German *Darlehenskassenscheine*. The French government incidentally regarded the pressure to refinance these short-term loans a larger problem than inflation caused by the increase in money in circulation.[53] This increase was by no means insignificant.

The total amount of *bons* issued between 1914 and 1918 was over 50 billion *francs*, in nominal terms (roughly $ 10 billion or £ 2 billion at pre-war values). The revenue for the government was much smaller, because almost half of the *bons* were used over the years to buy long-term war loans.[54] Nevertheless some 28 billion *francs* of *bons* remained in circulation, almost as much as the amount of *Banque de France* banknotes at the end of the war.[55] Evidently not all *bons* were used as money, but they certainly did not contribute to consolidation of the French national debt into long-term loans.[56]

The enormous amount reflects the popularity of the *bons*. During the war their volume remained rather stable, not only in nominal values but even if corrected for inflation – in contrast to the revenue of the German war loans. The financial instrument was a success, although this could not be foreseen at their introduction. Apparently, the French population possessed quite a lot of dispensable money, waiting for serious short-term investment opportunities. Indeed every prudent French head of a family had a safe in which he kept some cash, just in case.[a] The *bons*, moreover, had one important property in common with cash: they were in bearer form. Buying, selling and trading were not registered and the government had no insight into the financial position of the bondholders, which could be a very comfortable idea for many a Frenchman. Tax exemption of the *bons* therefore was recognition of current practice more than an incentive to buy them.[57] This incidentally did not restrict the popularity of the *bons* to France: up to the end of 1914 British and American investors bought the French *bons* to an amount of over 100 million francs.

Between the very short-term *bons* and the large war loans – to be discussed later – the French government introduced a third type of loan with an intermediate term: the *Obligations de la défense nationale*, Bonds of National Defence. The first *obligations* were issued in the spring of 1915 redeemable in five to ten years (there were different types in the course of the war), which made them more or less comparable to the German *Schatzanweisungen* issued in parallel to the German war loans. Such medium-term loans were not part of the floating debt and they indeed contributed to a consolidation of the national debt, thus

---

a   Frenchmen preferred to keep their money in cash (banknotes and coins) anyway, rather than the British who had more confidence in bank accounts, see for example **Eichengreen** (1995), p. 53.

decreasing the danger of inflation. The incentive for the investor was the advance payment of interest. At the moment of subscription, the investor immediately cashed 5% interest, free of tax. Financially, this meant an effective yield closer to 6% than to 5%, an indication that the French government was in urgent need of money.

The first issues of these *obligations* were used to annihilate the nasty July 1914 loan. In the first month of the war the price of this loan had fallen from 91 to 82, which made payment very unattractive for subscribers because they started with a loss. Ribot therefore offered the unfortunate subscribers the arrangement that the government would accept these securities at the original issue price if they were used to purchase new bonds, including the *Obligations de la défense nationale*. This opportunity received a massive response.[58] For the government the July 1914 loan became an intermediate administrative step in selling the obligations; the first issue of the *obligations* in November 1914 amounted to 4 billion *francs* and 3.3 billion of it was by means of converted July 1914 bonds. For the French government this meant additional costs, since it had to pay 5% instead of 3.5%. On the other hand, the higher interest rate would hold 5 or 10 years, whereas the lower rate would have lasted 25 years; furthermore the government saved some money by buying at the issue price of 91 instead of having to pay 100 at maturity (in 1939!). The most important benefit for the government, however, was that it kept up its credit status in the event of inevitable new large loans. The benefit for the investors was evident.

This system of conversion of loans had been applied to French government loans in the nineteenth century. In these cases it had been used to convert high interest bonds into bonds bearing lower interest to save interest payments.[59] In the case of the first *Obligations de la défense nationale* it worked the other way around in order to create attractive conditions to tempt old bondholders to invest in new loans. In the war circumstances, this policy was regarded as wise, not only by later commentators but also by contemporaries like Keynes who even qualified it as 'ingenious and sound'.[60] During the war, the principle of conversion of loans would be applied in Britain to such an extent that it could almost be called a trademark of British war loans (page 146 ff.).

French war loans: perpetual bonds sold at a discount

After the elimination of the July 1914 loan, the French government was in a position to issue seriously large war loans. This happened not before November 1915, when Germany had already successfully issued three war loans. The **first** French war loan, without a fixed amount, raised 13 billion *francs* thanks to an intensive propaganda campaign stressing patriotism. The loan was attractive for investors: the interest rate of 5% in combination with the issue price of 88 enhanced the effective yield to almost 5.7%. It was exempt from all taxes, which protected the investor against any future tax increase. And finally, it was a typical French perpetual loan: there was no fixed maturity date and the only obligation for the government was that it could not redeem the loan before 1931. The investor could count on fixed revenues whatever the market interest rate would be in the future. It was a familiar type of loan for the French investor; in fact the *rentier* was a characteristic element of French middle class in the 19th century.[61] In that period, however, the principal of a loan was not eroded by inflation, as it would be in the period 1915 until 1931. Investors – and probably the government as well – assumed that past results were a guarantee for the future. If people had known the future, the loan would have been less successful: in 1931 the value of the *franc* would be reduced to 20% of its 1913 value.

Anyhow, in 1915 it was a success. About 3.3 million Frenchmen and foreigners subscribed to the loan and two thirds of the 13 billion *francs* was 'new money', the other third being paid with *Obligations de la défense nationale* or converted older loans, including the July 1914 loan.[62] The revenue from the loan enabled the French government to repay an advancement of 2.4 billion *francs* to the *Banque de France* in cash. This transaction not only reassured the *régents* of the *Banque*, but it also contributed to combating inflation and increasing French credit status. Nevertheless, it took almost another year before the government issued a second large war loan. In the meantime, the government financed the war by the popular *bons*, *obligations* and by borrowing abroad (Chapter 10).

The **second** French war loan of October 1916 raised 10 billion *francs*; this was less than the first loan, but in this case 90% was fresh money (cash, bank deposits or *bons*); in absolute terms this was comparable to the fresh money of the first loan. The conditions were roughly the same as those for the first loan.[63] As these conditions were still considered very favourable for the investor, they met quite a bit of criticism. The respected French economist Pierre Paul Leroy-Beaulieu declared that it was impossible to find any other country in the whole world with a good credit status offering such attractive conditions.[64] The then former Finance Minister Louis-Lucien Klotz stated after the war that the French government lacked any rationality in interest rates on war loans.[65] [a] Despite these conditions, the loan itself was not a resounding success. One month earlier, the 6th German war loan had raised 10 billion *marks*,[66] not as much as the German government had wished, but nevertheless at that time equivalent to the 10 billion *francs* of the French loan.[67] The difference between France and Germany was that the French government was only partly depending on this large war loan. Almost one half of all money borrowed by France in 1916 (domestically and abroad) came from the short-term *bons*, a financial instrument of minor importance in German war finance.[68] Indeed, as far as the private capital market was concerned, France relied more heavily on short-term financial instruments than Germany, without consolidating this debt in long-term bonds.[b] Probably the most lasting result of the second French war loan was the famous poster of Jules-Abel Faivre with the text *'on les aura!'*: 'we will get them', a slogan and an image with an almost irresistible imaginative power.

French war propaganda: addressing all target groups

Like the German propaganda, the French government continuously developed more sophisticated methods to persuade investors to subscribe to war loans. The distinction became more pronounced between what we now call target groups. Schoolchildren were among these groups. Special training packages for writing and arithmetic were developed and distributed among teachers.[69] For language training for example there were exercises to conjugate irregular verbs like souscrire (subscribe): je souscris, nous souscrivons (I subscribe, we subscribe), etc. In mathematics, the pupils were to calculate how much interest a 'foreseeing head of family' who wished to save for his son's study would receive if he subscribed to a

---

a   Klotz indeed did not seek refuge in high nominal interest rates (page 141) when he succeeded Ribot a year later: he preferred the printing press, **Blancheton** (2001), p. 100.

b   Germany developed a large short-term debt as well, but this was mainly at the *Reichsbank*, not primarily by issuing government securities in the market.

war loan of 4% interest at an issue price of 70.8. Apart from an exercise in numeracy, this was obviously meant to penetrate the notion of war loans into society's capillaries. In the case that the problem would exceed the pupil's capacity, parents' assistance would extend the discussion to the family circle and unchain an undoubtedly animated (and hopefully positive) discussion about patriotic war finance.

The French government was remarkably little self-restrained in this target group policy, sometimes even contrary to regular policy. The posters for war loans for example were translated into regional languages such as Breton and Basque. In all other circumstances these languages had no right to exist in the centralised French governance system.[70] Apparently the end of raising money justified the means.

The last two French war loans were issued in the autumn of 1917 and 1918. At that time Finance Minister Ribot had been called to the high office of prime minister for the fourth time in his endless political career and Klotz returned to the Finance Department (French cabinets of the Third Republic were constantly playing musical chairs). At first sight it looked as if a new policy was introduced: the interest rate of the war loans was decreased a full percentage point to 4%, almost a pre-war level. This however was Klotz' window dressing, because the issue price of 68.6 implied that the government received considerably less value for money and the effective yield for the investor was still almost 6%, partly thanks to the advance interest payments. In reality the change was marginal. In contrast to previous loans, the **third** loan had a maximum amount of 10 billion *francs* with a life extended to 25 years. In order to reassure investors the government established a fund to purchase bonds to support the market if prices fell, thus protecting investors against losses. It resulted in proceeds of slightly over 10 billion *francs*.[71]

The tremendous success of the **fourth** (and last) French war loan can probably be attributed more to developments on the battlefield – and to the possibility to subscribe after the Armistice! – than to its financial incentives or propaganda efforts.[a] The loan raised no less than 22 billion

---

a   For Frenchmen the (incorrect) idea that prices would fall after the war and that war bonds were solid investments might have played a role as well; another, speculative, explanation is laundering of money earned in the black market.

francs, almost three times the proceeds of the simultaneously issued 9th German war loan.[72] If the outcome of the war were predicted in the autumn of 1918 from the success of war loans, it would have been perfectly clear who would win the war.

In the conditions of the fourth loan a special provision is worth mentioning: the option to pay in coupons of Russian government bonds and other Russian state guaranteed bonds. This was in fact a compensation for French investors who had bought these securities encouraged by French authorities, mainly before the war.[73] After the October Revolution in Russia payments on principal and interest were highly uncertain and indeed the bonds would eventually be reduced to collector's items.[a] When the French government was prepared to accept the coupons at 50% of their face value, investors at least saw some of their money back. Although this mode of payment was responsible for a negligible part of the loan (about 1.1%), for the French government it was a kind of moral duty (and one may assume that large holders of these bonds had some influence in government circles to suggest the policy). The result of course was, that French taxpayers were charged for the speculative investment policy of their compatriots, where it should be noted that, as always, taxpayers and investors partially overlapped.[74]

Overlooking French domestic war loans, one cannot escape the impression that France borrowed at a high price and at too short a term, as already remarked by contemporaries. The four large war loans alone had effective yields well above 5.5% and at the end of the war there was an outstanding short-term debt of 28 billion *francs* in the form of *Bons* and *Obligations de la défense nationale*.[75] In contrast to Germany, the war finance operation was ill prepared. The July 1914 loan had disrupted the financial markets at the worst possible moment. The initial refusal to increase taxes made the government a suppliant in the market and

---

a   From a strategic point of view French investments in Russia and in particular in Russian railways were by no means a waste of money. The unexpected rapid mobilisation of Russia in August 1914 was at least to some extent possibly due to the rail infrastructure constructed with French credits in previous decades. At a crucial moment in the war, Germany was forced to have a substantial part of its army on the eastern front, thus weakening its position on the western front and contributing to the defeat in the battle of the Marne, **Sauvy** (1984), part 1, p. 15; see also **Collins** (1973) for French strategic investments in Russian railways before the war and more recently **Horn** (2002), pp. 17-19 and **Clark** (2012), pp. 305, 352, 421.

even that role was at first played a little awkwardly. Government bonds were issued in the tradition of the *rentiers*, a system that worked well in the peaceful and stable *belle époque* years before the war but proved unable to cope with the unprecedented demand for money in wartime. Tax exemptions, generous conversion schemes and presents such as advance payment of interest finished the job. The result was devastating for France's future financial position: at the end of the war the national debt had risen to 170 billion *francs* or 170% of one year's GDP.[76] This was not only five times more than the already large debt at the eve of the war; more dangerously, a substantial part of the increase (more than 40%) consisted of short-term debts in the form of *bons* and *Banque de France* credits. This placed France in a vulnerable position for the years to come.

British war loans: large investors versus small savers

During the war Britain issued the least number of large (domestic) war loans of all belligerent countries: the first one in November 1914, the second one in June 1915 and the last and largest loan in January 1917. After the entry of the United States into the war and American government loans became available, no more large British war loans were issued until the Victory loan in June 1919, a few weeks before the Treaty of Versailles was signed; this fourth 'war' loan was mainly meant to cover financial support given to allies during the war.

Large domestic war loans were only a part of British war finance as far as borrowing was concerned. Being a centre of world trade, Britain had much easier access to the international capital markets than other countries, in particular Germany, Austria-Hungary, Russia and even France.[77] These highly advanced markets – of which Britain itself was of course a part – enabled the government to develop a broad and dedicated range of financial instruments; large war loans were just one of these instruments and they were used infrequently in order to consolidate shorter-term loans into long-term obligations. The three British war loans therefore cannot be separated from the other ways of borrowing. It was not only the *possibility* that enabled Britain to follow this policy; it was completely in line with orthodox budgetary *tradition*, a policy that had resulted in two realities: an unshakable confidence of the financial markets and a remarkably low national debt at the eve of the war. Whereas the national debt of Germany was 44% of one year's GDP and for France it was even 87%, Britain could boast of an amount as low as 28% in 1913, despite the wars it had fought and the large investments in the battleships programme.[78]

The **first** British war loan, issued three months after the beginning of the war, could hardly be called a success. It raised the fixed amount of £ 350 million, but only thanks to heavy pressure by the Treasury on the banks to subscribe; they were responsible for £ 100 million of the loan. The Bank of England itself subscribed for £ 150 million to prevent the loan from being a complete failure and to accomplish this, it even had to use some creative accounting.[79] The conditions of the loan were not particularly favourable to attract investors, either large or small. The interest rate was 3.5%. Indeed the effective yield was somewhat enhanced to 4% thanks to the issue price of 95 but even that was lower than the actual bank rate of 5%.[80] The exceptionally low issue price for British standards was motivated by the possibility of falling prices if the war lasted a long time; it ensured the investor an additional 5% at maturity date.[81] Whereas the loan was financially unattractive for large investors, small savers were discouraged for another reason: the minimum amount for subscription was £ 100, well above the average annual income.[82] In the unlikely event that they had saved such an amount, they would have to withdraw it from their account at the Post Office Savings Bank; it would have increased their revenue by 1% point at the risk of converting a solid savings account into a bond with fluctuating value. From the perspective of the government, it was not attractive either to encourage these small savers, since at the end it would have to pay the extra interest.

Due to these circumstances, the first British war loan was far from being a people's loan. There were only 100,000 subscribers, in sharp contrast to the first German loan issued a few months earlier: 1 million.[83] Lloyd George declared that it had never been his intention to address the masses of the population since big money was to be expected from large investors and banks only. He did admit that an appeal to the general public could have reached more people, but the revenue from small savers would not have led to substantially higher revenue from the loan.[84] From a financial point of view he was absolutely right as the results in Germany confirmed. But he overlooked the fact – and indeed in November 1914 this could hardly be foreseen – that a modern war is to a large extent a total war that requires mobilisation of *all* available means, including massive support of the whole population.[a] It was necessary to show the enemy that the nation supported the army and the navy in all respects, even if it would be less efficient from a financially rational point of view. A second argument was that collecting money from people who could offer hardly anything more than small savings from their weekly earnings, would immediately redirect any surplus money to the government without fuelling inflation. Men of means could more easily borrow from their bank to finance a subscription to a war loan, not particularly an inflation controlling mechanism. All these considerations made the first British war loan an instrument for the financial sector and the well-to-do.[85] This enabled wealthier people to make more profit on their capital than the working class, a point continuously stressed by the relatively small group of Labour Party members in Westminster, despite all parliamentary harmony in these first months of the war.[86]

In the **second** British war loan, the small saver received substantially more attention. Apart from political motives, combating inflation had become an important argument, a permanent issue in British war finance.[87] Increasing income remained not restricted to capitalists in the arms industry and its suppliers. The simple factory worker had also made some progress. In 1915 unemployment had fallen below 2% and it continued to decline.[88] Wages made an all-round rise, even without including overtime work. Women started to be employed in jobs that were hitherto restricted to men and boys. This allowed them a (small) income of their own and additional purchasing power that the government sought to skim in order to control inflation. They were a new target group for the war loan propaganda stressing not only the economic and financial argument, but above all the support for the men in the trenches.[89]

Initially Chancellor McKenna announced the second war loan in June 1915 without much noise in the neutral financial tradition for issuing government bonds. The prominent adman Hedley Le Bas who had gained experience in the famous Lord Kitchener campaign for volunteers, however, got wind of it. Perfectly in the style of his profession he literally

---

a   Many years later, this has been formulated to the point in Winston Churchill's famous blood, sweat and tears speech of May 1940. With respect to war financing, US Secretary of the Treasury William McAdoo's opinion was that 'any great war must necessarily be a popular movement', **McAdoo** (1931), p. 374; **ARST** 1917, p. 6.

stood at the doorstep of the Chancellor's private house at 36 Smith Square, Westminster, to persuade him of modern marketing techniques to attract large public support for the loan. The proposal fell on fertile ground and within a few days the Treasury provided a generous budget to promote the loan.[90] The propaganda was indeed unprecedented for this kind of a financial instrument and ordinary British citizens could subscribe at post offices directly for amounts as low as £ 5; or they could participate in an ingenious savings system with even smaller savings stamps of 5 s. Despite the campaign, contributions from the small savers were not abundant. The number of subscriptions was more than ten times higher than for the first loan, 1.1 million, but even that amount was lower than in any of the German war loans, including the disastrous loan of September 1918.[91]

The limited success in reaching larger classes of the population has been attributed to the fact that the British working class could be divided into two groups: those with a savings account and those who had no money in a bank at all.[92] The latter group lived, so to speak, from hand to mouth and was not inclined to save at the moment that earnings became a little higher than before the war. The first group was familiar with the Post Office savings book (or any other local bank) where they could regularly see their interest entered in the booklet and where the money could be withdrawn anytime. Buying a bond with a fixed maturity date would be a new and possibly uncomfortable way of 'saving'. Furthermore, although it was presented as a savings activity, buying government bonds was in fact an investment: bond prices could fluctuate. For the man in the street arguments like these were probably more decisive than fear of inflation, a phenomenon of greater concern for financial experts at the Treasury such as Keynes and his superior John Bradbury. Anyhow, the smaller denominations (certificates up to £ 5) contributed only £ 5 million, almost negligible when compared to the net proceeds of £ 610 million revenue for the Treasury.[93]

The predominant characteristics of the second war loan therefore were neither the contribution of small savers nor its interest rate of 4.5%.[94] More important was the customer loyalty programme that McKenna introduced, inspired by the French. Options for conversion of older bonds bearing lower interest were offered at a generous scale. Not only bonds of the first 3.5% loan could be used to convert, but also older

Consols (government bonds) bearing 2½% or 2¾%, although investors were obliged to bring a certain percentage of cash. Investors made massive use of these options. About £ 300 million of the revenue for the Treasury came from conversions, three times as much as had been subscribed to the first war loan by private investors.[95]

Movie star Marie Lohr buys a War Bond at a 'Bank Tank' placed in Trafalgar Square as part of a propaganda campaign, March 1918 (Illustration 9.4)

Source: © Imperial War Museums (Q 54384).

It would take one and a half years for the British government to float its third and last war loan before the Armistice. In December 1916 the Asquith coalition cabinet had fallen and the new Chancellor of the Exchequer, Andrew Bonar Law, announced the loan in January 1917. Its success was overwhelming: over 5 million subscriptions and net proceeds of £ 900 million fresh money, that is: apart from another £ 1.1 billion of conversions of older loans. This made the gross revenue over £ 2 billion and Bonar Law rightly received congratulations from his predecessor McKenna.[96] It was the largest war loan so far ever in any country and second only to the American Liberty Loan of October 1918 (as measured by the amount of fresh, unconverted money). It would also become the loan that kept alive the memory of the enormous financial efforts for the First World War for almost a century: final payments on the loan were made in March 2015 (Chapter 15).

Several circumstances contributed to this success. In the first place the government set up a fund to protect the bonds against a possible decrease in price. Banks offered their clients ample possibilities to borrow money to subscribe to the war loan. Furthermore, the loan had the option of tax exemption if the subscriber was prepared to accept an interest rate of 4% instead of 5%.[97] And finally, the propaganda machine turned at full speed with a sophisticated target group approach.[98] On the one hand, Bonar Law could address locally organised clubs of small savers (the War Savings Committees), while on the other hand appealing to the social responsibility of large ship-owners who made fortunes out of the war.

Evidently, Britain could show off this third loan, but there were two distortions. In the first place it was a huge amount indeed, but for a considerable part thanks to conversions from earlier loans. This can be seen if the second and third loans are taken together; then the amount of money produced by the population suddenly drops by £ 800 million.[99] In the second place, not all contemporaries realised that not only the amount was unprecedented, but inflation as well. Between the second and the third loan prices had risen by roughly 40%.[100] If measured in value, the real effort of the British population for the third loan was only 15% higher than for the second. On the other hand, it must be admitted that the population had endured another one and a half years of war, including the exhausting battle of the Somme. From that perspective, the proceeds of the second British war loan might without hesitation be called a formidable result.

The other side of this coin was a double mortgage on the financial future of the British government: a large sum of money borrowed for a long time at a high interest rate of 5%. Every six months, until 1947, the government had to pay £ 50 million in interest alone. In one respect, there could be some light on the horizon: the government had the option to redeem the loan completely, at three months' notice, after 1st June 1929. This offered the possibility to convert the loan into a new one at a lower interest rate, provided that interest rates fell and provided that the government possessed the amount of £ 2 billion to do so. It appeared to be a very wise option, as will be become clear in Chapter 14 (page 256). Taken together, the three large British war loans issued during the war raised the enormous net amount of GPB 2.3 billion.[a]

British war loans: a spectrum of financial instruments

The large war loans spread a part of the financial burden over a longer period. This part however was limited, because between the three large war loans, financial needs were covered by a system of short-term loans. This system comprised no less than four types of borrowing. The simplest one was the so-called *Ways & Means* financing, advances by the Bank of England. They were different from the normal peacetime financial transactions between a government and the central bank in one respect only: their amount. At the end of the war, the advances had grown to over £ 450 million.[101] This implied that an amount equal to almost one fifth of the total revenue from large war loans had been borrowed from the central bank at very short terms, as a floating debt.

Of more importance, however, were three types of short-term loans in the private capital market: *Treasury Bills*, *Exchequer Bonds* and (from October 1917) *National War Bonds*; their main differences were the maturity conditions, the frequency, the issue price and the interest rate.

The *Treasury Bills* were short-term government debt paper, issued with high frequency – sometimes daily – and for fixed denominations such as £ 1,000, £ 5,000 of £ 10,000 with maturities varying from three months to one year.[102] They bore no interest; the profit for the investor came from the discount price at which they were sold.[b] During the first week of the war, this brought the buyer a yield of 3.6%. In the summer of 1916, however, when the financial situation of the British government was awkward, the government was obliged to offer higher discounts, pushing up yields to 6.4% for one-year bills.[103] This shows exactly the strengths and weaknesses of the bills. By issuing them at carefully selected dates, the government could anticipate market circumstances and cover its financial needs at what were then attractive conditions. As the amounts and maturities were flexible, this type of borrowing

---

a   Converted at pre-war exchange rates, this was roughly half the amount of all nine German loans together and 10% more than the French loans.

b   This made the *Treasury Bills* different from the French *Bons de la défense nationale*, which they can be compared to in many other respects such as average term and type of investors.

resembled a continuous emission: borrowing on the tap, according to circumstances. During the first six months of the war, when other short-term investment options were difficult to find, it was a profitable financial instrument, both for the government and for investors. By offering different conditions, institutional investors could fine-tune their financial needs. The weakness of the short term was of course repayment of the bills, sometimes as soon as three months after they had been issued. In practice this often meant rolling-over at the same conditions, but not unusually the government had to offer higher discounts. Anyhow, the system required a perfect registration because practically every calendar day was an expiry date for some loan that the Treasury had to refinance. Nevertheless, the system of *Treasury Bills* worked during the whole war, except from small periods before the issue of large war loans to give investors an opportunity to build up sufficient capital for subscription to these loans. The system of the bills expressed the power, flexibility and development of the British financial markets, particularly in comparison with other belligerent countries in the First World War.[a]

Because the 'tap' could be controlled from day to day, the amount of outstanding bills changed continuously. Credits could be redeemed by the proceeds from war loans, for example. The simple facts, however, show that the number of bills issued had soared from a meagre £ 15 million in August 1914 to £ 1.1 billion in November 1918, or at a daily average rate of £ 650,000.[104] At the end of the war the bills were responsible for roughly 16% of the British national debt. Unlike the large war loans with expiration dates in the 1940s, the bills constituted an enormous short-term debt and the creditors could withdraw their money practically from week to week. This segment of British war financing in fact was not very different from the way the French operated.

Since the *Treasury bills* called on the financial markets from day to day, the yield of the bills, expressed as an interest rate, was a perfect indicator of the market situation, much better than the artificially stable bank rate. During the first years of the war, this interest rate rose steadily, expressing the growing effort of the British government to finance the war – for itself

---

a   **Balderston** (1989) even regards access to the international financial markets for short-term loans as the essential difference in war financing between Britain and all other belligerent countries.

and for its French, Russian and Italian allies as well. The rate culminated at almost 5.5% in the spring of 1917 when Germany had relaunched its unrestricted submarine warfare and the financial situation of the British government was delicate indeed.[105] The turning point came when the United States entered the war in April 1917; from that moment on Britain was no longer dependent on the commercial financial markets but it could rely on the almost unlimited support of the American government (Chapter 10). The yield on British three-month *Treasury Bills* immediately turned from an upward trend into a downward one (illustration 9.5). An independent observer knowing only these interest rates and without any knowledge of military or political developments would have concluded that a particular event had happened in the Great War in the first week of April 1917. It was in fact the decisive turn in war financing, as will be confirmed in Chapter 10.

The turning point in the interest rate on 3 months British Treasury bills: the Americans are coming! (Illustration 9.5)

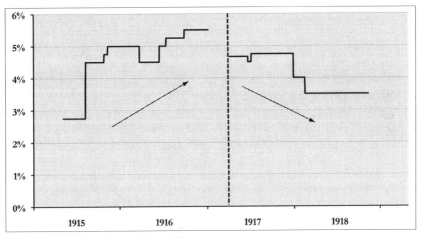

Source: based on data from Wormell.[106]

Between the short-term bills and the large war loans were the *Exchequer Bonds*, genuine government bonds with a fixed maturity date and bearing coupon interest. They had a life of roughly five years, sufficient for redemption when the war was over. The obvious objective of the Treasury was to be less dependent on the short-term bills without the pressure to have recourse to large war loans.[107] They were issued on a more or less continuous basis. In 1915 and 1916 the bonds (just like the bills) remained an instrument for the financial world, mainly banks, and the total amount issued was about £ 700 million.[108] From 1917 onward however, the *Exchequer Bonds* were successfully sold to the public at large under the appealing name of *National War Bonds* and bearing a fixed interest of 5%.[109]

The success of the bonds was due to the changed marketing strategy, directed towards the population instead of the traditional target group of financial institutions. At the end of the war, the outstanding amount of bonds was no less than £ 1.6 billion, equal to two thirds of the proceeds of all three large war loans together.[110] Actual subscriptions would have been even higher because the bonds had been embellished with options making them attractive for bondholders to use them before the formal redemption date. They could for example be used to buy bonds from the third war loan, which was profitable for the Treasury because it prolonged the maturity structure of the debt considerably. For bondholders it was also attractive that *National War Bonds* could be used to pay excess profits duty and inheritance tax. This latter option was frequently used: almost 20% of the tax that could be paid in this way was indeed paid by bonds.[111] For subscribers the bonds were also attractive due to the primary conditions; the combination of nominal interest rate, a life of five years and a premium at redemption date allowed for an effective yield well over 5%. In hindsight, we may be surprised why it took the British government so long before it introduced this financial instrument that the French had already successfully applied almost 2½ years earlier in the form of the *Bons de la défense nationale*.

As was the case with all loans at relatively high interest rates, the annual payments were the downside of the success. Initially it was £ 30 million, but it increased to £ 80 million, a serious burden for the budget. And the bonds would have to be paid back rather early after the war. Within 10 years, the government would have to pay the total amount of £ 1.6 billion of maturing bonds, a sum equal to more than a quarter of the 1918/1919 GDP.[112]

To sum up, Britain had found relatively easy solutions for its borrowing to finance the war, thanks to a well-developed banking sector, a considerable wealth gathered over centuries, an extremely good credit status, both domestically and abroad, and a successful although somewhat belated appeal to patriotism. A picture emerges of a broad, almost confusing range of tradable government securities that could be continuously converted and with all kinds of options to benefit from interest and tax profits. It was an ideal playing field for the banks that made money from buying and selling financial products, keen to protect their own interest and always willing to give the government unsolicited advice. On the other hand, it must be said, they did take risks and if necessary they were there when the Treasury was facing real trouble.

Meanwhile the British government had imposed upon itself – in all its tradition of sound financial management and with all rhetoric – a burden that exceeded the capacity of the Empire. The truth was, that Britain was among the victors on the battlefield, but financially it had lost its status as the world's creditor. Servicing the debt would become the most prominent political issue during the 1920s and beyond. The international financial scene would be taken over by American bankers.

American war loans: superlatives in many respects

The United States took a different position in the Great War, not only politically and military but also financially. Evidently their war reference was not the Franco-Prussian War or the Boer War, but the Civil War of 1861-1865. That war had been financed primarily by means of short-term loans and paper money. The loans had been bank credits where interest rates up to 6% had been not unusual.[113] Meanwhile, the printing press delivered the first official dollar notes as legal tender in denominations of $ 5, $ 10 and $ 20. It was the government's policy that this inflationary way of financing would not happen again in the First World War, although loans would again be dominant and provide for three quarters of war financing.[114]

A major advantage for the American government was the time for preparation. During its period of neutrality (August 1914 – March 1917) it could develop a policy of avoiding mistakes such as an inconvenient interest rate, impractical terms or addressing too narrow target groups. The propaganda machine had been developed as well and the issue of war loans can be characterized as American style: large, fast and exploiting all the opportunities afforded by new media. In one and a half years, between the declaration of war on Germany on 6 April 1917 and the Armistice on 11 November 1918, the four *Liberty Loans* raised $ 17 billion, or on the average $ 29 million *per day*! In 1919 the Victory *Liberty Loan* added another $ 4.5 billion. These amounts were huge indeed, but they were necessary: the United States had to finance not only its own military expenditure – including transatlantic transportation costs boosted by German submarine attacks – but it had also taken the responsibility of providing the credits that its allies needed to purchase military equipment from American industry. In the first half year from April until September 1917, credits to allies outnumbered the American own war expenditure by a factor of three (illustration 12.1, page 204).

The US government had adopted from the British the system of alternating large war loans and the issue of short-term treasury bills, but it reversed the pattern. Instead of a continuous flow of short-term bills interrupted by a few large loans, the American Treasury chose for large war loans as the primary instrument. Prior to these loans, it let the banks accumulate a stock of short-term debts in the form of *Certificates of Indebtedness* that could be converted into the *Liberty Loans* in due time.[115] In the placement of these *Certificates*, the new FED system played a significant role.[116] When the loans were announced, the banks collected the money from subscriptions to pay back the short-term credits. The loans themselves also offered opportunities for conversion to subsequent loans with higher interest rates; these options however were restricted in time or to the next loan; bondholders had to be alert in order to exercise their rights.[117]

The **first** *Liberty Loan*, issued in May 1917, had a fixed amount of $ 2 billion and (still) a modest interest rate of 3.5%.[118] It was 50% over-subscribed and over 4 million subscriptions could be recorded. This was more than two and a half times as much as the first German war loan if the size of the population is taken into account (103 million Americans versus 63 million Germans, respectively). Apparently, Secretary of the Treasury William McAdoo had more feeling with the markets – and with popular sentiment – than the banks that had suggested a much lower sum for this first loan.[119]

William Gibbs McAdoo (1863-1941), US Secretary of the Treasury, among many other businesses[120]

McAdoo held the position of US Secretary of the Treasury for almost six years, from 6 March 1913 until 15 December 1918. This period fully covered the First World War, and he was the only finance minister of all major belligerent countries to do so.

Before he was called to this office by President Woodrow Wilson, he had hardly any experience as a professional politician. Neither had he a reputation in the world of banking (he had been selling corporate securities in New York for some years, mainly from railroad companies. The various biographies and his own memoirs hardly give any particulars about this activity, except that he had developed a thorough knowledge of the financial position of all American railroad companies). His real capacity was that of an ambitious constructive entrepreneur, a man who could identify a small but accomplishable opportunity to achieve a large and enduring result. The construction of a railway tunnel under the Hudson River to connect Manhattan and New Jersey was such a challenge. After earlier attempts in the 1870s and 1880s had failed, McAdoo organised the necessary financial support by cleverly contacting and persuading wealthy investors, among whom J.P. Morgan (Sr.).[121] One of the financial pillars of the project was the development of large-scale office buildings combined with a passenger terminal at a high-potential location, the site of the later World Trade Center.

To the public, the enterprise brought a convenient way of travelling: from the opening in February 1908 the train service has been in almost continuous operation up to the present day. For the initiator McAdoo, it meant not only a secured income as the director of the Hudson & Manhattan Railroad Company; above all it realised what he was looking for: respect and honour,[122] a reputation as a successful businessman in the public-private domain and most of all a valuable *network in the highest financial circles and among decision makers. It gave the ambitious Southerner – born in Georgia, educated in Tennessee – his place under the sun in booming New York, where he had moved in 1892 and had tried to make his living like many anonymous others in law practice (he had studied law in practice and had been admitted to the Tennessee bar in 1885 after one year at the University of Tennessee followed by private instruction).*[123]

In the years 1910-1911 William McAdoo, averse to 'a state of indecision'[124] and always in search of new challenges, became seriously involved in politics. He played a decisive role in having the governor of New Jersey, Woodrow Wilson, nominated as the Democratic candidate for US presidency in 1912. After Wilson was elected president, McAdoo became one of Wilson's most important cabinet members as his Secretary of the Treasury. McAdoo has always vehemently denied the relationship between both events, and it must be said that his successes fully justified the choice: the adoption by Congress of the Federal Reserve Act in 1913,[a] the reform of the old tariff system and the introduction of income tax. In the crisis days of July and August 1914 when the war broke out in Europe, McAdoo acted resolutely by issuing emergency money and by having the New York Stock Exchange closed for five months. The closing of Wall Street prevented a gold drain from the country that would have been disastrous for the US banking system and American financial reputation. Thanks to the closing it became almost impossible for European investors to sell their American securities for dollars and subsequently converting them into gold; thus, the United States could formally and de facto maintain the Gold Standard – and therefore its financial credibility – simply because the flow of dollars from foreign transactions was blocked. At the end of 1914, the panic was over – in fact the European allies badly needed the dollars and gold began to flow into the US – and the New York Stock Exchange reopened. The following year the other measure, the issue of emergency currency, was also made undone, when the notes were gradually retired from circulation.[125] Recently, McAdoo's actions have been marked as

---

a   When the FED proved to be a success, as always many persons claimed to be its father – even those who had been the most fervent opponents, **Chase** (2008), pp. 312-313; William McAdoo can be counted among them, although the role of a determined midwife would probably be more appropriate.

major steps in shifting financial world leadership from Britain to the United States.[126]

During the war, McAdoo could claim the overwhelming success of the Liberty Loans of which he also introduced the name.[127] *In the meantime he established the Federal Land Bank system to support farmers – the Board being chaired by McAdoo, of course, just like the Federal Reserve Board – and life insurance for men in military service. When the war required an efficient transport system to bring material and ammunition to the ports of the Atlantic, a service that the competing railroad companies could not provide, he suggested President Wilson to place the railroads under federal control, led by a director-general whose name was unsurprisingly William G. McAdoo. In the last year of the war one might say that McAdoo for a good deal literally 'ran' the country. More than any other of his fellow cabinet ministers, he had direct access to the president, even on Sunday morning:*[128] *in May 1914 the 50 year old widower (his first wife had died in 1912) McAdoo had married Eleanor Randolph Wilson, the youngest daughter of the president, then 24.*[a]

Three days after the Armistice, McAdoo declared his resignation from the cabinet, partly for financial reasons: the salary of $ 12,000 of a US Secretary of the Treasury was a small fraction of what he could earn in business. In his five and a halve years at the Treasury he had transformed the once 'somnolent and gloomy institution'[129] *into a powerful and confident financial establishment that Wall Street had to take duly into account (he would never belong to the close friends of the big banks and the stock exchange, although he fully recognised their role in economy).*[130] *He used a broad interpretation of 'matters of finance', always trying to shift the demarcations with his colleague cabinet members in favour of the Treasury.*[131]

For McAdoo, the end of the war by no means marked the end of his career. Beside his business affairs in law and as a promoter of aviation (he frequently used his private Lockheed Vega monoplane),[132] *he remained*

---

a   One might note that he shared this characteristic of marrying his boss's younger daughter or protégée with his German and British colleagues Helfferich and Mc Kenna, see pages 104 and 217.

very visible in the political arena as an outspoken 'dry' in the period of prohibition and as an initially promising candidate for the Democratic nomination for US presidency in 1920 and 1924; in both cases he was beaten by candidates that would be swept away by Republicans Harding and Coolidge, respectively. One of the remarkable performances of the persuasive orator (both in public and in private) was his appeal at the Democratic convention in 1932 for the nomination of Franklin D. Roosevelt, as he had done twenty years earlier in 1912 for Wilson. He was a kingmaker without himself ever becoming king. Finally, McAdoo ended his political career as a senator for California from 1933-1938, the state where he had moved in 1922.

In 1935, at the age of 71, the ever-travelling celebrity McAdoo surprised political circles, close friends and the tabloids alike with the announcement of his marriage to a 25-years-old nurse, after his divorce from Eleanor Wilson the previous year.[133] It must have kept him young, as three years later he accepted the position of chairman of a withered steamship corporation to have it flourishing before long. McAdoo died in February 1941. His life reflects modern American history from his parents' move from Tennessee to Georgia during the Civil War, the development of railroads, the dynamic finance of New York in the early 20th century and finally to the year of the attack on Pearl Harbor, of which he had warned as one of the first frequent flyers. In this life, American financing of the First World War was just one episode.

An import technical characteristic of American war loans was its gold clause. Both interest and principal payments were guaranteed 'in United States gold coin of the present standard of value'.[134] This clause undoubtedly convinced subscribers that the *Liberty Loan* bonds protected their investment against possible future currency depreciations. If the German war loans had known this clause, the 1922/'23 inflation would have worked out for its bondholders very differently – provided of course that the clause had been respected. It must be noted, however, that even in the United States in 1933 the true (void) value of this clause would become evident, as we shall see in Chapter 14.

The first American war loan was very attractive for wealthy citizens, in particular when income tax rates were soon raised to about 70%. Thanks to tax exemptions on principal and interest, these subscribers received an effective yield largely over 10% on their risk-free investment in government securities.[135] [a] One might have expected less generous provisions from a Democratic president supported by a Democratic majority in Congress (and even a socialist representative).[136] In the **second** *Liberty Loan*, issued within five months after the first one, the tax exemptions were reduced, but not completely, while the interest rate was raised to 4%. The loan was again a great success. It was issued as a fixed sum loan, but the Treasury had promised that up to half of the oversubscriptions would be accepted. The loan eventually generated almost $ 4 billion from more than twice as many subscribers than the first loan had attracted.[137] This meant that at the end of 1917 every one out of eleven American citizens was a bondholder of a *Liberty Loan*, a rate that would even double for the third loan until at the forth loan one out of every five Americans had subscribed.[138]

The **third** loan, issued May 1918, was different from the first two loans in several respects. Apart from the slightly higher interest rate of 4¼%, it had a fixed life of ten years, whereas the previous two loans were double-dated: redeemable after five or ten years and ultimately payable after 30 and 25 years, respectively.[139] More important, however, was the announcement that despite the fixed amount of $ 3 billion, all oversubscriptions would be accepted. McAdoo could be reassured by the success of the previous loans to make this third one effectively an open-ended loan; it resulted in total proceeds of over $ 4 billion, slightly higher than the third one had raised.

All issues of *Liberty Loans* were accompanied by massive support from volunteers and professionals. Hundreds of thousands of volunteers participated, among whom groups of boy scouts, but also celebrities such as Mary Pickford, Al Jolson, Geraldine Farrar and Douglas Fairbanks gave evidence of their patriotic feelings in mass meetings. Charlie Chaplin even directed a propaganda movie at his own expense appealing to buy *Liberty Bonds*. A special National Women's *Liberty Loan* Committee under the presidency of Mrs. McAdoo (President Wilson's daughter) mobilised 60,000 women to sell bonds for the second loan and even

---

a   In fact, the tax exemption was so attractive that over two thirds of the bondholders did not exercise their right of conversion into subsequent *Liberty Loans* bearing up to ¾ percentage point more interest, **Gilbert** (1970), p. 172. This incidentally confirms the point that the interest rate is just one of the arguments in investing in (war) bonds, page 118 ff.

a tenfold for the forth loan.[140] For the average American citizen it was impossible to escape from this national mobilisation of money.

Fund raising American style: star tenor Enrico Caruso raises $2.2 million for the third Liberty Loan in a night at the opera with the assistance of the French Tricolour and a group of French 'Blue Devils' from the trenches (Illustration 9.6)

MUSICIANS RAISE $2,200,000 FOR LOAN

Crowd at Carnegie Hall Greets Pershing's Men and "Blue Devils."

THOUSANDS TURNED AWAY

James M. Beck Shows Close Relation of Music and Patriotism—Caruso and Farrar Sing.

Music paid tribute to patriotism last night in Carnegie Hall, where a crowd that filled the auditorium to overflowing was gathered by the Allied Music Trades and Associations of New York to boom the Third Liberty Loan. At the close of the meeting it was announced that $2,200,000 had been subscribed.

Source: *New York Times*, 1st May 1918.

During the campaign for the **fourth** and last loan during the war, in October 1918, mass campaigns were avoided. This had nothing to do with financial arguments but with health measures to prevent the spread of the Spanish flu. Public campaigns concentrated on canvassing individual households.[141] Despite these restrictions, the loan – this time it was again a double-dated one – raised $ 7 billion. It was collected by no less than 21 million subscriptions, the highest number ever recorded in any of the countries involved in the First World War.

The overall picture of the four American war loans is that a large amount had been raised in a relatively short time, partially by adopting successful marketing and financial strategies and avoiding failures learned by European countries; it was also bought at a relatively moderate interest rate. The large loans, including the post-Armistice Victory *Liberty Loan*, prevented the development of large short-term debts and a dangerous (although not negligible) increase in circulation of paper money. The massive campaigns resulted in a high rate of participation of all classes of the population, exceeding results in any other country. The contribution of small savers to the total result was not spectacular if measured in money, but it was impressive if measured in the number of subscriptions.

In one and a half years the lowest 20% of income households bought war bonds for $ 125 million.[142] The real benefit, however, accrued to the more wealthy classes thanks to tax exemptions and conversion options.[143]

Summary and conclusions

Large domestic war loans have dominated the picture of war financing both during the war and long after the Armistice. To some extent this is appropriate. Much effort had been spent on promotion campaigns accompanying the issue of the loans. The home front became engaged in the war in a more positive manner than by lists of casualties. In particular when developments at the military front were not encouraging the loan campaigns developed into unifying events; the proceeds were nevertheless higher when military successes could be celebrated. The amounts produced by the loans have indeed contributed to war finance, roughly for 60% (excluding foreign loans and central bank advances).[144]

Almost half of the money from large domestic war loans was raised in Britain and the United States; nominal values in own currency [in brackets indicative amounts in billions of 1913 dollars] (Illustration 9.7)

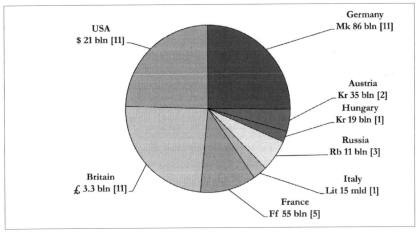

Source: calculated from Strachan, Roesler, Bogart, Brucker.[145]

The financial strength of the loans was that large sums of money became available in a relatively short period. The money was used for direct expenditure and to repay short-term advances from the central bank and other short-term loans. As long as the subscriptions were paid in cash or from existing bank accounts (fresh money), they contributed to combating inflation; in particular surplus war profits could be redirected into the treasury. In this respect domestic loans served three purposes, although they were not always communicated: war finance, solidarity and controlling inflation.

The large war loans, however, were only part of the story. They were issued at regular moments (Germany and, to some extent, the United States) or irregularly (France and Britain) to collect large sums to consolidate short-term debts into bonds with a time span of several decades. Between the large loans, the government's hunger for money was satisfied by short-term public loans such as the British *National War Bonds*, American *Certificates of Indebtedness* or French *Bons* (and *Obligations*) *de la défense nationale*. All belligerent countries had made use of these important complementary loans in the form of treasury bills or equivalent instruments. By doing so, they accumulated large floating debts – apart from central bank advances – that made budgets vulnerable for setbacks. It depended largely on the degree to which the government succeeded in the consolidation process whether this danger would be dominant after the war. In the United States it was hardly a problem thanks to the success of the last *Liberty* and *Victory Liberty Loans*. In Britain it led to a surmountable but painful process (Chapter 14). In France, however, the large floating debt, in particular due to the money-like *bons*, became a serious problem that – together with its other domestic and international debts – contributed to its financial misery in the 1920s. It explains to some extent the harsh demands in the Treaty of Versailles. In Germany these short-term public loans were of less importance as they formed only some 13% of the total domestic loans;[146] their role was in fact played by the even more harmful *Darlehenskassenscheine* and the printing press.

Apart from the first British war loan, all domestic loans were intended to be popular loans appealing to large classes of society. In financial terms, however, not a single loan could be so called. Despite large numbers of subscriptions for many loans, big money invariably came from large subscribers, be they wealthy individuals or institutions. The millions of small savers – directly or by special saving programmes – contributed a share not exceeding a few per cent of the total sum. The social impact went far beyond this financial contribution. German authorities succeeded in making the nine large war loans increasingly popular loans supported

Practically all countries used long-term and short-term loans parallel to each other; the illustration presents comparable types of loans by country; banknotes have been included as additional information only (Illustration 9.8)

		Britain	France	Germany	USA
War Loans	Long term	3 War Loans + 1 Victory Loan (1919)	4 War Loans (*Emprunts de Guerre*)	9 War Loans (*Kriegsanleihen*)	4 Liberty Loans +1 Victory Liberty Loan (1919)
	Medium term	Exchequer Bonds & National War Bonds	*Obligations de la Défense Nationale*	*Schatz-anweisungen*	
	Short term	Treasury Bills	*Bons de la Défense Nationale*		Certificates of Indebtedness
Paper money	Bank notes	Bank of England * notes (£)	*Banque de France* notes (*francs*)	*Reichsbank* * notes (*Marks*)	FED system notes ($)
					National Bank notes ($)
	Other notes	Currency notes (£)		*Darlehens-kassenscheine*	United States notes ($)**
				Reichs-kassenscheine	

* Also a limited amount of notes issued by a small group of private banks; in Britain notably in Scotland and Ireland. (**) gold and silver certificates not counted as paper money.[147]

by the German community until in the autumn of 1917 the lower and middle classes dropped out. British war loans were promoted heavily by modern marketing techniques, although they always kept some odour of the financial world. American war loans were real popular loans with participation rates up to 20% of the population; at the end almost every household was involved.

The modalities of the loans were not only dictated by market conditions. Culture and tradition played a significant role as well. This is shown by the French perpetual loans issued at low prices, the German loans with their uniform interest rate, British financial instruments always apprehensive about the interests of the financial markets and the massive American celebrity backed campaigns (and with large tax benefits for the super-rich). In all countries except Germany, the interest rate for large war loans increased during the war, but not spectacularly. In fact the rate reflected the demand for money only to a certain degree and for short-term loans in particular. The interest rate was more politically driven than by market conditions. Upward pressure on interest rates was diverted to the printing press for banknotes.

A final cultural difference with respect to war loans, was the attitude towards interest and principal payments. In Britain there was always the idea in the background that debts should eventually be paid back: servicing the debt. Indeed, one person's debt was another person's asset and a loan was simply a contract with an investor. Debts were just a particular sort of commodity that could bring profit by selling, buying and conversion. In this tradition it was not uncommon to make a reservation in the form of a sinking fund to save for redemption. In Germany and particularly in France, this tradition was completely absent. German authorities could not stop reminding the population and foreign investors that the true pillars of its credit status consisted of the productive power of its manufacturing sector and the industrious attitude of the population; this was supposed to be sufficient to ensure future repayments. It is hardly possible to catch German and French governments expressing explicitly a less solid financial moral. But at the end of the day, they seemed to be less embarrassed if not all loans were repaid to the penny.

It remains a matter of speculation for how long Britain could have maintained its system of short- and medium-term loans, with its large appeal to the banking system and the international capital market of private investors. The question has been made hypothetical by American participation in the war from April 1917 with its massive government credits to the allies. It is not impossible that the system could have held for a long time, because in the end it was not the financial resources as such that were decisive but the prospect of return on the investment in the form of a military victory.

10

Borrowing abroad: loyal allies or business relationships?

'They hired the money, didn't they?'
John C. Coolidge[a]

Loans, taxes and monetary financing were options open to every belligerent (and neutral) country. Borrowing abroad on the other hand was not available for every government. The possibilities for the Central powers and the Entente allies differed considerably. Whereas the latter had to appeal increasingly to the financial resources of their allies – in particular the United States, Germany was effectively excluded from access to the international financial markets.

Germany and the rest of the world

From the first days of August 1914 it was obvious that Germany could no longer appeal to the international financial markets in London. But even before the war, Germany had realised that borrowing abroad would be an improbable option for the country. Only countries that could be assumed to remain neutral were regarded as serious opportunities for credit. The German economist Dietzel, a strong advocate of borrowing, realised very well that for foreign loans his country had to resort to Belgium, the Netherlands, Switzerland and the United States (he did not mention Scandinavia).[1] He mentioned Belgium in the first place, which was not unreasonable in view of its economic position at that time. After the violence of breaching Belgian neutrality and its occupation, this option was obviously excluded and the number of creditor countries for Germany started to crumble as soon as the war broke out.

---

a   John Calvin Coolidge (1872-1933), 30th president of the United States (1923-1929); in 1923 he was vice president under Warren G. Harding; the exact date and source of the quote are uncertain (a 1924 conversation with Winston Churchill is sometimes referred to), but without doubt it expresses his opinion. Mrs. Coolidge later declared 'I don't know whether he said it, but it is just what he might have said', **Lathem** (1960), p. 151.

In Europe only the Netherlands, Switzerland and the Scandinavian countries were left.[2] Germany did find private creditors in these countries (apart from subscriptions by banks and individuals to German war loans). An explanation for these credits can found in the trade relations between Germany and these neutral neighbour states – despite British pressure to maintain an effective blockade. The credits were not intended to collect money in a general way for German warfare, but to finance specific purchases in these countries, in particular for foodstuffs.[3] As German exports, notably coal, decreased and the import of agricultural products rose, the deficit had to be balanced by credits (or, alternatively, by gold payments or the sale of foreign securities, methods that were less attractive or soon exhausted).

In peacetime, these credits would have been redeemed rapidly, during the war they accumulated. Although exact amounts are debatable, it is evident that the Netherlands was the largest creditor with a credit position of 1.6 billion *gold marks* ($ 400 million, £ 80 million) at the end of the war, according to the *Reichsbank*.[4] This was about one half of the total German external debt to neutral countries.[5] These credits were not loans from the Dutch (or Swiss etc.) governments, as this would have violated the country's carefully cherished neutrality. But even private banks in neutral countries were reluctant to grant large commercial credits; they had to be careful not to lose their own credibility in the City of London where one was not amused to see the German war machine being financed indirectly by neutral bankers.[6]

The only other large capital market was the United States and in that market Germany was not successful. Even in the years of American neutrality, before April 1917, German attempts to get credit had poor results and their contribution to German war finance was negligible. A first loan raised a modest $ 10 million; the total amount for the whole war has been estimated at about $ 30 million.[7]

It is not like the Germans did not try. In the first place they sold German war loans to American customers by intermediaries such as banks and stockbrokers. An appeal to patriotic feelings of German immigrants in the United States was not the predominant argument; besides, they were only a small market segment. A supposedly more convincing argument was found in potential market profits, both in value and in the dollar-*mark* exchange rate that was supposed to recover after the war.[a]

In the second place, physical circumstances were not favourable for the Germans. From the records of the German *National Debt Committee*, it appears that at several times amounts of German government securities had been transported to he United States to be sold there. A part of them had actually been sold, but in March 1916 there was still a pile of unissued paper in the German embassy in Washington. They had been invalidated and were waiting to be brought home 'if circumstances permit', that is when the blockade had been lifted.[8] The Committee, otherwise punctual in administrating the billions of German debt up to the second decimal, lost its grip on the matter; in 1918 it concluded that all relevant information would be published after the war.[9]

The absence of physical lines of communication between Germany and the United States is only part of the explanation for the meagre result of German attempts to borrow on the American market. The non-physical communication between the German government and the American financial world was underdeveloped as well. Indeed, in the United States there was a large minority of German immigrants and there were definitely connections with German banks and business firms. These companies however were beaten in many respects by the British who were literally and figuratively speaking the same language. In order to be successful in foreign capital markets, good relationships – and in particular good *personal* relationships – with prestigious banks are indispensible. At this point the British had advantages; a central personality in the American financial market, J.P. Morgan Jr. declared that he preferred to do business with the British (he even preferred London to New York as a place of residence).[10]

---

a   **The Economist** of 9 October 1915, p. 531, quotes an advertisement for the 3rd German war loan of September 1915, placed by the American stockbrokers house *Zimmermann & Forshay*. At least one customer had bought bonds for millions of dollars, as becomes clear from the records of lawsuits against the house many years after war by affected speculators – or should we say unsuspecting victims?, **UN** (2006), p. 46. During the war the securities were usually held for safekeeping in Germany, waiting for more reliable transport facilities to the United States. In practice this implied that at the moment of actual delivery their value had decreased considerably as a consequence of an exchange rate that had crashed instead of recovered.

These arguments, however important they may be, are all subordinate to economic reality: the pressure to obtain credits for Germany in the United States was simply much less than for Britain or France. These latter countries created large deficits on their balance of trade with the United States as a consequence of their massive import of American munitions, foodstuffs and clothing. These deficits had to be financially balanced in some way, and loans were the obvious way of compensation. Trade between Germany and the United States was modest and almost vanishing as a consequence of the British blockade.[11]

Britain and France enter the US private capital market

It is clear that the really large flows of international borrowing had to be found in the triangle Britain – United States – France and in particular in the axis US – UK with France as a supporting actor. During the first years of the war, it had been Britain that acted as the main public creditor, in fact the banker, for the European allies. The most important private capital market however was to be found in the United States, where the allied governments had to balance their trade deficits by loans on the private capital market, at least as long as the American government maintained its strict neutrality.

Initially the American financial market was a weak market for foreign government loans. The French had discovered this already in August 1914 and the British would find it out soon.[12] A shortage of money as such was not the main problem, although foreign investors had withdrawn short-term credits from the United States during the first months of the war. The United States itself was just recovering from a mild economic slump and within a few months the situation improved and capital became available in sufficient amounts. The US officially respected a policy of strict neutrality, but in practice it appeared possible to find a way round. It was more a matter of attitude and tradition.

Until the First World War, the United States had always been a borrowing country not a lending country. The large investments in its infrastructure such as railways had been financed to a considerable extent with capital from the Old World and the shareholders resided in Europe, in particular in Britain.[13] The very idea that American citizens would invest in foreign government securities instead of domestic industry was new. On the other hand, attractive yields and sufficiently elevated interest rates could convince banks to take the step. The problem was that dividends in the US were generally higher than in Europe and financial transactions were assessed by profitability, not by benevolence. Nevertheless, for those banks that were thinking strategically and wanted to expand their activities abroad, the new customers begging for credit from the other side of the ocean were interesting prospects. And so it happened.

A modest start and a symbolic success

The French – who had the most urgent need for money anyway – were the first to score a small success on the American market. In November 1914, just three months after the outbreak of the war, they negotiated a loan at the *National City Bank* in New York; the bank bought for $ 10 million French government securities at an interest of 5¾%, a rather favourable rate – for the investor that is, not for the French government for which it was one of the highest interest rates they had to pay during the whole war. Good personal relationships appear to have been conclusive in this arrangement.[14] In general however, negotiations between American bankers and French diplomats were far from smooth.[15] Both represented universes that had to meet only under the pressure of exceptional circumstances. On the one side there was the French bureaucratic and hierarchical approach; on the other side the more direct and personal American style that was much more in line with the British way of doing business.[a]

If we disregard the amount that was borrowed and its interest rate, this relatively small and short-term French loan was an important breakthrough in international borrowing with an unmistakably high symbolic value for all parties involved. The formally neutral American government allowed a commercial bank to give credit to the government of a belligerent European country in the form of US dollars against French treasury bills. Indeed, during the negotiations American policy had silently taken an important turn in October 1914. In August 1914 the hardliner pacifist Secretary of State William Jennings Bryan had declared that credits to belligerent countries were out of the question. In the next few months he was overruled by President Wilson thanks to

---

a   It should be noted, that this was the era when bankers were not mere employees with corporate responsibility but to a large extent really financiers taking risks with their private capital.

skilful lobbying, for example with the semantic argument that there was a fundamental difference between loans and credits. Whereas the former should not be given to foreign belligerent governments, nobody could seriously have objections to commercial credits if they were used to buy products of American industry.[16] It would last until March 1915 before the American government declared that it would not interfere in loans by private parties to belligerent governments.[17] In practice, this had been possible since October 1914, as the French loan proved. Wherever there is an economic will, there is always a political way.[a]

As regards the French, for them too the loan was worth far more than the $ 10 million. In the first place, French diplomacy – however clumsy it operated in the New World – had proved that there were options in the American financial markets, even for a party that had more to ask than to offer. In fact, the commercial environment of the American banking system was particularly rich in potential business partners and the French knew it. They succeeded in taking a relatively independent position by not dealing with *J.P. Morgan & Co.* but with its rival *National City Bank*.[b] During the rest of the war, the French government would successfully secure loans with several New York banks or syndicates.

A second, but at least as important symbolic value of the small loan was that France had shown that it was to a certain degree independent of Britain for its international loans. Just as London had always been the centre of global trade and international finance, the international part of war finance had to be controlled by the City – at least in the British view. Indeed, France had explored credit lines in London in the first days of August, even before the British Expeditionary Force appeared on the battlefield. Again, the background was formed by the import of British war supplies. After having made arrangements on shared purchase of ammunition and other material, the French government opened an account at the Bank of England with a credit limit of £ 400,000 (10 million *francs*), peanuts in the light of what was to come. There was no mention of other credits, while on the other hand France and Britain

---

a   Bryan resigned as Secretary of State in June 1915 soon after the sinking of the *Lusitania* when President Wilson adopted a less neutral attitude towards Germany.

b   It is by the way typical of the relationship between the competitors that the house of *Morgan* did not hesitate to subscribe to the loan as soon as it had been concluded.

had joined force in the military domain.[18] A political *Entente Cordiale* did not necessarily mean cordial financial relationships. On the contrary, there had been an atmosphere of mutual distrust from the beginning; during the war it gradually decreased, although with some unexpected outbreaks at critical moments and it never disappeared completely. The British were convinced of being well-organised and possessing superior knowledge of international finance. They had the idea that the French were fiddling around, for example by asking for credit and not being prepared to concede part of their immensely large gold reserves in exchange. Britain needed gold badly to maintain its international credit standing, as it was dependent on the convertibility of Sterling. The French from their side had no worries about credit standing; they had simply left the Gold Standard.[19]

The French for their part suspected the British of dragging their financial hegemony through the war and even aimed at concluding the war stronger than they had entered it – and most probably the French were right as shown by the words of McKenna (note p. 54). Furthermore, it was rather humiliating for the French sense of honour that the British treated them on the same footing as for example the Russians who were begging in London for credit and who were only heard if they were prepared to send gold. In French eyes warfare was more than just a matter of business. After all, so far France had paid a much higher price on the battlefield, as its losses had outnumbered British casualties by a factor of 10 until the end of 1914.[20] In such circumstances discussions about conditions of loans should be subordinate, at least from the French perspective. The language that was used in private shows little sympathy for their respective positions. Lloyd George spoke of 'our poorer allies', Ribot of 'certain national interests'.[21] No wonder that in the first phase of the war only the house of Rothschild with its French and British branch was prepared to step in with a credit of £ 2 million to the French government.

France becomes indebted to Britain

The first semi-government loan from Britain to France came in 1915, when the French had already secured their American credit. The Bank of England advanced £ 10 million (about 260 million *francs*) against French treasury bills at an interest rate of 5%. With this loan, France could continue purchasing war supplies in Britain. Although the Bank of England was the formal lender, it was in fact the British government that backed it, not the private capital market. During the war many of these loans would follow and at the end of 1918 the French government was indebted to the British for an amount of 11 billion *francs*, almost £ 420 million.[22] The major part of it, 80%, had been borrowed in the period before the United States entered the war.

It soon became evident for France that it had to give up its initial refusal to send gold – or at least to lend it temporarily. From April 1915 on, the usual arrangement was that the *Banque de France* provided gold from its reserves as collateral to an amount of 1/3 of the capital borrowed. In this way gold transfers from France to Britain accumulated to £ 110 million (3 billion *francs* at pre-war exchange rates) one third of which was actually sold and two thirds was lent for the duration of the war.[23] This usage of gold as a collateral for loans instead of using it as payments for products or exchange rate support has been described after the war as an efficient mobilisation of French gold stock.[24] For the French in any case it was a kind of justification for their grudgingly surrendering their carefully accumulated gold reserves. From a wider perspective, they certainly benefited from Britain maintaining its gold reserves; it allowed Britain to keep its credit status more or less intact and therefore resist successfully upward pressure on interest rates and downward pressure on exchange rates, both for Britain and France. Anyhow, it was a far more efficient use of gold than the Germans realised; they did not employ it to secure international loans and left it unproductively in the vaults of the *Reichsbank*.[a]

An overdraft account at Morgan's

In the meantime, the British government itself had deployed activities in the American capital market, but it had organised these contacts somewhat differently from France. The problem was, just as with the French, not to collect money as such but to get loans to pay the American suppliers of war material and foodstuffs. In order to coordinate these purchases (and the payments!) they contracted in January 1915 the

---

a   For domestic credit status gold reserves have limited value, in particular in a war economy. Only after a return to normal economic conditions when the war was over, German gold reserves could have had some value, but only when the war would have ended more favourable for that country.

bankers of *J.P. Morgan & Co*, who had a partner branch in London.[25][b] The bank became the exclusive agent for Britain and incidentally from May 1915 for France as well.[26] *J.P. Morgan & Co.* was commissioned to coordinate all purchases on the American market and to provide for the dollars necessary for the financial settlement of the transactions (the bankers received a commission of 1% for their activities).[27] The bank used several options at the same time: the sale of American securities held by British citizens and institutions, selling gold from the stock of the Bank of England and currency trading. It is evident that parallel to these trading activities banking facilities developed. Depending on the rhythm of deliveries and transactions, temporary deficits and surpluses occurred. These were kept in a current account that soon acted as an overdraft facility, the very *raison d'être* of a bank. This almost automatically opened a credit line for the British Treasury (and on its behalf the Bank of England). British gold reserves in Ottawa (Canada) and stock portfolios served as collateral. During the war, these advances of *J.P. Morgan & Co.* – in cooperation with other large American banks – to the British government fluctuated, but they increased unmistakably. In 1916 the average amount of outstanding credit was $ 100-150 million, in 1917 it was twice as much (illustration 10.1, left part).

The Anglo-French loan

The overdraft facility at *Morgan's*, large and increasing at it became, was peanuts if compared to the largest loan ever issued up to then (and long afterwards) by sovereign states on the international capital market: the Anglo-French loan of October 1915. It took long and tough negotiations for a syndicate of banks led by the same *J.P. Morgan & Co.* to define the conditions before it could bring the $ 500 million loan to the American market.[28][b] The loan not only expressed the gigantic need for money for the war, but also the wish of Britain and France to act together: each country took an equal share of $ 250 million.[c] It was an unprecedented amount for a five-year loan with an interest rate of 5% and an issue

---

a   Although *J.P. Morgan & Co.* had the advantage of a Paris branch, the choice for *MorganGrenfell* will not have been a coincidence: the senior partner of the London branch, Edward Charles Grenfell, was a director of the Bank of England, **Burk** (1985), p. 15.

b   The formation of the syndicate itself was not easy. *J.P. Morgan & Co.* could persuade only one Chigaco banker to participate: C.G. Dawes, whom we shall meet again in Chapter 12, **Dayer** (1976), p. 131.

c   Just to get an impression of the size of the loan: $ 500 million was about 70% of the whole US Federal budget in 1915, http://federal-budget.findthedata.org/l/34/1931.

British advances from J.P. Morgan & Co. increased at an average speed of $ 25 million per month from May 1916 until finally the American government itself acted as the main war creditor (April 1917) (Illustration 10.1)

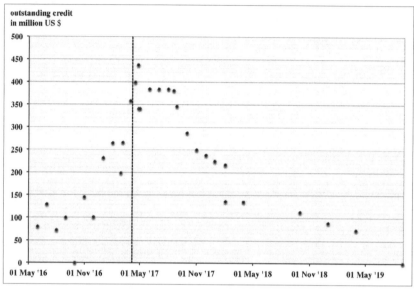

Source: chart based on data from Wormell.[29]

price of 98.[30] The syndicate emphasized to the American public that this was not a war loan for countries far away in Europe, but credits to support American exports. It was a national interest, not to be confused with taking sides in a distant conflict. This way of presentation was not unnecessary since sufficient opposition voices could be heard. They came not only from competitor banks outside the syndicate, but also from pacifist circles and German immigrants who threatened to withdraw their accounts from participating banks. Emotions were running high: 'billions of American money to bankrupt England, France and Russia' could be read at signboards in a demonstration at Wall Street.[a]

---

a   **The Economist** 2 October 1915, p. 499. Serious signs of opposition against such an overt and massive support to belligerent countries had been seen a few months before; J.P. Morgan Jr. ('Jack') had narrowly escaped an assassination attempt by what we would call today a lone wolf, a German immigrant, who had first exploded a bomb in the Capitol in Washington DC, (e.g.) **Harvard Crimson** 14 July 1942.

The whole story of the Anglo-French loan reflects the uncomfortable feelings in the American market towards credits to foreign powers. It needed a good deal of lobbying for the banking syndicate to float the loan and for the most part it was only successful among financial institutions and large industrial parties involved, not among individual investors.[31] For American standards, the yield of the investment was not particularly rewarding with an interest rate of 5% for such a large and high-risk loan. For the British and French governments on the other hand the price was high. Taking into account the redemption obligation in five years and the issue price below par, they had to pay almost 6%, much more than on their domestic loans and still apart from the exchange rate risk (the loan had to be repaid in dollars, whatever the exchange rate might be). The British parliament approved the loan but not without discussion. It was inevitable since the massive imports had slowly but surely decreased the exchange rate of Sterling.[32] A further deterioration would have made imports still more expensive; the worst-case scenario would be to decrease the imports themselves, which would have jeopardised the heart of warfare. But the Americans would not be happy too when Sterling slipped away with other currencies in its slipstream and affecting American export in general. The formal British defence for this loan therefore was that it was meant to secure the dollar-pound exchange rate and that it had nothing to do with arms purchases.[33]

Wanted: collateral
The Anglo-French loan was the last one that could be issued in the American market in good faith. Collateral would be necessary for all new loans, whether they were issued by France, Britain or by any of them on behalf of other countries. This was much easier for the British than for the French.[34] UK citizens and institutional investors such as insurance companies held large portfolios of American shares and bonds, in particular railway stock. The *Prudential Assurance Company* for example possessed no less than $ 40 million in American securities and it was prepared to make it available for the British government to fill a reservoir for continuing arms purchases in the United States – a short-term solution.[35] These acquisitions continued to take place in a rather *ad hoc* way until the British government started a campaign in the second half of 1915 to purchase these securities more systematically; it was not only directed towards institutional investors but in particular to individuals who were to persuade to hand over their American

stock to the government. They could sell them completely or just lend them. Although this practice on a voluntary basis was not without initial success, the flow threatened to dry after some time. Completely against the principle of liberalism and free trade, the British government exercised more and more pressure on its citizens to deliver their foreign securities. The list of eligible securities was continuously expanded and in May 1916 the British parliament even voted for a proposal to discourage ownership of foreign securities by imposing an extra tax of 10% on their dividends.

This roused a new flow of securities available as collateral for further loans on the American capital market. But again in March 1917 exhaustion came into sight even with the 10% extra tax. At that moment the British government started to requisition certain securities that had not been handed over – against payment, surely.[a] It has been estimated that the total amount of securities that the government mobilised (or rather: liquidated) voluntarily or enforced was about $ 1.4 billion (£ 300 million); two thirds were actually bought, the rest were lent to the government.[36] This is a considerable fraction of the securities held by British citizens and institutions. Before the war it had been almost £ 1.2 billion ($ 6 billion), but in October 1915 when the programme was discussed it had already decreased to £ 500-£ 700 million.[37] If this estimation is correct, the policy succeeded in mobilising 40%-60% of these securities.

It is good to take a step back to realise what this meant in economic terms. The purchase by the British government of securities from the population was just one financial link in the chain of wealth transfer from fighting Britain to producing America. The British government used the securities as collateral to secure loans in dollars in the American financial markets. These loans in turn were used to finance the purchase of the products of American industry, either for consumption by the British population or for destruction on the battlefields in Flanders, Gallipoli and the Middle East. By handing over the securities, the original holders – that is the British population – *at that very moment* refrained from

---

a   At about them same time, 22 March 1917, the German government took complete control over all foreign securities held by German individuals and companies, **RT** 321 nr. 744, p. 23.

its actual and future value in the form of capital and dividends. By this ingenious mechanism it was performed financially what was inevitable economically: war costs had to be paid one way or the other.

With regard to collateral, the Americans (and for that matter, the British as well) had less to expect from France. In the first place, the portfolios of French investors contained fewer American securities: $ 250 compared with the $ 6 billion of the British. Instead, in the years before the war, the French had largely chosen foreign investments in Russian state debt and Russian railways, which by the way amounted to the same thing as the railway bonds were guaranteed by the government. Those were not the securities that the Americans were looking for – if they could be sold anywhere at all.[38] Furthermore, the French government in the person of Finance Minister Ribot put less pressure on private investors than the British government did. The official explanation was that it would do more harm than good because it was a signal of decreasing credit status and it would divert from investments in their own government *obligations*. A deeper lying justification could be found in the policy that the state should be kept far from private property and it certainly should not offend the large class of *rentiers*.[39] Anyhow, the French programme to buy or borrow foreign securities from citizens and institutions raised about $ 350 million, a quarter of the British proceeds. These securities, it might be expected, were not all American, but also from neutral Scandinavian countries, the Netherlands, Switzerland, Latin America, etc.[40]

Although the French had fewer opportunities to provide collateral, they had access to one source of foreign exchange that most of the other countries lacked: foreign soldiers. Hundreds of thousands, later millions of foreign troops on French soil spent money. While the daily transactions were made in *francs*, the British government (and later the US government) compensated for it in strong pounds and dollars. It is estimated that Britain exported an amount equivalent to 4.3 billion *francs* to France, while the United States provided at least 5.7 billion *francs*.[41]

A race for foreign capital
After their concerted action in the large Anglo-French loan of October 1915, both countries regularly issued separate loans in the United

States, mainly through or with the assistance of the banking syndicate of *Morgan's* (illustration 10.2). Britain borrowed more than France. This was not only because they could provide larger collateral, but primarily because they had the burden of financing other countries. Apart from France, the allies Russia, Italy and Belgium had little or no access by themselves to the American financial market – and even if they had so, Britain would have been eager enough to act on their behalf.

In August 1916 Britain issued a new large loan on its own, ignoring agreements with France made in February of that year that they would coordinate actions and keep the other party informed. The French had just issued a large loan at an extremely high interest rate of 7¼% for the banking syndicate, and the British knew it; the interest rate could have been more confortable for both if the British and the French had coordinated their efforts.[42] A new issue of irritation had grown between the two countries while – and we should not forget that – in the trenches at the Somme British soldiers fell by tens of thousands each months and the French were hardly recovering from the slaughter at Verdun. It took a great deal of diplomacy to clear the air.

The underlying issue was that both European allies were fishing in the same financial pool in New York. This pool was large indeed and the British had no trouble as such that the French were active in it since it reduced the pressure on the London market. But the British preferred – to use the same metaphor – that the French used British fishing rods and brought their own bait in the form of gold and securities as collateral. And finally, the Americans were issuing the fishing licences; not only the American government that had already accepted the transactions, but above all the bankers. They looked at the war in Europe from their own perspective, which was primarily a business opportunity. Keeping in mind the words of Lloyd George that success means credit (page 90), they could ask a high price for their credit in 1916 and the spring of 1917 in the form of a high interest rate: there were hardly any successes to record.

The amount of large loans – against collateral and at high interest rates – increased for the British during the autumn of 1916 and in the spring of 1917 until it had reached some $ 130-$ 150 million per month, apart from the advances from *Morgan's* that grew at a rate of $ 25 million per month. It is evident that Britain could not have maintained this effort indefinitely, despite its large wealth, accumulated over decades and its efficient tax system. This is regardless of the question as to whether the American financial markets could have generated the money. Sooner or later the government would have to choose between three equally unattractive options: diminishing its own war efforts, restricting credit to other allies or resort to more monetary financing. In particular the credits to France and Italy were a heavy burden for Britain. In April they had grown to $ 1.2 billion (then £ 260 million).[43]

During 1916 and early 1917 the British government borrowed extensively in the American private capital market against high interest rates and with securities as collateral (Illustration 10.2)

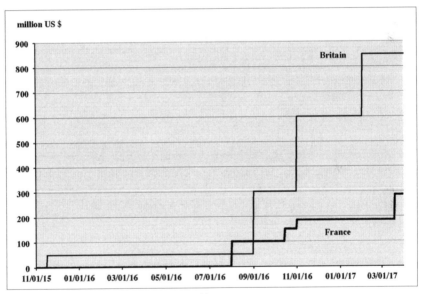

Source: Wormell, Jèze & Truchy, Nouaillat.[44]

It remains a matter of speculation what would have happened to British war financing if the United States had not abandoned its neutrality in April 1917 to enter the First World War on the side of the allies against Germany. It is indeed possible that Britain could have lasted much longer. The Empire could fall back on large financial resources especially if its dominions like Canada, Australia and New Zealand were taken into account as well as South Africa and the Indian subcontinent. Opinions among historians differ on this what-if question. Ferguson estimates that the financial participation of the United States was not decisive.[45] His main argument is that Britain had indeed borrowed enormous amounts of capital, but that it had lent still more: the net result was positive. Against this argument one can object that the balance was positive, but it was a paper surplus only. About three quarters of Britain's outstanding claims were on Russia; they proved to be irrecoverable after the war and could be considered questionable even during the war.[46] In Ferguson's view the idea of America's decisive role has been established by blindly following Keynes' scaremongering, who would have painted the British position too bleakly.

A somewhat different position is taken by Horn. He does not deny Britain's capabilities as such, but he points out that it was the support to its allies that would have eventually overwhelmed the country. If Britain had been unable to subsidise French purchases in the United States, things might have taken a different turn.[47] Strachan, finally, considers America's participations in the war as a – or maybe even: *the* – real turning point. He emphasises the fact that Germany made a literally capital mistake when it resumed the unlimited submarine warfare; within three months the United States entered the war.[48] In Germany, Helfferich had always used sound economic arguments and a sharp eye for the British position to prevent the military high command taking this step. Final decisions in Germany however were not made by politicians or economic specialists, but by the military commanders for whom the notion of 'America' and its economic power was far beyond their narrow-minded nineteenth century comprehension.[49]

A point that is often overlooked in this discussion is the radical change of time scale when the United States entered the war. Time is often a decisive factor in warfare. During the first months of the war – maybe even the whole first year – financial time was counted in months. The demand of months could be met with current revenue, accumulated resources and, in the case of Britain, with a few tax measures. From mid-1915 until the spring of 1917, it became clear that financing should be managed in other ways. In the field of ever growing loans abroad – necessary to balance trade deficits – a practice developed of time consuming negotiations with private investors. These negotiations took several months just to generate enough capital for a few months warfare. Furthermore, all these commercial loans were short-term. They had to be repaid within two or three years, but not unusually within just one year (with five years, the large Anglo-French loan was a remarkable exception). Negotiations for new loans started at the moment credits became actually available or even before that. The time scale was based on several months for raising a loan and on a few years to repay. This all changed instantly in April 1917. American government credits were arranged within a few weeks, there was no mention of a time for repayment. The time scale changed radically: credits became available almost instantaneously, maturity was indefinite.[a] The conclusion is inevitable: American entry into the war was a turning point indeed. The allied forces could not lose the war financially.

Russian and Italian loans in the international markets

Foreign loans of other allies generally were not issued directly in the private capital market and for good reasons. Russia, for example, was already overloaded with foreign debts at the start of the war; its credit standing was poor. Private investors were not expected to provide new large loans. Instead the British and French governments provided the credits to Russia and especially the British who required appropriate collateral in the form of gold deposits.[b] During the war, the Russian government had accumulated a foreign debt of roughly $ 3.6 billion, two thirds of which to the British government, one quarter to the French and the rest to the US.[50] These credits were mainly intended for the purchase of war material in Britain and the US, but a small part was earmarked for interest payments on old Russian government bonds.

Italian credits started with the negotiations about its conditions to enter the war on the side of the allies. Italy not only asked for (secret) promises about territorial extensions, notably from Austria (Südtirol / Alto Adige) and the Ottoman Empire (Dodekanesos). It also wanted a credit of £ 50 million ($ 250 million), a fact that is commonly overlooked in the military history of the war.[51] The credit was easily made available, even increased; at the end of the war Italy was indebted to Britain for

---

a   In practice it would to a large extent even be infinite, but that was of course not yet known in 1917, Chapter 13.
b   The logistics of these Russian gold deliveries is an interesting story by its own, see for example **Fisk** (1924), pp. 133-134.

an amount of $ 1.9 billion (£ 380 million), for $ 1.0 billion to the United States and for almost $ 200 million to France.

These credits taken together, the British government – and the Bank of England at its direction – credited Russia and Italy alone for $ 4.3 billion (roughly £ 850 million). To this can be added credits to France, $ 1.7 billion (£ 350 million) and some smaller amounts for example to Belgium, Serbia and Greece. These credits are incorporated in the British war expenditure in illustration 6.2, page 73. Apart from very small fractions in the second half of the 1920s, they have never been repaid (Chapter 12 and 13).

American government credits to the European allies

At the moment that the United States entered the war, the meaning of borrowing abroad changed overnight. On the physical battlefield in Northern France, it would take another seven months before the first American troops were actually fighting. In the financial war theatre, however, the deployment of American resources was immediate and tremendous. Already on 11 April 1917 the US government submitted a proposal for financial support to the allies.[52] Within three weeks after the declaration of war Congress had voted a credit of $ 3 billion to the allies, 30% more than the total amount of British and French loans on the private capital market in all preceding war years. Deliveries of material and foodstuffs were secured. Suddenly the British and French governments were no longer dependent on banks and private investors with their nasty conditions on interest rates and on collateral; conditions that became increasingly difficult to meet. On the other hand, the European countries did not receive cash. Just as with the private loans, the money did not leave the United States; it was passed on to the suppliers. And enormous these orders were: from the beginning of April 1917 until a year after the Armistice the allies would buy for almost $ 12 billion in the United States – measured in current prices.[53] The credits were simply booked on the account of the purchasing country, to be paid off somewhere in the future.

Britain and France used United States government credits to buy food,
ammunition and clothing; figures in million dollars (Illustration 10.3)

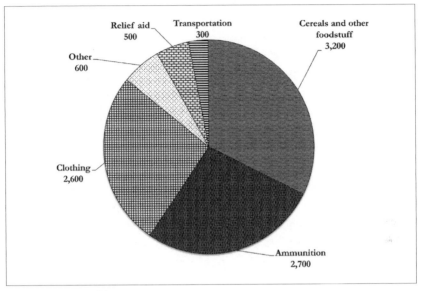

Source: *US Treasury.*[54]

In contrast to credits from private investors, the American nation was not motivated solely by commercial interests. In the discussions in the US Congress, members often referred to the aid that France had given to their country in the War of Independence, some 135 years earlier. The name Lafayette was mentioned and more than one deputy or senator suggested that France need not pay interest, or even that the credits would be a *gift*, not a *loan*. That was the way to do something in return.[55] It would however be curious to do the same kind of favour to Britain, the former colonial power that had been shaken off with French support. This made the argument less universal in the current situation. The French for their part appreciated these friendly feelings, but they had their pride. It was Ribot himself – at that time Foreign Affairs minister and for the fourth time in office as prime minister – who told the American ambassador in Paris that he hoped that Congress would make it a loan, not a gift. He added that France would appreciate if it would be free from interest payments during the war and some years afterwards.[56] The result was, that all allies were treated on the same footing: loans, to be repaid.

From the first instalment Britain received $ 200 million, France, Italy and Russia each half of it and Belgium $ 45 million.[57] It was only the beginning. Up to the Armistice credits would accumulate to over $ 7 billion, half of which was for Britain. The American government credits should be used to buy products from American suppliers. They were not intended to redeem existing private capital market loans, because that would amount to indirectly subsidising New York bankers by the American taxpayer, a practice that the American government – and in particular McAdoo – wanted to avoid at all price.[58] This probably did not happen directly but indirectly it was performed in a more sophisticated way as shown by the statistics. As soon as the pressure on private investors reduced, financial means became available for paying off these short-term private loans, in particular in Britain. This is clearly illustrated from the right part of illustration 10.1 where the decrease in British loans from *J.P. Morgan & Co.* is shown. Within a year, they were cut by two thirds. This meant that the banks received their money back, while the risk that is always attached to loans had been transferred to the American government. And, to extend this line to the end: the American government obtained the money for the credits to its allies by issuing large *Liberty Loans*. The risk therefore was again transferred to the subscribers on these *Liberty Loans* and finally to the taxpayers who had to pay for the interest and principal payments. The generously supplied credits in the end amounted to transferring financial risk from bankers (and their shareholders) to taxpayers.

Since the credits to allies were linked to the *Liberty Loans*, it was a matter of simple logic that the interest rates of the credits were also linked to those on the *Liberty Loans*. Initially one thought of 3%, but when the first *Liberty Loan* was issued, the rate had already risen to 3.5% and it soon increased to 4¼%.[59] During the first years of the loans, the debtor countries paid some interest, albeit in many cases (largely) from the proceeds of new loans.[60] From May 1919 until the end of 1922 interest payments were suspended altogether and the interest due was simply added to the principal.[61] But these issues touch post-war problems, to be analysed in more detail in Chapter 12.

A short summary and an uncomfortable perspective
All belligerent countries had recourse to foreign capital markets or allied governments to find means for war financing; they succeeded to

different degrees. Germany was least successful in borrowing abroad. It concluded commercial credits in neutral countries only – necessary to balance its large import surplus of agricultural products, mainly from the Netherlands. Neutral governments (among which the United States until April 1917) were not prepared to lend money and private investors were reluctant, in particular American bankers. During the whole war, Germany borrowed from the United States hardly 1% of the amount that its enemies received there in the private capital market, let alone the credits by the American government. Germany had to rely for 98% of its war finance on its domestic market.[62] From a financial perspective it was fighting against the rest of the world.

Britain acted as the banker of the group of allied countries, a role that it was eager to play. It did so directly by supplying government credits to France, Russia, Italy, Belgium and some smaller countries and indirectly by granting these countries access to its domestic private capital market – albeit to a limited extent. And Britain itself borrowed like most of its allies in the private American capital market, which means from banks, consortia and private investors. For Britain this was easier than for example for France, thanks to its enormous resources of foreign securities of 'western' countries such the US and Canada. By selling them or by using them as collateral they could be used to obtain supplies or credit. At the end of the war, Britain had provided for 18%-20% of its war finance on foreign credit markets. For France this share was slightly higher, but that country had more reasons to worry. Its debts were in dollars and pounds.[63] During the war it had taken advantage of the excellent British credit ranking and of the almost unimpaired exchange rate of the French *franc* that was unlikely to be maintained after the war.

At the moment that the United States entered the First World War (6 April 1917), the total debt *between* European allied countries had already accumulated to $ 3.8 billion.[64] Apart from that, allied governments had borrowed roughly the same amount from private investors and banks, mainly in the United States.[65] This mechanism of international borrowing produced a complicated interconnected system of debts. In principle, the British had no grounds to feel uncomfortable with it, as it bolstered the position of London as a global financial centre. Their problem, however, was twofold and both tendencies pointed in the same direction. In the first place, it was unmistakable that American bankers had growing fingers in the pie of international finance. They had the deepest pockets and they could dictate the conditions at which the European governments could obtain credit. In the second place, Britain felt especially that the comfortable portfolio of securities was dwindling at an alarming speed. Usage of American securities – either to buy products or to use as collateral for loans – initiated a gigantic mechanism of wealth transfer from Europe to America. These assets had represented a debt of the United States to Europe of a magnitude that could hardly have been redeemed in normal circumstances. But circumstances were far from normal during the First World War. In the words of McKenna, some years after the war: 'a capital liability which has been growing for over two centuries was almost entirely discharged in a few years'.[66] This fact marks the shift of global financial leadership from Britain to the United States.

American entry into the war was a turning point for France and Britain in their possibilities to borrow abroad (Illustration 10.4)

	the most important sources for foreign loans for:	
	Britain	France
until 5 April 1917 (32 months)	private capital market in the US ($ 1.5 billion)	private capital market in the US and in Britain ($ 0.7 billion and $ 0.5 billion, resp.) British government ($ 0.6 billion)
from 6 April 1917 until Armistice (19 months)	US government ($ 3.7 billion)	US government ($ 2.0 billion)

Source: composed from Moulton & Pasvolsky, Wormell, Burk.[67]

11

Monetary financing: the central bank as an ATM machine

'The Emperor: "We're out of money. Well, create it";
Mephistopheles: "I create whatever you want, and more that that".
Goethe, Faust[a]

Money in circulation

On the last day of July 1914, one day before the mobilisation would take place, less than 3 billion German *marks* were in circulation in the form of banknotes. Four and a half years later, in December 1918, it had soared to over 22 billion *marks*. Banknotes had increased sevenfold.[1] The *Reichsbank* had printed almost 20 billion fresh *marks*. Meanwhile the amount of *Darlehenskassenscheine* had grown from zero in 1914 to 10 billion *marks*. At the end of the war they represented one third of all paper money in Germany. Coins, on the other hand, had almost disappeared. Before the war, they circulated to an amount of almost 4 billion *marks*, at that time a larger value than banknotes; see illustration 11.1. And those coins that were used at the end of the war were pieces of iron, zinc and aluminium, instead of gold and silver.[2] The increase in coins and banknotes together during the war was 26 billion *marks*; the circulation of physical (cash) money at the end of the war five times as high as at the beginning.[3] Needless to say that the German economy – not to speak of wealth! – had not grown fivefold during the war. The increase in money in circulation was a visible manifestation of its loss of value.

Germany was a special example, but not particularly exceptional. All other countries increased the amount of money in circulation by printing banknotes. With this phenomenon there appears to hold what may be called the Law of the North Sea: the farther away from it, the larger the increase in money. In Russia the amount of money increased by a factor 12, in Austria-Hungary by a factor 10.[4] In France, where the *Banque de*

---

a   *'Es fehlt an Geld, nun gut, so schaff' es denn / Ich schaffe, was ihr wollt, und ich schaffe mehr',*
    Faust II, Act 1. The quote was reproduced on the front page of the publication *350 Milliarden Deutsches Volksvermögen*, **Steinmann-Bucher** (1909).

France issued notes at the government's request, it was roughly a factor 2.5, notably less than in Germany but nevertheless considerable. Britain and even the US did not escape the increase in money in circulation, but in comparison to the other countries, it remained reasonably under control.[a]

Restrictions removed on money creation

If it was so easy to increase the amount of money in circulation, why did not governments use this instrument much earlier to cover expenditure? In fact there were two obstacles and both were lifted in most of the countries when the war broke out.

The first restriction was convertibility. Before the war, banknotes had the legal status of a substitute for an amount of gold; the holder could at any time deliver the note at the central bank and require the corresponding amount of gold (or silver, depending on the standard used in the country). This right sets a limit to the amount of banknotes in a natural way. This principle of convertibility was removed during the mobilisation in every country. In Britain it was not formally abolished, but in practice it became highly restricted; see illustration 5.1 (page 58) for the parallelism of financial and military mobilisation. Removing convertibility (by law, or mostly by decree based on an old bank law) meant abandoning the Gold Standard and making paper money the only kind of legal tender. And it was the government that held the monopoly of issuing notes itself or it had transferred it as a privilege to the central bank.[b]

---

a   It should be noted, that the circulation of physical banknotes and coins is not a complete measure of the amount of money in a country. In particular in a country like Britain where already a century ago the banking system was highly developed, bank deposits were at least as important as cash. In Germany, and in particular in France, the population relied considerably more on physical money, preferably coins. Thus, in Britain not only the amount of cash increased, but also money in a wider sense, including bank deposits. Estimations using various definitions of money show that the total amount of money in a broader sense in Britain roughly doubled in the period 1913-1918, **Broadberry & Howlett** (2005), p. 219, based on data from **Capie & Webber** (1985).

b   These central banks were the *Bank of England, Banque de France, Reichsbank, Österreichisch-ungarische Bank, Banca d'Italia* and the various Eastern European state banks. At the outbreak of the war, the American FED was less than one year old; as a system of regional banks it would play a secondary role in war financing, apart from facilitating war loans, **ARST** 1917, p. 22. The Belgian National Bank suspended its activity in the occupied territories as a form of passive resistance; on 1st September 1914 all its possessions had been evacuated to Britain (a value of 2.7 billion *franks*, £ 100 million). Its task as an issuing institution was taken over by a joint stock bank under German supervision, the General Society (*Generale Maatschappij van België / Société Générale de Belgique*), **Zilch** (1994), pp. 123, 153.

The second restriction that was easily removed during the mobilisation was the legal ceiling to the amount of money that the central bank was allowed to bring into circulation (to be distinguished from the physical restriction imposed by convertibility). This ceiling was different by country, according to the organisation of the monetary system. Germany had a system of one-third-backing (*Dritteldeckung*, p. 50), which meant that for one third of all notes issued the *Reichsbank* should keep in its vaults gold or securities of comparable reliability. The War Acts of 1914 broadened this base of securities (which were by the way far from secure) practically in an unlimited way and this left the amount of banknotes free to grow. The German population was indoctrinated that the gold reserve of the Reichsbank was a guarantee for the trustworthiness of the currency and that it should be reinforced as much as possible in large patriotic campaigns of gold collection.[5] And it worked: at the beginning of the war, its gold reserves were 1.5 billion *marks* and it would increase to an average of 2.5 billion *marks*.[6] According to the one-third rule, this would have allowed for a banknote circulation of 7.5 billion *marks* but already in 1916 this amount was greatly surpassed. At the Armistice, it had soared to 17 billion *marks*. Apart from that, there were over 9.5 billion of *Darlehenskassenscheine* in circulation. Formally they were not counted as money, but the *Reichsbank*, holding one quarter of all these notes, used them as *backing* of its own banknotes; the effect was immense: with a gold stock of roughly 2.5 billion *marks*, the backing rate by gold was less than 15%, but when the paper *Darlehenskassenscheine* in the *Reichsbank* were counted as gold, the rate was 34%, just above the one-third-backing![7]

In France, there was no legally determined percentage for backing the notes of the *Banque de France*, neither by gold nor in any other way.[8] Before the war, the *Banque* itself maintained a gold reserve of about two thirds of the notes issued. On the other hand, there was a legal ceiling to the amount of banknotes in circulation. From 1870 on, this ceiling had been regularly raised by law, but at a very moderate average rate of 2% per year so as to adapt it to the expanding economy.[9] At the beginning of the war, when the circulation of banknotes was about 6 billion *francs*, the French parliament had relinquished its right to set the ceiling; from 5 August 1914 onwards, the maximum amount of banknotes in circulation could be raised literally by the stroke of a pen by presidential decree – an act performed many times. In the next four years of the war

In Germany, an abundance of paper money drove out coins from circulation (Illustration 11.1)

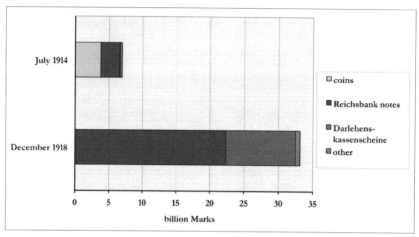

Source: Roesler, Holtfrerich.[10]

In France, the amount of banknotes grew considerably as well (Illustration 11.2)

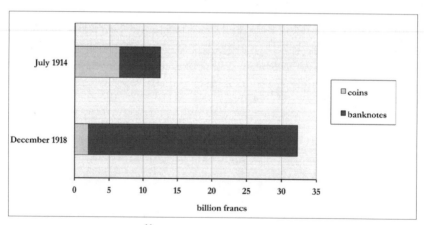

Source: *Banque de France*, Fisk.[11]

the limit would increase at an average rate of half a billion *francs* per *month*, followed closely by the actual amount of banknotes printed. Shortly after the war, the ceiling had been boosted to 36 billion *francs*, without any intervention of parliament. And even that was not enough; in the first year after the war the limit had to be increased again.[12] As

In Britain, currency notes added considerably to the notes in circulation
(Illustration 11.3)

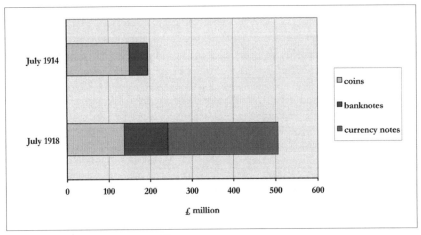

Source: Capie & Webber, Kirkaldy.[13]

In the United States, FED notes in circulation multiplied
(Illustration 11.4)

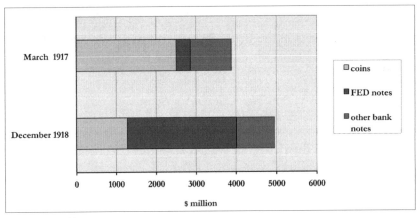

Source: BMS.[14]

a consequence, the backing of banknotes by gold had fallen form a comfortable 62% in 1913 to an alarming 11% at the end of 1918.[15]

In Britain, the situation was different. In the first place, there was not a single issuing institution; there were many. Beside the Bank of England, by far the most important one, there were private banks issuing their own banknotes, particularly in Scotland and Ireland (which was at that time an integral part of UK).[16] When the war began, as much as one third of all banknotes in circulation on the British Isles had been printed by Scottish and Irish banks. In August 1914 they were declared legal tender in Scotland and Ireland, respectively. All British issuing banks, including the Bank of England, increased their number of notes, so that at the end of the war, the circulation had roughly doubled.[17]

The second difference with the continental countries was the fact that the British government itself issued new paper money as legal tender in small denominations of £ 1 and £ 0.5. These *currency notes* were printed to provide for the immediate demand of day-to-day money. They were formally issued by the Treasury and found their way into the economy through (but not under the responsibility of) the Bank of England. At its counters, they could be exchanged for real Bank of England notes.[18] Initially, the currency notes had a gold backing, but in the following years government securities gradually replaced gold.[19] Through this mechanism, the reputation of the Bank of England remained unaffected. The public accepted and trusted the currency notes bearing the signature of John Bradbury, permanent Secretary to the Treasury, and of course the image of king George V, a symbol that had never been printed on the notes of the Bank of England.[a] As a consequence, the currency notes remained in circulation instead of being exchanged massively at the Bank of England.

During the war, the volume of these notes would increase considerably; at the end of the war the circulation was nearly £ 300 million.[20] Admittedly, this was much less than the sum of war loans at that moment. In addition to the increased volume of regular banknotes, however, the result was that the amount of money in circulation, in the form of coins and notes, at the Armistice was more than 2½ times as much as it had been at the outbreak of the war, illustration 11.3.

---

[a]   The production of the first currency notes was incidentally a perfect indicator of the poor financial war preparation in Britain. During the first week of August 1914, when the banks were closed, the currency notes had to be printed as a kind of emergency money on paper that was originally intended for post stamps, **Roberts** (2010), p. 169. The contrast could not have been larger with Germany and France, where the notes had been printed and stocked for years before the war.

In the United States the amount of FED notes exploded after the country took part in the war in April 1917. In the period of neutrality, the amount of FED dollars had grown, indeed, but at a very moderate average rate of $ 11 million per month. In less than two years from April 1917 until the Armistice however, this rate of increase of FED was tenfold, $ 114 per month; at the Armistice, the amount of FED dollars had increased from zero when the war broke out in Europe to $ 2,500 million.[21]

For all countries, the most direct way to contain the expanding volume of money would have been taxation. Apart form Britain, however, this happened sparingly. Long-term war loans offered a second possibility. Both methods, if applied, showed 'leaks'. Taxes levied on industry that led to higher prices were easily passed on to the buyers of the product – in the case of arms industry directly to the government itself. But even long-term war loans offered plenty of ways out to keep the money in circulation or even to increase it. It started with subscription to the war loans, where a down payment or a part of the purchase sum for the bonds could be made with money borrowed from the bank (if the buyer was sufficiently solvent, of course; a route for the financially secured only). Once the bonds had been bought and paid, they could serve as secure collateral for other loans, which amounted to unforeseen money creation. In Germany in particular, one could start with borrowing from the *Darlehenskassen* say 1,000 *marks* as an investment in the first war loan to end up with a value of 3,700 *marks* of government securities; it was a miraculous multiplication of money indeed and a kind of state-initiated pyramid scheme.[22] The German example, where the route was openly advertised in newspapers might have been exceptional by its scale, but it must have happened elsewhere too. Another mechanism to enlarge the money supply was offered by short-term war loans. Notably in France, the short-term *bons de la défense nationale* assumed the form of money, which meant that one could pay with it. Finally, it should be noted that price control was a very ineffective way to beat inflation; inflation was not overt, but suppressed as shown by queues, extended delivery times and flourishing black markets.

Central bankers in wartime
In normal times, the central bank is a lender of last resort in the financial system: the institution that can lend money to a bank when all other

sources fail. When there is a danger of bank runs, the central bank can support other banks by providing sufficient short-term credit. Commercial banks themselves are then enabled to give credit to industry and the financial process can be stabilised. During the First World War it was not the industry, but governments demanding the central bank credits; for them the central bank became the *lender of first resort*. It was much faster to get – or rather to compel – advances from the central bank, even faster than issuing war loans. A crucial point was not only the institutional power of the central bank or even its gold reserve; essential for speed were short communication lines between acting persons. The government in fact had to deal with one person: the governor of the bank, instead of a wider class of all kinds of stakeholders and interest groups.

The *Banque de France* had made arrangements with the government as early as 1911. The 2.9 billion *francs* mentioned in that agreement would only be the beginning. At the end of the war, the French state was indebted to the *Banque* for an amount of over 17 billion *francs*.[23] The growth of those short-term credits matched exactly the issue of new banknotes.[24] In Germany, the *Reichsbank* also credited the government for an enormous amount, a total of 27 billion *marks*, and issued a corresponding avalanche of notes.[25] In Britain, the Bank of England had provided advances for a total of £ 400 million, a relatively modest sum in comparison with the other two central banks (roughly 11 billion *francs* or 15 billion *marks*).[26]

Such amounts show that central banks had massively and without exception contributed to war financing with their printing presses and therefore inevitably to inflation.[27] Their cooperation was not always without reservations, but in the end they all collaborated. The extent to which the governors or presidents resisted or succumbed to the requirements of their governments varied from country to country, depending on the mental distance between both, on tradition and on the influence of the press and public opinion.[a]

---

a   The US FED is a special case. At the outbreak of the war, it was more or less *in statu nascendi*: the full Board took office on 10 August 1914 after heavy deliberations about the candidates. It lacked the tradition of the European central banks and still had to develop its prestige among the established financial institutions. The fact that the Board was housed in the Treasury building was not particularly emanating independence, **Silber** (2007), pp. 24, 118-119.

In France, the Board of directors (the *régents*) of the essentially private *Banque de France* were a little bit worried when the government appealed for more money within a few months. In September 1914 Finance Minister Ribot wrote an extensive letter in an attempt to remove these concerns. He promised that credits would be paid back as soon as possible, notably from the revenue of large war loans (that were not yet envisaged at that moment, by the way). He went so far as to declare that the government was prepared to pay 3% interest on credits that would remain once the war was over.[28] And of course he appealed to the patriotic feelings of the *régents*, but he refused to commit the government to a fixed date for redemption; the *Banque* was bound to yield. In the course of 1915, the *Banque* again declared its concern to the government; this time the increasing money supply was the issue.[29] The government had actually repaid some of the credits from war loans, but every new advancement surpassed redemptions on previous ones and the net outstanding credit only increased.[30] After the war, when national defence was no longer an argument, the *Banque* protested louder against the issue of new banknotes than it had done during the war.[31] But even in 1919 pressure from the government continued to be heavy and the *Banque* kept printing.[32]

The Bank of England, too, made the observation after the war that credits had assumed 'the nature of a continuous loan'.[33] It was cast in a politely formulated letter, but with unmistakable discontent. During the war, *The Economist* did not stop reminding the Bank and the government of financial orthodoxy that taught that monetary financing is no solution to a government's financial problems. In the last few years of the war, hardly a single issue of the influential journal appeared without mentioning the word 'inflation'.

The German situation was completely different. Until 1918 the i-word was not mentioned at all in the press, undoubtedly as a result of censorship.[34] The *Reichsbank* bluntly denied any relation between the credits it gave to the government and the banknotes in circulation, even after the war when censorship did not enforce the bank to do so.[35] At the same time in an attempt to keep up appearances, the population was encouraged to switch from cash money to bank accounts supposedly to smoothen money transfers and to modernise the financial system. Obviously it remained silent about the fact that this would not decrease the amount of money; it would only be less visible.

The question remains whether central bank directors were in a position to behave otherwise. A refusal to cooperate in credit supply would have been seen as unpatriotic conduct. In particular during the first weeks of the war it would undoubtedly have had personal repercussions for the governors concerned. But also during the rest of the war, their room for manoeuvre remained extremely limited. In the end, the interest of the nation would always prevail.[36] A more independent or reluctant attitude would have led to the government taking the initiative itself to printing as much money as it wanted or maybe even only threatening to do so. After all, the central bank derived its privilege to issue banknotes as legal tender by law. Notably in France, the *Banque* was well aware of this concession, which was given for periods of 20 years; of course, the concession was prolonged in 1920, as it had been done in 1897, but it remained a factor of consideration for the *régents*.[37]

The German *Reichsbank* was so strongly tied to government (the German Chancellor was formally president of the Board of Trustees) that an independent position was out of the question.[38] This relationship had still been strengthened by the common financial preparations in the years before the war. After all, the set of War Acts of 4 August 1914 had not been made without obligation. The *Reichsbank* had better be obedient, but even a light form of persuasion was absolutely unnecessary.[39] Subordination incarnated *Reichsbank* president Havenstein himself declared that extension of the money supply was necessary to provide for the demand that was caused by 'the general rise of prices'.[40] It was not until the summer of 1918 that the leaders of the *Reichsbank* expressed in internal communication their concern to the government about the increasing amount of money in circulation.[a]

In Britain, the Bank of England was in a more independent position relative to the government, which had after all already taken the initiative to issue its own notes. It was only during the second half of the war, that the Bank issued new notes in larger quantities.[41] Eventually, however, the Bank had to respect the government's demands.[42] In time of war, national interest prevailed over the private sector and the autonomy of

---

a   **Holtfrerich** (1980), p. 163. In the period of hyperinflation in 1923, it would appear that Havenstein still believed in these views, when he refused to see that money creation was not the solution of the problems but the cause of it (page 263).

the Bank was evidently limited, as was shown embarrassingly in the case of British gold reserves in Canada (pages 56, 57).

There was a second field of central banks' policy where severe restrictions were made. In normal times, an essential and exclusive right of a central bank is setting the discount rate (bank rate). The bank adjusts the interest rate in reaction to, or anticipating, economic developments. It is remarkable, that although the economies of the countries changed during the war at a scale and with a pace that had never been seen before, bank rates were kept as an apparent beacon of stability as if nothing had happened. Apart from the first weeks of mobilisation and war declarations around 1ˢᵗ August 1914, bank rate changes were extremely small or totally absent.[43] This was not only a psychological signal that everything was under control; it also reflected the circumstance that central banks had ceased to be autonomous in this field. In pre-war circumstances, a deficit in the balance of trade or an increased demand for industrial credit would have led to the decision to increase the discount rate. During the war however credit demand was not driven by productive investments but by government imposed production. Import surpluses were not economically driven but politically induced. And finally, a high interest rate was the last thing the government wanted, as it was the largest borrower of all.[44] Pleas for higher interest rates, as they were uttered sometimes in the scientific literature ('higher bank rates now!' – 'hinauf mit den Bankraten!') met with no response.[45] Reality was that discount rates were political interest rates.

The significance of monetary financing
Monetary financing played an important role in war financing. To determine the *exact amount* however is a different question and data presented in the literature show a large range.[46] In the first place not only physical banknotes should be taken into account, but bank deposits as well (and even distinguished according to term). The most tangible indicator of monetary financing in all countries is the rise in price level or cost of living: in France and Britain it roughly doubled, in Germany it tripled.[47]

The development over time is at least as important as the amount of money itself. And then the borders between monetary financing, taxation and loans become a little blurred. If one looks at the war period alone, say 1914-1918, then only the increase of money supply counts that was realised *during* the war. Monetary financing however did not stop at the Armistice; in fact it went on after the war had ended, in France and Germany even at an accelerated speed. Monetary financing became more and more a tax on capital, as far as the latter was held in cash or securities. A clear distinction between monetary financing and taxation gradually disappeared, as did the border between monetary financing and loans. Indeed, looking back, all nine large German war loans could be labelled as monetary financing (and the French ones for say three quarters).[48] The most visible *impact* of monetary financing therefore remains the enormous rise in prices.

If we restrict ourselves to the increase in money in circulation in the form of coins and banknotes, we see confirmed the large differences between countries. In Britain, this increase amounted to roughly 10% of the pre-war GDP, in France it was about 33% in Germany almost 50%.[49] To some extent, these differences can be explained by the greater significance of bank accounts in Britain, whereas on the continent cash was predominant. The situation in Germany in particular was alarming, or rather, should have been perceived as alarming. The amount of paper money in circulation – largely not backed by gold! – equalled half a year of national income.[50] This raises the question whatever could be done to set it right? The only realistic answer is: by a victory on the battlefield and imposing reparations to the rest of Europe (as Germany started to do with Russia in the Treaty of Brest-Litovsk). History decided otherwise and Germany followed the path of economic chaos and hyperinflation.

Conclusion

In all European countries monetary financing was an important tool in the repertoire of governments to provide for their large demand of money at a short term. It was a practical instrument and printing bank notes during the first few months of the war was both inevitable and effective. For politicians it avoided awkward discussions about taxation. Once started however, the inflationary spiral was almost impossible to break. The government's interest was simply too large.

In issuing fresh banknotes, the central banks had to follow the government's directions, whether they liked it or not. In fact collaboration was the only possibility, under threat of being completely bypassed.

Furthermore, all countries created mechanisms for an increase in the amount of money in circulation, whether overtly or more obscured. In Germany the *Darlehenskassen* offered interesting extra facilities, in Britain the Treasury itself printed scarcely backed currency notes and in France the *bons*, intended as short-term loans, practically acted as banknotes. In all these cases the central bank was 'spared' and its credit standing remained apparently untouched.

The great flood of new money brought into circulation during the war provided the foundation for future economic disruption. After the war, all European governments were faced with the choice to let it happen in the form of continuously increasing inflation, or to resort to a policy of rigorous deflation. The first option inevitably led to massive impoverishment of the middle classes, in particular when inflation developed beyond control; the other option brought economic misery as well among vulnerable parts of the population. Again, every country made its own choice as will be seen in Chapter 14.

Before that, however, we shall first deal with the most intriguing question of the large debts between governments – the consequence of massive international borrowing. During the war, these debts had started as almost invisible phenomena for the general public and a concern for the financial leaders only; after the war, however, they would be the basis for decades of discord between former allies. The inextricably linked German reparations question resulted in a continuation of the war by other means.

Episode III

1920-2015

The debts question: a century of small payments and large cancellations

12

Back to normalcy: mission impossible

'Ja, mach nur einen Plan.
Sei nur ein großes Licht!
Und mach dann noch 'nen zweiten
Plan Geh'n tun sie beide nicht'
Bertolt Brecht, 1928[a]

1918: continuity in war financing

On 11/11 of the year 1918, when 'the guns fell silent', the end of shelling was in fact the only thing that really changed. Practically all other operations that had determined the previous four years continued as if nothing had happened. Even the massacre continued, as the Spanish flu had silently taken over the role of the war machinery.

War funding also continued in the first months after the Armistice. Indeed, spending went on at the same rate: there was no peace, just an armistice. The armies of millions of soldiers continued to be fed and clothed and provided with ammunition; transportation costs to be made. And, once the men were demobilised, their integration into civil society and into a peacetime economy would require immense efforts. In particular in Europe, large spending on social security could be foreseen. On the Western front only (not to speak of the Eastern theatre), physical damage was enormous and the population of Belgium and northern France were in need of social relief programmes.

On the supply side of the war, current contracts for deliveries had to be bought out. So, paradoxically, in the winter of 1918/'19, when the war seemed to be over, war expenditure was higher than in any period during the war. American war expenditure, for example, peaked in December 1918 and January 1919 (illustration 12.1).[1]

---

a   'Yes, make a plan / be a great light / and after that, make a second plan / they both will not work', Song of the Insufficiency of Human Endeavour (*Lied von der Unzulänglichkeit menschlichen Strebens*), Threepenny Opera, **Bertolt Brecht** (1898-1956).

When hostilities ended, money flows went on; American expenditure for the war peaked in December 1918, after the Armistice (Illustration 12.1)

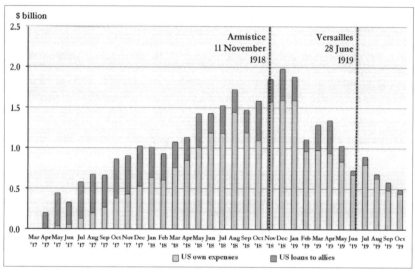

Source: calculated from US Treasury data.[2]

On the funding side, existing plans for tax increases remained implemented, war profit taxes persisted, and monetary financing by printing money was not abolished or even diminished, in any case not on the European continent. Large war loans were issued, although the names were slightly different, as the *Victory Loan* and *Victory Liberty Bonds* of 1919 in Britain and the US show. Finally, the American Treasury continued to make available enormous sums of money for the allies, France, Britain and Belgium, but also for a growing list of other countries, among which new emerging states such as the Baltic States, Czechoslovakia and Yugoslavia.

The only thing that really changed in financing the war was the market for army supplies: the dump store. Governments could try to recover some of their spending by selling old (or new and unused) material. In particular, the US wanted to get rid of ammunition, vehicles, horses and clothing, quickly becoming idle on the former battlefields in northern France. In any case, it would save shipping capacity. On the other hand, as the box shows (next page), this presented the government with unexpected problems as a consequence of the international character of the war. After all, the contribution of selling this material was relatively small, a matter of a few per cent of all war expenditure.

The dump store, Act I: France and the US as competitors in second hand trade

After the war, governments tried to sell surplus material on the civil market, to recover a modest share of war expenses. Germany, for example, collected a onetime revenue in the fiscal year 1921 of no less than 3.8 billion marks (at that time about $ 40 million) from selling surplus army and navy material.[3] At the same time, the British government earned £ 160 million ($ 600 million) for the same sort of actions.[4] The United States was most favourable, however, in using this funding channel. After the boys went home, it sold surplus material in Europe at a value of $ 820 million and saved large repatriation costs.[5] The larger part was acquired by France, Poland and by some new Central European states, but individuals, companies and organisations also bought their share, totalling $ 110 million. Horses in particular were popular, not only in France, but also in defeated Germany. The Americans could sell their 180,000 horses (and mules) at good prices at auctions, receiving no less than $ 35 million in cash.[6]

Almost half of the $ 820 was a lump sum of $ 400 million, paid by the French government for the bulk of the American surpluses, regardless of their quality, location, condition or market value. After the deal, France could resell it to individual buyers and keep the revenue, while the United States government would not have to bargain with a multitude of private traders (of course, personal belongings of the soldiers were excluded, as well as horses and other animals).[7] The sum of $ 400 million was the result of relatively short but tough negotiations between the US and France. It was, to be honest, more a diplomatic agreement than a commercial transaction. Apart from time pressure on the American side (the army was already sailing home), two financial issues dominated the negotiations: import duties and exchange rates.

The French, keen on keeping the price as low as possible, put forward that the material had been brought to France without properly paying import duties. Indeed, circumstances were exceptional, but duty *regulations had to be obeyed. The amount of lost earnings for the French state was estimated at about $ 150 million. This sum, according to the French, had to be subtracted from the estimated value of the material, $ 580 million. After some discussions, the total sum to be paid by France was concluded at the round sum of $ 400 million.[8] France won this first battle of negotiations. The 115,000 Americans who lost their lives on the battlefield did not count at that moment.*

The Americans, however, hit back by demanding that the amount of $ 400 million would be paid in dollars, not in Francs of an uncertain future value. France could not possibly pay that amount in cash and the Americans were prepared to lend the money by means of a 10-year bond at an interest rate of 5%. Since payments on both principal and interest should be made in dollars, France bore the exchange rate risk. By mid 1919, when the agreement was made, the exchange rate was 7.25 francs for one dollar. In 1920, the franc had fallen to almost half of this value: 14 francs to the dollar and in July 1926 it even dropped to 41 franc to the dollar.[9] Measured in francs, the French government had to pay 5 times as much as originally concluded. In France, the war supplies deal evoked bitter feelings, deteriorating the already uneasy relationship between the two countries.[10] The whole affair would find a surprising aftermath

To be continued (page 222).

After the war, the differences between countries in their way of financing the expenditure did not diminish; instead, they increased. Germany called upon printing bank notes more and more, resulting in 1923 in a disastrous hyperinflation. France resorted to gain time by relying on future German reparations that would end all its financial troubles. Britain stressed the restoration of the pre-war system of financial solidity, whatever the price. For the Americans, finally, it went without saying that the generously provided loans should be repaid. 'Back to normalcy' was the slogan, following the first priority of repatriating the boys from the European battlefields.[a]

---

a   President Warren G. Harding (1865-1923), in a speech in May 1920 while competing for presidency, an office that he would hold until his sudden death in August 1923.

It would take, however, a long time before the relations were 'normal' if ever this state would be reached. Pre-war conditions had changed, or rather they were destructed. Increasing expenses in the first months after the Armistice would soon diminish, but costs for veterans and widows would lay a heavy burden on government budgets for decades. In the first place, however, the unprecedented debts were the real headache: short-term loans from the central banks, treasury bills in the hands of banks and private investors, large war loans subscribed to by millions of citizens and loans provided by foreign governments.

In fact, the large war loans were the least of the problem, since their interest and principal payments were spread over a long period. The short-term debts formed a more serious danger, in particular in France. Any moment that such a loan expired, governments hoped and expected that they would be rolled over, but this was not guaranteed. Governments were completely dependent on the good will of the creditors and their alternative options for investments, which could be more profitable in other sections of the (peace) economy. Both types of loans, however, were fundamentally *domestic* problems. They represented government debts of the nation to its own citizens. National wealth was not affected, in principle, by clearing domestic debts. Only the *distribution* of wealth between social groups might be altered.[11] Of course, such redistribution could cause immense human and social suffering. The liquidation of all savings of the German middle classes through *in*flation was a traumatic event (page 270).[12] In Britain, miners' strikes during the 1920s were reactions to the wealth reduction of the workers, this time precisely by a policy of *de*flation. Such debts between groups in society are very interesting as they have left deep scars, but they form a subject of domestic policy, not of war finance. Therefore, in Chapter 13 this matter will only be touched upon in relation to war financing in the way it has been described in the previous chapters.

Not: who is to blame, but: who has to pay, that was the question

The real obstacle to return to pre-war 'normalcy' was the accumulation of loans *between* countries. At the end of the war, $ 16 billion was the total amount of outstanding loans between the allies, measured in 1918 dollars.[13] The problem was, that these debts were highly intertwined. Britain had borrowed from the US, but the British Empire itself had lent heavily to France, Italy, and Belgium and, not in the last place,

Russia. In the period of reconstruction, roughly until 1922, the group of debtor countries grew to over 15 different countries, tied together in an inextricable tangle.[14] France, for example, had accumulated large debts in both the United States and Britain, but it had claims on Belgium, Italy, Russia, Rumania and a series of other countries. Even Italy, a debtor to all large western countries, had supported Rumania with loans and after the war also the new European states of Czechoslovakia and Poland.

At the end of the war a complex system of inter-ally debts had been built up; this would only grow in the following years by reconstruction and relief loans (Illustration 12.2)

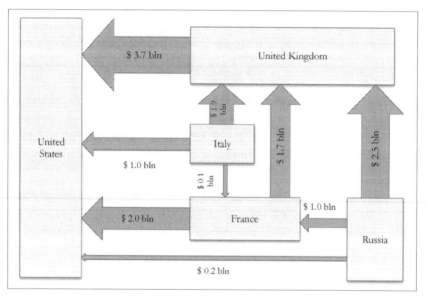

Source: Moulton & Pasvolsky, Self.[15] Smaller debts (Belgium, Commonwealth, etc.) neglected.

From a purely accounting viewpoint, the countries took different positions. Britain, for example, at the time of the Armistice had lent $ 7.0 billion, itself being a debtor to the United States only for $ 3.8 billion. This meant an ostensibly splendid positive balance of $ 3.2 billion. One might say – and indeed it was said at that time and long afterwards – that Britain had made a profitable deal with banking during the war. In reality, the British position was not that fortunate at all, because debts differ in quality. The major part of the British loans, to the tune of $ 2.5 billion, had been made to czarist Russia, debts rejected by the Soviet government. This item alone reduced the British surplus to $ 0.7 billion, provided all claims but those on Russia could be collected. This simple example illustrates that it was not a matter of merely cancelling debts against each other. The value of some debts, for example those of Britain to the US, was simply much larger than other debts, such as the Russian debts, although the numerical values could be the same.[16]

Apart from the values of the debt, there was the problem of priorities. Which debts should be paid first if a country had two creditors and scarce resources? Italy is a good example. From its total debt of $ 3 billion, two thirds was to Britain, one third to the United States and a rather small amount of (net) $ 75 million to France. If Italy paid France, it could relatively easily restructure its debt position by reducing its creditors by one. In that case, however, the US and Britain would have to wait longer for their money.[17] But Italy itself had a claim on Rumania, a debtor country to the United States too. If the Rumanians would give priority to paying off the Americans instead of Italy, would that imply that Italy could postpone its payments to the US until it had itself received the Rumanian money? Maybe Rumania would wait until it received reparations form its neighbour country Bulgaria and from Germany?[18]

In the reparations theatre itself, Rumania was but a minor player. France expected by far the largest reparations payments from Germany. At the same time, it had the largest foreign debts of all continental countries, while the once prosperous northern region of the country was ruined. It was evident, that France could never pay off its debts to its allies without decades of extreme austerity and an enormous decrease in the standard of living, unless... indeed, unless it received large German reparations.

Obviously, everything was connected to everything. A way out seemed impossible, and in fact it was not reached. Therefore, two issues come together in the debt settlement question of the Great War: the inter-ally debts and German reparations as imposed by the Treaty of Versailles.[a] Both will be dealt with in the remainder of this chapter.

---

a   Reparations were also imposed on Germany's allies Austria, Hungary, Bulgaria and the Ottoman Empire at the corresponding treaties of Saint-Germain-en-Laye, Trianon, Neuilly-sur-Seine and Sèvres (replaced by Lausanne), respectively. Of course, the real issue was Germany.

The two mutually affecting issues: the inter-ally debts and German reparations* (Illustration 12.3)

	inter-ally debts	reparations	political context
1918-1921	accumulation	fixing the amount	Versailles 28 June 1919
1922-1930	restructuring through bilateral agreements; partial payments	restructuring through international plans; partial payments	Ruhr occupation; January 1923- August 1925

*   A more detailed table can be found on page 238.

It was quite obvious for the Europeans at the end of the war, that the inter-ally debts and German reparations were inseparable, just as it is for the present-day spectator with all hindsight. For the US at that time, however, the two issues were absolutely distinct. Loans to allies were commercial transactions, whereas reparations were a matter of settling the bill for warfare, a strictly European affair. The American position can hardly be summarised shorter than by the words: 'debts are debts and reparations are fines.'[19] The United States had not ratified the Treaty of Versailles. They could make no claims (and in fact they did not) under article 231 of the treaty, which placed the responsibility of the war exclusively on Germany.[20]

This controversy implies that it is impossible to give a strictly chronological analysis with all its implications and details. This would obscure the light on the losers and victors, as it would not make clear who would eventually pay for the war. At the end of this chapter (page 238), a table shows some important events in their chronological order.

I have chosen rather to present the inter-ally debts between the two World Wars as a tragedy in three acts: accumulation, restructuring and (eternal) postponement. The same procedure has been followed in the settlement of reparations: fixing the amount, restructuring and eventually cancellation. The two processes mutually influenced each other in long controversies and clashes in international debt conferences. These conferences were interesting events for the diplomats involved and profitable for French (and other) luxury hotels and congress resorts. The debtor countries eventually saw their debts decreasing with every new agreement; delaying appeared a better strategy than paying. In 1931 it was the bold initiative of President Herbert Hoover, urged by the economic crisis (and by interested banks and bondholders), to declare unilaterally a one-year moratorium on all inter-ally debts. This financial armistice marks the beginning of the common third part in both plays: postponement until they would be forgotten by everyone but the bookkeepers and historians.

For the sake of completeness, it should be remarked that inter-ally debts were not restricted to the 'western' allies. On the defeated side of the European Central powers, debt positions had also been built up, mainly from Austria-Hungary, the Ottoman Empire and Bulgaria to Germany. The inter-government debts between these countries were much smaller than on the western side and also less complicated as they were all directed towards Germany.[a] Of the total amount, $ 0.6 billion in 1918, about 80% was a debt of the recently broken-up Dual Monarchy.[21] A settlement of these debts was irrelevant for Germany. The Treaty of Versailles stipulated that Germany transferred all its financial claims on the governments of Austria, Hungary, Bulgaria and Turkey to the western allies, 'in particular, any claims which may arise, now or hereafter, from the fulfillment of undertakings made by Germany during the war'[22] Thus, Germany was simply excluded from the settlement of these debts.

The Drama of the inter-ally debts, Act I: accumulation

Debts between the allies were gigantic. In the period of 20 months that the US participated actively in the war, from April 1917 to the Armistice in November 1919, it had given credit to European allies to the amount of $ 7.3 billion; half of this sum was borrowed by Britain, the rest by France, Italy, Russia and Belgium.[23] Before April 1917, private American banks had given loans to France and Britain (Chapter 10). In the first year after the war, both countries had to pay off the bankers for some hundred million of dollars each. On the near horizon, there was also the redemption of the large private Anglo-French loan of 1915, which was

---

a   Financial cooperation between Central powers was far less sophisticated than among the Entente (including the United States as their 'associate'). Despite all difficulties that would arise during the war, France and Britain had started regular consultation about financial and economic issues as early as August 1914, **Horn** (2002), p. 38; for Germany and Austria-Hungary this kind of coordination was remarkably poor, at least during the first period of the war and in particular in view of their close military (and political) collaboration, **Popovics** (1925), p. 124.

to mature in 1920, an inescapable obligation of $ 500 million for both countries together.

After the Armistice, credit demand remained high and the American government continued acting as the big lender of last resort. Although new loans to Britain, France and Italy gradually decreased, these countries alone received advances totalling $ 1.9 billion in 1919-1920. At the same time, devastated areas, notably in northern France and Belgium, had to be reconstructed; in Central and Eastern Europe, from Finland to Yugoslavia, large investments had to be made to organise more or less stable societies. Belgium, for example, received as much after the Armistice as it had received before, at an average daily rate of $ 140.000, rounding up to a total of $ 315 million over the period 1917-1920.

The last advances made by the United States to European allies (apart from relief programmes), was on 20 September 1920, when France received $ 20 million.[24] It was a welcome bonus for France, because it arrived just in time to lighten the forthcoming redemption of their part of the large Anglo-French loan, $ 250 million to be paid by mid-October 1920.[25]

Altogether, up to and including 1922, the United States government supplied loans to the European allies – for warfare and relief – to an amount of $ 12 billion dollar (in currency of that time, of course; in present-day value, it would be orders of magnitude larger, see Annex).[26] At the moment of granting these loans, it was implied that they would bear the same interest as the *Liberty Loans* by which they had been funded: originally 3¼%, later 4½%. Payments on interest, however, were hardly made; the US Treasury simply added arrears to the total amount outstanding. Payments on principal were completely out of the question and even maturity dates were undetermined. During the war, other priorities prevailed; servicing debts was a matter of 'after the war'.

But after the war, the situation had changed; in Europe, but certainly in the US. The first signs could be seen in the preparations of the Paris Peace Conference, which would ultimately lead to the Treaty of Versailles on 28 June 1919. France made its first attempt to consider all financial aspects as one comprehensive issue, and in particular it wanted to establish a link between the inter-ally debts and German reparations.[a] This position was understandable. As long as no arrangements had been made on reparations, it was unclear for France, but also for Italy, how it could ever repay its debts to the Americans and to Britain. Unfortunately for the French and the Italians, the issue was not even put on the agenda of the peace conference.

The British, having a net positive balance on their debts, were prepared to discuss a cancellation of debts. In the months after the signing of the Treaty of Versailles, they suggested making a generous gesture: restructure all outstanding debts between governments and resume business as usual. This was in line with a tradition already followed after the Napoleonic wars in the early nineteenth century.[27] In this view trade and prosperity would benefit more from debt restructuring than from rigidly sticking to (economically impossible) repayments.[b]

For the American government, however, cancelling debts was out of the question. Its viewpoint was that the credits represented commercial debts, to be repaid like any other obligations in business life. Congress did not stop reminding the US Treasury that it was a matter of loans, not gifts. Successive Secretaries of the Treasury declared that the United States could not bear the burden of the entire world, and certainly not Europe's financial needs. A serious point of concern was that the US had no control over tax policies in the European countries. Indeed, the United States had financed its own part of the war for one third from taxation, whereas European countries had been negligent, resorting to loans and monetary funding by central banks. With respect to France, but also to some other continental powers, the Americans had a point.[28]

---

a   See, for example, **Moulton & Pasvolsky** (1932), pp. 53-57. This idea of linking issues of financial and strategic political nature is a strong and persistent line in French foreign policy. For example, in 1931, after the default of the Austrian *Creditanstalt* (page 239), France was prepared to support Austria with a loan on the condition that the proposed Austrian-German customs union should be called off. A recent example is France accepting German unification in 1989/'90 provided that the Euro would be introduced, implying that Germany would give up its *mark*.

b   As early as in the 1920s, the internationally oriented Harvard economic historian **Gay** (1926) had pointed to this British tradition that went back to Lord Liverpool: 'in case of war, if you can give at all, give and do not lend' (circa 1816).

A new American Secretary of the Treasury, David Houston, explained in March 1920 the position of its government in an extensive letter, formally sent to the British embassy, but in fact directed towards all European allies.[29] European countries had to blame themselves for their failure in repaying debts. The US government had noticed that they had not even made budgetary reservations to pay interest. They were lax in taxation, wasted their money, and refused to save costs by disarmament. Furthermore, he stated – without mentioning names – that some European countries created too much paper money. They were incompetent in stabilising exchange rates. Instead of keeping talking about reparations, they had better adopt a policy for Germany and Austria to contribute to the economic rehabilitation of Europe. European countries did not restore private initiative, unnecessary economic barriers still existed, and free trade remained hampered. Houston's letter was a mix of financial, economic and moral arguments and a sermon not to be misunderstood: a loud and clear 'no' to any attempt to cancel debts. The sprit was unmistakably isolationist. It foreshadowed the American aversion to European affairs that would contribute to the landslide victory of the Republicans Warren Harding and his running mate Calvin Coolidge in the 1920 presidential elections.

Meanwhile, the Europeans struggled with their reparations. It was evident, that somehow, they would be imposed, but how, and even how much, remained unclear. At this crucial point, the Treaty of Versailles, in all its extensive text of 75,000 words, paradoxically had only given some global indications.

The Tragedy of Reparations, Act I: – fixing the amount
Reparations imposed on Germany by the Treaty of Versailles have been the subject of deep emotions, ever since they were written in the treaty. Up to the present day discussions have not silenced, among the general public and scholars alike.[a] Many aspects have been dealt with, from historical, political, economic, legal and moral viewpoints. This chapter restricts itself to facts and backgrounds relevant for the inter-ally debt question and for the history of (not) paying.[30]

---

a   *WorldCat* gives over 3,000 publications on the combination *'reparations'* + *'Germany'* of which one third was written in the period 1918-1932; emotionally charged discussions on internet continue up to today.

The first thing to notice is the big difference between the reparations of Versailles and those of 1871. In the latter case, the total amount to be paid by France, 5 billion *francs*, was already mentioned in the preliminary treaty of 1871, in fact an armistice. After Versailles however, it took almost 2½ years before the total sum was finally fixed. This is a striking difference, if one realises that in a period of 2½ years, France had already almost completely paid off its debts in 1873.[a] The big contrast of course was, that in 1871 there was one victor, whereas in 1919 a coalition of powers had won the war and each one had its own interests. How to divide the loot *among* them was probably an even larger problem than the amount of it, although about the latter there were also divergent views: how much could be extracted from Germany?

The notion of Germany's capacity to pay had already been mentioned in the Treaty of Versailles, but merely in a legal, not in an economic sense.[31] The only concrete point was Germany's obligation of an amount of 20 billion *marks*, to be paid by Germany by 1st May 1921, in cash or in kind. It was meant as a provisional sum pending a final settlement that was to be concluded before that date. From that date on, Germany would then be given a period of 30 years to pay, a period that could be extended if necessary. Incidentally, it is often forgotten that the treaty even provided that part of the reparations could be cancelled – by mutual agreement, of course.[32]

After many rumours, speculations and suggestions, finally on 5 May 1921, the London *Reparations Commission* proposed a sum of 132 billion *gold marks*, to be paid by the defeated countries to the victors.[33] Although the 132 billion *marks* were to be paid by all Central powers together, it was clear that the burden fell almost entirely on Germany.[34] Evidently, the contributions of the successor countries of the fragmented Austria-Hungarian Empire, the small and agricultural Bulgaria and the old Ottoman Empire, transforming into modern Turkey, would be negligible.

---

a   This short period of amortisation also reduced significantly the difference between the principal to be repaid, the total payments including interest, and the present value of these payments; in the case of German reparations this distinction was absolutely unclear, and hence fully open to political interpretation, see pages 217, 218.

Something should be said about this total sum of 132 billion *marks*. In Germany, everyone was perplexed and it was considered as devastating for the nation for generations. It has undoubtedly contributed to the myth of reparations, not only in Germany but also abroad.[35] In reality, it had been reduced to 50 billion *marks* in the very proposal. The majority, 82 billion *marks*, was immediately postponed. It was a debt on paper, possibly to be paid eventually, as it was politically motivated.[36] Ten years later, Lloyd George declared that none of the directly involved politicians had ever taken these 82 billion *marks* seriously.[37] It just served the political intention to show the population in the victor countries that Germany would be seriously punished.[a] In subsequent negotiations and in payments, these 82 billion *marks* would play a relatively insignificant role. For agitators, however, the 132 billion *marks* would remain an easy target, as indeed for critical commentators in the allied camp.[38] The only amount that should be taken seriously, the 50 billion (gold) *marks*, amounted to roughly $ 12 billion, at pre-war exchange rates.[39]

Karl Helfferich – after the war (continuation from page 83)

After the war, Karl Helfferich's career was somewhat sidetracked. A temporary position at the German embassy in Soviet Russia could not be called successful. In Berlin, it was Hjalmer Schacht who succeeded

Havenstein as president of the Reichsbank, not Helfferich.

In the Weimar Republic, however, Helfferich's star began to rise again. He obtained a great response to his agitation against anything even remotely leftish. The stab-in-the-back myth might not be his creation, it certainly was his darling. Anyone who had the slightest inclination to meet the allied demands of reparations could be sure that he would be burnt down by Helfferich's

---

a   An interesting and readable account of the issue has been given by Gaston Furst, member of the Belgian delegation in the *Reparations Commission* and former artillery commander, **Furst** (1927), in particular p. 130 ff.

attacks. Commentators have held his speeches in the Reichstag responsible for a climate where political murders (such as those on Foreign minister Walther Rathenau and Armistice negotiator Matthias Erzberger) became a normal phenomenon.

Karl Helfferich was a leading member of the German National People's Party (Deutschnationale Volkspartei) and at a meeting in Hamburg on 1ˢᵗ April 1924, he was cheered loudly while people shouted 'Hail Helfferich'[40] Undoubtedly, he would have had a splendid future in Germany in the interwar period, with his combination of financial intelligence and extremely right-wing political views. Fate decided otherwise. Less than four weeks after his Hamburg performance, on the night of 22 to 23 April 1924, he was killed in a tragic railway accident in the Swiss city of Bellinzona, travelling home from a visit to the Italian villa of his parents-in-law (Four years before, at the age of 48, the confirmed bachelor Helfferich had married the widow Anette von Müffling, no lesser person than the daughter of Georg von Siemens, founder of the Deutsche Bank and 14 years his junior).

In modern Germany, almost all traces to Helfferich seem to be effaced. In Neustadt an der Weinstraße, where he was born, one can find the only street in Germany that bears his name, the Karl Helfferichstraße. It received its name by the City Council in 1933, voting unanimously, in honour of his 'indefatigable battle against democracy, corruption and Erzberger'.[41] In the same session the Nazi-dominated Council also decided to rename the Neustadt Market Square (Marktplatz) Adolf-Hitler-Platz, this decision was reversed long ago.

The London Agreement of 1921 thus settled the 'total' reparations bill for Germany, but the annual payments on interest and principal were yet to be decided. At this point, the Agreement was just as indeterminate as on the total sum. Germany was to pay an **annuity** of about 3 billion (gold) *marks*, corresponding to a rate of 6% of 50 billion *marks* (5% on interest and 1% on principal). The 'about' meant that the 3 billion (gold) *marks* could vary slightly from year to year: it consisted of a fixed amount of 2 billion (gold) *marks* and another 1 billion (gold) *marks*, representing a quarter of Germany's export value. This latter value might fluctuate, but it had been included in the Agreement deliberately, to make a connection between reparations and the development of

Germany's economy, its 'capacity to pay'. Payments themselves were to be made in cash (gold or foreign currencies, such as dollars) and/or in kind: coal, timber, chemical products, dyes, cattle. It remained unclear, however, how long these annuities should be paid; periods of 30 of 35 years circulated, but no one really knew.[42]

All things considered – the total amount, the ambiguity of the amount (including or excluding interest), the export depending annuities and the maturity date – the London Agreement for German reparations was misleading, vague and vulnerable to manipulation. It was no sustainable solution to the reparations question, and it would soon prove to be none.

What did Germany really pay? During the period 1920 until August 1924 (when the London Agreement effectively ended), Germany paid the equivalent of some 8.8 billion (gold) *marks*, the major part of it in kind, less than 20% in cash.[43] The first payments, in the period between the signing of Versailles and the London Agreement were almost completely in kind, in particular timber, coal and railway equipment.[44] From 1921 on, Germany soon lagged behind in cash payments. Emphasis shifted more and more towards deliveries in kind, but soon these showed arrears as well. The majority of the *Reparations Commission*[a] finally declared Germany in default on reparations. In January 1923, French and Belgian armed forces invaded the Ruhr region, a territory they would occupy for two and a half years.[45]

The Drama of the inter-ally debts, Act II: restructuring

While Europeans were busy quarrelling about reparations, Americans wanted to leave the war behind them. On 2 July 1921, President Harding had declared the end of the war, which meant that the credit line from the US to Europe was discontinued. Now was the time to prepare the bill and to make arrangements for debt settlements. For the US government it was clear that loans had to be paid back, and with interest. To this end, bilateral agreements would have to be made with individual debtor countries, without consideration of such distracting issues as reparations.[46]

---

a   France, Italy and Belgium versus Britain.

This settlement would prove to be a long-lasting process. Negotiations alone would consume almost as much time as the whole war in Europe had taken, from April 1922 to the spring of 1926. A special commission of Congress, the *World War Foreign Debt Commission*, was to prepare the settlements. The commission had instructions to negotiate agreements by which loans would be redeemed: within at most 25 years and bearing an interest of at least 4¼%. This soon proved an impossible task. The capacity to pay for any European country was absolutely insufficient to meet such requirements. At the end of the process, in the spring of 1926, the actual result was that the United States had to write off more than 40% of the debts, taken over all countries together.[47]

Britain was among the first group of countries to make arrangements to settle their bill. In the agreement, the total amount (principal) was settled at $ 4.6 billion. The interest rate was quite moderate, 3.3%, and the repayments schedule extended over no less than 62 years. This was in all proportions against the instructions Congress had given to the commission, but there was no other option than to agree. As a consequence, the annual instalments were – at that time! – manageable for the United Kingdom. Initially it amounted to $ 25 million on principal and $ 135 million on interest, to be paid in dollars, of course.[a] In the course of the decades, the interest payments would decline, while payments on principal would increase, keeping the total annuity relatively constant from 1933 onwards, as in an amortised loan. When the arrangement was signed, June 1923, the last payment was scheduled for 1984. This would not be reached by far (page 248).

After signing agreements with Britain, Finland and a series of Central European countries, the United States gradually but unmistakably took a more lenient attitude. Countries that signed later came off much better than Britain and Finland. France, for example, succeeded in procrastinating the negotiations until April 1926 and managed to achieve an average interest rate as low as 1.6%, mainly because it was

---

a   The business-like approach of the Americans in the inter-ally debt question influenced relations between Britain and the US negatively for decades, in fact until the Second World War. Self (2006) gives an extensive description of this 'unspecial relationship'. Although there was less openly displayed enmity than between France and the US (page 220), relations were cool to say the least. It was thanks to Hitler that the relationship became warm again.

exempted from interest payments during the first 5 years. By this result, France succeeded in cutting the outstanding debt by half. Although it had an original debt of $ 4.2 billion on principal and interest, the agreement reduced it by $ 2.2 billion. This meant, that France was obliged to pay effectively the full amount on the loans received *after* the war, but only one third of the debt accumulated *during* the war. No less than two thirds of the loans France had received between April 1917 and the end of 1918 were cancelled.[48] From an American viewpoint, this settlement was regarded fair; Secretary of State Frank Kellogg even called it 'generous'.[49]

The French had a completely different view on the matter. The fundamental background was, of course, that even in the mid-twenties, the US government resolutely refused to talk about a connection between inter-ally debts and reparations. As German reparations lagged behind, France had postponed its payments on American loans again and again.[a] In the summer of 1926, when the agreement was finally signed between the French ambassador in Washington, Henry Bérenger and the United States Secretary of the Treasury Andrew Mellon, the atmosphere in France was grim, almost hostile. American tourists in Paris were threatened and jeered. In July 1926, when the news of the agreement had spread, a group of 20,000 disabled veterans (*mutilés de guerre*) demonstrated in a silent march at the American embassy.[50] Now the euphoria from wartime was forgotten, the excitement in February 1917, when the United States had broken diplomatic relations with Germany and had chosen the side of France and Britain. At that time an enthusiastic audience had cheered the American Ambassador in the box of the *Opéra Comique*; the performance of *Madama Butterfly* had been interrupted and the orchestra spontaneously had started playing *Yankee Doodle*.[51] Undoubtedly in 1926 many Frenchmen would have regretted the once chivalrous attitude when they preferred a loan to a gift. What was left in France in the Mellon-Bérenger era, were feelings of bitterness, expressing what was felt as a great injustice: *La Grande Injustice*.[52] No wonder, that it would take another three years and much political quarrelling before the French Parliament finally ratified the agreement. Which, by the way, did not entail sustainable payments. To be true, the future annuities were 'much higher than

---

a   The only substantial payments France made were interest payments on the loan for war supplies (the inventory of the 'dump store'), page 222.

France [was] ever likely to pay' as *The Economist* rightly concluded as soon as the agreement became known.[53]

While Britain started paying off its debt to the United States, France applied all sorts of arguments to wriggle out (Illustration 12.4)

FRANCE'S DEBTS TO AMERICA

MARIANNE: PLEASE, SAMMY SHOW ME SOME COMPASSION
JONATHAN: HE PAYS OFF HIS DEBTS, DOESN'T HE ?
MARIANNE: YES, BUT HE GOT ALMOST AS MUCH PROFIT FROM THE WAR AS YOU DID !

Source: Johan Braakensiek in *De Amsterdammer, 20 December 1924.*

If the Americans were fair to France, still better off would be Greece and Italy. They arrived at settlements that wrote off 67% and 75% of their debts, respectively. These arrangements reflected the poor payment capacity of those countries. From the US point of view, however, all agreements, even the most severe ones with Britain, Finland and the new Baltic States Estonia, Latvia and Lithuania, were concessions to the original demands stated by Congress: interest rate at least 4¼% and repayment within 25 years. These indeed, were the conditions of the *Liberty Loans*, by which the loans to the allies had been financed. Servicing these *Liberty Loans*, that is paying bondholders for interest and principal, was an obligation of the American government, to be paid from the federal government's revenues, that is taxes. Thus, by 'restructuring' the debts of the allies – cancelling a total amount of $ 5.2 billion – the burden was invisibly shifted to the American taxpayer. And there was more to come.

The dump store, Act II: Who laughs last

In order to finance the purchase of American army supplies, France had negotiated a $ 400 million loan with the United States government. It paid grudgingly the annual interest of 5% or $ 20 million, in expensive dollars due to the unfavourable exchange rate.[54] Redemption of the loan would take place at the end, after 10 years. In the Mellon-Bérenger agreement, the principal of $ 400 million was simply added to the total French debt, which itself was 10 times as high. By doing so, the burden of this 'dump loan' was included into the annuities of the agreement, to be paid until 1987. Interest payments that had already been made on the 'dump loan' since 1925 were redefined in retrospect as the first annuity payments of the Mellon-Bérenger scheme. This relabeling from interest payments into payments on principal, however, could not take place as long as the French Parliament had not ratified the Mellon-Bérenger agreement, of which it had been made part. And if it was not ratified at 1ˢᵗ August 1929, the expiration date of the 10-year 'dump loan', the whole principal of $ 400 million would fall due to the US government at once. This was a situation that the French government wanted to avoid at all costs as it would imply a formal default. Since the Americans did not intend to give in and the issue dragged on for almost three years; finally, under the pressure of the rapidly approaching maturity date, the French Parliament ratified the agreement in the end of July 1929.[55] At that moment the 'dump loan' was part of a regular scheme with repayments extending over almost 60 years.

Real payments would not last until 1987; actually, they held for two years only, until the Hoover moratorium (page 210). So the end of the affair was that France won the last and final stroke from the Americans. Total payments on war supplies were effectively reduced to some six years of interest payments on a sum that had already been cut back by charging import duties.

In the greater context of financing the war, this is but a detail. Nevertheless, it is a striking example of the success of procrastination, legally airtight, politically feasible, but not a whit better than what the Germans contrived with their reparations bill.

The debts to the United States were not the only ones to be settled. In Europe, the British had by far the largest claims outstanding.[56] Although they had originally proposed a total cancellation of all debts, the American attitude forced them to revise this idea. They concluded debt settlements with their debtor countries, from Rumania (October 1925) to Yugoslavia (1927). *Pièce de résistance*, of course, was the agreement with France, signed in July 1926.[57] It provided increasing annuities, until eventually a total sum of £ 800 million would have been paid in 1989.[58] This may appear as a large amount, in particular if expressed in French currency: about 100 billion *francs* at 1927 values. In reality it meant that Britain cancelled over 60% of the French debts, or about £ 375 million. Altogether, Britain has written off no less than £ 950 million on its loans to allies. Although the largest amount was on the Russian loans,[a] just as in the American case Italy was treated extremely mercifully; 87% of its debts to Britain were cancelled. This loss had to be borne by the British taxpayer, who had to pay for servicing the large British war loans with their high interest rates, much higher than its debtor countries had to pay according to the settlements (France: 1.5%, Italy: 0.0%).[59]

Just as it did in the negotiations with the United States, France tried to link payments on loans to Britain to German reparations. It expected more sympathy at the other side of the Channel than of the Atlantic. After all, Britain had earlier showed some inclination to forgive debts in general. The British Chancellor of the Exchequer, at that time Winston Churchill, replied in a polity formulated letter, that France's capacity to pay would of course be taken into consideration. However, in the case of German arrears, Britain itself could run into trouble. In that case, all creditors of France would have to be dealt with in the same way;[60] thus, in the end it would (again) depend on what the United States would do. In view of the American attitude in this matter, the British commitment was rather unsubstantial and France was left empty handed. Again, everything depended on progress on the reparation issue.

The Tragedy of Reparations, Act II: – reducing and restructuring

Meanwhile on the European front of reparations, it became clear in 1923 that something had to be done. A permanent occupation of the Ruhr region and a German economy in disorder would certainly not

---

a   Roughly £ 520 million.

contribute to a sustainable economic recovery in Europe. The London scheme was practically dead and some new scheme had to be developed, but how?

Two successive plans would settle the issue and both resulted in a considerable decrease in the reparations bill: the Dawes scheme of 1924 and the Young scheme of 1929. It was characteristic of the shift in economic and financial power from Europe to the United States, that both schemes (preceded by plans) bore the name of American capitalists, the presidents of the commissions that made the proposals. The first one was Charles Dawes, a banker from Chicago;[a] the second one was Owen Young, industrialist and chairman of the board of *General Electric*. Both captains of industry were wealthy and they even refused to be paid for their work on the commissions, including many trips to Europe.[61]

The Dawes scheme

The first commission of experts to pull the reparations problem out of the doldrums was installed at the end of 1923. It was presided by Dawes, with Young as one of its members. The main problem was to really determine Germany's capacity to pay by rigorous economic analysis. Next, a proposal was to be made for German payments.[62] In the background, the occupation of the Ruhr region continued, but the *Dawes Commission* kept well away from this tricky political issue. The proposal, soon to be known as the Dawes plan or Dawes scheme, consisted of three interconnected components: (1) an amount to be paid annually by Germany (the annuity), (2) a guarantee that Germany would meet its obligations and (3) an international loan.[63] Together, they would replace the complicated London scheme of 1921.

(1) *The annuity*

Germany was to pay every year an amount of 2.5 billion *marks*, which included both principal and interest payments. This full amount was to be reached in 1929; in the preceding years, it would gradually increase, starting with 1.0 billion *marks*.[64] The financial sources that Germany would apply were a mortgage on its railways, tax revenue and the international loan, the third part of the plan (to be discussed later).

---

a   He would soon receive the Nobel Peace prize (1925, together with Austen Chamberlain) and serve as vice president under Coolidge (1925-1929).

The fixed annuity was a simplification compared to the London scheme, with its complicated dependence on Germany's export. As vague as the London scheme, however, remained the maturity date: when would these payments end (or: ever end, as it was felt in Germany). Politically, this was as far as the commission could reach, in view of the conflicting interests of France and Germany. In fact, the finite lifetime of the plan had been built in, more or less deliberately. The plan undoubtedly meant a reduction of the 50 billion *marks* to be paid by Germany. The real reduction rate however cannot be calculated, because neither the London scheme, nor the Dawes plan set an end date to the annual payments.[65]

(2) *A guarantee for payments; the Dawes solution to the transfer problem*
The reason for a guarantee for actual payments can be traced back to a fundamental problem of reparations, the so-called transfer problem (see box, page 226). The very essence of reparations is, that capital flows have to be generated between countries for political reasons without an economically identifiable counter flow of goods or services. Receiving countries expected the money in their own currency or alternatively in gold, British pounds, American dollars or any other practical currency, but certainly not in German *marks*.[66] The German government, on the other hand, could only extract *marks* from the German economy, notably by taxation. The Dawes plan relieved Germany from its responsibility to exchange these *marks* into foreign currency, to formulate it kindly; one might also say that Germany was not trusted to do so. Germany's responsibility would end as soon as the money (in *marks*) was placed on a special account at the *Reichsbank*, whatever the transfers would show (at least up to an amount of 5 billion *marks*). The *Reichsbank* itself lost its independence and was placed under international supervision.[67] It was the task of a new international committee, the *Transfer Committee* (which included Germany), to take care of a proper usage of these funds, in order to exchange them into foreign currency. 'Proper' here meant that the exchange rate of the German *mark* would not be allowed to fall if Germany's export surplus would be insufficient. In this way, the Dawes plan aimed at solving Germany's capacity to *pay*; its capacity to *produce* was beyond all doubt.[68]

It remains an open question whether the transfer problem was actually decisive for Germany's incapability to pay reparations in the 1920s.

Discussions among experts continue up to the present day (see box). Anyhow, Germany could not use the argument in view of the solution proposed by the Dawes plan.

The transfer problem

For a receiving country, say, Belgium, reparation payments were only meaningful if they represented a real value for the country itself. German marks would only have such a value up to the level where they could be used to pay for Belgian imports from Germany. Any marks received in surplus would be potentially worthless, even at stabilized exchange rates (unless they were accepted by third countries, just shifting the problem). Gold would have this real value, but gold reserves of Germany, or any other country, were absolutely insufficient.[69] This implied that Germany had to pay in foreign currency, (in this case) Belgian franks, or even American dollars by which Belgium could pay off its loans to the United States. For the German government to obtain foreign currency, two conditions had to be fulfilled: (1) a net German export surplus, although not necessarily to the receiving country; (2) a taxation system to extract this surplus from the economy; after all, it was by business that trade flows were realised, not by the government that was to pay the reparations bill.

It should be noted that there exist other means to transfer capital (or wealth) from one country to the other. An obvious way is a loan on the international capital markets, precisely the third component of the Dawes plan. Other ways are more rigorous, such as sending labour force abroad or ceding territory. It had indeed been proposed that Britain and France could diminish their war debts to the United States by handing over some of their possessions in the West Indies.[70] The transfer problem as such was primarily caused by requiring payments in cash. Deliveries in kind may give some (temporary) mitigation, but they immediately reduce export opportunities for third countries that would otherwise have sold the product on the world market. Britain, for example, was absolutely not in favour of Germany paying its reparations to Italy in coal, an important British export product.

> *There exists a rich literature about the transfer problem, in particular in the wider context of the effects on the economies of the countries involved. The level of the discussion was effectively set by the famous Keynes – Ohlin – Rueff debate in 1929 (The Economic Journal, 1929, Vol. 39, pp. 1-7, 172-182, 388-408). A recent analysis and discussion points is given in Brakman & Van Marrewijk (2007) and references therein.*

(3) An international loan

The third component of the Dawes plan was a loan by the German government on the international capital market; it would be the most lasting element of the Dawes plan. The loan would guarantee that Germany could pay its first few annuities in foreign currency, because the loan was issued in New York and London, in dollars and pounds, respectively. A transfer problem did not exist. The terms of the loan were very favourable (for the investor, to be sure; not for Germany); the interest rate was 7% and it was issued at a large discount, the price being set at 92. The loan would mature in 1949 (after 25 years) and the issuing consortium lead by *J.P. Morgan & Co.* had stipulated that German customs and excise duties were collateral to the loan. Together, these conditions made the Young loan undoubtedly one of the most attractive 'after-war' loans in modern history: the effective yield was no less than 7.7% and the amount of $ 220 million (800 million *marks*) was easily raised. Half of the amount subscribed to the Dawes loan was by American investors; a quarter was British (illustration 12.6).[71] One last subtle point however had to be arranged: investors wanted to be absolutely sure that they would get their money back. In the Treaty of Versailles, reparations had been given absolute priority above all German external payments. The Dawes plan, therefore, repealed this condition.[72] It was the first step in shifting reparations from an uncomfortable arrangement between governments towards the more familiar situation of a country borrowing from private investors.[a]

---

a   One might observe the belated similarity with the French reparations in 1871 (page 32).

Dawes and Young bonds (Illustration 12.5)

Source: author's collection.

The success of the Dawes loan boosted confidence in the international financial system. Germany not only resumed its reparation payments, it also restored international confidence in its credit position; as a consequence new credits became available. Although this initially enhanced international confidence, it had a drawback. It initiated an international circuit of (mostly short-term) capital flowing from one country to the other that would dominate the rest of the 1920s. Foreign investors lent money not only to German industry and the government, but also to German regions, communities and public utilities.[73] The largest overall creditors were American investors, but in commercial business credits, Dutch investors were predominant.[74] Part of the money was really invested in the German economy (or 'wasted' in local infrastructure and social welfare projects[75]), but another part was used at least indirectly for paying reparations to France, Britain, Italy, Belgium and a few other claimants. Those countries, in their turn, could use the money to repay part of their debts to the United States and some mutual debts. This closed the circle and there is some truth in it when it is referred to as American reparations to Germany.[76] Evidently, it was not a sustainable solution.

Private investors in many countries subscribed to the international loans in 1924 and 1930, by which Germany paid part of its reparations (Illustration 12.6)

| | sums subscribed, rounded | | | |
| | Dawes, 1924 | | Young, 1930 | |
country of subscription	$ million	share	$ million	share
United States	110	50%	100	28%
Britain	55	24%	60	16%
France	15	6%	100	28%
Netherlands	10	5%	30	8%
Sweden	5	3%	30	8%
Switzerland	15	6%	20	5%
Belgium	5	3%	5	1%
Italy	5	2%	5	2%
Germany	-	-	10	2%
Total *)	220	100%	350	100%
Net proceeds	800 million *marks*		1,270 million *marks*	

*   Due to rounding, the amounts in units of 5 and percentages in integers, their sum is not necessarily equal to the 'Total' row.

Source: The Economist, BIS.[77]

The carrousel was to turn for several years. In 1928 the engine started sputtering in the beginning of the wave of speculation on Wall Street, and finally in 1929 in the crash of the stock exchange it failed completely. Short-term American loans that had always been rolled over without questioning suddenly were called back on maturity.[a] Up to 1929 the loans had contributed to Germany meeting the reparations requirements according to the Dawes scheme: an amount of almost 7.5 billion *marks* during the period 1924-1929.[78] Thus, the major part of the payments had not been done with money earned but with money borrowed.

a   Already in 1928, interest rates on brokers' loans to speculators became much more attractive in New York than loans to municipalities in Germany, see for example **Galbraith** (1961), p. 49.

1928 was also the year that the Dawes plan wore out. After all, it was meant as a temporary solution to end the Ruhr occupation and the impractical London scheme. Nobody had really been happy with it. The Germans the least, for they still had to pay year after year, without any glimpse of an end. Moreover, they lived under the tutelage of the *Transfer Committee*. The *Reichsbank* was under supervision of foreigners and the *Agent General* of the *Reparations Commission* and president of the *Transfer Committee*; the American Seymour Parker Gilbert was effectively a viceroy of Germany.[79] Neither were the French content. Whereas they had presided over the mighty *Reparations Commission* (with a double vote for the president!), they were now just one of the members of the American-dominated *Transfer Committee*. For them, the Dawes plan meant the end of the Ruhr occupation, thus giving up political power. For the British, it became clear that the Americans had taken over financial leadership in Europe, or at least on the continent. The only party that could be satisfied, at least for the time being, were the American bankers, who had placed another prestigious loan in the financial market, and who could arrange many other credits in its slipstream.

The Young plan
The next step in the reduction of the German reparations came five years after the Dawes plan: the Young plan of 1929. The new plan met the generally felt need for a 'final liquidation of the war'.[80] The arrangement was to be prepared by an expert group, this time also comprising Germany. It was essentially an American plan, although the United States itself would participate only marginally.

In comparison with the old Dawes plan, the new Young plan showed three essential differences: (1) a total amount to be paid, not just annuities, (2) a link with the inter-ally debts and (3) transfer became a German responsibility.[81] Furthermore, one new institution, the *Bank for International Settlements* (BIS) replaced the variety of committees. One element was common to the Dawes and Young plans: an international loan to provide Germany with foreign currency for the first few years.

(1) *The annuities and the total amount to be paid*
According to the now familiar method, the annuity was split into two parts.[82] The first, 'unconditional' part would be a fixed amount of 675

million *marks* annually to be paid over 37 years, until 1966.[83] The other part, called 'conditional', was flexible up to a certain degree. Although the scheme mentioned explicit amounts, Germany was permitted to postpone payments by one or two years. This part anticipated a situation of negative economic developments that would prevent Germany from paying in foreign currency without jeopardising the exchange rate of the *mark*. This implied dependence on economic development as well as an assessment of it. The unconditional and conditional parts taken together were less than the former annuity of 2.5 billion *marks* of the Dawes scheme; on average, taken over 37 years, the reduction was 18%.[84] Thus, Germany had achieved another reduction, apart from the new international loan.

(2) *The link with the inter-ally debts*

For the present-day observer, the link between the Young plan and the inter-ally debts agreements shows as an ingenious piece of bookkeeping tinkering under political boundary conditions. It was a double link: in maturity dates and in annuities (see the box, below). The scheme reduced the value of the German debt to 34 billion *marks*, as compared to the original value of 50 billion *marks* of 1919 (the realistic value, not the fancy 132 billion *marks*, evidently).[85] Taking into consideration what already had been paid, this meant a reduction in value of about 15%-20%.[86]

The Young plan: reparations and inter-ally debts: tightly linked but formally separated

The annuities of the reparations payments in the Young scheme were to be paid 59 years, exactly equal to the maximum period of the inter-ally debts. After 37 years of unconditional payments, another 22 years would follow, not specifically called conditional or unconditional. When all payments on inter-ally loans had passed, ultimately in 1988, all reparations would also terminate. This was the link in time span, but there was more.

The amounts of the reparation annuities in the last period of 22 years were exactly equal to the annuities of the inter-ally debts schemes. This implied that in these years, at that time still in the remote future, only net

---

flows of money would remain, while among the allies only net mutual settlements were left over. Finally, the level of the conditional part was carefully fine-tuned to guarantee a surplus over the inter-ally debts; thus the unconditional part would always be available, irrespective of possible German arrears in the conditional part.[87]

This intricate scheme linked the implementation of the reparation payments to the agreements on inter-ally debts, although there was no formal politically agreed relationship; the only formal connection concerned the hypothetical situation that if inter-ally debts were reduced (read: if the United States cancelled part of its claims) reparation payments would also be reduced, according to a specified scheme. This connection was laid down in a separate 'concurrent memorandum'.[88] The formal separation between the two issues even went so far that the United States did not participate in the Young agreement, as is had always denied the relationship. In December 1929 the US government concluded a separate agreement with Germany, analogous to those with the allied debtor countries. But – oh wonder! – the annuities and the time scale of this agreement miraculously fitted into the Young scheme.[89]

(3) *Germany becomes responsible for transfer*

In the Young plan, it was Germany's responsibility to deliver the reparations payments in foreign currency. The *Transfer Committee* and the function of *Agent General* were abolished and the *Reichsbank* was released from its external supervisors. In other words, Germany was considered sufficiently full-grown to receive its full financial autonomy. A new international loan would give it a start to continue reparation payments. This loan was issued in 1930, simultaneously in New York, London and some other European capitals, in local currencies. The total sum was $ 350 million (1.3 billion *marks*), larger than the Dawes loan and at a lower interest (5.5%), adapted to the meanwhile decreased international interest rate. Nevertheless and possibly inspired by its rather low price (it was issued at 90), the loan was fully subscribed, in Germany even three times oversubscribed.[90] In particular investors in Germany's business partners and former neutral countries such as the Netherlands and Sweden subscribed to the Young loan. In contrast to the Dawes loan, American and British investors were much more reserved (illustration 12.6).[91] This reflects a trend: after the Wall Street crash, Anglo-Saxon investors appeared less interested in continental Europe.

A novelty in the Young plan was the establishment of the *Bank for International Settlements* (BIS), with its seat in (neutral) Swiss Basel.[a] The underlying idea was, that settlement of reparations should be removed from the political domain and trusted to an independent financial institution. The BIS would take over the duties of the *Reparations Commission*, which was formally still operational under the Treaty of Versailles. Furthermore, it would administer the Dawes and Young loans, acting as a trustee for the creditor countries vis-à-vis Germany. The BIS soon extended its activities as a real supranational banking institution, acting as a bank for central banks and an international platform for financial consultations.[92] Within one year, all European central banks were shareholders of the BIS. The American FED was represented only indirectly, another point where the United States did not participate on equal footing in the Young plan.

The Young plan itself was formally and officially settled at a meeting pretentiously named *Conference on the Final Liquidation of the War*, that took place in two rounds in The Hague, Netherlands.[93] The first session was in August 1929, the final one in January 1930.[94] Just four months separated these two dates, four months, however in which the world and its economic perspectives had changed dramatically. Two events made that the settlement of neither reparations, nor inter-ally debts could be maintained in the way they had been arranged by the autumn of 1929.

---

a   The seat should be in one of the former neutral countries. Amsterdam was regarded as too much an outpost for German bankers, while France lobbied for francophone Brussels. The outcome was Basel, where the BIS is active up to the present day. For a history of the alleged independence of the BIS of political influence during its first decades, see **LeBor** (2013) and for the discussion on the seat **Houwink ten Cate** (1989), pp. 118, 135, 136.

Successive reparation schemes became more and more specific, while the amounts decreased (Illustration 12.7)

	London scheme	Dawes plan	Young plan
initial year	1921	1924	1929
total sum of reparations	132 billion *gold marks*, of which 50 billion *gold marks* considered seriously	undetermined (formally: London scheme)	35 billion *reichsmarks*
to be paid annually (annuity)	3 billion *gold marks*	increasing, from 1 up to 2.5 billion *gold marks*, to be reached in 1929	varying around an average of 2.0 billion *reichsmarks*; at most 2.35 billion *reichsmarks*
duration of payments	undetermined	undetermined	59 years
transfer-mechanism	undetermined	responsibility of Transfer Committee; account at the *Reichsbank*	responsibility of Germany; account at the BIS
relation to inter-ally debts	none	none	no formal relation, but fully synchronised in annuities and duration
international loan	none	German External ('Dawes') Loan	International ('Young') Loan
- amount		800 billion *marks*	1,270 million *marks*
- interest rate		7%	5.5%
- term		25 years (until 1949)	35 years (until 1965)
miscellaneous			BIS established (1930)

The Drama of inter-ally debts and the Tragedy of Reparations, a shared Act III: postponement & cancellation

The first event shook the financial world. In the months between August 1929 and January, the New York Stock exchange crashed. Whereas the *Dow Jones Industrial Index* peaked in the week after the first session of The Hague Conference, reaching an all time high of 381, in the beginning of January 1930 it had fallen to 244; one third of the stock market value was lost within three months.[95] It was largely speculative paper value that had evaporated, but those affected felt it as a real loss, and it would not miss its effect in the financial and soon in the economic world.[a] Short-term credits stopped being rolled over and the merry-go-round of international capital flows halted.

---

a   This was only the beginning. One year later, the index would be halved to less than 170; in the summer of 1932 it bottomed at 41, indicating that almost 90% of the (largely speculative) stock market value had evaporated since the peak. We mention in passing that it is a myth that the real speculative boom before the crash took place in 1929; careful statistical analysis shows that it happened in 1928, **Gumbel** (1954), pp. 45-46.

Exhausted politicians in the early morning hours at the Hague Confe-
rence on the Young plan, January 1930 (Illustration 12.8)

From left to right: Louis Loucheur (France, Labour minister), André Tardieu (France, Prime
Minister), Julius Curtius (Germany, Foreign minister), Henri Chéron (France, Finance
minister).[96]

Source: candid photograph by Erich Salomon © Reproduced by permission of the National
Gallery of Victoria, Melbourne.

Yet, confidence did not crash immediately, but with a time lag. The
Young loan was not unsuccessful when it was issued in the summer
of 1930; at that time feelings were that the crisis might be grave, but
not catastrophic. Spreading of the crisis from the financial sector to
the rest of the economy, however, led to a collapse of production, mass
unemployment and a corresponding loss of purchasing power among
the population worldwide. The capacity to pay rapidly broke down in all
countries, Germany, the former allies and neutral countries alike.

A second ominous event happened in Germany in the period August
1929 – January 1930, between the two sessions of The Hague Conference.
This time, it was political. All countries expected that Germany would
accept the Young plan, perhaps with some muttering. After all, it had

quite a few positive elements: France would evacuate the Rhineland five years earlier than agreed in the Treaty of Versailles and the tutelage of the *Reichsbank* was terminated; furthermore Germany had once more gained some time with its successful procrastination strategy that might bring further reductions in the future. Indeed, the politicians in the German *Reichstag* would finally approve the results of The Hague Conference, which included the Young plan, in March 1930; it was a clear majority of 265 against 192.[97]

The German population, however, had developed a growing aversion against the plan already in the summer of 1929. They reasoned that payments would last almost 60 years, meaning 'penal servitude up to the third generation'.[98] Moreover, simply adding all annuities resulted in an amount of 115 billion *marks*;[99] this was noteworthy approaching the original and cursed 132 *marks* of Versailles, especially if it was taken into account that during the period 1919-1929 billions of *marks* had already been paid. In such circumstances, the difference between principal and interest played no role anymore (indeed, the Treaty of Versailles, the London scheme and the Dawes plan had been extremely vague in this respect). The visible reduction, hopefully expected by the Germans, appeared dissipated. Leading German politicians on the other hand were more optimistic, although they were careful not to express openly that in their view the Young plan was just an intermediate step, to be reconsidered within the next five years.[100]

In the meantime, right wing parties in Germany collected the necessary signatures for organising an official plebiscite against the Young plan. It was held on 22 December 1929 but it received less than 14% support among the electorate. The poll itself was a failure for the organisers, but it placed them unmistakably in the spotlights and in particular Adolf Hitler's Nazi party NSDAP.[101] In the elections of September 1930, the NSDAP would win 95 seats in the *Reichstag* and become the second largest party in Germany.

Conclusion

In successive steps the total sum of German reparations has been decreased and payments themselves were in arrears, in particular in the first five years. A considerable part has been paid in kind, not in cash. Around 1930 Germany had paid in cash only about 11% of the imposed reparations, by the most favourable assessment. During the second half of the twenties, a continuous influx of American capital had enabled Germany to pay. Not without a sense of truth, this flow has been called American reparations to Germany.

Part of the reparations bill had been funded through two large international loans. As the interest and principal payments on these loans had to be made to private bondholders, the very existence of these loans reflected the end of the conditions of the Treaty of Versailles. Indeed, the treaty stipulated that German payments to governments had absolute priority above all other debts. Individuals might be in a weak position against a debtor state, but in the years after Versailles they gradually increased their weight, at the expense of the governments of the receiving countries. Starting with the Dawes plan, private bondholders stood first in row to be paid.[102]

The link between reparations and inter-ally debts, denied by the United States and emphasised by all other victor countries, had only complicated the solution of both. It needed a long series of diplomatic conferences to reduce them. There is certainly some truth in the word of the British historian A.J.P. Taylor that 'the only economic effect of reparations was to give employment to a large number of bookkeepers'.[103] This however is only half of the truth, since it can easily be extended to the inter-ally debts; moreover, business was not restricted to financial experts, but also comprised French, Swiss and Dutch hotels and restaurants, and not to mention American bankers.

Looking back at the decade of debt settlements, one must conclude that the programme Keynes had proposed as early as 1920 had been largely realised.[104] These points of action were (1) revision of the Treaty of Versailles; (2) settlement of the inter-ally debts; (3) an international loan and the reform of the currency. The second action would find its conclusion – though not its solution – in the 1930s. A forth and final point of the Keynes programme concerned the relations of Central Europe to Russia. This would require at least another 60 years to be settled, that is until the fall of the Berlin wall. But even today this remains an unresolved question as developments in Ukraine show.

A short chronology of events in international debt reduction after the First World War, part I: 1918-1930 (Illustration 12.9)

		inter-ally debts	reparations	political/military
1918	11 Nov.			Armistice
1919	28 June			Treaty of Versailles
1920	28 Sept.	last advances by United States to France		
1921	5 May		London Conference; total amount fixed and arrangements for German payments	
	2 July			US president Harding declared end of the war
1922	18 April	start of the activities of the US World War Foreign Debt Commission		
1923	11, 13 January		Germany declared in default on reparations	occupation of the Ruhr region by France and Belgium (until August 1925)
	1st May	US concluded first foreign debt settlement (with Finland)		
1924	9 April		Dawes scheme	
	15 Oct.		Dawes loan issued	
1925	19 October	first European debt settlement: Britain with Rumania		
1926	29 April	debt settlement US-France signed		
1929	7 June		Young scheme	
	20, 26 July	debt settlement US-France ratified by French parliament		
1929 - 1930	August, January		The Hague Conference on the Final Liquidation of the War	
			Austrian reparations cancelled	
1930	26, 27 Feb.		BIS established	
	12 June		Young loan issued	
	30 June			last allied occupation troops leave Germany (Rhineland region)

Table to be continued on page 251 for 1930 and later years.

13

The Financial Armistice of 1931

'We were responsible for their having to hold the line, and we advanced the money which made it possible for them to hold it. But I believe part of that expense should now be borne by the United States'
John J. Pershing, 1924[a]

The impact of the economic crisis

1931 would be the year of truth, and indeed, it had a good start. It was the first full year of the Young Plan and Germany had transferred – through the BIS – an amount of almost 1.4 billion *reichsmarks*.[1] During the American fiscal year July 1930 – June 1931, the European allies had paid $ 235 million on principal and interest, the largest amount paid so far.[2] Even France, after five years exemption from interest payments, fully met its obligation of $ 39 million in cash. Never again would such amounts be recorded.

The Young Plan was a product of the late 1920s, when the sky was bright. In the new decade, however, the economic climate worsened month after month. In 1931 unemployment in industry had increased to 25% in the US and even to 33% in Germany.[3] Excessive borrowing, both in Europe and in the US, in the previous years inevitably invoked a crisis in the banking system. The first casualty in Europe did not fall in Germany, but in Austria. In May 1931, the major bank *Creditanstalt* was about to fail. This bank (which had been forced to merge with another feeble bank) was highly involved in almost every branch of the Austrian economy: it was too big to fall. The government initiated a rescue operation, but the very idea that the largest bank of Austria could not meet its obligations ignited a chain reaction of lost confidence in the whole European

---

a   August 1924, quoted by **Gay** (1926), p. 400. Pershing (1860-1948) was commander of the American armies in France during the First World War.

banking system. In particular in Germany, account holders and foreign creditors withdrew their money, because it was (not unjustly) assumed that the financial situation in Germany and Austria was more or less comparable.[4] From May until July 1931, German solvency fell by the day.[5] This was not only threatening the system of inter-ally payments, dependent as they were on German reparation payments, but, more importantly, it jeopardised German credits in the private financial markets, among which the Dawes and Young loans stood first in line.

Gold and foreign currency in the vault of the *Reichsbank* were rapidly exhausting, and the bank had to raise its discount rate drastically to 7% in June, the start of a rally that would end up in a discount rate of 15% at the end of July, only surpassed by the fancy rates during the 1923 hyperinflation.[6] Such high interest rates not only hampered credit supply for domestic business, worsening the already grim economic climate: unemployment in Germany rose more than in any other country and improvement was not to be expected.[7] Above all, the classical reaction of the *Reichsbank* was a signal for foreign investors that Germany was in a precarious situation and short-term credits were in danger. In June, Germany declared that reparation conditions could no longer be met. Meanwhile the country was actively trying to negotiate a standstill on private foreign loan obligations. In the summer, when it became inevitable, many creditors preferred the chance of at least a partial payment to a sure loss.[8]

Not only in Europe were banks in trouble. In the United States several smaller banks had to close in 1930 and 1931.[9] The larger banks began to fear that all credits to Germany could be lost if the country was not able to service its debts. And Germany had many short-term loans: almost 60% of the credits were to mature within three months![10] If a domino effect started, the larger banks would not be left untouched. It was Thomas Lamont, leading partner of *J.P. Morgan & Co.*, who suggested President Hoover declare a suspension on all exiting intergovernmental debts.[11] In a situation of crisis, such a bank holiday could restore calmness and trust in the market.

President Hoover announced the moratorium on 20 June 1931, just 10 days before the beginning of the new fiscal year. It was generally received with enthusiasm. Only the French showed some hesitation but more for psychological than for economic reasons: the Americans had not consulted them in advance in this unilateral step; they nevertheless agreed on 7 July.[12] The moratorium was essentially a banker's action, as it covered only the intergovernmental debts: the inter-ally debts and reparations. Government debts to *private* bondholders, among which of course the Dawes and Young loans, were excluded from the moratorium. Furthermore, the moratorium would only hold for the American fiscal year 1931/'32. Finally, Hoover explicitly declared that the intention of the moratorium was to give the European countries some relief in the economic crisis situation, but that it implied in no way that the debts would be cancelled or even reduced. Congress explicitly confirmed this in its joint resolution of 23 December 1931.[13]

In the course of 1931, the initial relief gradually turned into concern: what should be done at the end of the moratorium year, in June 1932? The Hoover moratorium painfully illustrates the familiar saying that if someone borrows $ 100.000 from a bank, he (or she) has a potential problem, but if the bank has granted someone a credit of $ 100 million, the bank itself might face a serious problem. Indeed, the American government obviously took the largest burden by refraining from the $ 250 million (mainly consisting of interest) that it would have received in the current year. At that time, this was a huge amount, as it consisted of a non-negligible 13% of the federal budget.[14] (Apart from that, American banks and private creditors had supplied loans to German public and private debtors to the amount of $ 2.4 billion; their exposure to a German default was serious indeed.[15])

Meanwhile, the international economic and financial situation declined sharply, not only in Germany. In September 1931, Britain was forced to leave the Gold Standard; a range of other countries followed. The depreciation of Sterling increased the next instalment to the United States, as measured in pounds, by not less than a third.[16] The world realised that not only Germany could fail, but even the most reliable link in the international financial chain, Britain, was likely to go on default. Something had to be done.

The Lausanne conference
All developments obviously pointed in the same direction: from debt suspension to debt restructuring. Precisely this was concluded at the

conference in the Swiss city of Lausanne in the agreeable environment of Lake Geneva in the summer of 1932. In fact, the Lausanne settlement merely confirmed what had been practice in the current year. Again, it was Germany that attained the best part of it. Germany was obliged to pay a single lump sum of 3 billion *reichsmarks* to satisfy all remaining reparation debts. However, even this largely reduced amount was not to be paid immediately and in cash; it was to be deposited in bonds at the BIS in Basle (which in fact highly resembled the 'C'-bonds of the London agreement of 1921). The bonds, bearing an interest of 5%, would be kept in the vault of the BIS for three years, only to be sold on the market if conditions were favourable. If the BIS was unable to sell the bonds, the unsold part would automatically be cancelled after 15 years – and so it happened.[17]

The Lausanne settlement effectively put an end to German reparations on 9 July 1932. This was three weeks before 31 July when Hitler's Nazi party won the general election and became the largest political party in the country, without however obtaining an absolute majority. It is a myth that the Nazis ended payments of reparations, a commonly heard statement. In fact, they had been successfully renegotiated and reduced to nil by the politicians of the Weimar Republic, the scapegoats of Hitler and his henchmen.

Nevertheless, there remained much fuel for their agitation. Although payments to foreign governments had stopped, obligations on the private capital market were still alive, and among them the Dawes and Young loans were the most obvious ones. Economically, this was a much more delicate subject, even for the Nazis. In contrast to the reparations, a default on these *private* loans would immediately affect the fragile reputation of Germany's solvency and hence the possibility to call upon the international capital market.

The Dawes and Young loans were only a small part of the total amount of Germany's debts; for the Nazi government, however, they had a special meaning since they were – not only emotionally – connected with the reparations, the humiliation of Versailles. They could be presented as the continuation and inheritance of the reparations, although they were quantitatively only 4% of them: 2 billion *marks* as the principal of the Dawes and Young loans together against the original 50 billion *marks* on reparations. Payments on the Dawes and Young loans therefore were reduced by Hitler step-by-step, just to maintain credibility as a debtor country as long as Germany needed international financial support (see box). From 1933 on, bondholders in former neutral and allied countries received fewer and fewer payments on their bonds; since, at the same time, bond prices on the stock exchange kept falling, they lost both on their revenue and on their capital. Through this large detour and after many years, they contributed to the German funding of the Great War. It has been cynically called a kind of reparation (*'Wiedergutmachung'*) paid by the winners to the defeated.[18]

During the Second World War, Germany immediately stopped paying bondholders in countries with which it was at war. For British and French bondholders, this was as early as the summer of 1939, for American bondholders in 1941. Bondholders in neutral Switzerland received their money until the end of 1944, when even they were left out in the cold.[19] This meant a – temporary – end of payments connected to the First World War. It was not until 1953 that they would be resumed to a certain degree, as we shall see in Chapter 15.

Nazi Germany succeeded in reducing its debt obligations step by step[20]

The first step was a unilateral cancelling of the gold clause in the Young loan and the American issue of the Dawes loan. After the devaluation of the dollar (and other currencies) in 1933, Germany kept paying in nominal amounts, instead of the gold value. In the second half of 1933, redemption payments of the Young loan were suspended, only interest was paid; at that moment, the older Dawes loan was still fully serviced (apart from the gold clause).

The next step was the announcement that all payments would be suspended starting July 1934. This was too ambitious a measure: in bilateral agreements with countries where the bonds had been issued (and where bondholders were residents), arrangements were made for partial continuation of interest payments. At that moment, Germany could not yet finance its (civil and growing military) investments without international private credit. The agreements, however, were always of a temporary character and the conditions could be changed in Germany's favour at arbitrary moments. As Nazi Germany felt itself stronger and less dependent on foreign credit, bondholders had to make ever more concessions. For example, the interest rate in the British issue of the Dawes loan was reduced from 7% to 5% in 1938. Bondholders had hardly any other option than to agree (the bond price itself had already lost about 60% of its original value by mid-1938).21 It is obvious, that these bilateral arrangements completely undermined the role of the BIS as an independent trustee for the bondholders.

The Lausanne agreement was a purely European affair between Germany and the countries claiming reparations. It was not the comprehensive settlement of all war debts, including inter-ally debts. One crucial condition, present in the minds of all participants at the conference, was not settled: how to proceed if the United States kept their position and claim payments on the outstanding debts? Diplomacy constructed a solution in the form of a *gentlemen's agreement* attached to the Lausanne settlement. All inter-ally debts between the contract partners, *i.e.* the European countries involved, would be postponed until the parliaments had ratified the agreement. And they would do so provided that their own debtor positions had a 'satisfactory settlement', which meant if they were freed from American claims.[22] Given the American position this was out of the question and the ratification never took place. But German reparation payments, as well as European inter-ally debt payments stopped, never to be resumed again.

All together, Germany had paid 21.5 million *marks* over the period 1920-1931.[23] It depends on the criterion to decide which part of the total debt this amount represents. If the London scheme, 132 billion *marks*, is taken as a reference, Germany paid 16%. If the 'C'-bonds are disregarded and the more realistic reduced sum of 50 billion *marks* was the real burden, Germany would have paid 43% of it. But even these figures are hardly realistic. In the first place, this calculation completely neglects interest. If interest had been taken into account, only at most a third was paid, in fact about 11%, even in the reduced case when the total amount of 50 billion *marks* were taken as a reference.[24] In the second place, most of the debt had been paid in kind, not in cash. Only about one third of the payments were actually made in cash.[25]

The default on inter-ally debts

Thus, reparations came to a standstill in the summer of 1931. But also payments on the inter-ally debts were not seriously resumed. There was only one country that met its obligations completely after the end of the Hoover moratorium: Finland, and it would maintain this loyal attitude until the end, in 1984 (see box, page 246). Britain started to resume its payments at the expiration of the moratorium, but only in full for the first instalment of $ 100 million in the second half of 1932 (it paid in gold). The next payment was a symbolic token payment of $ 10 million, where $ 76 million was required.[26] Moreover, this amount was not paid in cash or in gold, but in silver. Payment in silver was allowed – exceptionally – by the agreement, but the signal was clear: Britain showed its good intentions as a reliable debtor, but it was unable to pay in dollars or in gold. In an explanation, the British ambassador explicitly referred to the transfer problem. The country could only pay in dollars if it had a trade surplus with the United States, but that was impossible due to American import restrictions.[27] Only once more, at the end of 1933, would Britain pay a token payment of $ 7.5 million (where $ 106 million was required), and that was the end of Britain as a trustworthy debtor in international loans. The American Congress adopted the Johnson Act forbidding new loans to foreign governments that had failed on earlier loans.[28] Although Britain eventually failed, in the meantime it had paid by far the largest part of its debts of all countries: no less than 87% of all payments that the United States received in the period 1923-1933 had been paid by the United Kingdom.[29] The country expressed that it had gone to the limits of its possibilities.[a]

---

a   **Self** (2006), p. 202. The British argument incidentally had a high pot-calling-the-kettle-black value; Britain formed a trade block of its own together with other Commonwealth countries; worldwide nineteenth century fee trade with the rest of the world had long ceased to be a policy principle.

Only Finland and Hungary paid their debts
to the United States in full

Finland deserves a special mention in the settlement of inter-ally debts. In the first place, Finland was the first country to conclude an agreement on the debts to the United States. In the second place, it was the only country that would pay to the cent its debt of $ 22 million ($ 9 million repayment on principal and $ 13 million interest) according to the original scheme agreed on 1ˢᵗ May 1923. Only during the Second World War, was there an interruption of a few years, understandingly accepted by the American government and paid afterwards with compensation for lost interest.[30] At the Hoover moratorium Finland had suspended its payments, like all other countries. But at the end of the year, it was the only country to promptly resume the payments, including the additional annuities to compensate for the loss of one-year arrears. It brought the 'brave little country' much goodwill among the American population.

After the Second World War (in fact from the end of 1943) Finland again paid in conformity with the agreements. It became a painful discrepancy with other countries that paid nothing at all (but in the meantime took permanent seats in the UN Security Council and were prominent members of the World Bank and the International Monetary Fund!). In 1949 the US Congress decided that the loyally paid amounts would in some way be designated for Finland's own benefit. The money would be paid into a fund for scientific and educational development.[31] Thanks to this fund, Finnish scientists could be trained and participate in the US scientific environment; higher education in Finland was boosted through American literature and investment in technical equipment during the 1950s and 1960s.[32] It is an intriguing question to which extend the later successes of Finnish technology (Nokia) and the renowned quality of the Finnish educational system can be traced back to this positive heritage of... the First World War.

As with most other countries, Hungary did not resume its payments after the end of the Hoover moratorium. Even in the preceding years, it had not paid in dollars, but in the then national currency pengö, referring to the transfer problem.[33] In 1937, however, Hungary suddenly resumed its payments, be it at a considerably reduced form as a token: only 1% interest on principal, no amortisation payments and temporarily for three years. Nevertheless, the American government welcomed this gesture 'with gratification' as a 'noteworthy wish and effort of the Hungarian Government to meet its obligations', but it also stated that, of course, this did not imply by any means an end of the obligation to finally meet the debt in full.[34] Just as in the case of Finland, the Second World War ended the Hungarian payments, but they were not resumed. After 1945, Hungary, in contrast to Finland, was behind the Iron Curtain, an impermeable barrier for this kind of transfers.

The early 1970s, however, brought a certain kind of détente in the relationship between the United States and Hungary. In the period 1976/'77, communist Hungary paid in one lump sum all overdue payments, to the amount of $ 3 million. In the following years the annuities were resumed according to the original scheme of 1924.[35] Just like the Finnish, who were rewarded with the education programme, the Hungarians received in exchange a recompensation with a high symbolic (and material) value. In 1978, President Jimmy Carter had the golden crown of King Stephan and other jewellery transferred to Budapest from Fort Knox, where they had been kept since the end of the Second World War.[36] The crown, dating from about the year 1000, is the symbol of Hungarian sovereignty. It seems natural to assume a link between the repayment of the old debts and the return of the treasure a year later. Establishing this link unambiguously will probably be a challenge as long as official diplomatic documents are not yet published.

By 1933, all other countries had already thrown in the towel. France and Belgium did not even keep up appearances by means of a token payment after the end of the Hoover moratorium. All together, up to 1932, European countries had paid about 7.5% of what they would have to pay in 62 years. With 50 years to go, this was the end of the payments of the inter-ally debts of the First World War, up to the present day. They 'sputtered out like a candle in the rain.'[37]

From July 1931 on, repayments of European allies on their war debts to the United States stuck at 7.5% of the agreed amount (Illustration 13.1)

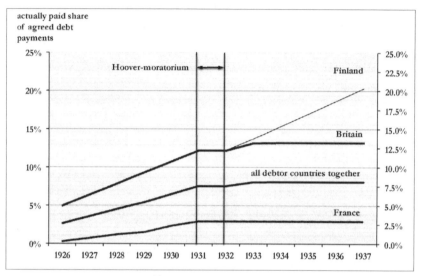

Source: **ARST**, issues 1926-1937.[38]

An estimation of the total American losses

As a consequence of the suspension of the payments by the Hoover moratorium, the American government lost $ 240 million in the fiscal year 1931/'32. This is the amount often mentioned in the literature, but it was only the beginning. In the end, the Hoover moratorium was not a suspension but an indefinite postponement. The total American loss due to this fact alone can be estimated at $ 7.6 billion, as measured in dollars of that time.[39] Looking back, this implies that the US had to write off an amount comparable to 10% of the GDP of the Hoover moratorium year.[40] This comes on top of the earlier reductions made in the period 1922-1926, when the debt settlements had been agreed (page 218 ff.). When both reductions are taken together (that is: if all *real payments* are compared to the *original debts* in 1922), the European allies have paid back only 12% of their debts and the American losses increase to $ 10.5 billion (in dollars of the year 1922!).[41]

Conclusion and reflection

The enormous debts between countries, built up as a consequence of the First World War, have been paid back in very small part. The economic crisis of the 1930s meant the end of money transfer, both for inter-ally payments (to the United States and inter-European) and for German reparations. As a result of the Hoover moratorium, only private bond-holders remained as serious creditors. And even they would not get their money back in full, as will be seen in the next chapters.

The American government was left with a huge unpaid bill. Already in the early 1920s, the loans from the war period itself had been largely written off. For the post-war loans for relief and reconstruction, debt settlement schemes were agreed, which were *de facto* cancelled with the Hoover moratorium. These loans to the allies, however, had been paid from the revenues of the *Liberty* and *Victory Loans*, and the American government was obliged to pay them back to the (American) bond-holders from the federal budget, that is to say, by tax income. So finally, about 85% to 90% of this bill ended up with the American taxpayer.

Considerable differences can be distinguished between the payment attitudes of the countries involved. It is easier to illustrate this assertion with examples than to support it with scientific facts. Just as in the case of German reparations, it is difficult to separate the economic impossibility to pay, from the political purpose of not willing to pay.[42]

In its ethics of repayment, Britain went much further than all other countries (except Finland). The British had been brought up in the tradition that debts must be paid; otherwise, the very base for trust would vanish and trade would become impossible. It is no surprise that Britain paid the major part of the money that the Americans received. This undoubtedly had a deeper meaning than just servicing debts in a financial sense. It was a means of showing the former colony that the British Empire was solid, and superior in financial management. After leaving the Gold Standard in 1931, the token payment of 1933 and the final ending of all payments in 1934, the country had to admit bitterly that it had burdened itself with a debt too large to bear.

France, on the other hand, has continuously striven to reduce its debts and to postpone them as far as it could. All available arguments were thrown into the battle: moral, diplomatic, legal.[43] A moral argument, indeed, was the number of soldiers fallen on the battlefield; the country had undoubtedly made a sacrifice that was beyond expression in monetary terms. Of all large western countries, in relative terms France counted the largest percentage of men killed and the United States the least.[a] To what extent this may count as an argument for not paying voluntary agreed debts, is a question of politics and morality. After all, America was the least responsible for this 'European' war. Furthermore, there is the remarkable detail of the French levying import duties on American equipment landed in French harbours (page 205). It is difficult not to see this as a trick to reduce another part of the debt. Also, it should be remembered that France was second to last to arrange an agreement with the United States for debt settlements and subsequently it took another three years for the French Parliament to ratify it. Finally, France immediately seized the opportunity of the Hoover moratorium to stop once and for all the payments on the debts. And the country got away with it.[b]

It is more difficult to make a general statement about the German attitude towards debts, because of the instability of the country in the interwar period. Nevertheless, some conjectures can be made. Unmistakable is the German feeling that the country had not been done justice. Both for the government and the population, this formed a convincing argument to be reluctant in servicing debts, without any recourse to economic and financial restrictions. Within this state of mind – and in complete contrast to the British tradition – denying a moral obligation exculpates one from paying a financial debt. After all, in the German language both 'debt' and 'guilt' are expressed by the same word *Schuld*.[44] This might – subconsciously or not – have made financial debts more difficult to separate from moral debts. It was only after the Second World War, when the German Federal Republic realised that the country was not only financially, but even more morally ruined, that this mental association would lead to redemption of the existing financial debts (page 274).

---

a   3.4% against 0.1% as a percentage of their population, **Broadberry & Harrison** (2005), p. 27.

b   This is consistent with France's earlier attitude in the negotiations about the Anglo-French loan in 1915: whereas the British delegation was eager to arrive at a low interest rate, the French were more interested in borrowing a huge amount. Costs had not their highest priority, **Wormell** (2000), p. 168, **Nouailhat** (1979), p. 279.

Timetable of developments in the debt problem after the Hoover moratorium until the Second World War (Illustration 13.2)

		inter-ally debts	reparations	political/military
1931	20 June	Hoover Moratorium		
	23 December	United States Congress against reduction or cancellation of debts		
1932	June & July		Lausanne Conference: *de facto* end of reparation payments	
	after 1st July	6 countries discontinue payments		
1933	30 January			Adolf Hitler German Chancellor
	4 March			Franklin D. Roosevelt US President
	after 1st July	another 6 countries pay only a token payment or nothing at all		
1934	after 1st January	only Finland continues payments		
	and later years	Hungary temporarily resumes payments (1937)	Nazi Germany reduces payments on Dawes- en Young loans	

14

Clearing domestic debris

'Here is the gratitude of a nation to those who were pressed and forced during the war to give up their gold for the predatory war of the German imperialists by every means of moral pressure, and who are now being robbed by those self-same big capitalists'
Karl Korsch, 1925[a]

While the settlement of inter-ally debts and reparations dominated the international scene, domestic debt servicing remained a subject for violent discussions for national politicians. It was an issue in all nations, except in those countries that had ceased to exist and where new leaders simply ignored the problem: Tsarist Russia, the Ottoman Empire and, partially, Austria-Hungary.[1] The successors took no responsibility at all for domestic debts. Other countries, with sufficient continuity of government, could still make different choices in dealing with the problem.[2] In finding their way, governments appeared to be led more by cultural, historic and political circumstances than by financial or economic reasoning. In that respect, there was not so much difference between the post-war period and wartime itself. Indeed, governments had the same menu to choose from as during the war itself: levy taxes, issue a loan or create money. Apart from that, they had the possibility of flatly repudiating the debt, for example by introducing a new currency. Of course, decent countries do not resort to such measures, or only tacitly by creating (hyper) inflation...

---

a   Karl Korsch (1886-1961), deputy of de *Kommunistische Partei Deutschlands* (KPD) in the *Reichstag*, when voting on the Act on redeeming public debts (see page 264), 16 July 1925, **RT** 386, p. 3219, *'Hier handelt es sich um den Dank des Vaterlandes an die, die im Kriege mit allen Mitteln des moralischen Drucks gepreßt und gezwungen wurden, ihr Gold für den Raubkrieg der deutschen Imperialisten herzugeben, und die jetzt von diesen gleichen imperialistischen Großkapitalisten ausgeraubt werden [und für sie auch noch die Kosten des verlorenen Krieges allein tragen müssen]'* (and who have to bear exclusively the cost of the lost for them).

Britain: financial solidity above all

The predominant concern of the British government was to restore and maintain the pre-war financial solidity of the country; servicing the debt by paying interest and principal was the method to achieve this.[3] By the time the war was over, the country was overloaded with debts. It had not only financed its own war efforts, but also supplied European allies with credit. The national debt had multiplied tenfold in the period 1914-1919: from £ 700 million to almost £ 7,500 million. This was 150% if expressed as a percentage of one year's GDP (1918).[4] In modern ratings this would be called a junk state. During the war, the national debt had grown fastest of all countries involved and it was also by far the largest of all.[5] Moreover, almost 20% of this enormous debt was held in foreign currency, in particular American dollars. This was in great contrast to the pre-war period; since time immemorial, Britain had been free from debts overseas. This splendid situation had to be restored by all possible means, in order for the country to recapture its unique position in the financial world.

During the First World War Britain's public debt increased more than in any other recent war (Illustration 14.1)

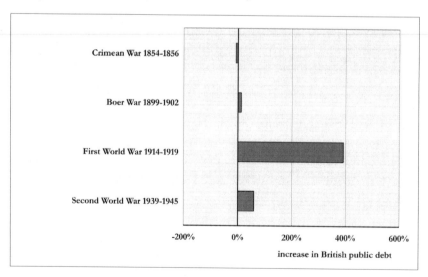

Source: author's calculations based on BOE3C.[6]

Servicing the debt laid a heavy burden on the British budget. To get an impression of the way in which the war had disrupted the treasury, one should realise that in 1920 interest payments alone exceeded the total pre-war budget.[7] Admittedly, this was in nominal terms, including inflation, but this hardly lessened the government's concern. And indeed, the debts were outweighed by at least the same amount of claims abroad, but this accounting truth did not automatically imply real relief. Proceeds from these claims were not guaranteed and could not be used beforehand for redemption of Britain's own debts. Russian repayments were not to be expected anyway and France made its payments conditional on receiving sufficient German reparations. Britain had a serious problem indeed, and the most urgent issues to be tackled at home were the huge short-term debt and the large long-term loan of 1917 with its high 5% interest rate.

Reducing the short-term domestic debt had the highest priority, so it received most attention in the period 1920-1922. This was, however, much easier said than done, because other debts were also crying out for redemption. Solidity in the financial arena required that the British punctually serviced their part of the Anglo-French loan, expiring October 1920. The American bankers simply expected their $ 250 million back. This commitment alone would need 5% of the budget and there were many others duties to be fulfilled.[8] Without additional measures, the government would face many years of deficits and consequently a loss of solvency.

British politicians therefore opted for a reduction of the national debt by a primary budget surplus, that is, apart from the high debts burden. This method required a rigid tax policy. Consequently, in the budget proposal for 1920/'21, taxes on cars, alcoholic beverages and tobacco were increased, although the war was over. In the meantime, the government tempted holders of short-term treasury bills to convert these into long-term bonds at a lower interest rate. This policy was not very successful, because the government had little to offer. Apart from political uncertainty about German reparations and Irish independence, to name a few, it was in particular the high interest rate in the market that prevented investors from responding to the government's wishes. Early in 1920, interest rates were at 6% and even increasing during the year to 7%.[9] This was much more attractive for an investor than long-term government bonds. It would take almost two years, until 1921, for interest rates to decline, and in the summer of 1922 they had reached the pre-war level of 3%. From that moment on, short-term debts could be consolidated more easily into long-term debt.[10]

When the interest rate had fallen to 'normal' proportions, the most serious problem of the Chancellor of the Exchequer was the millstone of the 1917 war loan, with its huge amount of £ 2 billion and an interest rate of no less than 5%, to be paid for many decades to come. Servicing this debt only, would require the unimaginable share of 14% of the budget, year after year.[a] This was more than just a financial challenge; it was a political problem. It implied a transfer of wealth from all taxpayers to the relatively well-to-do bondholders. In a way, this had been all in the game and it was the inevitable consequence of financing the war by borrowing. It became really inconvenient, however, when the roaring twenties were over with the Great Depression starting in 1929/'30. Everyone in British society had to make sacrifices, be it in the form of lower wages, higher taxes of even unemployment. Many people in the United Kingdom asked themselves, and openly, why those bondholders, who received a comfortable 5% while prices were falling, should be spared. And why was it necessary to send taxpayers' money abroad to foreign bondholders? This latter argument was somewhat exaggerated, as they probably formed less than a quarter of all bondholders, but nevertheless, it could be used as political pressure.

The opportunity to convert the loan had in fact existed since June 1929. In 1917 when the loan had been issued, one of the conditions, wisely anticipating developments, stated that the loan could be redeemed at par on or after 1ˢᵗ June 1929 after three calendar months' notice.[11] From the beginning of 1931, interest rates had sufficiently fallen, but the government hesitated to initiate the operation. It was risky indeed, since it came down to refinancing no less than one third of the whole national debt, and asking investors to accept substantially worse conditions. And circumstances were unfavourable. After all, 1931 was the year of the banking crisis in Germany, the Hoover moratorium and finally Britain

---

a   This and other background information about the conversion have been derived from **Wormell** (2000), p. 589 ff. As a reference, one must realise that at the moment (2016) interest payments are 5% and 7% of the British and United States budget, respectively, **UKBUD** 2016, p. 6 and **USBUD** 2016 Historical Tables, Table 3.1. It should be noted in passing that interest payments for the United States are estimated to rise above the level of 10% in 2019, ibid.

would be off gold.[12] The announcement to convert the 1917 war loan at the same time as abandoning the Gold Standard would rightly have been understood as a declaration of bankruptcy.

The new year 1932 was considered more appropriate. After three years of recession, the bank rate continued to fall and on 30 June, the Bank of England decided to fix it as low as 2%.[13] This was not just a pre-war level, it was outright a nineteenth century interest rate, and even then exceptionally low.[14] It was the moment for the government to act. It decided to refinance the 1917 loan at 3.5%, well above the market rate. A difference between 5% and 3.5% seems little, but for bondholders, it would mean an immediate loss of 30% of their annual revenue. The government therefore, would have to apply much persuasion to seduce bondholders to convert their securities voluntarily. It followed the same strategy as during the war, calling on patriotism to relieve the country from this heavy burden. Those who responded quickly would receive a one-off bonus of 1%, but those who did not respond to the call were assumed to have agreed with the conversion. The governor of the Bank of England described the procedure as 'voluntary-forced'.[15] The trick worked, thanks to heavy pressure on the banks to participate with their own bonds of the loan. With a sigh of relief, Chancellor Arthur Neville Chamberlain could declare in December 1932 that the conversion had been successful. It would save the government each year £ 42 million of interest payments.[16] Thus, on the 1st of December 1932, the third war loan of Bonar Law, dating from 1917, had been converted into what has been known since as the 3.5% War Loan.[17] As a perpetual loan, it had no definite expiration date and indeed it has been traded for over 80 years on the stock exchanges in London, and later in Frankfurt (see page 281). For the bondholders the conversion meant a financial loss and a delayed contribution to the funding of the Great War, only compensated by a good feeling of patriotism. For the UK as a nation, it was not a formal bankruptcy, but only thanks to the reaction of the bondholders. It was true, that the government had the right to redeem the loan before maturity, but it simply did not have the money to do so. Only by forcing the bondholders to convert – in fact levying them a tax – could it refinance the loan at lower conditions. It was the only time in modern history that the United Kingdom was that near a state of failure.[18]

After the fall of the coalition cabinet of Asquith in December 1916, Reginald McKenna radically retired from political life. The many remaining years of his life, he would successfully lead one of the largest and prestigious banks of the world, the (London, City &) Midland

Bank, nowadays part of the HSBC. He rejected repeated requests of Conservative Prime Ministers Bonar Law and Stanley Baldwin to become Chancellor in their cabinets (and the only time he was inclined to do it, there was no constituency vacant). The door to active politics was definitively shut, and the last liberal Chancellor had left the scene.

Yet, he would play his principal role at two decisive moments in British financial history. The first occasion was in 1925, when Winston Churchill struggled with the question of restoring the Gold Standard. As an advisor to the government, McKenna admitted with great reluctance that returning to gold would be politically inevitable, but in practice it would be 'hell'.[19] Solidity would be restored, but Stirling would be too expensive, leading to unemployment and social disturbances.

The last time McKenna took a position of principle was in 1932, at the occasion of the conversion of the 1917 war loan from 5% tot 3.5%. The Midland owned no less than £ 30 million of these bonds and conversion would mean a loss of interest of almost half a million pounds each year, a sacrifice he could not defend to the bank's shareholders. As a compromise, the Bank of England bought £ 25 million of the 1917 bonds and the Midland needed only £ 5 million to convert. Reginald McKenna had played for high stakes, as he acted in the interest of the bank and not in his personal interest. With this action he probably spoilt his last chance to receive a peerage, an honour by which so many of his former colleagues had been recognised.[20]

Reginald McKenna died in 1943; his wife Pamela, 25 years his junior, would survive him by only two months.[21]

Germany: inflation and hyperinflation

Financial solidity and a strong currency, the central theme in Britain, were not on the German agenda. What counted was he problem of how to finance the enormous deficits after the war. During the post-war years 1920-1923, government spending exceeded revenues on average by a factor of 2.5.[22] Not only regular expenditure contributed to this deficit, but also the losses on state enterprises. In particular, the national railway company, the *Reichsbahn*, laid a heavy burden on the budget. This public enterprise counted one million employees,[a] five times as many as all government officials of the whole *Reich* (apart from the local and regional levels), while the revenues were far from proportional.[23] Besides, there were the reparations, but even without those, the deficits would be enormous.[24] In fact, they amounted to less than half of the deficit, except in the year 1922.

Just as in Britain, the German government could resort to three policies: taxes, loans and creating money. It was Finance Minister Matthias Erzberger[b] who energetically introduced one tax law after the other. Among these were the first permanent income tax at national level and taxes on war profits and excessive capital gains.[25] Initially, in 1921 government revenues undoubtedly improved, but the delay in materialisation soon flattened the effect. Quickly the accelerating inflation eroded the revenues faster than the tax measures could make

---

a   From 1917 to 1919 the number of employees of the German railways had grown by 350.000 or almost 50%, **Sühl** (1988), p. 63. This cannot possibly be explained from increased transportation demand; it reflects an employment program for war veterans and excess staff in the arms industry.

b   Erzberger (1875-1921) was the man who had signed for Germany the Armistice agreement in Compiègne at 11-11-1918.

them grow. Meanwhile, tax ethics in Germany broke down after the reparations bill was presented, in particular the incomprehensible amount of 132 billion *marks*. Why should one pay taxes if all revenues would immediately be transferred into the hands of the victors? The centrum (that is, Catholic) politician Erzberger did not make friends with this policy and he became increasingly a target for attacks of the right wing Helfferich; in August 1921 he was assassinated in the Black Forest by right wing extremists. The legacy of his tax reforms is not in the revenues they generated, but in the shift of tax levy from the regional and local level to the *Reich*. In other words: it was not the German treasury that benefited from his short term in office, but German unity.[26]

Increasing state revenues did not stop with Erzberger's dead. In 1922, one of his successors, Andreas Hermes, introduced a mixed tax-loan construction, the so-called *Zwangsanleihe* (forced loan).[27] All capital owners were obliged to subscribe in a bond issue of the *Reich*, in such a way that higher wealth implied a higher share. The first three years of this 'loan' was a thinly disguised tax: the bondholders received no interest or any redemption payments at all. After these three years, the government would pay 4%, increasing to 5% in later years. It was not foreseen when the loan would mature, but undoubtedly it would take a long time.[28] Formally a loan, it was a wealth tax in practice. Initially, the total revenue was estimated at 70 billion *marks*, but inflation soon made this amount rise rapidly. A few years later, when the German financial system was completely re-established after the hyperinflation, the *Zwangsanleihe* would reveal itself as a downright tax (page 264, note a).

Neither taxes nor loans, however, under whatever names they were presented, were the most important means for financing the government deficits in Germany in the early 1920s. The approved instrument remained monetary financing: printing money, just as in the last period of the war. At ever increasing speed, the *Reichsbank* bought short-term government bills, thus inflating the economy with billions of new *marks*. The excesses are well known (see, for example, the box on page 262) and they would have been amusing, if they had not had a disastrous effect on the already unstable German economy and hence on the complete social and political system.[29]

The German inflation and hyperinflation form a much-discussed subject in a wide range of publications, both popular and academic.[a] This analysis goes far beyond the scope of this book; we leave it to the observation that the relationship between inflation, reparations and the political climate during the Weimar Republic is less straightforward than is sometimes assumed.[30] The only interest here lies in the effect it had on the large national debt that had been built up to finance the war.

Three conclusions about the German inflation appear to be uncontested. In the first place, the fact that inflation had already started well before the end of the war, even though the German financial elite denied it. It was at best ignored and in any case it was no point of concern, in contrast to Britain. In the second place it was an illusion that printing money could lighten the burden of reparations, as they were expressed in *gold marks*. This was already evident before a specific amount was known (May 1921) and in any case from that moment on. And in the third place, it is easy to see that inflation always favours debtors and disadvantages creditors, since the value of the debt automatically decreases as it is expressed in nominal values. The largest debtor in Germany in the early 1920s was undoubtedly the German Republic; consequently the government had the largest interest in inflation.

The value of the old domestic war loans decreased rapidly. The bondholders, in fact millions of Germans, saw their capital melting away week after week. Those who possessed their bonds in bearer form could try to sell them to some speculator who saw a bright future – or to keep them and wait for better times themselves. Many people, however, lacked the possibility of selling on the stock exchange, as they had their bonds registered by name. At the time of issue, this was an attractive opportunity, as it yielded a discount on the price (page 128, note a). The government indeed saved some money by not printing actual bonds by only writing a name in the register (the *Reichsschuldbuch*) and this small advantage had been given to the bondholder. In 1923, however, the advantage of the simple procedure turned into its opposite. The

---

a   It is remarkable that the vast majority of studies and theoretical papers on inflation concentrate on *macro*economic data such as development of prices, money in circulation, wages and exchange rates. They try to find relations to confirm or to refute – statistically or otherwise. Confirmation of theories with *empirical* information at the *micro*economic level, such as motivations of consumer and producer households, is scarce to say the least.

administration of the register became a serious burden, in particular for the small denominations of 100 of 500 *marks*. Although they were practically worthless, they still needed the legally required activities such as the administration of an equally worthless interest. What had started as an attraction to involve small savers now had turned into a millstone. The government decided to redeem *en bloc* all war registered bonds under 5,000 *marks* and cancel them from the *Reichsschuldbuch*.[31] For the government, this saved a lot of purposeless work; for the bondholders, it meant the replacement of a claim by another worthless piece of paper. Although it violated the law, these 900,000 (!) small bondholders were not notified individually, to save costs. In 1923 Germany, some laws were just bypassed. Bondholders were supposed to accept the action; in fact they were trapped. As some kind of compensation they received a 'bonus' in the form of 150% of the par value. The simple truth is that 150% of nothing remains nothing. The whole operation can be rightly characterized a domestic default.

Some excesses of German hyperinflation and the last years of Havenstein

Germany would not be Germany if it had not translated inflation into its legislation. A fine example is the Act on the impact of currency depreciation in tax laws, dated 15 March 1923.[32] It simply stated that the word 'hundred' should be replaced by 'thousand', although it was not very systematic: at some other place '50' should be read as '5,000'. Furthermore, it was stated that arrears in tax payments would be punished with 15% each month (without compound interest). Thus, after half a year, tax obligations would be automatically increased by 90%. It was, however, profitable for the taxpayer to wait this long as in the meantime the value had decreased to less than 10%. Together with the fine, this meant that the real burden had been reduced to one fifth, just by waiting six months! The superior German legislation was hopelessly overtaken by the developments.

It was not only legislation, in fact all authorities responsible for monetary policy failed. President of the Reichsbank was still Rudolf Havenstein. He once more deployed his talent as an organiser, which had been so successful in issuing the war loans. In a memorandum to the government dated 5 September 1923, he stated that he was fully in control; in particular he boasted on the practical aspects of money supply.[33] In order to produce the necessary amounts of banknotes, he had contracted no less than 11 large printing companies in the then occupied territories of Germany, working in shifts. The transport problem also needed his attention. Just to avoid tedious checks at the borders by the French and Belgian occupation armies, he chose for an alternative route through the Netherlands, taking extra costs for granted. In the summer of 1923, he even established an airlift via London to supply Cologne every day with billions of marks in banknotes ('operating very well'). On one occasion this went wrong, when a plane carrying 5,000 billion marks had to make an emergency landing in Belgium. The crew refused to give information about their origin and destination of the money aboard. They were arrested and only in October, in the middle of the Ruhr occupation, the diplomatic incident was appeased.

It is a personal tragedy that Havenstein did not realise that printing and shipping banknotes was not the proper solution for a failing economic, financial, fiscal and social policy.[a] Throughout the time of the hyperinflation, Havenstein was in charge of the Reichsbank, literally until the hour of his death. On 29 November 1923 he collapsed and died of a heart attack, indeed in his official residence in the building of the Reichsbank. At that moment he had already lost control over the German financial system to his successor, Hjalmar Schacht, who would be president of the Reichsbank from 1923-1930 and in the period 1933-1939.

After the registered bondholders had been tackled, it was the turn of the bonds in bearer form. On 20 November 1923, the value of the new *Rentenmark*, that was to become the new *reichsmark*, was pinned by

---

a   Havenstein kept thinking of money in terms of paper, although he had always advocated for cashless payments. If he had known that the FED and the European Central Bank could provide the economy with hundreds of billions (dollars and Euros) just by pushing the button and calling it Quantitative Easing or other fancy names, probably he would have realised that all the printing and distribution work could have been skipped.

Hjalmer Schacht at 1,000,000,000,000 old *marks*. That measure not only stopped the hyperinflation and restored confidence, but it also reduced the existing national debt to manageable proportions.[34] At that time, the outstanding debt of all war loans amounted to approximately 50 billion (old) *marks*, in nominal terms (one half of the original 100 billion *mark* bonds and treasury bills had already been redeemed or bought back).[35] Measured in new *reichsmarks*, this amount, which had been so painfully brought together during the war, represented a value of one trillionth of its value, 5 *pfennig*, an almost insulting tip when ordering a drink in a café.

It is often heard, that the bondholders lost everything; this is not true, they lost *almost everything*. This is what happened. After hyperinflation, the complete German financial system had to be rebuilt. All debts and claims, such as mortgages and insurance rights had to be reconsidered and government debts formed no exception. In the summer of 1925, the *Reichstag* passed a law called the Act on redemption of public debts.[36] It took some political deliberations, but at the end bondholders got some compensation, although it was more window-dressing than substantial. For every 1,000 (old) *marks* of bonds, they received bonds of a new issue; this new issue was to pay 125 *reichsmark*, thus enhancing the factor of one trillionth to a factor of one eighth. Redemption of these bonds, however, would take place by drawing lots, during a period of no less than 30 years. Interest would not be paid on principal, but only as a lump sum at expiration. In practice, this could mean, that a bondholder who had supported his beloved country in September 1914 with the then considerable amount of 1,000 *marks* for a war loan, might receive as late as in 1955 12.5% of his original subscription (plus a little delayed interest).[37] Up to the moment that one's lot was drawn, which would take 15 years on the average, the money was effectively lost, and almost 90% was lost anyway.[a] The big winner was the government. Undoubtedly, there were speculators who bought large blocks of bonds at bargain prices, just to take the chance of being drawn early and taking the 12.5% in 1925.[38] The majority, however, of the German middle class

---

[a] The Act on redemption of public debts incidentally settled a few other inconvenient 'details'. It declared that all circulating *Darlehenskassenscheine* could not be converted into new *reichsmarks*, which made them worthless (it should be remembered that at the end of the war one third of all currency in circulation consisted precisely of these notes). Bonds of the forced loan of 1922 were also excluded from conversion, making this so-called loan a real tax instead of a loan.

saw their wealth going up in smoke, the more so if they had been more devoted patriots.[39]

Thanks to inflation, Germany had effectively coped with its domestic debts, in fact much faster than Britain (that would take its time to 2015 to redeem the last war loan, page 282). It would be an exaggeration to declare that Britain was without social stress in the twenties and thirties. In Germany, however, the political consequences were catastrophic.

France: depreciation of the franc

Germany was an extreme example, but France also suffered from high inflation in the first half of the 1920s. It was not uncommon that prices rose by 10% or more in one year (illustration 14.2). Domestic debts (in nominal *francs*) diminished year after year, and again it was the French government that benefited most. Purchasing power of interest payments lost two thirds of its value between 1919 and 1926 – not to mention the price of the war bonds on the stock exchange. As in Germany, bondholders were hit hard in this 'euthanasia of the *rentier*' (Keynes).[40]

Inflation in France was generally high in the 1920s, often in double digits (Illustration 14.2)

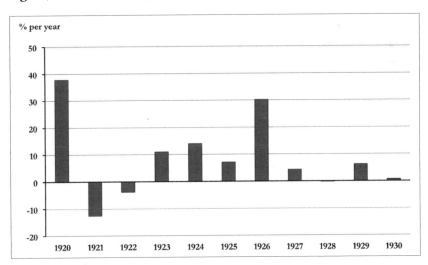

Source: INSEE.[41]

Inflation enabled the government to shift part of the burden of the debt abroad.[a] An investor in a neutral country such as Switzerland or the Netherlands who had subscribed to the last large French war loan (page 121), was to lose a great deal of his money. By 1926, the exchange rate of the French *franc* against most other currencies had fallen to 20% of its pre-war value.[42] Thus, the annual interest payments in *francs* yielded only one fifth of what a similar Swiss or Dutch loan would have brought. Moreover, the investment itself had also lost 80% of its value, as the bond price had fallen proportionally. In economic terms, this loss represents the contribution of foreign (in particular neutral) investors to the French war financing.

The background of financing by inflation in France was different from that in Germany and the differences were tax revenue, the policy of the *Banque de France* and the expected reparations from Germany. Due to retardation effects, taxes had formed a substantial source of revenue in the first few years after the war – in great contrast to the war period itself. In 1920 and 1921, for example, the war profits tax yielded five or six times as much as in the war year 1918.[43] In the meantime, after the Armistice, the French government kept appealing to the *Banque de France* to print bank notes in exchange for treasury bills. Between September 1918 and September 1920, circulation of bank notes increased by 25%, but then its growth fell sharply.[44] After the war, the *Banque de France* was less and less inclined to finance budget deficits by monetary financing, although it had from time to time to give in to the financial demands of the government.[45]

When the war profits tax source dried up, new and additional taxes should have replaced it. In France, in the early 1920s, this kind of unpopular measure was politically out of the question. The more so, when in May 1921 the German reparations bill had been presented, of which France was to receive at least 50%. All hopes were focussed on the flood of gold from Germany that would fill all budget deficits. In Germany, reparations were used as an argument against taxes since the revenue would just have to be sent abroad. In France, on the other hand, it was felt that domestic tax increase would be a signal to Germany, that the

---

a   Of course, this was not restricted to France. Germany also profitably made use of it (page 94, note b).

expectation of receiving reparations was low, in particular because they could be regarded as unrealistically high.[46] Any tax increase therefore was avoided, apart from the fact that is was unpopular in France anyway.

From 1923 on, it gradually became evident in France and among the allies, that neither reparations nor the Ruhr occupation would bring miracles. Meanwhile, political controversies blocked every kind of reform. Right and left alternated permanently on the political scene. In the period 1920-1926, the average term of a French government was less than six months, and no less than 10 finance ministers appeared (and disappeared). Both parliament and government preferred inflation to tax increase and they exerted pressure on the *Banque de France* and thus, after a few years of relative stability, in 1924 the circulation of bank notes grew again.[47]

The combination of political instability, expanding inflation and doubts about reparations made the country vulnerable to the financial markets, whether rightly or wrongly. In 1925, the *franc* lost another third of its value against the dollar. New calls on the *Banque de France* to print banknotes brought France in serious danger of high inflation. Finally in 1926, after a change of government, the *franc* stabilised at 20% of the pre-war value (illustration 14.3).[48]

Immediately after the war, the French franc depreciated quickly; subsequently in the period 1920-1920 the exchange rate fell once more with over 50% (Illustration 14.3)

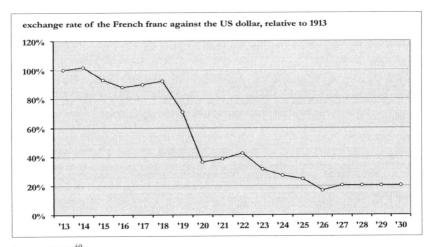

exchange rate of the French franc against the US dollar, relative to 1913

Source: BMS.[49]

Needless to say that the depreciation of the *franc* was by no means comparable to that of the German *mark* in the same period; it was, however, exceptional for a currency of a modern and developed economy. It was very inconvenient for the holders of French government securities, who apparently had forgotten the lesson of the bad *assignats* issued during the French Revolution.[50] On the other hand, it turned out very profitable for foreigners, in particular American citizens who could afford to buy real estate in France for a bargain price.[51] For the French government, the depreciation of the *franc* had two sides. On the one hand, together with the inflation, it reduced the domestic debt. On the other hand, however, it worked out counterproductively for French debts to the United States and Britain, denoted in dollars and pounds, respectively, as they became more and more expensive. This explains to a certain degree the stubborn efforts of France to elude these debts or at least to postpone them until other countries' debts became just as unbearable (Chapters 12 and 13).

United States: roaring twenties and gold clauses declared void

After the war, the United States was free from foreign public debts.[a] The only government liabilities due to the war were the payments on principal and interest of the four large *Liberty Loans* and the 1919 *Victory Liberty Loan* of 1919; together they represented an amount originally exceeding $ 21 billion.[52] The US government expeditiously tackled the redemption of the loans, thanks to a sinking fund established during the war. In contrast to (continental) Europe, the maxim was: 'the war debt should be paid, not perpetuated, and the time to pay it is as soon as possible after the end of the war.'[53] Firstly, the focus was on short-term debts; they were partly redeemed and partly consolidated into long term bonds.[54] During the 1920s, the American government paid off the loans with such impressive speed (at a rate of $ 1.3 billion on the average each year), that at the economic crash of 1929, only 40% of the original *Liberty Loan* debts were left, partly by conversion into long-term bonds.[55]

The United States performed this on its own strength. The contribution of payments received by the US government from former allies on their

---

a   Furthermore, existing pre-war *private* debts, for example railway shares held by British investors had been greatly reduced (Chapter 10).

debts was far from significant; its share was about 15%.[56] This swift annihilation of the domestic debt is an indicator of the strength of the American economy in the 'roaring twenties'; it is the more remarkable in view of tax reductions on higher incomes by successive Presidents Harding and Coolidge, initiated to make funds available for industrial investments.

The golden years came to an end with the crash of 1929. The following depression would have one important effect on the outstanding *Liberty Loans*, notably on their gold clause. This clause stated that 'the principal and interest thereof shall be payable in United States gold coin of the present [*i.e.* at the moment of issue] standard of value' (pages 158, 159). This clause had been a dead letter as long as the gold value of the American dollar was stable. This changed during 1933 and 1934, when President Roosevelt took steps against the economic crisis. One of his first acts in office was to forbid hoarding of gold. The next step was the obligation to give in gold (apart from jewellery and the like) at the exchange of paper dollars at the official rate of $ 20.67 per ounce. During 1933, this exchange rate was continuously adjusted, until it ended in early 1934 at $ 35 per ounce. The dollar was effectively off gold and it had lost 41% of its former value and against currencies still on gold, such as France, Belgium and the Netherlands.

Apart from the direct economic effect of making American products cheaper in international trade, the measure by itself showed determination and therefore contributed to restoring confidence.[57] On the other side, however, it raised the question about the relevance of a gold clause. Would the bondholders receive their payments in dollars at the original 1917 or 1918 gold value or at the new $ 35-rate? No wonder, the government decided for the latter. Bondholders had to accept a loss of 41%, which they not unjustly regarded as expropriation in view of the text of the declaration of issue. Congress had already legalised this practice by a resolution to pay 'dollar-for-dollar', with the reasoning that acting otherwise would violate previous legislation on the possession and hording of gold.[58] All gold clauses, including those on *Liberty bonds*, were declared void. Bondholders took action, but eventually they failed; a few diehards appealed to the Supreme Court. The Court produced an astutely phrased majority decision, declaring that, indeed, Congress had acted unconstitutionally, but, on the other hand, the plaintiff had not made clear the amount of his loss and in fact, it was impossible to establish it. His claim was rejected.[59] By this trick, the American government placed itself in the company of all other nations that had diminished their First World War debts in an improper way, be it only for a small part. That is to say, it also shifted part of the burden to those who had in good faith supported the war financially by subscribing to gold claused war loans.[60]

Conclusion

Each country found its own way of dealing with its domestic debts. The Anglo-Saxon countries Britain and the United States attempted to convert short-term debts into long-term ones and to obtain budget surpluses to pay off the loans as soon as possible. The principle of a sound budgetary policy dominated, in order to guarantee confidence and a reputation for solidity on the financial markets. Psychologically, this reflects the desire to return to the pre-war situation, as if nothing had happened.

The United Kingdom was the typical example of this policy. During the 1920s and 1930s, the government was preoccupied with converting the enormous debt and reducing the burden of interest and principal. Re-establishing the Gold Standard – at the pre-war rate! – was the ultimate indicator, at the expense of international competitiveness and hence employment. The country came a long way in this policy through harsh austerity and thanks to the loyal taxpayer. But eventually, the government had to appeal to patriotism, as if it was still wartime, to get rid of a substantial part of the domestic debt. The Americans came a lot further on the way, supported by their decade of a booming economy; but finally in the 1930s, even they had to capitulate, as they were obliged (or seduced?) to repudiate the gold commitment of the domestic debts.

On the European continent, debts were taken less seriously. France could not escape inflationary funding by postponing tax measures and awaiting the expected gold flows from German reparations. Germany itself wiped out its domestic debts in a ruthless hyperinflation. This traumatic experience and its social and political consequences seems to have become an anchor in German minds ever since. This heritage of the aftermath of the First World War is present today in European policy: the requirement that the Euro should be a strong currency, the

European Central Bank located in Frankfurt and the rigorous rejection of Eurobonds and the resistance against a form of 'quantitative easing' by the European Central Bank, they all echo the inflation of 1923 when the German middle class in effect paid for the Great War by loosing all its capital. It is this *experience*, probably even more than rational economic models, changed international relations or technological progress that seems unforgettable, even after three generations.[a] Few things are so disruptive in society as money losing its meaning.[b]

All belligerent countries failed to some extent in meeting their domestic war debt obligations; some countries failed completely (Illustration 14.4)

	default types on war debts or currency	period
Russia	state bankruptcy; foreign debts cancelled	1918
Austria-	hyperinflation; *krone* fallen to 0,007% of pre-war value *	1921/'22
Hungary	hyperinflation; *korona* fallen to 0,007% of pre-war value	1923
Germany	hyperinflation; *mark* fallen to 1 trillionth (10^{-12}) of pre-war value; roughly 90% of domestic war loan debts cancelled	1923
France	inflation; *franc* fallen to 20% of pre-war value in 1928	1913/'28
UK	'voluntary-forced' conversion of war loan from 5% to 3.5% interest	1932
US	gold clause in war loans abrogated after dollar devaluation	1933

* At dollar exchange rate.

Source: Reinhart & Rogoff, Hanke & Krus, BMS, The Economist.[61]

Looking back at the practices deployed by the various countries in handling their domestic war debts, one can only conclude that they all failed, be it to varying degrees. Doubtful measures were not avoided. In doing so, governments not only recognised the loss of wealth due to the war, but they did it in an obscure way, as had been foreseen by Gladstone 70 years before on the occasion of the Crimean War (page 117).

---

a   It seems no coincidence that one of the more thorough books on inflation is called The *Experience* of Inflation, **Feldman** *et al.* (1984).
b   Here the famous quotation in **Keynes** (1920), p. 220 applies: 'Lenin was certainly right. There is no subtler, no surer means of overturning the existing basis of society than to debauch the currency'.

15

Two Wars later

'Consideration of governmental claims against Germany arising out of the first World War shall be deferred until a final general settlement of this matter'
Agreement on German External Debts, London, 1953[a]

After the Second World War, the discussion about debts from the previous World War was temporarily postponed, but not for long. In fact, settlement of the debts arising from the war of 1939-1945, including Marshall Plan aid settlements, put the old debts on the agenda again. Two milestones mark this settlement of World War I debts in the second half of the 20th century: The 1952/'53 London Debt Conference and the 1990 Treaty of Moscow. The two events were separated by almost forty years of Cold War blocking any discussion of the German part of the debt that still existed from the First World War. And even after 1990, only the German part of the debts question, originating from the reparations, was finally resolved. The inter-ally debts have been no subject of serious international settlements since the Lausanne conference in 1932.

The London Debt Agreement of 1953
In 1945, the old German debts were far from done and dusted. The circumstances, however, were not favourable to a solution. Germany was occupied and quartered. It was absolutely unclear which institution could be held responsible for the old debts. The German Federal Republic, comprising the three western occupation zones, and the German Democratic Republic (DDR), the Russian zone, were not established until 1949. In the meantime, there was no question of payments on old debts, such as the Dawes and Young loans. This meant not so much a problem for foreign governments, but the more so for private bondholders (assuming that their securities had not already been lost during the war). Indeed,

---

a   **London Agreement**, 27 February 1953, article 5, sub 1.

273

they had only partially received interest payments since 1933, whereas payments on principal had been discontinued altogether since 1934.[1]

Small problems, like those of the private bondholders, sometimes find their solution in a wider context. This context was the Cold War. The western allies US, Britain and France realised the significance of a prosperous country on the western side: the German Federal Republic. Anything that could hamper its development, including war debts, should be removed as far as possible. They were inclined to assume a mild attitude towards the German Federal Republic during the early 1950s.[2] This time, it was also in the interest of the Germans themselves to achieve a quick settlement. In the first place, it would restore their access to the international capital markets, highly necessary for the reconstruction of the bombed-out country.[3] Moreover – and this marks a crucial difference with the situation of 1918 – the German Federal Republic had a *moral* interest. It was of existential importance for Germany to be accepted in the ranks of decent countries, from which it had been excluded by the Nazi regime. A settlement of old debts, even at a price, would be a step in the right direction.[a] After all, Germany in the 1950s and 1960s, the country of Konrad Adenauer and Ludwig Erhard, was a completely different state to that of Karl Helfferich and Paul von Hindenburg in 1920.[4] At least as important was the position of the United States. After the First World War, its predominant attitude was isolationism; after 1945, its policy was to build an economically strong and politically stable western capitalist alliance against the Soviet Union. The United States realised that they had to act fast. They wanted to avoid the long and paralyzing negotiations of the 1920s, when individual countries competed among each other with their claims on Germany. This threatened to happen again at the end of the 1940s, when countries tried to 'defreeze' the debts that had been frozen some 15 years before. The United States concluded that only an international conference could solve the problem.[5]

It was in London, more specifically in Lancaster House, where the Conference on German External Debts would take place during 1952. In

---

a   Apart from – and in the first place – financial compensation to holocaust victims, survivors and descendants. The first steps to this end were taken almost simultaneously to the London debt conference, at a conference in the village of Wassenaar, near The Hague, Netherlands, see also note 4 on page 351.

February 1953, the final agreement was signed.[6] The importance of the conference greatly exceeds the rather technical subject. In fact, it formed the indispensable basis for European political and economic integration in an Atlantic context. To mention a few consequences, shortly after the agreement, the German Federal Republic became a member of the International Monetary Fund and the World Bank. The significance of the conference and the agreement has long been neglected and only recently, after the German unification and current debt crises, attention and appreciation for the negotiators has been revived.[a]

The London Agreement on German External Debts provided settlements on a variety of old German public debts, including Prussian state debts. In those cases where a solution was not yet possible, a clear procedure for the future was agreed upon, as we shall see later.[7] In relation to the financing of the First World War, two provisions of the agreement are interesting. The first one concerns the Dawes and Young loans and the second one concerns the issue of reparations.

The Dawes and Young loans were tackled by the usual procedure in debt relief: splitting, postponement and decreasing interest rates Bond-holders were offered an exchange of their original securities into a new loan with a longer life, 27 years, and a lower interest rate. For the Dawes loan, the interest rate was reduced from 7% to 5% and for the Young loan the corresponding reduction was from 5.5% to 4.5%.[8] The German Federal Republic became responsible for payments on interest and principal for this new loan, a total amount of 1.5 billion *marks* (in 1970 value).[9] This meant that the total German debt – apart from reparations! – was reduced by roughly 50%.[10] The escape route that had undermined the Dawes agreement in the period 1925-1929 was cleverly blocked: Germany should make its 'payments for current transactions', that is from an export surplus, not by capital imports through new loans.[11] The BIS was entrusted with the actual banking operations, just as in the interwar period. The issue of reparations (of both World Wars) was settled by a procedure arrangement (page 279).

---

a   The London German Debt Conference, for example, received much less attention than the well-known Bretton Woods Conference (1944), where the international system of exchange rates was established, together with the Wold Bank and the International Monetary Fund.

Of course, private bondholders of Young and Dawes bonds were free to accept or reject the offer. In reality, they had little choice, because the proposal was part of an agreement between their governments and the German Federal Republic. Private lawsuits to claim their old rights on Germany would certainly lack support by their own government and were deemed to be lost. From a wider perspective, the 50% cut they suffered formed another, and belated, contribution to the financing of (the German part of) the First World War.

German unification and the last mile

By the London Agreement of 1953, the German Federal Republic had confirmed the old debts of the German *Reich*.[12] Payments on the new loan created no problem. Thanks to the German 'Economic miracle' (*Wirtschaftswunder*), Germany enjoyed a comfortable trade balance surplus, starting in the early 1950s (and up to the present day). Indicators for this economic expansion were the *Volkswagen* vans, *Grundig* radio sets and *SieMatic* kitchens finding their way all over Europe and paid for in foreign currencies, by which the loans could easily be serviced.[a] The transfer problem that had formed – rightly or wrongly – a serious issue in the 1930s played no role. On 1st June 1980 the German Federal Republic paid the final annuity.

At that moment, everything seemed settled, but for two tricky points in the 1953 London Agreement, that had been deliberately addressed but solved only by prescribing a procedure. The first issue was the *territory* of the German Federal Republic as compared to the former German Reich; the second point was no less than reparations, both from the First World War and the Second World War.

It was clear to everyone that the territory of the German Federal Republic did not coincide with the former *Reich*. The difference was not made up of territories such as former East Prussia and parts of Silesia; the real issue was the DDR, formally the eastern (Russian) occupation zone. This country was not a party to the London Agreement, but the German Federal Republic acted as if it represented Germany in its entirety. Although this was clearly a point of concern, it opened a political window to leave out part of the old debts, while at the same time

---

a   Apart from the enormous influx of dollars through the American occupation army.

addressing them. An excellent opportunity to circumvent this potential bottleneck in the negotiations in 1952 was formed by... the Dawes and Young loans. Although the German Federal Republic resumed payments from 1953 onwards, an exception was made for the arrears in interest payments for the period 1-1-1945 until 15-4-1953! It was recognised by all parties involved that the German Federal Republic alone could not be held responsible for those arrears. This may seem strange in the light of the fact that the Germans did commit themselves to paying old Prussian debts, but it offered an opportunity to postpone part of the burden; after all, diplomacy is a matter of give and take and not necessarily logically consistent. And it was by no means a financial detail. The original Young loan had an interest rate of 5.5% and for the Dawes loan it was even as high as 7%. A period of 8 years of interest on a 7% loan implies a burden of 56% of the total amount of outstanding bonds, disregarding compound interest. A rough estimate of this interest burden arising from the Dawes and Young loans amounts to over 600 million *marks* in 1953 ($ 150 million or £ 50 million, in 1953 values).[13] The political compromise in London was, that payments of this part of the Dawes and Young debts would be postponed until German (re-)unification.[14] In 1953 circumstances, this meant: indefinitely. Bondholders of the new loans received a certificate that entitled them to receive payments (at reduced rates) if ever this situation happened. For over 40 years, this certificate was a mere slip of paper, representing the value of a collector's item, with no more status than old Russian railway bonds.[15]

Unlikely events, however, sometimes happen. In 1989 the Berlin wall fell and by 3 October 1990 German unification was a reality. At that time, the provisions of the London Agreement automatically came into force. The German Federal Republic, now representing the whole of Germany, immediately issued a 20-year loan to provide for the outstanding claims over the period 1945-1953. The bondholders saw their certificates turned into a real asset and they (or their heirs) could cash.[16] The total amount of outstanding certificates, reduced by earlier redemption, was about 220 million *marks* ($ 135 million in dollars of 1990).[17] The final payments were made on 3 October 2010. By that date, almost a century after the beginning of the Frist World War, this part of the debt problems had come to a relatively decent end.

After the London Debt Conference of 1953, bondholders of the original 1924 Dawes and 1930 Young loans received a claim to compensate for unpaid interest by the Nazi regime; the claim could be cashed 'in the event of the reunification of Germany' (Illustration 15.1)

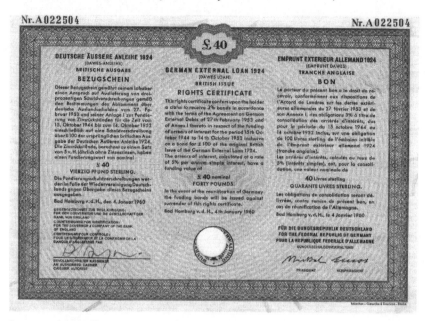

Source: author's collection.

In 2010, Germany made the final payments on the loans related to the First World War: nearly € 70 million, an amount negligible as compared to the actual debt burden (Illustration 15.2)

Item	Credit financing scheme	Amount for 2010	Amount for 2009
		1,000 €	
2.1.1.3	Federal Treasury Bills...	1 440 676	1 548 912
2.1.1.4	Promissory Note Loans..	555 599	528 800
2.1.1.5	Federal Bonds..	34 000 000	36 000 000
2.1.1.6	Cleared Foreign Debts (**London Debt Agreement**)	**69 950**	1 443

Source: translated excerpt from the German Federal Budget, *Bundeshaushaltsplan* 2010.[18]

In October 2010, German (and other) newspapers proclaimed that Germany had paid off the reparation debts. This is too simplistic a statement. In reality, as we have seen, it was the last payment on German loans dating from the 1920s and issued at that time to provide for a (small) part of the reparations. These loans had not been serviced by the Nazi regime from 1993 onwards. In 1953 part of the obligations had been postponed for 40 years, consented by the western allies. It was that part that was finally redeemed in 2010.

Reparations themselves formed the second tricky issue that had been deliberately circumvented in the London agreement. Indeed, they had been dealt with effectively in 1932 in the Lausanne settlement, an agreement that had never been ratified (page 244). The London Treaty dealt with private claims, but explicitly excluded *government claims* on Germany arising from the First World War. This implied that reparations were left out, but the treaty also described the procedure to deal with the question. Article 5 stated that they 'shall be deferred until a final general settlement of this matter'.[19] By the same article, similar claims arising from the Second World War were also postponed by a slightly different phrasing 'until the final settlement of the problem of reparation'. Both formulations refer to an indeterminate future, rather an event than a definite point in time; it strikingly resembles the postponement of the interest arrears question of the Dawes and Young Loans to the as then unpredictable German unification.

In this case the tricky issues were solved by explicitly ignoring them. This happened in the treaty ending the Second World War, the so-called Two-plus-Four Treaty, also known as the Treaty of Moscow. On 12 September 1990 the still formal powers of occupation France, Russia, Britain and US on the one hand and the German Federal Republic and the German Democratic Republic on the other hand, concluded the Treaty on the Final Settlement with Respect to Germany. It was a peace treaty in all respects, except in name, and as 'a masterwork of diplomacy' that even found its place on the UNESCO World Heritage List since 2011.[a] The stipulation in the 1953 London Agreement that reparations should be settled in a 'final general settlement' implied that a said settlement would be the last word. The Two-plus-Four Treaty, by its name and scope cannot be regarded in any other way than this very final and general settlement. No more is ever to be expected and in international law, the Two-plus-Four Treaty is indeed regarded as such.[20] On the point

---

a   The difference with the Treaty of Versailles could not be greater. In 1919, the diplomats needed almost 200 pages, 40 articles and nearly 75,000 words. The Two-plus-Four Treaty counted only 5 pages, 10 articles and 2,000 words. Admittedly, it had been preceded by 40 years of Cold War; http://www.unesco.org/new/en/communication-and-information/flagship-project-activities/memory-of-the-world/homepage/.

of reparations, however, the treaty contains no single reference, proviso, exclusion or whatsoever, whereas at the same time it is a *final* settlement. The conclusion is obvious: all remaining reparation claims, if any, have been silently buried never to be revived again. More than 70 years after Versailles, First World War reparations were officially settled.

Inter-ally debts and the rest...

The London conference dealt exclusively with German debts. Inter-ally debts resulting from the First World War were not subject for the negotiations. In fact, at that time they had been discontinued for twenty years, since the Hoover moratorium of July 1931.[21] In Europe, the bulk of the debts resulted from borrowing from Britain, but the majority was formed by the loans that the United States had given to its allies. In 1934 this was an unpaid bill of $ 11 billion. As a consequence of the annuity scheme, where interest payments dominated in the first years, the outstanding debt on principal was almost completely intact. As the debtor countries (apart from Finland) had stopped paying completely, the US government added the interest accrued but not received to the total debt year by year. It was a matter of concern for the Americans and from time to time the government wrote letters to the allies to draw attention to their default. In practice, however, the United States lacked power resources (or the desire) to actually collect the debts.[a]

After the Second World War, inter-ally debts arising from that war got priority over the old debts. As a matter of fact, these new debts were partially forgiven and the remainder was paid off according to agreed schemes, whereas the old First World War debts only increased by unpaid interest. By 1953, British Second World War debts to the United States had already shrunk to $ 2.4 billion, while World War I debts had risen to $ 17 billion![22] The United States government had stopped sending reminders, but internally the increasing arrears were recorded – up to 1975 even with the accuracy of dollar cents. A revival of the attention for the old debts came after 20 years, in 1973. The American

---

a   For example, Department of State Bulletin, 21 December 1940, p. 565 ff. Undoubtedly, the United States possessed sufficient coercive power in financial terms to call their allies to order. To actually use them, however, was in the end a matter of political judgement. Apparently, the United States government did not seek a war on debts with its important customers. During the Second World War, it supplied Britain with ample financial means (by means of the lend-lease construction to circumvent the Johnson Act), without requiring any payments on the old First World War debts.

Senate initiated a hearing on all American claims, in connection with the enormous aid programmes for developing countries.[23] Senators blamed government officials that they wiped out existing debts, without properly informing Congress and disadvantaging the taxpayers, their voters. At that occasion the old First World War debts reappeared on the scene, in fact at the moment when Second World War debt had been repaid almost completely. In the meantime, First World War debts to the United States had grown to $ 25 billion, in 1973 dollars.[24] In the Senate hearing, the government declared once more that it had always maintained the position that that there was no relationship with the likewise unpaid German reparations, as the allies claimed. However, it admitted that 'there is a linkage in reality' and the debts meant 'immensely complex political and economic issues'.

Nevertheless, the American government continued with painstaking accuracy recording the ever-growing debts. At the end of 2009 – the last year in which the data were published in detail on a regular basis – the score had risen to over $ 40 billion of arrears on principal and interest.[25] It is illusory, that these debts will ever be paid; in fact they could have been cancelled as early as in 1934, saving a lot of paperwork. Although $ 40 billion is a large amount of money, in the perspective of, say, the actual American government deficit, it is almost negligible. If all debtor countries repaid their whole First World War debts to the US now, this would reduce the American federal debt by 0.2%.[26] If, to start with, they resumed interest payments only, the effect on the federal budget would be practically unobservable.[27]

Until recently, there was only one reminder of the war debts alive and well: the large (domestic) British War Loan of Bonar Law of February 1917. After the successful conversion by Neville Chamberlain in 1932 (page 257), it had survived both the Second World War and the Cold War under the name of the United Kingdom 3.5% War Loan. Until March 2015 it was traded daily on the London and Frankfurt stock exchanges. Today, it would have been a real perpetual – one hundred years lasting – loan. Until 2015, not a penny had been paid on principal, but the more so on interest: 3.5% meant an annual burden of £ 70 million ($ 105 million) for the loyal taxpayers of the United Kingdom of Great Britain and Northern Ireland, to be paid to the bondholders, be they original, heirs or investors. Just as in 1932, market interest rates have dropped in recent years, well below 3.5% and on 3 December 2014 Chancellor George Osborne announced a complete redemption of the loan.[a] For the UK Treasury it was their contribution in the centennial commemoration of the Great War as a 'fitting way to remember that extraordinary sacrifice of the past'.[28] The bondholders received their investment back, financed from new loans at a lower interest rate. The direct link with the First World War is not visible anymore, but the money for servicing the new loans has still to be collected from the taxpayer, although the burden is substantially lighter. It is an echo of German Finance Minister Karl Helfferich's prophesy almost exactly a century before, in August 1915: 'may *they* drag it down through the decades to come, not *we*'.

---

[a]   In the course of 2014, the bond price (code: GB0009386284) had already increased almost to par. Undoubtedly speculation about a redemption in view of the low market interest rate and the commemoration of the War have contributed to this development.

Epilogue

Our journey has taken us from 1870 until today. It is now time to look back and make some overall remarks. The Great War lasted four years and consumed an astronomical amount of money: roughly the equivalent of between $ 35 and $ 40 trillion in today's money. It is no wonder that it caused decades of financial problems and that we are still dealing with the legacy of a war that changed the world.

The immediate impact of the war was a dramatic decline in prosperity and a global re-allocation of wealth. Moreover, as we have seen in numerous examples in the previous chapters, the financial flows were visible indicators of economic processes that were taking place. These outcomes fully justify a detailed consideration of the financial aspects of the war.

Not only do the financial mechanisms reveal the underlying material costs of the war, but how those mechanisms were used by governments gives us insight into the cultural differences between countries – differences that are often ignored in economic and financial theory. Since cultural changes occur very slowly, experiences from as long ago as the First World War are not only historically interesting, they also help us to understand the present-day behaviour of countries and governments. In the next few pages we will formulate and substantiate six different findings. The main messages are:
1 The First World War was fought on credit
2 Belligerent countries exploited and exhausted their economic and natural resources; details of the financing reveal this exploitation
3 Global financial power shifted from Britain to the United States
4 The American taxpayer acted as the lender of last resort
5 Countries differed considerably in their attitudes to the ethics of debt repayment
6 In general, the idea that governments repay a substantial share of large debts they incur is illusory.

(1)   Credit was the ultimate financial fuel of the war machine

Scarcely any country in history has fought without borrowed money. Kings and emperors have always resorted to bankers for loans to cover their war expenditure and many a respectable banking house has flourished on the financial demands of belligerent monarchs. The First World War was no exception. A dominant characteristic of the war was the large-scale borrowing required to finance it. At least three-quarters of the total expenditure was raised by borrowing, and in many continental European countries the proportion was considerably larger.

What was new in the First World War was the international scale of borrowing, at least on the part of the Entente powers. Practically every country borrowed from several other countries, both in the private capital market and from allied governments. It was a world war not only geographically and in its destructive impact in material and human terms, but also in its financial dimensions. And it was this system of reciprocal debt, created in the heat of the war, that was to disturb international relations in the decades after the war.

In the years before the Great War it had been proclaimed that a modern industrial war would end quickly due to the lack of financial resources. The costs would simply be too high. Those prophecies soon proved unfounded. With the financial system that was in place, including central banks, bank accounts and paper money, governments were able to borrow continuously as long as their populations had sufficient confidence in the value of money. The war did not stop for monetary reasons as long as the material resources in the form of shells, men and horsepower were not exhausted. Borrowing kept the machine going. Although there was not necessarily a policy of flagrant deception of the public, we can legitimately conclude that many governments did not tell their people the true story of impoverishment and the consequences of borrowing. Particularly in countries with a poorly developed parliamentary tradition and a heavily censored press, governments had *carte blanche* to abuse public confidence in the value of money and in the authorities that were supposed to safeguard its value.

The lesson to be learned is that the financial system as such is not designed to avert war; rather it offers a broad spectrum of ingenious instruments to accommodate and to continue and protract war.

(2) Countries draw on their economic resources

Ultimately, the only economic resources from which the war (or any war) could be paid were production, consumption and capital – including human capital. Every government was forced to fall back on these resources to finance the war. Taxes on income and consumption were insufficient to cover the costs to any appreciable extent, even in countries such as Britain and the United States with a well-developed income tax system. In Europe, governments had to mobilise and liquidate the enormous wealth and capital that had been accumulated in the closing decades of the nineteenth century, an age of relatively great prosperity. War loans, gold surrender campaigns, estate taxes, the sale of securities and the printing of money were all instruments used to free up this capital for its eventual destruction on the battlefield.

The **German** government's major source of income before the war, revenues from customs duties, quickly dried up as a result of the British blockade. The country was also cut off from the international capital markets, while its allies – Austria-Hungary, the Ottoman Empire and Bulgaria – were more of a burden than a help. Thus, the country depended entirely on its own resources, apart from some commercial credits from neighbouring neutral countries to buy food. Domestic physical resources – labour and food and chemicals production, for example – were exploited with harsh and detailed regulation, almost to the point of being dictatorial. Heavy charges were levied on conquered areas in the west and in the east to support the German war machine financially. Domestic financial assets were liquidated by means of ingenious legal instruments such as the system of *Darlehenskassen*. Inflation was an effective instrument for hidden taxation of financial capital.

Accordingly, Germany exhausted its capital in all its manifestations: human, financial and material. Financial authorities concealed the true state of the country's finances, in much the same way as the military leaders withheld information about the increasingly precarious situation at the front from the public. In both cases, it was a recipe for disbelief and discontent when the war ended. It might have worked in the event of a victory in a short war, in which case the defeated enemy would have to pay the bill to redeem the domestic war loans and *Reichsbank* advances, a policy openly communicated by the government, but that dream was shattered by the Treaty of Versailles.

France employed an improvised method of financing throughout the war. It entered the war with an enormous national debt and a formidable stock of gold in the vaults of the *Banque de France*. Taxation was a taboo for the French government before 1916; it only became more than negligible when the war was over. From the outset, France tried to secure international loans, both from its ally Britain and in the United States. In the process, it took advantage of Britain's high credit status in the international financial markets. However, France was reluctant to pay the price of supporting this status in the form of collateral in gold. The domestic war loans were a mix of perpetual loans in the tradition of the nineteenth-century *rentier* and a variety of very popular short-term loans. The term to maturity of some loans was so short that they practically constituted monetary financing; in combination with the printing of banknotes they contributed to inflation and to an enormous rise in short-term debt, adding to the already gigantic national debt with which the country had entered the war.

One might say that France survived the war financially – as it did military – thanks to its alliance with Britain and the United States. Its delicate financial position would come to light after the war with the crash in the value of the *franc*. Inflation was the inevitable post-war reaction to insufficient taxation and expensive borrowing during the war. The inflation largely wiped out the government's domestic debts, at the expense of the holders of war bonds. It was, in the words of Keynes, a silent euthanasia of the *rentier*.

Britain paid its share in the financing of the war mainly with a variety of loans raised by its banking system domestically, in the Commonwealth and internationally. During the war, taxes were a welcome additional source of income for the government.

Like other countries, Britain had to have recourse to its capital, but this was less visible than in other countries. A relatively large part of its wealth was tied up in portfolios of American securities, which until the beginning of 1917 provided a sufficient buffer for direct payments and could be used as collateral to secure private loans in the US. The British government succeeded in mobilising these assets through a combination of persuasion and legislation. The effect was that within a few years the United States was relieved of a foreign debt that had been built up over centuries. This represented the real loss of wealth suffered by the United Kingdom: the financial flows were just its materialisation. Instead of being a global creditor, Britain became a debtor state.

The **United States**, on the other hand, took advantage of its period of prosperous neutrality. While most European countries had to switch to a war economy, the US economy essentially remained a peacetime economy. Wealth was generated without the material burden of the war. Instead of eating into its national capital as the belligerent countries were doing, the United States was able to increase it. Not surprisingly, since wealth is generated by production, not by destruction. To express it cynically, the US was able to invest even more in the European war machine.

American industry flourished thanks to the demand from Europe for war supplies and foodstuffs. This offered a sound basis for heavier taxation in the public domain, as well as generating resources for loans by private bankers. The United States was able to finance almost a quarter of its war expenses through taxes, the largest percentage of any of the belligerent countries. That share could have been even higher if the country had not assisted the European allies with credits on such a grand scale – the loans tipped the balance in favour of the Entente because they were practically unlimited in volume and, even more importantly, were provided swiftly.

Furthermore, the United States was able to avoid mistakes made by other countries, such as setting interest rates too high or using the more harmful financial instruments of short-term borrowing and massive monetary financing; it could employ good practices such as organising large war loans promoted by large-scale marketing campaigns. Finally, its institutional facilities, notably the FED system (although it was still barely operational) and a flexible income tax system, were in place at the right time.

(3) Global financial power shifted from Europe to America
Although it was formally contrary to the early policy of the Wilson administration, in financial terms the United States had taken sides in the European war long before it became involved military and politically. Belligerent Entente governments already started borrowing heavily in the

American financial markets in November 1914 to finance their massive purchases of war equipment and foodstuffs. And American bankers were all too eager to help them, provided that the return was attractive and there was solid collateral. These markets effectively remained closed to Germany and its allies as they had hardly any trade relationships with the United States.

Between August 1914 and April 1917, US bankers controlled financial relations with European governments. From April 1917, the US government took over with a model for financing the war that more or less resembled the system for a short war that the European countries had hoped to use but had failed to establish. In effect the war only lasted for two years for the US (from April 1917 to Versailles) and during that period it was in a position to take the lead in financing the entire war. After the war the domestic loans could be quickly repaid, while at the same time the heavily progressive taxes were reduced.

Britain, on the other hand, started the war as the banker of the Entente countries, in much the same way as it had financed wars in previous centuries. Flourishing trade during the war, but particularly after the war, was expected to generate the revenues to cover the costs. Business was the driving force behind the financing of the war and financial credibility was the ultimate article of faith. The First World War was to prove different, however. It would cost Britain more in real financial terms than any war it had ever fought previously and up to the present day, including the Second World War.

What started out as a limited campaign to support Belgian neutrality with an expeditionary force of volunteers ended with the conscription of an army of over two million men to serve on the Western front alone. Meanwhile, the country wanted to preserve its dominant role in international finance not only during the war, but more especially in the post-war period when, it was believed, trade would resume as if nothing had happened. Britain therefore supported its European allies with loans, but many of those countries proved to be questionable debtors: all of the loans to Russia had to be written off and France and Italy paid back only a fraction of theirs. For good reasons from their point of view, but at the expense of Britain.

Large imports from the US obliged Britain to balance the trade deficit with American loans, initially from private bankers and later with enormous credits from the US government. When the Treaty of Versailles was signed, the United Kingdom was indebted to the United States government to the tune of about $ 4 billion, or £ 900 million, in 1919 values. This was an unprecedented level of external debt for the country. Moreover, the country had sold off a substantial proportion of its financial assets in the US, thus losing all the recurrent revenues it had enjoyed in the past.

By 1919 the old pre-war relationships between Britain and the United States had been reversed. The United States had enormous financial claims abroad, while it was practically free from external debt. American bankers and investors continued to provide loans to European countries, and Germany in particular (until 1929). The legion of American bankers that dominated post-war European finance clearly demonstrated the country's financial supremacy. The result was that American financial power had grown at the expense of Britain's. In all fairness, the war exceeded the British Empire's financial strength. For the United States, the First World War was simply a business opportunity that it grasped unreservedly.

He who pays the piper calls the tune. The United States continued to intervene in European financial affairs long after the war ended. In the aftermath of the financial crash of 1929, one European country after another threatened to default on inter-ally debts – and Germany on its reparation payments. President Hoover's moratorium in June 1931 effectively brought an end to all debt repayments between governments.

Twenty years later, after the Second World War, the United States again took the initiative to clean up Europe's financial affairs. The London Debt Agreement of 1953 resolved the issue of Germany's outstanding obligations, notably the debt arising from international loans it had used to make reparation payments from the First World War. For the German Federal Republic, the agreement restored the financial credibility that the country had in fact lacked since 1914.

(4) The taxpayer: seemingly spared but in reality hard hit
Borrowing and printing banknotes helped to defer the direct effect of the financial burden of the war to the future, but in the end only

taxation could fill the gap between government revenue and escalating expenditure on destructive power. However, as Adam Smith remarked 240 years ago, governments are reluctant to openly pass on the bill for a war to their taxpayers.

In France and Germany tax measures were virtually absent until 1916, when it became clear that such a policy could not be maintained. Interest on war loans was absorbing an increasing share of the budget and war profiteers could afford to live in luxury while the vast majority of the population were seeing their standard of living decline. But even then the tax measures were insufficient. Tax revenues started to grow in the early post-war years, but it was too little and too late. As both direct taxation of income and property and even duties on food, beverages and 'luxury' goods could not fill the gap, inflation, the invisible tax on capital, eventually did the job. Since inflation is not explicitly a tax, it was difficult for governments to be blamed politically, but the effect for the taxpayer was the same as a double-digit tax (or almost 100% in Germany's case) on everyone's savings.

The loyalty of the British taxpayers has been mentioned before. During the war they were expected to pay from the first war budget in 1914 onwards, and were still paying for the war loans almost a century later. It was the same tradition that had gradually reduced the British national debt in the nineteenth century after the Napoleonic wars.

The role of the American taxpayer was crucial in financing the First World War. From April 1917, the US government effectively assumed financial responsibility for the war from the European Entente allies. This was not done entirely without self-interest, as it provided continuity for American industry and agriculture. European governments were freed from tiresome and expensive borrowing in the American private capital market. They quickly received generous loans from the US government, which were in turn funded from the large *Liberty Loans*. This shifted the risk of the loans from the banks and their depositors and shareholders to the government and hence to its ultimate creditor, the American taxpayer, who in fact acted as the lender of last resort.

It was only after the war that this would manifest itself. The US government recovered only a fraction of the loans made to the allies. As early as the beginning of the 1920s it had to write off part of the debt when it made long-term debt settlement schemes with its debtors. These schemes provided for lower – sometimes considerably lower – interest rates than the US government itself had to pay on the *Liberty Loans*. But even these arrangements for reduced payments, which were intended to continue until the mid-1980s, were often not fulfilled. After the announcement of the Hoover moratorium in 1931, when all international payments were suspended for one year, most of the debtor countries defaulted on their obligations – with the notable exception of Finland. Incidentally, the moratorium itself weakened the position of the American taxpayer to the benefit of bondholders of German international loans who continued to receive their money – at least until Hitler seized power in Germany.

It is no exaggeration to say that a considerable part of the unpaid bill for the First World War was silently shifted to the American taxpayer, who had to pay the interest and principal on the *Liberty Loans* in as far as they had been used to provide financial support for the allies. This financial loss for the US was only veiled by the strong economic growth in the country during and after the war (up to and including the next world war), despite the depression of the 1930s. The other side of the coin for the taxpayer was the expansion of the private sector – industry, banks and agriculture – for whom the war generated a lot of new business and contributed to the general prosperity.

(5) So many countries, so many customs: the ethics of servicing debts

After the war every government was left with enormous debts – to their own citizens through war loans, to private investors on international markets, and to governments of allied countries. For the defeated countries, these problems were overshadowed by the size of the bill for reparations. No government – victorious or defeated – avoided the temptation of reducing this imposed or self-created debt burden. The options were allowing the currency to depreciate, perpetual procrastination, reducing interest payments, paying off gold-secured loans in paper money and, finally, flatly refusing to pay.

Remarkable differences became apparent between countries in their attitudes to debt servicing. In **Britain** the intention had always been that loans would be properly redeemed in order to maintain the country's status as a reliable debtor. In the first decade after the war it scrupulously paid its annuities on the American loans. After the Hoover moratorium it made heroic attempts to persevere with this policy, but in 1933 it defaulted on its debts. By then it had repaid more than any other country, · but even that was only a small portion of its total debt.

Domestically, the bondholders of the large war loan in 1917 suffered when in 1932 the government forced them to accept a substantial reduction in payments with an appeal to their patriotism – as if it was still wartime. Nevertheless, the spirit of tenacity was not lost. The British taxpayer continued to contribute to the interest payments on a war loan originally issued in 1917 for another 80 years. It was only in March 2015 that the Chancellor of the Exchequer finally repaid it in full – that is, refinanced it at a lower interest rate. Since then, the burden is invisible in the large anonymous mass of the national debt.

France, on the other hand, excelled in procrastination pending receipt of German reparations. It used the moral argument of the sacrifices it had made on the battlefield, which were indeed the largest of all the Western countries. It was second-to-last in reaching agreement with the US on a settlement scheme, which took three years to be ratified in parliament, and it immediately seized the opportunity of the Hoover moratorium to end repayments of the debts once and for all. Within a decade, inflation had reduced the French government's domestic debts to one fifth of their original value, which affected residents and foreign investors in war bonds alike.

In **Germany** domestic debts were effectively wiped out by inflation. The devastating effect on society of the hyperinflation of 1923 has left its traces to the present day in Germany's aversion to anything that resembles (or actually is) monetary financing. After the First World War, Germany's fundamental international obligation was the bill for reparations, which the country regarded not as a debt but as an undeserved penalty. Not surprisingly successive German governments tried to reduce it, and ultimately succeeded. Even before the Nazis came to power, the reparations were practically abolished. It was only after the Second World War that Germany, seeking to restore its moral standing in the world, would resume payments on old international loans that were originally used to make reparation payments. From that moment on, German governments strictly observed the policy of servicing its debts, until the final payments were ultimately made in 2010.

The **United States** was free from external debt after the war. The official policy of repaying the domestic Liberty Loans as soon as possible was successful. With respect to international loans, the role of the US government was to a certain extent ambiguous. On the one hand, it demanded punctual repayments after the war, but on the other it took protectionist measures that made it very hard – not to say impossible – for the debtor countries to earn the dollars needed to make those payments. Things were different during and after the Second World War. The unpaid accounts from the First World War did not deter the US from once again writing out large cheques, even to those countries that were still in default on their earlier loans. These new loans and the *Marshall Plan* aid have been repaid – insofar as they have not been cancelled – whereas the First World War debts are still outstanding. First World War debts have easily survived all the veterans.

These observations show the differences in the behaviour of countries in the aftermath of the Great War a century ago. One might think of them just as historically interesting phenomena. They are not, however, the inevitable consequences of some 'natural' laws of economics or finance. It is precisely those differences that reflect the fact that choices can be made, and that customs and culture can play an important role in those choices. Since cultures change slowly (if at all), these differences in behaviour of countries can still be seen today by anyone who has an eye for them.

(6)   The illusion of international debt repayments
Despite numerous international conferences, settlement schemes and 'final' agreements, only a small fraction (in the order of 10% to 15%) of the debts between allied governments arising from the war has been repaid; this is roughly the same fraction as Germany has paid for reparations. A legion of diplomats constructed payment schemes, with annuities running into the millions and calculated down to the last penny, which would continue for generations. They have all failed with two minor exceptions (Finland and Hungary). This comes as no surprise because these 'settlements' merely reflected the balance

of power at the time they were made – as agreements generally do – rather than a serious analysis of the parties' capacity to pay. From the early 1930s, the US government in particular had to confine itself to sending regular payment reminders, which were answered in polite diplomatic terms but not with money.

For the debtor countries (and Germany in the case of reparations) delaying was a better strategy than paying, quite apart from the issue of separating the economic impossibility of paying from the political unwillingness to pay. Curiously, repayment of international debts by governments to *private* investors appeared to be more sustainable than debt repayments between *governments*. German reparation payments constitute the most obvious example. In 1919 they still had absolute priority over any payment by the German government to external creditors. This changed when part of the debt was privatised through the Dawes and Young international loans: private bondholders were paid in full, while allied governments had to be content with reduced payments. Private claims were also exempt from the Hoover moratorium. One might even say that this was the very purpose of the moratorium from the bankers' perspective. Payments to private bondholders by the German government continued (apart from complications in the Second World War) until 2010, and by the British Treasury on a domestic war loan until 2015. These obligations easily survived reparation payments and war debts between European countries and to the United States government, which had effectively ended in 1931. The debtor countries simply defaulted and got away with it.

It is too simple to attribute the failure to repay debts between governments to a collective unwillingness. The annihilation of these debts reflects the illusion that financial obligations with a political basis can be regarded and treated as commercial transactions. What remains is the uncomfortable feeling that it took a very long time indeed for this truth to be realised. Politicians and populations clung too long to the idea that after the war they could return to the pre-war status quo and simply pick up the thread as if nothing had happened. That is a lesson that transcends the First World War; it still holds true today, but seems to have been forgotten. Public international debts between governments that will take half a generation or more to be repaid might as well be restructured from the beginning in order to avoid creating expectations that are illusory. As the Germans say: better an end with pain than pain without end.[a]

---

a   *Besser ein Ende mit Schrecken als ein Schrecken ohne Ende.*

Annex

What is the meaning of a sum of money of 1914-'18 a century later?

The first question on reading the billions of money spent on the war is: how does this translate into present-day values? Most people have a vague notion that $ 100 or £ 100 in 1916 is worth much more than the same amount of money nowadays, but it remains unclear exactly *how much* more. Many sources in financial war history do not even raise the question and equally often questionable assumptions are made. One of the few books that pay explicit attention to the question is **Ahamed** (2010), who gives some rules of thumb to translate sums of money from the 1920s to the current context.

There is no single conversion factor
The crucial point to understand is, that there are different translations for different purposes. A tax-free threshold of £ 160 in 1914 translates differently into a corresponding amount nowadays than an increase of £ 160 million of national debt. After all, in the first example, we want to get an impression of the impact on the individual wage earner. In this case, purchasing power development from 1914 to 2016 provides the benchmark, or at least a good proxy. In the case of national debt or war expenditure, however, we are talking about developments at the macro economic level of a country as a whole and not of consumer goods or the labour market. Wage index data or consumer price index values are less appropriate in that case; the scale and structure of the economy of a country has changed too much over a century. For example, the first US *Liberty Loan* raised $ 2 billion by a population of 103 million ($ 19.42 per capita). The same loan in 2016, just to keep pace with the actual population (over 321 million), should have raised over $ 6 billion. Thus, without any inflation, growth of wealth, change in standard of living, a simple factor of three would be necessary to translate the 1917 amount. Since much more has changed than population only, such translations factors are not adequate.

Amounts at a national level should be gauged against the size of the national economy. A usual measure for the size of the economy of a country is its gross domestic product, GDP.[a] National efforts, debt, expenditures and revenues are best translated using the GDP and its development. For example, British military expenditure in 1908 (the time when large battleships were ordered) was about £ 70 million per annum. As compared to the 1908 GDP of £ 1,978 million, military expenditure represented 3.4% of GDP.[1] In 2015 values, with a British GDP of roughly £ 1,800 billion, this would amount to £ 60 billion on military expenditure, a factor of roughly 900 as compared to the original £ 70 million of 1908![2] The actual UK budget for defence is £ 46 billion (in relative terms roughly three quarters of what is was in the era of dreadnought building).[3]

For the United States, with a dollar value of the GDP of $ 18,000 billion in 2015, the corresponding amount of 3.4% would be $ 600 billion per year for military expenditure, a numerical factor of 1,700 with respect to the original £ 70 million.[4] This amount of $ 600 billion is not only of the order of magnitude of the actual (2015) US military expenditure: $ 598.5 billion, it is almost exactly the same amount.[5] Thus, the burden of British military expenditure of 1908 (including the Dreadnought programme) as compared to the national economy is equivalent to present-day US military expenditure. Apparently, it is the military burden of a world power.

The multiplication factors mentioned above (900 and 1,700) are much higher than frequently found in publications where sums of money are unduly translated into current values by means of consumer price indices.[6] The order of magnitude given here is the same as the rule of thumb given by **Ahamed** (2010) in the translation of macro economic data from the 1920s and 1930s to 2010, a factor of 200.[7]

Data issues
There are three complications, however, in using these factors. In the first place, a practical point. The whole notion of GDP was developed

---

a   Recent discussions on the value of GDP for measuring the 'real' size of the economy are beyond the scope of this book; see **Stiglitz et al.** (2009). It is hard enough to obtain reliable historical data for GDP, let alone for a more inclusive GDP.

in the 1930s. Original sources dating from before that period at best mention a 'national income', which is not necessarily equal to modern internationally concluded definitions of GDP. Fortunately, time series that have been reconstructed afterwards, such as **BOE3C, CEPII, HISTAT** and **Johnston & Williamson** (2016), fill the gap.[8] They are not available, however, with a sufficient degree of accuracy for all countries; in particular for countries like Austria-Hungary or Serbia that disappeared, it is difficult obtain historical GDP data. But even for those countries with an uninterrupted economic history, there are sometimes large disturbances and conflicting data, urging researchers to make acceptable compromises.[9] This is even more acute in periods of war than in peacetime.

In the second place, there is the problem of exchange rates, both during the war and later. Until August 1914, all countries involved adhered to the Gold Standard, which pegged the exchange rates (see column '1913' in illustration A.1).

Exchange rates for some currencies[10] *(Illustration A.1)*

currency	exchange rate (currency per 1 US $)			change in value against US $		
	1913	1919	1928	during WW I	9 years after war	1913-1928
British *p and sterling*	0.21	0.23	0.21	-9%	+10%	0%
French *f anc*	5.18	7.31	25.50	- 29%	-71%	-80%
Belgian *f ank* (1)	5.22	7.83	35.90	-33%	-78%	-85%
Italian *l ia*	5.26	8.80	19.02	-40%	-54%	-72%
German *mark*	4.20	32.85	4.19 (2)	-87%	(1)	(2)
Austrian *krone*	4.96		7.11 (3)		(2)	(3)
Russian *rouble*	1.94	(4)		-73% (4)		

1) From 1926-1944 the official Belgian currency was the *belga*; 1 *belga* = 5 *frank*.

2) After the 1923 hyperinflation, the value of the *reichsmark* was formally one trillionth (10^{-12}) of the pre-war value of the (gold) *mark*. A comparison of pre- and post-1923 currencies has no significance.

3) Austrian *schilling*, with a value of one ten thousandth of the former Austrian-Hungarian *krone*. A comparison between both currencies is without significance.

4) In 1919, after the Russian Revolution, several currencies were circulating simultaneously ('Tsar', 'Duma', 'Kerensky' and 'Soviet' *roubles*); exchange rates varied wildly; change during the war is based on the last-used formal rate of $ 0.14 of December 1918, **The Economist** 7 December 1918, p. 787.

During the war, these fixed exchange rates were maintained formally, but in reality exchange rates diverted from their pre-war value, sometimes considerably.[11] In particular in trade relations with neutral countries, risk premiums (on buying) or discounts (on selling) were applied varying over time.[12] This does not make it easier to compare GDP values expressed in local currencies. **Bogart** (1920) systematically applies pre-war exchange rates to convert European currencies to dollars, whereas they diverted more and more as the war proceeded. Simply adding annual figures expressed in these 'floating' dollars necessarily leads to incorrect results. Incidentally, it must be noted that the largest changes in exchange rates occurred *after* the war (the last 3 columns of table A.1). **Ferguson** (1998), p. 323 uses 'appropriate average dollar exchange rates' to convert European currencies into dollars. Exchange rate fluctuations have been taken into account, but it is unclear how country specific inflation has been incorporated.

A third and final complicating factor is the framing of GDP itself, as it refers by definition to the *national* economy. 1% of the British GDP (2015) is £ 18 billion/year, 1% of the US GDP of the same period is $ 180 billion/year.[13] Using the average dollar-pound exchange rate for 2015 (1.528 $/£), we arrive at £ 118 billion/year. This is obviously much higher than the British figure, reflecting the difference in scale of the two countries; the amounts *per capita* are of the same order of magnitude but still unequal (£ 275 /year/capita for UK and £ 366 /year/capita for United States, expressed in Sterling). Per capita figures can be compared, but cannot be added for different countries or different years. This example makes it clear, that exactly the same relative burden of 1% of GDP translates into different figures in a comparison from then (1914-'18) to now. In other words, each country translates the past into the present from its own perspective.

All three factors – development of the national economy, fluctuating exchange rates and the frame of reference – play their role in the assessment of expenditures as they were made during the war a century ago in a wide range of countries. The total amount has been estimated at $ 215 billion in nominal values for the period 1914-1918/'19, which amounts to roughly $ 80 billion in pre-war value (1913 dollars). This total amount is the result of adding current expenditures from different countries during a period of about six years, in all sorts of existing and vanished currencies, the conversion being made by country with price indices to a year of reference and than translated into dollars of that reference year (or, in the case of **Ferguson** (1998) with average exchange rates).[14]

Finally, translation of all currencies into US dollars as a common unit suggests – albeit probably not on purpose – a relationship with the American economy, a relationship that was absent in most of the original data. Nevertheless, some common denominator has to be applied and the US dollar has replaced Stirling as the *de facto* international currency since the First World War (and undoubtedly after the Second world War). In view of the continuity of debt settlements, the dollar is a logical choice, but we have to be aware that projection from then to now with the development of the American economy as a frame of reference is to some degree distorting. Keeping this in mind, in terms of the United States economy the following can be said.

Results

Translating 1913 dollars into current (2015) dollars on the basis of GDP implies a factor of 456.[15] The total war expenditure of $ 80 billion in 1913 if it had been made completely by the United States, would be worth $ 36,000 billion now, again in US terms. That was the total amount spent during almost six fiscal years, so it amounts to roughly $ 6,000 billion per year. Taking into account the uncertainties in the assumptions (number of years, indices, exchange rates) this amount should be taken as a point in a *range*. But even if it were only 2/3 of it (or 3/2 times as high), it represents a sum of an astronomical order of magnitude. Just for comparison: total US expenditure in the Iraq and Afghanistan wars together (until February 2017) was $ 1,580 billion, in current prices;[16] other estimates mention even higher amounts, such as $ 3,000 billion and beyond.[17]

American expenditure in the First World War was $ 17 billion, in 1913 dollars, the equivalence of $ 7,500 billion in current dollars. This shows that the United States paid (in relation to its economy) more than 4.5 times as much for the First World War than in the Iraq and Afghanistan Wars taken together (7,500 / 1,580) or 2.5 times as much if the higher estimate is used; in either case these recent wars have not even approximated the American expenditure in the First World War.

Furthermore, American military involvement in the Great War lasted at most 2.5 years – and this is taken very broadly –, whereas the other wars lasted 14 years. It is an intriguing question whether the 'low tech' trenches warfare in 1914-'18 as compared to modern 'high tech' warfare contributed to this enormous discrepancy, but this question remains beyond the scope of this book.

Glossary

(expressions used in the context of this book; concepts may have a different meaning in other contexts)

annuity
A sum to be paid every year (or any other fixed period) consisting of interest and amortisation payments. The ratio between both parts generally changes over time while their sum is kept fixed. Annuities typically appear in mortgages (amortised loans), starting with high interest payments and low amortisations. Interest payments diminish over time while the amortisation share increases.

bill (of exchange)
A written order signed by one person to instruct another person (usually a bank) to pay the bearer a specific sum (ultimately) on a specific date. The sum of money can be expressed in a different currency than used by the signatory and the location where the sum is to be paid generally differs from the signatory's. The bill of exchange, in particular the Sterling bill, was widely used in nineteenth century international trade.

central bank
An institution in a nation (or a group of nations bound by a common currency) holding the exclusive right of controlling money supply. In practice this means, among other things, fixing discount rates, issuing bank notes, discounting government and commercial bills, acting as a lender of last resort for commercial and savings banks and high level communicating about economic developments. A central bank generally has exclusive rights, laid down in relevant bank acts, for example the monopoly of issuing bank notes as legal tender.

conversion / convert
Replace a loan by a new loan. Used for offering the opportunity to replace existing bonds with a low interest by new ones with a higher interest (or, conversely, the obligation to replace a high-interest bond by a bond with a lower interest).

convertibility

The right of holders of banknotes to have them exchanged at a bank into bullion (gold or silver bars of pure quality) or in another currency. Often at a rate previously defined by law and the bank having the legal duty to do so. Depending on legislation varying by country, this could be done at commercial banks, the central bank or the treasury.

discounting (a bill or a cash flow)

Discounting is the process of determining the present value of a payment or a stream of payments that is to be received (or paid) in the future. Given the time value of money, a dollar or a pound is worth more today than it would be worth tomorrow. Discounting is the primary factor used in pricing a stream of tomorrow's cash flows.

The expression discounting is used for two related notions:

a) comparing sums of money that are paid at different times; for example, $ 100 paid now will have grown next year by accrued interest. When the interest rate is 5%, $100 now is comparable to $ 105 in one year; the other way around, $ 100 next year is equivalent to 100/105 of it now, which is $ 95.24. A sum of money to be paid (or received) in the distant future therefore represents a much lower figure now; for example $ 1 million to be paid 59 years later corresponds to a fraction of $(100/105)^{59} = 0.056$ (rounded) of that amount now, $ 56,000. This principle of discounting has nothing to do with inflation (although the value of the interest rate used can be influenced by inflation).

b) trading a bill for cash before its expiration date by transferring all rights and obligations, in which case the buyer pays less than the face value by subtracting a discount percentage. By selling the bill, the seller converts its future claim into a real and immediate value; this has as price, expressed by the discount.

discount rate (bank rate)

The interest rate at which commercial banks can borrow money (short-term credit) at the central bank.

effective yield / gross redemption yield

The yield of a bond taking into account the initial price, years to maturity and interest rate. Technically, it is the rate of interest, which, if used to discount future dividends and the face value at redemption, makes the present value equal to the price of issue.[a] If the bond price at issue is below par (less than 100%, usually simply referred to as 100), the effective yield is higher than the nominal interest rate; how much it exceeds the nominal rate depends on the years to maturity, other factors being equal.

face value (nominal value)
The value of money or financial assets is the nominal value as printed on the currency or the document, in contrast to the value in trade; this latter value can be different for example caused by inflation. As a rule, the real value is less than the face value, but in certain cases it can be higher; tickets for pop concerts, for example, are sometimes traded above face value. At the issue of bonds, the government can deliberately create a difference by selling a bond below par, for example a £ 100 bond at £ 96, thus making it more attractive.

The nominal interest rate of a bond is the percentage as specified in the conditions, in contrast to the real interest rate or the effective yield.

Gold Standard
The monetary system in which the value currency of a country has a value directly linked to gold. Countries 'on gold' convert paper money into a fixed amount of gold (measured by mass and fineness). When several countries adhere to this principle, exchange rates are also fixed, apart from possible small temporary fluctuations. During the last quarter of the 19th century and until the outbreak of the First World War, most countries were 'on gold'. To be effective internationally, the Gold Standard system has the following requirements: unlimited convertibility of national currencies (including paper money) against gold at fixed prices, no restrictions on private ownership of gold, free and unlimited exporting and importing of gold and, finally, a universal trust that everyone obeys these conditions. Every country was free to be on gold; there was no formal international supervisory institution. The decision to adhere to the Gold Standard could be based on economic grounds or prestige considerations.

gross domestic product (GDP) / gross national product (GNP)
GDP is the total amount, expressed in monetary terms, of all goods and services produced in a country in a particular period of time, generally taken as a year. Formally GDP should therefore be expressed in (billions

---

a   Bank of England, Explanatory Notes – Yields.

of) \$/year, £/year, etc., although the '/year' is generally but unduly omitted. GDP is the most frequently used figure to express material wealth of a country.

GNP is an analogous concept, but relates to the goods and services produced by companies and individuals based in the country, irrespective where they are produced, domestically or abroad. The difference between GNP and GDP is that the latter uses territorial boundaries, whereas GNP uses legal boundaries.

legal tender

An object (coin) or document (banknote) that by law everyone has to accept as payment of debts. Generally, legal tender is country specific. For example, Bank of England notes are legal tender in England and Wales, banknotes issued by Scottish banks are not legal tender (not even formally in Scotland), Euro's are legal tender in the Eurozone, not in the United States, the American dollar is not legal tender in Europe, etc. Legal tender, however, does not coincide with acceptability. Shopkeepers in border regions generally accept other currencies. Conversely, gas stations may refuse banknotes in large denominations for security reasons. Credit cards, traveller's cheque and bullion are not legal tender.

money

An officially-issued legal tender generally consisting of currency and coin. A more abstract definition is: 'a documented promise of value of general validity' (Schmölders).

moratorium

A government measure by law or decree to postpone the obligation to pay debts of individuals, companies or institutions; a complete moratorium delays all payments, but usually it is restricted to interest and redemption payments and bills of exchange, while payments of wages, pensions and rents remain unaffected.

perpetual (loan/bond)

A loan or bond without a fixed maturity date. The debtor has to pay a fixed amount of interest annually (or semi-annually), but there is no obligation to pay back the principal at a well-defined date; this can continue indefinitely, unless the conditions stipulate that the debtor has the option to redeem the loan (voluntarily) after a specified number of years.

present value
The current value of a future amount of money or a flow of future amounts. The present value is calculated by means of the technique of discounting.

real interest rate
Nominal interest rate minus inflation rate (approximately). In case of high inflation, the real interest rate can become negative, implying that borrowing is more profitable than saving.

sinking fund
A reservation made by a company or a public body such as the government that issues bonds; by making small annual reservations in the fund the whole principal can be repaid at maturity date. The institution of a sinking fund enhances an investor's confidence that (s)he will be paid back; for long-term loans where risks might be considered large, it acts as a kind of growing collateral.

Notes

Preface

1   **Keegan** (2000).

2   **Tuchman** (1962), p. 100.

Chapter 1 – War financing

1   Paraphrased from **Burkheiser** (1941), p. 37.

2   http://www.bankofengland.co.uk/about/pages/history/default.aspx#2.

3   **Roesler** (1967), p. 195; **Fisk** (1922), p. 4 (pensions not included).

4   Based on GDP data from **Ritschl & Spoerer** (1997) and **CEPII** (variable 'PIBQ').

5   See also **Ferguson** (1998), p. 130.

6   For example **Einzig** (1935), p. 28.

7   The British economist Arthur Cecil Pigou has explained the concept of war costs as early as in 1916, in an article that reads very modern for current researchers in cost-benefit analysis, **Pigou** (1916), p. 14.

8   This monetising exercise poses large dilemmas and challenges. **Edelstein** (2000), p. 349, for example, points out that the average income in the 1950s and 1960s was larger than in in the 1920s and 1930s. In strictly economic reasoning, this would imply that a soldier fallen near Château-Thierry in 1918 would be less valuable than a comparable casualty in Normandy in 1944, because the latter would have realised more wealth in his lifetime than the former – if both had not been killed. From an ethical perspective, this is problematic, to say the least.

9   Ibid., p. 349.

10   See for example **Broadberry & Howlett** (2005), p. 222 ff., on British war economy.

11   Maintaining a professional army indeed enhanced *government expenditure* in the pre-war years compared to countries with a conscription system. This does not imply however that the *costs* for British society as a whole were necessarily higher as well. At the macro economic level it was merely a transfer of wealth from one group (all taxpayers) to the other (the professionals in the British Expeditionary Force and in the Royal Navy). Conscripted men would have to be extracted from the regular economic process of production in other sectors of the economy. One could even argue that recruitment of volunteers achieved a better allocation of human resources in comparison with an indiscriminate draft for military service regardless of physical and mental ability; the total costs for society might well be lower for a professional army than under a conscription system. For a more extensive discussion of this interesting question, in particular regarding the size of the army, see **Brauer & Van Tuyll** (2008), pp. 298-307 and references mentioned therein. Anyhow, Britain introduced conscription early 1916 after intense political tensions.

12   **Pigou** (1941), p. 30, makes a somewhat refined distinction in four categories: depletion of existing capital, augmented production, reduced personal consumption and reduced

investment in new forms of capital. The last three of these are highly related to national income. **Burkheiser** (1941), pp. 38-39, distinguishes foreign loans as a separate category, but in fact they are simply a form of creating negative national capital. See also **Roesler** (1967), p. 151.

13 **Pigou** (1941), p. 74; also **Roesler** (1967), p. 158; **The Economist** 12 August 1916, p. 279.

14 This refers to the 'veil of money' that hides the 'real' economic process. The notion of veil of money (German: *Geldschleier*) appears frequently in the earlier (1908) writings of Schumpeter, **Klausinger** (1990).

15 **Pigou** (1940), p. 48.

16 See also **Hardach** (1987), p. 154.

17 **Roesler** (1967), p. 152; also **Steinmann-Bucher** (1909) and **Helfferich** (1914), pp. 114-115, where the amount is estimated at 310 billion *marks*.

18 Background information on this highly interesting monetary union (from an historic perspective) can be found in **Einaudi** (2000) and references therein. The reference work for the Gold Standard is **Eichengreen** (1995).

Chapter 2 – French reparations

1 RGBl. 1871, Nr. 26, p. 215 ff., http://de.wikisource.org/wiki/Friedens-Präliminarien_ zwischen_dem_Deutschen_Reich_und_Frankreich.

2 The details are in Article 7 of the Treaty of Frankfurt: France should pay 2 billion *francs* within one year, of which 1.5 billion *francs* in 1871. The remaining 3 billion *francs* would bear 5% interest, RGBl. 1871, Nr. 26, p. 223 ff., http://de.wikisource.org/wiki/Friedens-Vertrag_zwischen_dem_Deutschen_Reich_und_Frankreich.

3 Calculated from the French GDP of approximately 19 billion *francs*, from **ESFDB** based on data from **Bonney** (2010). **Ritschl** (1996), p. 185, mentions 20%, but that is related to the somewhat higher GDP of 1869.

4 **O'Farrell** (1913), pp. 2, 19.

5 Eligible currencies based on the Gold Standard (Britain), Silver Standard (The Netherlands) or a mixed standard (Belgium). These currencies were considered to be as safe as gold.

6 Ibid., pp. 3-5; **Von Renauld** (1901), p. 73; **Moulton & Pasvolsky** (1932), p. 18.

7 This is the general picture; for qualifying remarks on the use of bills, see **Kindleberger** (1984), p. 248.

8 A detailed description of the role and practice of bills of exchange is given by **Brand** (1921), Chapter I.

9 **O'Farrell** (1913), p. 4. The short-term loans were mainly contracted by Prussia.

10 For details on the loans, see **Kindleberger** (1984), p. 243 ff.

11 **O'Farrell** (1913), p. 10; **The Economist** 22 March 1873, p. 345.

12 **Kindleberger** (1953), p. 319 ff.

13 In the French tradition the loans were perpetual (see Chapter 9), **Leroy-Beaulieu** (1874), p. 838.

14 Calculations based on **Bonney** (2010), presented in **ESFDB**. It should be noted that the loans to finance the reparation debt was not the only source for the rise in French national debt. Investments in a large system of inland waterways also contributed to this increase, **Eichengreen** (1995), p. 78.

15 National debt taken as the item 'RENTE' (long-term debt) conform **CEPII**, http://cepii.fr/francgraph/bdd/villa/mode.htm; GDP data before 1890 are not available from CEPII; they have been taken from the GNP time series derived by Bonney as published in: **Cardoso & Lains** (2010), conform **ESFDB**, http://esfdb.websites.bta.com/table.aspx?resourceid=12302. Unfortunately, these data are available for periods of 5 years only, which underestimates the increase during 1871 and 1872: the increase will be even more pronounced than in the illustration. For the years after 1890, the Bonney data are only slightly different from the CEPII data.

16 **US Department of Commerce** (1976), Western Europe includes Germany, Britain, Ireland, Scandinavia and other NW European countries; during the same period 7.8 million people emigrated to the United States from Central and Eastern Europe and 4.4 million from southern Europe (mainly Italy).

17 The amount of 20% is an indication. There is some discussion in the literature about reliable historical GDP data for Germany, **Ritschl & Spoerer** (1997), **Burhop & Wolff** (2005); in an unpublished paper, the latter authors mention a share of 15%-20%, **Burhop & Wolff** (2002), p. 15; although they do not mention a nominal German GDP value, this would imply a nominal German GDP of 20-27 billion *marks* 1870/'71, which seems (too) high considering a contemporary GDP/capita value in comparison with France for example.

18 A lively view on German inflation and speculation during the early 1870s from a French perspective (not without some gloating) is given by **Serrigny** (1909), p. 379 ff.

19 **Burhop & Wolff** (2005), p. 647; an assessment of economic developments in Germany in the period 1870-1873 is subject to scientific discussion, brought about by data problems. Undisputed facts are the initial rise and subsequent sharp fall in the stock exchange index, and the boom in newly established banks of which a considerable part went bankrupt within a few years, **Pohl** (1978), pp. 20-22.

20 **McKenna** (1922); **Sauvy** (1984), Part 3, p. 26; neither author gives more specific sources.

21 **Guyot (1919)**, p. 7. Based on an original debt of 5 billion *francs*, this would have accrued at 5% interest over 47 years (1871-1918) into roughly 50 billion *francs* instead of 60 million *francs*. The journalist started with an initial amount of 5.69 billion *francs*, **Martin** (1999), p. 45; this seems to be too high, even if all costs are taken into account; **O'Farrell** (1913), p. 2, mentions a gross amount of 5.32 billion *francs*, a reasonable amount if the interest on the 3 billion *francs* of the debt is taken into account.

22 **Bastable** (1903), pp. 646-649. At the eve of the war the French national debt was 65% of one year's GDP, **Hautcœur** (2005), p. 185; also **CEPII**: 66%; the corresponding data for Britain are 30%, **BOE3C**, for Germany 10%, based on **Lotz** (1927), p. 125 and **Ritschl & Spoerer** (1997), p. 38 and **HISTAT**, and for the United States 7.5%, **Reinhart & Rogoff** (2011); all data are for 1913, but vary (insignificantly) depending on the exact date of reference (end of fiscal year vs. calendar year). For Italy, the national debt was almost 70% of one year GDP in 1913, **Reinhart & Rogoff** (2011).

Chapter 3 – *La Circulaire bleue*
1 **Horn & Imlay** (2005), pp. 719-723.
2 **Ramon** (1929), p. 427.

3   **Ahamed** (2010), p. 70. Roughly 40% of the increase in gold reserve took place at the expense of a decrease in silver, **Petit** (1929), p. 717.

4   French sources, such as **Serrigny** (1909), p. 108 ff., point out that Pallain initiated measures from his first day in office, but mainly behind the scenes.

5   **Horn** (2002), p. 23; **Horn & Imlay** (2005), p. 725; **Petit** (1929), p. 717. It is not yet fully clear whether the accumulation of gold was and end in itself or primarily driven by economic developments, *Banque de France*, 2014 and 2017, private communication.

6   The sources on the Russian gold stock at the eve of the First World War are not unanimous. **Strachan** (2004), p. 38, refers to data from Michelson *et al.* (Michelson, A.M., P.N. Apostol en M.W. Bernatzky (1928), *Russian public finance during the* war, New Haven, Yale University Press), which imply that the value was 4.6 billion *francs* (£ 185 million); **Brand** (1921), p. 29, mentions £ 125 million, corresponding to 3.2 billion *francs*. As regards Britain, although it had evidently no gold mines in Europe, it had access to – or in fact control over – South African gold supplies, **Harris** (1931), p. 302.

7   **Strachan** (2004), p. 6. In 1913 the *per capita* gold reserve in Britain was less than £ 1, the total 1.7% of one year's GDP. There are rational economic and monetary explanations for the difference between gold stock in France and Britain, notably the international and flexible financial market in London and the fact that Sterling was in fact the world's monetary standard. In the background a cultural factor seems to be involved in the almost obsessive way the French approached gold. The French *franc* was backed by gold for almost 70%, one of the highest (if not the highest) rates for any currency, **Jèze & Truchy** (1927), p. 239. It is not unlikely that the traumatic experience of the (paper) *assignats* from the time of the French Revolution still played a role.

8   Currencies have been converted at pre-war (gold based) exchange rates. Original data from **Petit** (1929), p. 717, **Zilch** (1987), p. 114; population data from **CEPII** (France, variable 'POP') en **HISTAT** (Germany; Sensch, J., *Geschichte der deutschen Bevölkerung seit 1815*. GESIS Köln, ZA8171 Datenfile Version 1.0.0 and Diebolt, C. & O. Darne, *Die Reichsbank 1876 bis 1920*, GESIS Köln, ZA8144 Datenfile Version 1.0.0, variable: *Durchschnittlicher Goldbestand*); GDP data from **CEPII** (France, variable 'PIBQ') and **Ritschl & Spoerer** (1997).

9   *Conventions* 11-11-1911, art. 1.

10   French GDP in 1911 was 46 billion *francs*, **CEPII**, variable 'PIBQ'.

11   *Loi du 5 août 1914*, art. 4. **Lachapelle** (1915), p. 233 mentions that the conventions were published by the Finance Department in December 1914; they had been mentioned however already in the Act of 5 August 1914. It should be noted, that it was not the first time that agreements with this intention had been made between the *Banque* and the government. The amount of the agreement of 1911, however, was considerably larger; previous agreements of 1890, 1896 and 1899 to amounts of 350 million francs were overruled by the new agreement. Secret negotiations between the government and the direction of the *Banque* date from at least as early as 1890, **Vignat** (2001), p. 147.

12   Sources are, among other things, the article at the occasion of his appointment at the *Banque*, **L'Illustration** (8 January 1898, p. 29, also the source of the picture), the funeral oration of **Robineau** (1923), the PhD thesis of **Vignat** (2001) and genealogical research by the author. Vignat remarks that biographical information about Pallain is hardly available and by all means insufficient for a scientifically sound biography.

13   **Robineau** (1923).

14   There exists a remarkable document, the *Convention* (1910), signed 18 March 1910 by both brothers-in-law in their capacity of Finance minister and Bank Governor, respectively. It concerned an interest-free loan to the government for assistance to flood victims.

15   *Banque de France* (1914).

16   After the 1907 banking crisis Senator Aldrich made a trip to Europe to explore experiences and to collect good practices in order to decide whether it would be wise for the United States to establish a central bank and if so, in which form, **Aldrich** (1908). It would take more than 5 years before the United States created the Federal Reserve System in 1913, after lengthy and difficult political discussions and much pressure from Aldrich himself. For details on the discussions and their circumstances, among which the crucial Jekyll Island negotiations, see **Ahamed** (2010), pp. 70-71.

17   *Banque de France* (1980/1997), p. 77.

18   **L'Illustration** (1898), p. 29.

19   **Horn & Imlay** (2005), p. 727.

20   *Banque de France* (1908).

21   The instruction (the *Circulaire bleue*) is undated. In view of Pallain's energy and drive, one may assume with good reason that it was sent out before the Agreements of November 1911 but after the decision to print banknotes in December 1908.

22   *Banque de France* (1980/1997), *Cahier Anecdotique* nr. 7, pp. 11, 16.

23   In its preparation the *Banque* had concentrated on the Eastern regions. A German attack from the North through neutral Belgium was considered less probable, also in financial circles. When the attack nevertheless came from the North according to the Schlieffen Plan, evacuation of the Northern offices was organised rapidly and successfully, **Vignat** (2001), p. 383.

24   See the quote and footnote on page 35 and page 42.

25   See also **Horn** (2002), p. 23.

Chapter 4 – *Finanzielle Kriegsbereitschaft?*

1   The *Reichsbank* was founded 1ˢᵗ January 1876 based on the Bank Act of 1875, **RGBl.** 1875, Nr. 15, § 12, p. 180; see also **Zilch** (1987), p. 13 ff.

2   When the war broke out, the envisaged increase was not yet reached; the level was 205 million *marks* in gold and 6 million *marks* in silver, **Roesler** (1967), pp. 23-24.

3   **Roesler** (1967), p. 45.

4   For example **Von Renauld** (1901), **Riesser** (1909/1913), **Dietzel** (1912). A comprehensive list is given in **Holtfrerich** (1980), p. 104 ff.

5   One of the discussants, the economist Heinrich Dietzel, expresses the options in the title of his book: 'War tax or War loan?' See also **Roesler** (1967), p. 34, and **Strachan** (2004), pp. 98-99.

6   **Roesler** (1967), p. 24.

7   The effective date was 1ˢᵗ January 1910, **Riesser** (1912), p. 149.

8   The monthly data show a net increase in July of 118 million *marks* of coins (+ 3%); in this same period, the circulation of *Reichsbank* notes increased by 502 million marks (+ 21%), **Roesler** (1967), p. 218. **Ramstein** (1923), p. 40, mentions an amount of 230 millions *marks* of silver, nickel and copper coins put into circulation during the weeks around the outbreak of the war; this amount cannot be verified from the monthly data.

9   **Hardach** (1987), pp. 151-152; the specific notion *gesetztreu* appears in the German edition
      only, **Hardach** (1973), p. 164.
10   **RT** 315, Nr. 9; also Nr. 26, p. 102-114.
11   Session of the Prussian Cabinet 31 May 1891, in: **Spenkuch** (2003), Band 8-I, nr. 53.
12   **Riesser** (1913), p. 144.
13   The formal status of the *Darlehenskassenscheine* was a debt certificate in bearer form, as a
      receipt for the acceptation of the pledged material. The material could consist of real
      non-perishable (physical) goods, but also of financial assets, such as stock or bonds. For
      physical goods, normally half of the value (in exceptional cases up to 2/3) was paid in
      Darlehenskassenscheine. **RT** 315, Nr. 9.
14   **Zilch** (1987), p. 122.
15   **Hardach** (1987), p. 156; also **Roesler** (1967), pp. 41-43.
16   The right to fix the amount of *Darlehenskassenscheine* was in the hands of the *Bundesrat*, the
      Federal Council. This institution was appointed by the German States, it was not elected. In
      practice it was an instrument of the regional kings, archdukes and other princes, dominated
      by Prussia, the king of which was one and the same person as the German Emperor.
17   'The fiction that paper be gold' (*'die Fiktion das Papier Gold sei'*), **Bendixen** (1919; first
      edition 1916), p. 28. Bendixen was a banker from Hamburg with a more realistic view
      on finance than the authorities in Berlin. See also **Feldman** (1985), pp. 34-36, for the
      reception of this criticism in Germany and the fiction of the one-third-backing system
      (*'Dritteldeckung'*).
18   The value of the notes issued was accounted by the National Debt Administration (*Reichs-
      schuldenverwaltung*) in the National Debt as short-term (floating) debt, **Lotz** (1927), p. 22.
      The ultimate backing was of course the material pledged at the *Darlehenskassen*. They had
      the right to sell the goods publicly if the original pledger did not show up.
19   **RT** 315, Nr. 9, §2; see also **Roesler** (1967), pp. 41-43. The laws gave the government *carte
      blanche* to pursue all kinds of intervention through the *Bundesrat*. For example, already in
      September 1914 all gold clauses in contracts were rendered ineffective, a measure that could
      only be reversed by the Chancellor, not even by the *Bundesrat* itself! **RT** 315 nr. 26, p. 7. For
      the Bank Act, see **RGBl**. 1875, Nr. 15, pp. 177-198 and for the *Reichskassenscheine* before
      the war **Roesler** (1967), p. 208.

Chapter 5 – *The City*
1   **Horn** (2002), p. 4.
2   **McKenna** (1948), p. 170.
3   **Eichengreen** (1995), p. 43.
4   **CMD** (1905) 2384 and for the secret clauses **PP** (1911), Vol. CIII, Cmd. 5969: *Declaration
      between the United Kingdom and France Respecting Egypt and Morocco*. On the *Entente
      Cordiale* and its role in French-British relationships in the preparation of the war and during
      the war, see **Bell** (1996) and **Greenhalgh** (2009).
5   **Horn** (2002), pp. 23-24. In later years, it appeared that cooperation between government
      departments had been rightly identified as an important issue, as it would emerge in the
      problematic cooperation between the War Office, the Ministry of Munitions, the Board
      of Trade, the Admiralty and the Treasury and their respective leaders (Kitchener, Lloyd
      George, Runciman, Churchill and McKenna, mainly in the period 1914-'16).

6   **Horn** (2002), p. 25.

7   For the specialised network of financial institutions in London (and their role at the outbreak of the First World War), see **Horn** (2002), p. 8 ff., but also **Roberts** (2010) and **Brand** (1921), p. 21 ff. for technical details.

8   During the war, the interest rates on *Treasury Bills* (and to a lesser extent on war loans) replaced the bank rate as an indicator for the price of money and capital, **Roberts** (2010), p. 170.

9   Biographical information derived from, among others, **Burk** (2008), **Ahamed** (2010) and **Horn** (2002).

10   **London Gazette** (1914), p. 10688, 15 December 1914.

11   **London Gazette** (1917), Supplement, p. 8794, 27 August 1917.

12   **Ahamed** (2010), pp. 78-79.

13   **Horn** (2002), p. 173; **Ahamed** (2010), p. 83.

14   **Ahamed** (2010), p. 105.

15   Quoted in *Geoffrey Madan's Notebooks*, **Gere & Sparrow** (1981), p. 87.

16   **Hardach** (1987), p. 140. Legal dates may differ from *de facto* dates. For example in France the *Banque de France* terminated gold issue at the mobilisation decree and therefore it actually suspended the Gold Standard, which was confirmed by law a few days later; gold exportation was formally prohibited by decree on 3 July 1915, *Décret 3 juillet 1915*. The German Reichsbank suspended convertibility unilaterally on 31 July 1914, **Lotz** (1927), p. 18. In Britain, the moratorium had been issued on 2 August 1914, primarily as a reaction on the financial crisis, not on the war as such, **Kirkaldy** (1921), pp. 6-7, **Strachan** (2004), pp. 8-9; although Britain did not formally suspend the Gold Standard, in practice there were several restrictions in connection with a highly discouraging policy, **Harris** (1931), p. 308 ff. For US export restrictions, based on the Trading with the enemy Act, **USSAL** 1919, vol. XL, p. 411, see **FRB**, June 1989, p. 426 and **Brown** (1940), p. 34, where also a more general discussion on the reality of keeping up the Gold Standard can be found (p. 28 ff.); although there was no formal or even *de facto* restriction on US gold export, the outflow was more or less automatically reduced by the closing of the New York stock exchange on 31 July 1914 (until 12 December 1914), page 156. The operation, together with prohibitive insurance rates might be called an 'informal' export ban, ibid., p. 18; see also **Silber** (2007), p. 35.

17   **Vignat** (2001).

18   For example **Horn** (2002), p. 9.

Chapter 6 – War expenditure: beyond comprehension

1   **Breyer** (1973), p. 52. Other quantitative details about battleships, ibid., passim. For conversion of currencies see the Annex 'What is the meaning of a sum of money of 1914-'18 a century later?'.

2   **Helfferich** (1919), Band II, pp. 137-138.

3   **ARST 1920**, p. 338, in current dollars.

4   **FRB**, April 1918, p. 275.

5   **Fisk** (1924), p. 16.

6   Ibid., pp. 163-164.

7   **Bogart** (1920), **Fisk** (1924). For a reflection on the measurement problem, see also **Broadberry & Harrison** (2005).

8   RT 306, p. 35.

9   **Hardach** (1987), p. 152. Russia also applied this system of a normal budget parallel to an extraordinary budget.

10   See for example the analysis in **Broadberry & Harrison** (2005), p. 22 ff. In practical terms this amounts to first applying a price index by country to obtain pre-war or 1914 values, followed by a conversion into a common currency, usually American dollars. Exchange rates used are typically pre-war values based on gold parity. See for details the Annex 'What is the meaning of a sum of money of 1914-'18 a century later?' and the note on sources, page 357.

11   For example **Hardach** (1987), p. 153, for the period 1914-1919 (6 fiscal years), **Ferguson** (1998), p. 323 (for a selection of the countries, 5 fiscal years and partly using a different method). One of the first calculations, **Bogart** (1920), p. 267, already resulted in an amount of the same order of magnitude.

12   The data in **Ferguson** (1998), p. 323, appear to take into account exchange rate changes only, resulting in a kind of current dollars. Exchange rate changes, however, reflect only partially inflation rate disparities between countries, in particular in wartime. Thanks to the fact that official exchange rates of Sterling and *franc* (to the dollar) were still approximately equal to their pre-war value, the *nominal* value in this calculation differs not much from the method with fixed exchange rates by year, except for Germany and Austria-Hungary. In 1913 dollars, the values from Ferguson differ from the **Fisk** (1924) values and calculations based thereupon.

13   Ultimately based on **Fisk** (1924). Indexation based on development of wholesale prices. The Fisk data for this index are not fundamentally different from those presented by **Holtfrerich** (1980), p. 15, after a recalculation from calendar year to fiscal year.

14   They are only partially incorporated if loans were issued in the last few years of the war to cover this expenditure and as far as the interest on these loans has been taken into account; in practice, this will be negligible.

15   Based on **Broadberry & Harrison** (2005), p. 15. It should be noted that their data refer to total government expenditure, not only war expenditure. By assuming that roughly three quarters of pre-war government was not war-related at all and continued as expenditure during the war, an estimate can be made of the war-related part. For France this is in line with estimates based on annual expenditure; German data are indicative due to lacking reliable GDP data.

16   The amount of *total* government expenditure given by **Broadberry & Harrison** (2005), p. 15, (35%-37%) is somewhat low if compared to the data from **Balderston** (1989), p. 227, that give rise to a share of 50% as well. A rate of 35% on the other hand is reasonably in line with older data from **Fisk** (1922), p. 11.

17   **Broadberry & Harrison** (2005), p. 15 (Austria-Hungary) and **Fisk** (1924), p. 21 (Austria-Hungary and Italy).

18   **UKBUD** 2015, p. 6 and p. 109. http://www.ukpublicspending.co.uk/uk_defence_spen ding_30.html.

19   When calculating such long-term effects, care must be taken to avoid double counting and omissions; for example, if a loan during the war is counted as war expenditure, later redemption of the loan should be subtracted, possibly at a discounted value, etc.

20   Mainly based on the original data and checked calculations from **Fisk** (1924). There is not a large discrepancy with more recent calculations. The main differences arise from the period

chosen: six fiscal years 1914-1919 (or 1914/'15-1919/'20 in the case of broken years) and the index numbers used to recalculate them to 1913 values. These choices are appropriate, but different choices can be defended. For Britain the Fisk data are in good agreement with the data from **Balderston** (1989), p. 227, in which the period is restricted by one year. For Germany the Fisk and Balderston data largely agree up to and including 1917/1918; Balderston however correctly includes the German federal states, thus increasing the German expenditure by 13% with respect to the value for the German *Reich* alone. For the latest war years Fisk uses German wholesale price indices that agree with the data from **Holtfrerich** (1980), but for Germany the cost of living index is probably more realistic than the wholesale price index; the latter has been used in illustration 6.2. The total value for France given by Fisk is in agreement with **Hautcœur** (2005), p. 186, if it is assumed that French loans to allies have been left out. **Soutou** (1991), p. 284, however mentions a higher amount.

21   **Von Renauld** (1901), p. 107. The GDP value used by Von Renauld, 18 billion *marks*/year in 1901, is too low, as is the value for German national wealth. In the table his values have been corrected following **Ritschl & Spoerer** (1997) and **Helfferich** (1914), p. 114, respectively, the latter indicatively recalculated to 1901. For details on the real expenditure, see note 20 above to illustration 6.2.

22   **Bogart** (1921), p. 83, mentions daily values of the order of $ 20-$ 55 million, for all belligerent countries together.

23   **Holtfrerich** (1980), p. 105.

Chapter 7 – Sources for funding: a menu with limited choices

1   For example **Holtfrerich** (1980), p. 99 ff.

2   **Burkheiser** (1941), p. 59; **Pigou** (1941), p. 72.

3   **RT 306**, p. 38.

4   The regular budget for the fiscal year 1915/'16 even showed a surplus. As a man of law, Helfferich correctly reported that this surplus was merely of a technical nature; the large expenditure for warfare (*'aus Anlaß des Krieges'*) had been transferred to the extraordinary budget. For the *Reichstag* members it was no issue, it even led to cheerfulness (*'Heiterkeit'*), **RT 306**, p. 34.

5   **Horn** (2002), p. 82.

6   Sources for this short biography include the comprehensive biography by **Williamson** (1971), the paper by **Wunder** (2004) about his city of birth and **Helfferich** (1919) himself. For the role of Helfferich after the war, see page 216. Photograph: author's collection.

7   For example: **Helfferich** (1923).

8   **Williamson** (1971), pp. 117-118; also **Zilch** (1994), p. 104 ff.

9   **RT 355**, p. 7997. It took place in the *Reichstag* debate on reparations arrangements with France that had been initiated earlier by Foreign Secretary Walther Rathenau. The debate was held on 23 June 1922; the next morning Rathenau was assassinated.

10   See also **Williamson** (1971), p. 413.

11   **Höll** *et al.* (2007), p. 1419.

12   **Reinhart & Rogoff** (2009), p. 61 ff.; also **Eichengreen** (1988). The same argument: credit status as the big stick, would be used in the 1920s and 1930s in attempts to transfer German reparations from public to private (market) debts, thus commercialising reparations. In

contrast to French reparations after the Franco-Prussian War, it was only partially successful, Chapter 12 and **Gomes** (2010), p. 173.

13 **Keynes** (1924), p. 80.

14 For example **Pigou** (1941), p. 72 ff., **Dietzel** (1912), p. 20 ff., **Holtfrerich** (1980), p. 99 ff., **Strachan** (2004), pp. 63, 115-116; also **Ritschl** (1996), p. 177 ff. on the Ricardian theory about equivalence of taxation and financing by government bonds.

15 **Gilbert** (1970), p. 86 ff.

16 For example **Balderston** (1989), p. 234.

17 See also **Pigou** (1941), p. 81; **Dietzel** (1912), p. 26.

18 This of course depended on the alternative use of the capital lent to the government (the opportunities) and the use of capital not lent. From an economic viewpoint, some comment could be placed on the efficiency argument.

19 **Dietzel** (1912), p. 35 ff.

20 See also **Strachan** (2004), p. 116.

21 The fact that *all* taxpayers had to contribute to interest payments, both the rich and the poor, did not necessarily imply that capital was categorically taxed less than labour. There is some evidence that at least in Britain capital was levied more severely than labour, **Nason & Vahey** (2007). For countries with high (post-war) inflation, such as France and in particular Germany and Austria-Hungary, this must certainly be the case, at least for capital in the form of cash (Chapter 14).

22 For example **Ferguson** (1998), p. 130 ff.

23 **Münkler** (2013), pp. 590 and 593-593, points out that in 1916 the German government had limited possibilities to take initiatives for peace, because it had to consider the interests of bondholders of war loans fearing that their investment would not be paid back (or only partially).

24 The role played by media is a subject by its own; see for example **Di Jorio et al.** (2012) and **Kang & Rockoff** (2006).

25 David Lloyd George, quoting himself in 1933 from a document dated November 1916, Lloyd **George** (1933), p. 340.

26 For example Helfferich in the German Reichstag, 10 March 1915, **RT 306** p. 35 ff., Bonar Law in the British Parliament, 26 February 1917, **HC**, 1695-1697.

27 In Britain several other banks, notably in Scotland and Ireland, had the right to issue banknotes. In Germany too, there were few banks with this privilege, but at a much more modest scale, **Holtfrerich** (1980), p. 49.

28 For example **Hardach** (1987), p. 154.

29 A documented illustration of this effect of pushing up prices by the government is found in Austria-Hungary, where the army commanders ordered that for requested material twice the normal market price should be paid: speed had a price, *Die Österreichisch-ungarische Bank*, http://www.oenb.at/Ueber-Uns/Unternehmensgeschichte/1878-1922.html.

30 For example **Holtfrerich** (1980), p. 11.

31 Ibid., pp. 64-65.

32 For example **The Economist** 12 August 1916, p. 280, 9 September 1916, p. 435 and 23 June 1917, p. 1145.

33 For example **Einzig** (1935), p. 36; **Hardach** (1987), p. 149; **Roesler** (1967), p. 179.

34 **Strachan** (2004), p. 130.

35 Keynes (1924), p. 42. In the argument the (classical) assumption has been made of an unchanged rate of circulation.

36 In Germany for example one could pledge war bonds at the *Darlehenskassen* for a value of 75% of their face value; after such a transaction, three quarters of the original war bonds re-entered circulation in the form of *Darlehenskassenscheine* or just money in a different form; a description has been given by **Bogart** (1921), p. 190 and **Strachan** (2004), p. 124. In France the *bons de la défense nationale* did the same trick (Chapter 9) by being used as banknotes in disguise. In fact even in Britain, there was no effective obstacle to prevent money that had been tied up in long-term bonds to re-enter circulation, at least partially, **Strachan** (2004), pp. 116-117.

37 In the Second World War countries occupied by Germany have contributed considerably to finance the Nazi war, **Occhino *et al.*** (2006).

38 **Van Langenhove** (1927), p. 167; **Zilch** (1994), p. 183 mentions an amount of 2.28 billion *franks* as the German levies on Belgian provinces. The official rate of exchange was the pre-war parity 100 *franks* equals 80 *marks*.

39 **Flama** (2009/2010), p. 121 ff., based on publications in the German *Verordnungsblatt*, nos. 80, 259 and 333.

40 **Zilch** (1994), p. 208.

41 Louis Dubois, quoted by **Lewandowski** (1923), p. 54, from an annex to the Transactions of the Chamber of Representatives of 18 December 1918.

42 This is an indicative estimation because it is based on nominal amounts, converted at fixed, pre-war rates of exchange. At the Eastern front Germany indeed applied this model of war finance by imposing reparations in the Brest-Litovsk and Bucharest Treaties. Russia had to pay 1.5 billion *marks* in addition to 250 tonnes of gold, **Zilch** (1994), p. 377.

43 **The Hague Conventions** (1907).

44 For example **Ferguson** (1998), p. 254.

45 **Breyer** (1973), pp. 136, 138, 148. The ships were the *Agincourt*, *Erin* and *Canada*, respectively, used by Britain in the battle of Jutland. Originally the Agincourt had been commissioned by Brazil, but it was taken over by the Ottoman Empire in January 1914. The amount of £ 7.5 million in 1911 represented roughly 3.4‰ of the British GDP of that year. Transferred to the impact on today's national economy, this would mean roughly £ 6 billion for Britain or $ 60 billion for the United States.

46 **RT 306**, p. 34: '*Wir werden nicht darauf verzichten können, und wir denken nicht daran, darauf zu verzichten, daß unsere Feinde – abgesehen von allem anderen – uns für den materiellen Schaden aufkommen müssen, den sie mit diesem frevelhaft angezettelten Kriege angerichtet haben*'.

47 This is based on the value of *gold marks*, the currency in which reparations were expressed. War expenditure for the allies is taken as the round value of $ 60 billion in 1913 values, corrected for inflation just as the *gold marks* were effectively corrected for inflation. The pre-war exchange rate was 4.20 *marks*/$. Only reparations in cash have been taken into account, not reparations delivered in kind.

48 This is in fact not very different from large private acquisitions such as a house. Few people can afford to buy a house from their current income; most of them have to apply to savings or loans, see **Pigou** (1941), p. 73.

Chapter 8 – Taxes: an inconvenient option for politicians

1   For example **Hamilton-Grace** (1910), p. 18.

2   **Knauss** (1923), pp. 175-176, **Ferguson** (1998), p. 232, **Balderston** (1989), pp. 226-229.

3   **McAdoo** (1931), p. 384; **Synon** (1924), p. 223.

4   In the fiscal year ending 30 June 1918, 32% of American government expenditure (including war expenditure) was covered by normal revenues, but without the loans to the allies it would have been 49%, **ARST** 1918, p. 4.

5   **Bogart** (1920), pp. 161-181; **Knauss** (1923), pp. 174-175; **Ferguson** (1998), p. 323; **Strachan** (2004), pp. 66, 80, **Balderston** (1989), pp. 226-229. There is a range of uncertainty where the data in various sources do not agree, due to different reference periods, inclusion or exclusion of levels of taxation, attribution to categories and progress in knowledge.

6   **Von Renauld** (1901), p. 52. Only in the American War of Independence, Britain financed a war over 95% by loans; also **Hamilton-Grace** (1910).

7   **Strachan** (2004), p. 48; **Daunton** (2002), pp. 10-11.

8   An important background was that tax rates that had been increased to finance the Boer War were not (accordingly) decreased after that war, **Balderston** (1989), p. 233.

9   **Kirkaldy** (1921), p. 214, reproduced in **Broadberry & Howlett** (2005), p. 216.

10   £ 47.2 million on total revenue of £ 198.2, ibid.

11   **Strachan** (2004), pp. 67-68.

12   For example **Strachan** (2004), p. 48. In matters of finance Lloyd George relied heavily on advice from his friend Lord Reading (Rufus Isaacs), Lord Chief Justice, who would play an important role in the negations with the US about war debts, **Horn** (2002), p. 34.

13   **Bogart** (1920), pp. 9-10; **Strachan** (2004) p. 69, gives slightly different rates for the base rate.

14   Tax revenue based on **Broadberry & Howlett** (2005), p. 216, which are derived from **Kirkaldy** (1921), p. 214; GDP data converted to fiscal year based on *Bank of England* data, **BOE3C**.

15   The main sources are **McKenna** (1948), **Horn** (2002) and **Farr** (2005a/b). Photograph: *Library of Congress*.

16   **Howe** (2010), **Farr** (2008); **McKenna** (1948).

17   **McKenna** (1948), p. 166.

18   Ibid., p. 26.

19   Ibid., pp. 236-238; also **Horn** (2002), p. 101.

20   **Horn** (2002), p. 101.

21   Ibid., p. 35.

22   Ibid., p. 180.

23   **Lloyd George** (1933), p. 187.

24   **Farr** (2005a), p. 222. It is no accident that Jekyll Island (Chapter 5) bears the same name; it was named after Sir Joseph Jekyll (1663-1738), a distant ancestral relative of Pamela.

25   The genealogy of the Horner-Graham-Jekyll families can be found in **http://www.stanford.edu/group/auden/cgi-bin/auden/individual.php?pid=110113&ged=auden-bicknell.ged&tab=4.**

26   **Farr** (2005b), pp. 33-35.

27   **Strachan** (2004), pp. 68-69.

28 **Bogart** (1920), pp. 17, 21.

29 **Strachan** (2004), p. 78.

30 *The Economist* 25 September 1915, p. 463; also **Bogart** (1920), p. 17.

31 As a standard for pre-war profit the taxpayer could choose the average of 2 out of 3 years before 1914; in case of slump conditions, the taxpayer could even choose 4 out of 6 years, **Bogart** (1920), p. 17.

32 Ibid., p. 20.

33 Ibid., p. 38.

34 **Broadberry & Howlett** (2005), p. 216, derived from **Kirkaldy** (1921), p. 214.

35 **Strachan** (2004), pp. 73-76.

36 Ibid., pp. 76-77; **Bogart** (1920), pp. 26-27.

37 **Bogart** (1920), p. 38, **Knauss** (1923), p. 136; **Strachan** (2004), p. 77, mentions a slightly different percentage.

38 **Einzig** (1935), p. 41.

39 **Roesler** (1967), p. 196.

40 The SPD had received 34.8% of the votes, which made it more than twice as large as the second party, the (Catholic) German Centre Party (*Zentrumspartei*) with 16.4% of the (popular) votes. Source: http://de.wikipedia.org/wiki/Reichstagswahl_1912.

41 This had been a political demand of German socialist already laid down in their Erfurt Programme, **SPD** (1891).

42 For example **Strachan** (2004), p. 97 and **Ferguson** (1998), pp. 115-117.

43 **RT** 306, p. 2

44 **Helfferich** (1923), pp. 213-214.

45 **Roesler** (1967), p. 96.

46 Ibid., pp. 195-196.

47 Ibid., p. 197. The percentage applies to the normal (*'ordentlicher'*) budget only. The extra-ordinary budget (*Außerordentlicher Haushalt*), where the war related expenditure was charged and its financing by credits could be found, was 7 times larger than the normal budget. When both ordinary and extraordinary budget are taken together, the rise in interest obligations increased from 5% to 15%.

48 **RT** 325, nr. 1879.

49 **Hardach** (1987), p. 161.

50 **Jèze & Truchy** (1927), p. 204 ff.

51 Ibid., p. 225.

52 Ibid., pp. 226-227.

53 Ibid., p. 204; **Schmidt** (1974), pp. 112-114.

54 **Hardach** (1987), p. 161.

55 In 1916 debt related payments, mainly interest, took two thirds of the regular government revenue, in 1917 this increased to 80% and in 1918 even more than 100% of the government revenue had to be paid for servicing the debts. **Jèze & Truchy** (1927), p. 212; evidently, this concerned – just as in Germany – the regular budget, not war-related expenditure.

56 Based on revenue during the years 1916-1919 from **Jèze & Truchy** (1927), p. 203 and the total amount of current expenditure that was used in illustration 6.2; **Hardach** (1987), p. 162 mentions a lower amount of revenue (800 million *francs*), but this is without the year 1919 that has been included in the total expenditure used here.

57   In particular the parliamentary budget committee stressed this point, **Klotz** (1924), p. 59 ff.

58   **Jèze & Truchy** (1927), p. 152.

59   Ibid., p. 207.

60   **Strachan** (2004), p. 85.

61   **Jèze & Truchy** (1927), p. 152. In this case, inflation has been approximated by using the *franc*-dollar exchange rate for the period 1917-1921.

62   **ARST** 1913, pp. 13, 41.

63   **ARST** 1913, p. 42, **Bastable** (1927), p. 488.

64   **ARST** 1914, p. 43.

65   In France income tax would contribute 7% to total government revenue in 1918 and 1919, **Fisk** (1922), p. 186; in Germany income tax as such remained absent, **Roesler** (1967), p. 196.

66   **ARST** 1915, p. 53; 1916, p. 32; 1917, p. 56.

67   **ARST** 1918, p. 126.

68   The economic arguments used, mainly based on the benefits of free trade, are given by **McAdoo** (1931), pp. 194-203. The other financial policy issue of the Wilson Administration was to establish the FED.

69   **ARST** 1915, p. 20. For the same reason the corporation income tax lagged behind, ibid., p. 17.

70   **Gilbert** (1970), p. 26, 27.

71   **ARST** 1915, p. 51. In mid-1915 the budget estimate for the fiscal year 1916/'17 showed an increase of expenditure by $ 167 million and 77% of it was for military purposes (still apart from investment in rivers and harbours), ibid., p. 72.

72   Ibid., p. 51 and **Gilbert** (1970), p. 54. Government revenue in the fiscal year ending 30 June 1915 was $ 700 million, ibid., p. 53, GDP recalculated for the fiscal year roughly $ 38 billion, **Johnston & Williamson** (2016). GDP data from this source differ slightly from those given in **Gilbert** (1970), p. 202.

73   **Kirkaldy** (1921), p. 214, **BOE3C**.

74   **ARST** 1916, p. 113.

75   **Gilbert** (1970), p. 82 ff.

76   Ibid., pp. 84-95.

77   **ARST** 1917, pp. 9, 22, 43,

78   **USSAL** 1917, vol. IXL, pp. 756-757 and **USSAL** 1919, vol. XL, pp. 300-301, summarised in **Gilbert** (1970), p. 96.

79   **McAdoo** (1931), pp. 372-373; also **Gilbert** (1970), p. 84, **Graig** (2013), pp. 165-166.

80   This rate was for the calendar year 1918, **USSAL** 1919, vol. XL, pp. 1062-1064, for personal incomes over $ 1 million in 1918 (12% normal rate plus 65% surtax); **Gilbert** (1970), p. 111; **Strachan** (2004), p. 156, mentions a tax rate of 67%, which holds for the previous year, note 135, (page 330) and **Rockoff** (2005), p. 321, a rate of 70.3% for 1918 based on US Bureau of Census data; differences are probably a consequence of conversions from fiscal to calendar years.

81   **ARST** 1916, p. 110.

82   Ibid., 1915, p. 51.

Chapter 9 – Domestic war Loans: a patriotic mortgage on the future

1   All countries issued war loans, with the exception of countries such as Belgium or Luxemburg that had largely or completely lost their territory. Neutral states like the Netherlands, Sweden and Switzerland called them 'mobilisation loans' or 'crisis loans'. The propaganda in these countries was less patriotic, but the amounts raised were significant.

2   Details on the contribution are given in note in notes 145 (page 330) and 20 (page 316).

3   An early overview has been given by **Lasswell** (1938 [1927]); see also **DiJorio** *et al.* (2012), **Kang & Rockoff** (2006).

4   For example **Pigou** (1941), pp. 92-94; also **Rockoff** (2012), pp. 114-115.

5   **Pigou** (1941), pp. 87, 93.

6   **Jèze & Truchy** (1927), p. 264 ff. This was a French tradition; it was not unusual to enhance interest rates of 5% to 6% by setting issue prices of 82 or 84. The large loans of 1871 and 1872 to finance the reparations were examples of this policy, **Bastable** (1903), p. 646, **Kindleberger** (1984), p. 243 ff.

7   **Kirkaldy** (1921), p. 126.

8   RT 306, p. 454. **Bogart** (1920), p. 224 explains the German issue prices close to 100 as a reflection of the depreciated currency, by which the real issue price had fallen to, say, 60; this seems hardly an argument, because the value of the bond was reduced by the same factor, unless it would have been expressed in gold, which was not the case. It seems more likely that a passion for (apparent) stability was the decisive factor.

9   This holds only if other conditions are disregarded. A higher interest rate can be beneficial for the government (at the expense of the investor) if the government has the *right* – but not the *obligation*! – of redemption before maturity date. Indeed, refinancing at a lower interest rate can be advantageous and the probability that interest rates decrease is evidently higher in the case of initially high rates, **Wormell** (2000), pp. 74-75; but the market might have anticipated this in the actual price of the bond, as the government has to redeem at the issue price, not at the market price. Economically this is a matter of asymmetric information: only the government knows if and when it will exercise this right (see also page 122, note a). It should be noted that the relation between interest rate and price at issue, although it is a matter of elementary financial calculus, was not completely understood during the First World War even in the highest financial circles. **Wormell** (2000), p. 320, points out that the director of the prestigious London City and Midland Bank, Sir Edward Holden, overlooked the discount effect in the discussions about the conditions of the 3rd British war loan.

10   *Algemeen Handelsblad*, 19 October 1918, p. 4, **KB**.

11   In neutral countries confidence in stable exchange rates and credit status of Germany was unscathed at least until the end of 1917. The influential Dutch *Algemeen Handelsblad* wrote on 22 September 1917, p. 5 at the occasion of the 7th German war loan that 'solvability [of Germany] was not based on gold reserves or stocks of goods but on the labour force, the spirit and entrepreneurship of the German people. And in this we trust boundlessly'.

12   See **Wormell** (2000), pp. 101-102 for a discussion on the amount of the first British war loan.

13   McKenna in Parliament, 21 June 1915, **HC**, 999.

14   RT 315, nr. 26, p. 96 (Annex 1).

15   It also prevented an upward pressure on interest rates for subsequent loans, **Bogart** (1921) pp. 221-222. As a consequence the general interest rate could remain lower, which made industrial credit more available.

16 **Wormell** (2000) p. 372; **Kang & Rockoff** (2006) p. 12.

17 **KwBl.** (1918), nr. 14, p. 4.

18 **Kang & Rockoff** (2006). In fact the evidence is indirect: an econometric analysis of bond price developments of *Liberty Loans* is used, not statements made by investors themselves.

19 If Austria and Hungary are taken together as one entity, the Dual Monarchy Austria-Hungary surpassed Germany because both parts of the empire issued separate domestic loans: 8 for each part, with some of the Hungarian loans even split into two issues, **Bogart** (1920), pp. 251-252, and another four Hungarian loans issued privately directly to banks, making a total of 17 different Hungarian loans, **Popovics** (1925), p. 81.

20 **Roesler** (1967), p. 206, **Helfferich** (1923), p. 213. At pre-war values the total amount is $ 24 billion or £ 4.8 billion.

21 **RT** 315, Nr. 26, p. 98.

22 Ibid.

23 '*Mutmaßungen*', ibid., p. 95.

24 **Angell** (1913), p. xi, quoted by **Ferguson** (1998), p. 135. Neither of the sources mention a date, but it may be assumed that it was in or about 1910. In the summer of 1910 the German 3% loan was priced 82.5 (**The Economist** 27 August 1910, p. 453); the lower price was a reflection of the lower credit status of Germany: before the war it had to pay a risk premium of at least ½% point in comparison with otherwise equivalent British or French government securities, **Ferguson** (1998), p. 131.

25 **RT** 315, Nr. 26, p. 95.

26 Biographical data mainly derived from **Ahamed** (2010), **Achterberg** (1969), http://kulturportal-west-ost.eu/biographies/havenstein-rudolf-2/ and **Zilch** (1987). Photo: *Library of Congress.*

27 **RT** 306, p. 35. In the neutral Dutch press for example *Algemeen Handelsblad* 29 September 1914.

28 **Zilch** (1987), p. 63.

29 Ibid., p. 126.

30 Quoted in **Feldman** (1993), p. 795.

31 **Fürstenberg** (1965), p. 166.

32 **Wirtschaft und Statistik** (1925), p. 42.

33 **RT** 315, Nr. 74, p. 26 ff.

34 **RT** 306, p. 36.

35 In the neutral American market, a German-oriented bank offered the bonds at a price of 84, see page 167.

36 **Hamilton-Grace** (1910), p. 54. Military developments were not the only explanatory factor for fluctuations in war loans proceeds. A poor harvest or political issues were other causes, for example **Deist** (1970), p. 801.

37 For example **Roesler** (1967), p. 78.

38 **Strachan** (2004), p. 125.

39 + 17% in the third quarter of 1917, **Holtfrerich** (1980), p. 15.

40 This direct advertisement campaign remained restricted to the 7th loan. The 8th and 9th loans were only formally announced (in German) without moral arguments; potential investors were simply referred to their bank for details. For earlier loans Germans living abroad had been contacted only through official representations such as the German embassy or consulate.

41   **Roesler** (1967), p. 206. Purchasing power development has been taken as an indicator for inflation; annual data (for example **Ferguson** (1998), p. 331 and **Feldman** (1993), p. 83) all trace back to **Wirtschaft und Statistik** (1925) as quoted in **Bry** (1960), pp. 440-445. (Incidentally, it should be noted that the purchasing power data (*Lebenshaltungskosten*) for the years 1913-1919 are missing in the appropriate Table I on p. 5 of the *Sonderheft*, but implicitly available – and obviously used by Bry – from a table on p. 40; consequently the **HISTAT** database mentions the data only indirectly, ZA8584, Table B.3.01). Bry also presents 'graphically' interpolated monthly data; for illustration 9.3 annual data have been recalculated to issue dates of the loans by polynomial interpolation; the difference with the Bry data is negligible and would be invisible in the illustration. Using a different indicator for inflation such as the total amount of money in circulation (available on a monthly basis from **Roesler** (1967), p. 216) gives a similar picture, as does a correction on the basis of wholesale prices. Purchasing power (as well as money in circulation) is a good indicator for the sacrifices of the people in subscriptions for war loans, as they had to compete with other expenses. The alternative of indexing with GDP development is less adequate here because it does not reflect choices of individuals, still apart from the fact that reliable GDP data on a monthly basis are illusory.

42   http://archive.org/details/1917-06-xx-Rudolf-Havenstein.

43   **KwBl.** (1918), nr. 5, 6.

44   Bids with payments in war bonds would even receive priority over those in cash, **KwBl.** (1918), nr. 2. This obviously violated the law stating that banknotes were legal tender and that everyone, including the government, had to accept them. The proposal meant that the government openly resorted to illegal methods to promote the war loan.

45   The exact rate depends on the indicator used to measure inflation; food prices had risen by 0.4% per month in the 12 months preceding March 1918, wholesale prices by 2.9%, according to **Holtfrerich** (1980), p. 42 and p. 15, respectively. A rise in food prices was limited by government measures, whereas wholesale prices would reach consumers with a time lag. Everyone might expect in March 1918 that prices would continue to rise at least at the rate of the preceding year. The interpolated data in **Bry** (1960), pp. 440-445 show a monthly increase in cost of living of about 1.25% in the first 3 months of 1918.

46   The leaders of political parties in the Reichstag issued a declaration that war loans were truly a safe investment, **Bundesarchiv**, *Plakat* nr. 001-005-018, October 1918.

47   **Jèze & Truchy** (1927), p. 259 ff.

48   The bank had been pressed by the Finance Department to subscribe and large brokers were assumed to have speculated, ibid., p. 260; also **Keynes** (1971-'89), volume XVI, p. 51.

49   According to **Klotz** (1924), p. 62, the original idea was not Ribot's, but proposed by the financial statistician Alfred Neymarck.

50   Two of these advantages of the *bons* were that they would be accepted for subscription to war loans at face value instead of the market price (although corrected for accrued interest) and the possibility to use them as collateral for loans at the *Banque de France*, **Jèze & Truchy** (1927), pp. 248-249. Meanwhile normal treasury bills remained in circulation.

51   Ibid., pp. 246-247. Despite the extended distribution channels, the *bons* remained an instrument for the larger investors: almost 60% of the subscriptions in 1915 were made for amounts of 10,000 *francs* or more, **Charbonnet** (1922), p. 172.

52   **Jèze & Truchy** (1927), p. 252.

53 **Strachan** (2004), p. 141.

54 In fact 45% was used in this way, **Jèze & Truchy** (1927), p. 250.

55 Ibid., p. 238; **Bogart** (1920), p. 110: 29.1 billion *francs* on 31 October 1918 and 30.3 billion *francs* by the end of 1918.

56 Obviously such amounts could never have been issued according to the original legal restrictions: in July 1914 the ceiling for treasury bills was 600 million *francs*. This restriction was raised frequently, initially by decree and after December 1914 by parliamentary consent. It resulted in the dozens of billions at the end of the war, **Charbonnet** (1922), pp. 156-157.

57 **Jèze & Truchy** (1927), pp. 248, 253.

58 Ibid., pp. 257, 261.

59 **Bastable** (1903), pp. 647-648.

60 **Keynes** (1917-'89), volume XVI, p. 52; **Jèze & Truchy** (1927), p. 261; **Wormell** (2000), p. 105.

61 **Martin** (1999), pp. 20-21, referring to Weber, E. (1986), *France, fin de siècle*, Cambridge MA, Belknap Press, points out that French society in the Third Republic was solidly based on a bourgeois middle class of *rentiers*.

62 **Jèze & Truchy** (1927), pp. 274-275. 'New money' in this context comprises purchases done by means of the *bons*; by their short-term and bearer character they were more or less equivalent to cash, in particular when the date of maturity was within the period that subscriptions had to be paid. Jèze & Truchy consider converted *obligations* as 'new money', but this is questionable because they were medium-term loans.

63 The option to convert old 3% bonds had been cancelled The other conditions were an issue price of 88¾ and an interest rate of 5%, tax exempt and paid in advance.

64 **Bogart** (1920), p. 89.

65 **Klotz** (1924), p. 62.

66 The 10 million *marks* were the proceeds of the war loan proper, without the (much smaller) simultaneously issued treasury bills.

67 The German *mark* had devalued stronger than the *franc*. As there was no direct currency trading between *marks* and *francs*, exchange rates with the dollar have been used. In September 1916 the rates were 5.89 *francs* to the dollar and 5.82 *marks* to the dollar, **The Economist** 9 September 1916, p. 434. This gives an approximate rate of 1.01 *francs* to the *mark*. Both rates in then neutral New York contain an unknown risk premium, which is irrelevant as only indicative rates are necessary.

68 **Bogart** (1920), p. 90.

69 **Di Jorio** *et al.* (2012), Annex.

70 Ibid.

71 Half of the amount was paid by *bons* and *obligations*, **Jèze & Truchy** (1927), p. 280.

72 The German loan raised roughly 8 billion if measured in *francs*. Because in October 1918 New York had ceased to be a neutral market, in this case two intermediate currencies have been used to convert *marks* to *francs*. At 10 October 1918 in New York, $ 1.00 was equivalent to 5.48 *francs* and to 0.33 Dutch guilders, while in Amsterdam 1.00 *mark* was traded for 0.33 guilders, **The Economist** 12 October 1918, p. 460. Combining these three values gives a rate of approximately 0.80 *francs* to the *mark*. These calculations are of course indicative. It should be noted that the pre-war (par) level was the inverse: 0.81 *marks* to the

franc. This incidentally shows that near the end of the war German currency had depreciated considerably stronger than French currency.

73   **Jèze & Truchy** (1927), p. 281.

74   The British government felt such a moral responsibility as well, but rather with respect to the banks. In 1915 the government had pressed the banks to invest in Russian government securities at unfavourable conditions. In January 1918 the government offered the banks to buy them off with a special loan with more favourable conditions, permitting these banks to sell the Russian bonds, **Wormell** (2000), pp. 736-738, **Fisk** (1924), p. 140.

75   The total amount of *bons* issued in the period 1914-1918 was 51 billion *francs*; 24 billion *francs* of it had been used to purchase war loans; apart from that there was an amount of 900 million *francs* of outstanding *obligations*, **Jèze & Truchy** (1927), pp. 250-274.

76   The amounts mentioned in the literature show slightly different values, possibly due to varying reference dates. **Sauvy** (1984), part 3, p. 6, mentions 33 billion *francs* before the war and 175 billion *francs* at the end of 1918, the latter value containing 43% short-term debts. The data in **Ferguson** (1998), p. 325, for France are based on **Fisk** (1922), pp. 26-28 (except for 1914): 114 billion *francs* in 1918 en 171 billion *francs* in 1919. The **CEPII** data (variable 'DETTE') are 124 billion *francs* and 178 billion *francs* for 1918 and 1919, respectively. The GDP values for 1918 and 1919 are 78 billion *francs* and 105 billion *francs*, respectively, according to **CEPII** (variable 'PIBQ'); this leads to a debt ratio of 160% to 170%. Ferguson's value for (1st January) 1914 is in line with the **CEPII**-data 32.8 billion *francs* and 33.5 billion *francs*, respectively. **Hautcœur** (2005), p. 186, agrees with the **CEPII**-data.

77   **Balderston** (1998), *e.g.* p. 239.

78   **Ferguson** (1998), p. 127.

79   The Chief Cashier and his Deputy subscribed in their own names for large amounts to the loan to avoid that the weekly publications of the Bank would show large amounts of government securities. They borrowed the money from the Bank to do so, **Wormell** (2000), p. 82.

80   **Wormell** (2000), p. 86, **BOEBR**.

81   Lloyd George in Parliament, 17 November 1914, **HC**, 372-373.

82   The average annual wage in 1913 in Britain was £ 62; in the sector with the highest wages, iron and steel industry, the average was £ 99, **Feinstein** (1990), pp. 603, 604, 609.

83   Lloyd George in Parliament, 27 November 1914, **HC**, 1554; **Wormell** (2000), p. 82; **Strachan** (2004), p. 148, mentions 25,000 individual subscriptions.

84   Lloyd George in Parliament, 17 and 19 November 1914, **HC**, 374 and 623-624.

85   Wealthy investors could make use of a special credit facility at the de *Bank of England*: advances for a period of 3 years at an interest 1% point below the official bank rate, which implied 4% interest, the effective yield of the war loan. Characteristics of the loan are given in **The Economist** 5 December 1914, p. 992.

86   Arthur Henderson in Parliament, 19 November 1914, **HC**, 612 ff.

87   **Strachan** (2004), p. 148.

88   **The Economist** 19 February 1916, p. 313.

89   **Kirkaldy** (1921), p. 126.

90   **Hiley** (1987), p. 38. The (initial) advertisement budget was £ 100.000.

91   **Bonar Law** in Parliament, 26 February 1917, **HC**, 1698; **Roesler** (1967), p. 207.

92   **Kirkaldy** (1921), p. 130.

93 The amount mentioned is from **Wormell** (2000), p. 118, based on *National Debts* (*annual returns* 1916, p. 34). This amount includes £ 24 million through savings banks. **Kirkaldy** (1921), p. 127, and **Bogart** (1920), p. 13, present slightly different amounts without specifying sources.

94 The increased interest rate of 4.5% was relatively high for British standards. This reflects the fact that in mid-1915 the government was obliged to offer more to the investor. As the issue price was 100, the effective yield was also 4.5% (in fact fractionally higher because the first interest payment had been advanced).

95 **Wormell** (2000), p. 118: £ 290. **Strachan** (2004), p. 149, mentions £ 313. The amounts given by **Kirkaldy** (1921), p. 129, and **Bogart** (1920), pp. 12-13, if corrected for exchange rate conversions, are £ 305 and £ 277 million, respectively.

96 **Kirkaldy** (1921), p. 141; also Bonar Law in Parliament, 26 February 1917, **HC**, 1701. The conversion right was not only backwards, but also forwards. Subscribers had a guarantee that they could use the loan without loss to subscribe to future loans. This was indeed a risk for the Treasury, because it would always be obliged to borrow at the highest interest rate. On the other hand, the Chancellor might have reasoned: secured is secured.

97 To collect taxes from bondholders for received interest was felt as pumping around money. This could be avoided by giving tax reductions, where the French system provided an example. Therefore, the government offered the loan in two options: either a tax-free ('tax-compounded') loan at 4% or a (normal) 5% loan subject to income tax. This provided an investor to subscribe to the loan that best suited his or her financial situation. In practice, the tax-exempt option was hardly chosen (for only 2% of the total amount). Apparently the public judged that taxes were not prohibiting – or they supposed to avoid taxes by other, less visible ways. Nevertheless, the policy made some sense. In the next months it became evident that taxes might rise; this pushed up the price of tax-exempt bonds, whereas the price of the normal bonds fell, **Kirkaldy** (1921), p. 138.

98 **Wormell** (2000), pp. 332-342.

99 Due to the multitude of conversion options, an overview of *net* revenues of British war loans requires some calculations and the results are not always published in an easily accessible way, **Bogart** (1920), p. 14; **Kirkaldy** (1921), p. 129; **Wormell** (2000), pp. 118, 339.

100 Interpolated annual data from **BOE3C** lead to 34%; the more detailed monthly wholesale data from **Fisk** (1924), p. 350 lead to an increase of 42%; the cost of living data from **Ferguson** (1998), p. 331, interpolated, even result in an increase of 50%. Both index figures and reference data for the loans contain some variation.

101 **Wormell** (2000), pp. 732-733.

102 In the second half of 1916 there were even bills, called *War Expenditure Certificates*, with a life of 2 years, **Wormell** (2000), p. 196.

103 **Kirkaldy** (1921), p. 153; **Wormell** (2000), p. 94.

104 **Kirkaldy** (1921), p. 162; **Wormell** (2000), p. 731, gives amounts at the end of the fiscal year (31 March).

105 It should be noted that this happened at the moment that Germany issued its largest loan until then (in nominal amounts).

106 Data from **Wormell** (2000), pp. 94 and 352. In specific periods, for example between January and April 1917 no *Treasury Bills* were issued. Before April 1917 the average annual *increase* was 1.5% point; after April 1917 the average *decrease* was 1.1% point.

107 **Wormell** (2000), p. 209.
108 **Wormell** (2000), pp. 95, 100. Sources are not completely consistent about the total amount, for example ibid., pp. 95, 199, 353, 737; **Kirkaldy** (1921), p. 172. Besides, the total amount issued is not highly relevant in view of all kinds of conversions, for example at the occasion of the third war loan. The only thing that matters is the amount outstan-ding at the end of the war, £ 380 million, a sum that had to be repaid within a few years, **Wormell** (2000), pp. 412, 425, 565.
109 Or 4% free from tax, as an option.
110 Reference date 31 March 1919, **Wormell** (2000), p. 360.
111 **Wormell** (2000), p. 364. This distracted the bonds from circulation, a contribution to combating inflation.
112 Calculated with GDP data from **Broadberry & Harrison** (2005), p. 219.
113 **Bogart** (1921), p. 297 ff.
114 **McAdoo** (1931), pp. 372-374.
115 **ARST** 1918, p. 20.
116 **ARST** 1917, p. 22.
117 Details of the terms and conditions as well as the amounts of bonds surrendered for conversion during the war, are given in **ARST** 1918, pp. 67-69.
118 The First Liberty Loan Act provided for an amount of $ 5 billion, of which $ 3 billion was to be used to establish credits to allied countries, **ARST** 1917, p. 17.
119 **McAdoo** (1931), pp. 382-384; **Strachan** (2004), p. 156; **Bogart** (1921), p. 208. More critical remarks about the policy of McAdoo were also heard, in particular his stressing of patriotism, the low-interest policy and the generous tax and conversion facilities, **Gilbert** (1970), pp. 120-124. The official source, **ARST** 1917, p. 7 mentions that 'more than 4,000,000 men and women subscribed', whereas Bogart gives 4.5 million.
120 Of all finance ministers in this book, McAdoo has the largest amount and variety of biographies and, as a consequence of his large network, he is mentioned in many other histories. The main sources for this sketch are, in reverse chronological order, and generally without explicit notes: **Craig** (2013), **Chase** (2008), **Silber** (2007), **Broesamle** (1973), **McAdoo** (1931) and **Synon** (1924). Photograph: *Library of Congress*.
121 **McAdoo** (1931), p. 95.
122 **Chase** (2008), p. 55 ff.
123 Although the FED website (http://www.federalreservehistory.org/People/DetailView/226) indicates that McAdoo actually graduated from the University of Tennessee, this fact is not confirmed in any of the six biographies mentioned here.
124 **McAdoo** (1931), p. 161.
125 **ARST** 1915, pp. 491, 585.
126 **Silber** (2007).
127 **ARST** 1917, p. 5.
128 **McAdoo** (1931), p. 497.
129 **McAdoo** (1931), p. 407.
130 Ibid. (1931), pp. 239-241.
131 **Craigh** (2013), p. 105 ff.
132 **Chase** (2008), p. 292.

133 His bride Doris Isabel Cross is often referred to as '26'. This is correct if she was born on 1st April 1909; other sources, however, mention 8 November 1909 as the day she was born; in that case she was actually 25 at the date of the wedding, 15 September 1935.

134 For example in the 1st Liberty Loan Act of 24 April 1917, **USSAL** 1919, vol. XL, p. 35.

135 **Bogart** (1921), pp. 210-212, based on the tax rates of the War Revenue Act of 1917; **Kang & Rockoff** (2006), p. 30, calculate an effective yield of over 13%, based on the highest tax bracket of 73% in 1920 for those who at that time held the bonds.

136 **Kang & Rockoff** (2006), p. 12; http://en.wikipedia.org/wiki/65th_United_States_Congress.

137 **ARST** 1917, p. 10.

138 **ARST** 1919, p. 225; **Bogart** (1920), p. 182. It should be noted that the numbers of purchases are not necessarily a reliable indicator for the number of participants; **Gilbert** (1970), p. 123 points out that banks and other corporations declared extra dividends to enable their employees to subscribe to bonds; **Kang & Rockoff** (2006), p. 23 describe the process as a collective purchase by companies, which distorts the one-to-one relation between subscriptions and participants. **McAdoo** (1931), p. 409, mentions the fact that people subscribed in two or three places to the same loan, reducing the number of subscriptions to subscribers by roughly a factor 0.8. And finally, all numbers of subscribers are for individual loans. In order to calculate the total amount of subscribers to *any* loan, it would be necessary to use identification data for all loans and correct for overlap.

139 **Bogart** (1920), p. 182.

140 **McAdoo** (1931), p. 407.

141 **Bogart** (1921), p. 223.

142 **Kang & Rockoff** (2006), pp. 24-25.

143 **Strachan** (2004), p. 158.

144 Based on the amount of total expenditure (illustration 6.2; for Germany national expenditure only) and the amount of the loans (illustration 9.7). Evidently, the share of 60% depends on the reference periods, both from expenditure and from loans taken into account.

145 As usual, sources are not always consistent. Values presented are nominal, in their own currency; the proportions in the illustration give an indication, in the same way as the values in brackets approximate values in 1913 (billion) dollars. Recalculations to these values have been made consistent with the procedure for expenditure (illustration 6.2). Loans have not been corrected for conversions (pages 147, 148), German loans have been corrected for simultaneously issued treasury bills based on **Roesler** (1967), p. 206. For French loans, the amount received by the Treasury has been used; this could be as low as two thirds of the face value as a consequence of the lower issue price (page 139). The pre-war Italian Mobilisation Loan of January 1915 and the American post-war *Victory Liberty Loan* of April 1919 have been counted as war loans, but the French July 1914 loan is not regarded as a war loan. Data for Austria and Hungary are from **Brucker** (2010), p. 143, as are the corresponding index values. Data for Russian loans are from **Bogart** (1920), p. 141, and **Strachan** (2004), p. 131. Short-term credits and central bank advances have been left out, as well as foreign loans (for which, see Chapter 10).

146 **Roesler** (1967), p. 206.

147 **BMS** (1943), p. 409; **Elwell** (2011), pp. 6-8.

Chapter 10 – Borrowing abroad: loyal allies or business relationships?

1   **Dietzel** (1912), p. 62.

2   Also: **Frey** (1994), p. 350, note 101.

3   In mid-1916, while the battles of the Somme and Verdun were fought, all dairy products for the German troops were imported from the Netherlands, **Frey** (1994), p. 339. An analysis of the German and British agricultural sector can be found in **Broadberry & Harrison** (2005), pp. 18-22. In Germany, agricultural productivity was low and labour-intensive. It had to compete with the army for its primary input factors: labour force, horses and nitrates. The government bought production surpluses of farming households at prices that were kept artificially low in order to keep food prices low for the urban population. There was no incentive for farmers to increase production, while the black market was stimulated. In fact the agricultural sector of the economy behaved as if it were a neutral foreign country. The British agricultural sector on the other hand was relatively small (food was imported), but flexible. Market incentives pushed the farmers to produce more, **Broadberry & Howlett** (2003), p. 7. For Austria, this mechanism of decreasing agricultural production as a result of government regulations to keep prices low has been observed by **Redlich** (1925), p. 166.

4   For example **Euwe** (2010), p. 224, **Strachan** (2004), p. 166, **Frey** (1994), pp. 350, 353. Discussions may arise from definitions about what should be included, at what time and about the exchange rate. For German-Dutch relations in general during the war, see **Frey** (1998).

5   **Frey** (1994), p. 353.

6   **Frey** (1994), p. 336, **Strachan** (2004), p. 165.

7   Sources are not unambiguous, **Strachan** (2004), p. 165, ranging from $ 27 million tot $ 35 million. For German attempts to enter the American market see also **Tooley** (2005), pp. 67-68.

8   **RT** 315, nr. 101, p. 2 (session of 20 May 1915), and **RT** 319, nr. 434, p. 12 (Annex I, dated 25 March 1916). Also **Lotz** (1927), pp. 115-119.

9   **RT** 322, nr. 1263, p. 9, 30 January 1918.

10 **Strachan** (2004), p. 164. Jack Morgan (J.P. Morgan Jr.) spoke both German and French. He called New York a city under construction, 'half-paved and half-finished', **Horn**, (2000), p. 91.

11 **Brown** (1988), p. 39. This made dollar loans to Germany highly risky.

12 **Jèze & Truchy** (1927), pp. 308-309.

13 Ibid., p. 311.

14 In particular the French banker & lawyer Maurice Léon, **Nouailhat** (1979), p. 103 ff.

15 **Horn** (2000), pp. 97-98; also **Nouailhat** (1979), p. 103, **Strachan** (2004), p. 187.

16 A detailed analysis of the American policy change has been given by **Horn** (2002), p. 60-62.

17 Ibid., p. 61; **Nouailhat** (1979), pp. 105-106.

18 On the economic and financial ties between France and Britain in relation to the military and political cooperation, see for example **Greenhalgh** (2009) and **Bell** (1996).

19 **Horn** (2002), p. 37 ff., pp. 55-56 and pp. 91-92. For the French side of the matter, also **Petit** (1929), p. 191 ff. For France, gold backing was important for domestic reasons because the French monetary system was largely based on coins and banknotes, in contrast tot Britain where cheques and bank accounts were predominant. During the 1930s France would be one of the most stubborn defenders of the Gold Standard.

20 Roughly 850,000 against 85,000, http://hsc.csu.edu.au/modern_history/core_study/ww1/overview1914_18/page137.htm#anchor165302.

21 Lloyd George, quoted by Sir Edward Grey, **Horn** (2002), p. 41, Ribot to the French ambassador in London, Paul Cambon, ibid., p. 43.

22 Based on **Horn** (2002), p. 183: £ 417 million, derived from British sources. **Jèze & Truchy** (1927), p. 286 mention a total amount of 13 billion *francs*, but possibly some credits may have been repaid; based on the amounts of individual loans, ibid. pp. 299-307, the amount is roughly 10.8 billion *francs*, depending on exchange rates.

23 **Petit** (1929), p. 716, presents detailed information on the gold shipments from France to Britain; based on the pre-war exchange rate, the total amount of 2,840 million *francs* corresponds to roughly £ 113 million; **Horn** (2002), pp. 91 and 205 rightly remarks that precise figures are not clear, as is also evident from **Jèze & Truchy** (1927), pp. 299-300; the order of magnitude, however is beyond discussion.

24 **Jèze & Truchy** (1927), pp. 298-300. On the return of the gold lent by the *Banque de France*, see **Harris** (1931), pp. 306-307, and, for a detailed account on the negotiations, **Moreau** (1991 [1954]), pp. 233-252 and **Moreau** (1937), p. 299 ff.

25 **Wormell** (2000), pp. 161-162. The British merchant bank was *Morgan Grenfell*. See also **Horn** (2000) and references mentioned there about the *Morgan* imperium.

26 **Nouailhat** (1979), pp. 242-243.

27 In fact 1% of the net price of purchases above £ 1 million and 2% below that amount, **Burk** (1985), p. 22.

28 **Nouailhat** (1979), p. 275 ff., **Burk** (1985), p. 65 ff.

29 **Wormell** (2000), p. 160.

30 **Wormell** (2000), pp. 170-173. For the syndicate banks, the issue price was 96, leaving them a 2% bonus.

31 See also **Burk** (1985), pp. 73-75.

32 In August 1915 the exchange rate had slipped away to $ 4.70, more than 3% below par, the pre-war gold-based value of $ 3.86½ to the pound, **Wormell** (2000), p. 163.

33 McKenna in parliament: 'this loan explicitly is not being raised for the purpose of paying for Government purchases of munitions in America. [...] it is for the purpose of maintaining the exchange', 12 October 1915, **HC**, 1254.

34 See for example **Horn** (2002), p. 89.

35 **Wormell** (2000), p. 163; **Dennett** (1998), p. 206. An enlightening description of the story behind the scenes of this transaction has been given by Lord Beaverbrook, quoted in **McKenna** (1948), p. 238.

36 **Wormell** (2000), p. 179, calculations based on an average exchange rate for 1916; also: **Kirkaldy** (1921), pp. 184-195.

37 **HC** (12 October 1915), 1236. In 1910 it was estimated between £ 900 million and £ 1 billion, **Horn** (2002), p. 89. These are estimates, because the securities were privately owned by individuals and by institutions; they were partly registered and partly in bearer form. Even the report of the prestigious *Cabinet Committee on the co-ordination of military and financial effort* (Asquith, McKenna and Austen Chamberlain), published in April 1916, could not mention more accurate figures than an amount not exceeding £ 300-£ 400 million for American stock held in Britain at that time, **Horn** (2002), pp. 119-120. Anyhow, British interest in the American economy were 'very, very considerable', paraphrasing a governor of

the Bank of England.

38   The pre-war amount of foreign financial assets held in France has been estimated at 40-50 billion *francs*, or $ 8 à 9 billion, **Jèze & Truchy** (1927), p. 297; **Horn** (2000), p. 96, mentions a comparable amount of 40-45 billion *francs*, based on data from Milward. Also ibid., p. 141.

39   **Horn** (2002), p. 130.

40   **Jèze & Truchy** (1927), p. 303.

41   Ibid., p. 289, note 2, based on data from Klotz in 1919 and **ARST** 1919, p. 66.

42   **Horn** (2002), pp. 136-139.

43   **Moulton & Pasvolsky** (1932), p. 425. In a note to Cunliffe of 9 April 1917, Keynes mentions an amount of £ 243 million as the credit outstanding to France alone as quoted by **Horn** (2000), p. 96. At the average exchange rate of 1917, this would indeed imply roughly $ 1.2 billion, 6.6 billion *francs*. Moulton & Pasvolsky adjust for gold shipments from France to Britain (see note 23) and arrive at an amount of $ 560 million for credits to France, almost £ 120 million. The corresponding amount for Italy is $ 670 million, £ 140 million.

44   The graph presents the amount of outstanding loans of at least $ 50 million in current dollars. Sources are: **Jèze & Truchy** (1927), **Wormell** (2000), **Nouailhat** (1979). The 'kink' in the French data of October/November is caused by a series of loans issued almost simultaneously by the French cities of Paris, Bordeaux, Marseille and Lyon. Although they were formally municipal loans, it was evident that they were effectively intended for the French government.

45   **Ferguson** (1998), pp. 326-329.

46   At the time of the Armistice Russia's debt to Britain was $ 2,470 million; the British surplus of receivables over debts was $ 3.230 million, **Moulton & Pasvolsky** (1932), p. 426.

47   **Horn** (2002), pp. 164-165.

48   **Strachan** (2004), pp. 202-203.

49   **Williamson** (1971), pp. 156-157, 164; **Helfferich** (1919) part II, p. 384 ff.

50   These data and the Italian data are based on **Moulton & Pasvolsky** (1932), p. 426, derived from **Fisk** (1924), p. 21. These are 'current' values, converted by Fisk from the original currencies to dollars by means of fixed exchange rates, just as the Russian and Italian amounts.

51   It has been remarked by **Strachan** (2004), p.184 and already by **Fisk** (1924), p. 148.

52   **McAdoo** (1931), p. 375.

53   **Moulton & Pasvolsky** (1932), pp. 427-428. This amount is in current dollars, accumulated over all years concerned.

54   **ARST** 1920, p. 338. Amounts are in current dollars running over the period 6 April 1917 to 1st November 1920.

55   **Fisk** (1924), pp. 160-169. For the French side, see **Homberg** (1926), pp. 27-29.

56   **FRUS**, 1917, Supplement 2, p. 522.

57   The French ambassador, Jusserand, was 'piqued' for receiving only half the amount of Britain, since his country belonged to 'first class countries, too', **McAdoo** (1931), pp. 394-395.

58   In July 1917 rumours had reached McAdoo that some British government officials might have the intention of filling the *Morgan* overdraft gap with US government credits, **Synon** (1924), p. 266.

59   **ARST** 1917, p. 18; from 15 May 1918 the interest rate was formally 5%, **ARST** 1920, p. 56.

60   **ARST** 1920, p. 57.

61   Ibid. p. 58 ff.

62   Based on the share of foreign credits (including the negligible American loans) in the total amount of German loans, comprising the war loans and short-term debts as per 31 December 1918 as given by **Roesler** (1967), p. 205.

63   The data for Britain are consistent in various sources: **Wormell** (2000), p. 733: 17.3% in 1919, **Petit** (1929), p. 327: 18.2%; **Broadberry & Howlett** (2005), p. 221, mention 'less than one-fifth', in fact 18.8%; **Fisk** (1924), p. 340, gives 20%, based on expenditure converted to pre-war values. French data show a somewhat larger variation, most probably caused by reference date and exchange rates: **Patat** *et al.* (1986), p. 33, 18.1%, **Martin** (1999), p. 20, 19.8%, and **Fisk** (1924), p. 340, even 26.1% in 1913 dollars.

64   **Moulton & Pasvolsky** (1932), p. 425, excluding a debt of $ 540 million of Commonwealth countries to the European homeland.

65   Ibid., p. 35. In these data the British overdraft account at *J.P. Morgan & Co.* appears to have been disregarded; it has been taken into account in **Burk** (1985), p. 265, with data based on **Morgan** (1952), pp. 230-235; this correction has been made here as well.

66   **McKenna** (1922).

67   **Moulton & Pasvolsky** (1932), pp. 35, 425, 426; **Wormell** (2000), pp. 152-156, 160; **Burk** (1985), p. 265. All amounts are in nominal dollars, outstanding on the first days of April 1917 and 11 November 1918, respectively.

Chapter 11 – Monetary financing: the central bank as an ATM machine

1   **Roesler** (1967), pp. 216-218.

2   **Helfferich** (1923), pp. 164, 207.

3   This increase is almost half of one year's pre-war GDP, expressed in nominal *marks*: 56.6 billion 1913 *marks*, **Ritschl** (2005), p. 44.

4   **Ferguson** (1998), p. 330; **Popovics** (1925), Table II.

5   **Roesler** (1976), p. 38.

6   Ibid., pp. 208-210.

7   Ibid., pp. 208-214.

8   Pallain, in **Aldrich** (1908), pp. 18-19.

9   Calculated from the Law of 29 December 1871 and the Law of 29 December 1911 and relevant intermediate laws.

10   **Roesler** (1967), pp. 216-218; **Holtfrerich** (1980), pp. 48-51.

11   Circulation of banknotes is well-documented, **BDFB**. The amount of gold and silver coins that were actually in circulation (not hoarded) is much more uncertain and estimates vary largely. **Fisk** (1922), p. 41, mentions 4.8 billions *francs* in mid-1914, **Saint Marc** (1986), pp. 25, 27, quotes various sources, giving considerably higher amounts, ranging from 9-12 billion *francs*, in line with **Jeanneney & Jeanneney** (1985), p. 295, and **Sicsic** (1989), p. 728. This was only the beginning of the war. The amount of these coins in circulation and used as legal tender at the end of the war is expected to be much lower. Following a suggestion of the *Banque de France* the rounded values used here are 6.5 billion *francs* for mid-1914 and at most 2 billion *francs* at the end of 1918.

12   *Loi du 5 août 1914*, **Décret** *25 février 1919*.

13 **Capie & Webber** (1985), pp. 368-370 (end of July data), notes in circulation including those issued by Scottish and Irish banks, but not including notes held by the Bank of England, **Kirkaldy** (1921), p. 50, with a negligible time difference. The number of *gold* coins held by banks in July 1918 was estimated $ 40 million, **CCFE**, 13.

14 **BMS** (1943), p. 409-410; 'coins' include gold and silver certificates; 'other bank' notes include United States notes, issued by the Treasury; for details see ibid., p. 404 ff.

15 Circulation amounts as per 31 December conform **BDFB** and gold reserves taken from **Horn** (2002), p. 91. Circulation values in Horn, derived from **Saint Marc** (1986), p. 28, are annual averages; at the end of 1918 circulation was 30.3 billion *francs*.

16 **Kirkaldy** (1921), pp. 40, 41. Here 'private' banks means: all commercial banks; in Britain there was a distinction between real 'private banks' (privately owned, mostly by partners, type: Rothschild) and Joint Stock Banks (Ltd. / Corp., type: HSBC).

17 Ibid., pp. 41 and 50; also **Broadberry & Howlett** (2005), p. 219.

18 Subsequently they could be converted into gold according to the Currency and Bank Notes Act of 6 August 1914, art. 1 sub 3.

19 The backing of currency notes by gold in the Bank of England had decreased to 17% in 1918. As the Bank of England was obliged to accept currency notes for conversion into its own banknotes, the final backing rate of paper money by gold is determined by these banknotes *plus* the currency notes. This rate had decreased to 26% in August 1918, **Kirkaldy** (1921), pp. 26 and 50.

20 **Capie & Webber** (1985), p. 370.

21 **BMS** (1943), p. 409-410. Data are at the end of the month; 31 October 1918 data have been used as a proxy for the Armistice.

22 *Kölnische Zeitung*, 2 September 1915, quoted by **Bogart** (1921), p. 189.

23 **Jèze & Truchy** (1927), p. 233, **Horn** (2002), p. 170. The reference date is 31 December 1918.

24 From the detailed half-yearly data in **Ramstein** (1923), pp. 76-77, the correlation can be calculated as statistically highly significant, as was to be expected from the very mechanism.

25 **Holtfrerich** (1980), pp. 64-65. In this case the correlation between banknotes in circulation and short-term government debt at the *Reichsbank* (*Schatzanweisungen*) is also almost perfect.

26 Taken at an average 1918 exchange rate. These advances comprised not only the so-called ways & means credits (£ 230 million), but also the government's account at the Bank of England to enable the issue of currency notes, backed by debt certificates, **Wormell** (2000), p. 351, **Kirkaldy** (1921), p. 24 ff.

27 In Central and Eastern Europe countries such as Austria-Hungary and Russia, where government control of national banks was much larger, checks on money creation were correspondingly lower, **Strachan** (2004), pp. 129, 133.

28 **Finances** (1914). The words were carefully chosen: 'at the end of hostilities', not 'at the end of the war', which would have implied a peace treaty. Pallain evidently wanted to avoid that the government used endless peace negotiations as an excuse to prolong the favourable credit facilities.

29 **Vignat** (2001), p. 490.

30 **Jèze & Truchy** (1927), p. 234.

31 **Vignat** (2001), p. 636 ff.

32 **Jèze & Truchy** (1927), p. 235.

33 **Kirkaldy** (1921), p. 48: Letter from the Bank of England to the Chancellor of the Exchequer, 22 September 1919.

34 **Roesler** (1967), p. 131.

35 According to **Roesler** (1967), p. 137, the word 'inflation' was never used in *Reichsbank* publications during the war. It appeared however in their War Economy Papers (*Kriegswirtschaftliche Blätter*), **KwBl.** nr. 13, undated, presumably August 1918, albeit in quotation marks: *"Inflation" (Notendruckerei)'*

36 **Blancheton** (2001), p. 85.

37 **Vignat** (2001), for example p. 8 ff., p. 18.

38 § 25 of the Bank Act of 1875, **RGBl.** 1875, Nr. 15, pp. 177-198; see also **Zilch** (1987), pp. 13-17, and **Roesler** (1967), p. 169, on the (in)dependence of the *Reichsbank*.

39 See page 130 about Havenstein's character.

40 **Holtfrerich** (1980), p. 162: *Verwaltungsbericht der Reichsbank* 1915, p. 4; also **Roesler** (1967), p. 82, pp. 168-171.

41 In de period until the summer of 1917 the amount of banknotes increased by roughly 40%, a relative modest growth in comparison with other countries; only in or about October 1918 the rise would be 100%, **Kirkaldy** (1921), p. 41.

42 It was perhaps even more in its exchange rate and bank rate policy that the Bank became subordinate to the government, rather than in monetary financing.

43 After the turbulent days of July and August 1914, the (British) bank rate was pegged at 5% from 8 August 1914 until 11 November 1919, with one exception during the second half of 1916 (6%) and the spring of 1917 (5.5%) until the United States entered the war, **BOEBR**. The German discount rate was also 5% since December 1914 (and in the earlier war months temporarily 6%), **Lotz** (1927), pp. 91-92. The *Banque de France* discount rate was 5% from 20 August 1914 until April 1920 5%, **Blancheton** (2001), p. 90.

44 **Pigou** (1941); also in passing **Horn** (2002), p. 172.

45 **Wicksell, K.** (1916), quoted by **Roesler** (1967), pp. 169-171.

46 Monetary financing in France for example has been estimated at 13% of the total war expenditure, against 87% for loans, **Occhino** *et al.* (2006), table 3; this agrees with the *Banque de France* credits based on short-term government bills, **Jèze, & Truchy** (1927), p. 336. For the US the same source mentions 9%, quite comparable to the 10% given by **Kang & Rockoff** (2006), p. 27. However, when the complete monetary system is taken into account, that is: including loans given by banks to subscribers on war loans (with the purchased *Liberty Bonds* as collateral), the percentage of monetary financing in the United States is as high as 40%, ibid., p. 28.

47 Based on **Maddison** (1982), p. 238 and quoted for France and Germany in **Ferguson** (1998), p. 331. Original data for France (index 213) in **INSEE** 1966, p. 405, for Britain (index 203) in **BOE3C** and for Germany (index 304) in **Wirtschaft und Statistik** (1925).

48 **Hautcœur** (2005), p. 188, for example estimates the 'tax' imposed by inflation at 40% of the annual GDP in 1920. The franc would lose another half of its value afterwards.

49 Based on GDP data from **BOE3C, CEPII** (variable 'PIBQ') and **Ritschl & Spoerer** (1997), respectively.

50 The share was even larger, because GDP had fallen rather than grown during the war (but not sufficiently known to serve as a base for accurate calculations).

Chapter 12 – Back to normalcy: mission impossible

1 At the end of the Second World War in 1945, the United States would remember very well that war expenditure had been larger in the six months after the Armistice than in the six months before 11 November 1918, **ARST** 1945, p. 332.

2 **ARST** 1919, pp. 26-27. Amounts in current dollars and corrected for regular (non-war) expenditure.

3 **RT** 376, nr. 5557, p. 12. Roughly $ 40 - $ 50 million in dollars of that period, at violently fluctuating exchange rates.

4 **Kirkaldy** (1921), p. 212. Data for the fiscal year 1921/22, roughly over $ 600 million.

5 **Parker** (1920), p. 5.

6 Ibid., pp. 31, 113.

7 Other exceptions were material promised to third countries and Red Cross material, ibid., p. 26.

8 Ibid., pp. 27, 106. The agreement gave the United States (not France!) the option to choose for payment in francs, which laid any exchange rate risk fully on the French side.

9 **Sauvy** (1984), part 3, p. 397, **BMS** (1943), p. 670.

10 **Homberg** (1926), p. 50.

11 This distribution might give rise to wealth effects, for example when one group uses resources in a more productive way than the other, therefore: 'in principle'.

12 In fact, this had already been realised during the war when wealth had been parted with, although it was not yet realised; after the war it was merely executed.

13 **Moulton & Pasvolsky** (1932), p. 426, based on **Fisk** (1924), p. 345.

14 Mutual loans between Commonwealth countries are disregarded in this system.

15 **Moulton & Pasvolsky** (1931), p. 426. Their values are in dollars and based on **Fisk** (1924), p. 345, who converted amounts in other currencies to 1913 dollars (at gold parity), regardless of the year of the loans. This implies that the amounts due to the US are nominal values as per November 1918 but flows between other countries are indicative and need not correspond exactly to amounts agreed between those countries. A specific British-Argentinean loan increasing the British debt to $ 3.8 billion has been left out. It should be remarked that exchange rates at the end of 1918 were not extremely far from those in 1913 (Britain – 2%, France – 8%; outlier Italy – 33%). The amounts mentioned by **Self** (2006), p. 15, without a source and date of reference are higher, probably because they refer to debt positions around 1921. The same must hold for the data given by **Sauvy** (1984), part 3, p. 62, *'à la fin de la guerre'* (at the end of the war).

16 For example **Wormell** (2000), p. 478.

17 If Italy would spread all its payments in annuities over 40 years, Britain and France would receive *annually* as much as the whole Italian debt to France ($ 75 million).

18 For Belgium this was probably even more relevant than for Italy. Italy changed its position from neutral to belligerent voluntary, whereas Belgium had been an occupied country and a battlefield from the first day of the war. At the Armistice, its debts had grown to $ 1.1 billion, half of which to France, one third to Britain and the remainder to the US. All parties involved – at least on the victors' side – agreed that Belgium had an enormous legitimate claim on Germany. But would that imply that the US had to wait for repayment from Belgium until Germany would pay Belgium?

19 A quote, via-via of a mayor of New York, **Self** (2006), p. 197.

20 *'[...] Germany accepts the responsibility of Germany and her allies for causing all the loss and damage to which the Allied and Associated Governments and their nationals have been subjected as a consequence of the war imposed upon them by the aggression of Germany and her allies'*, **Versailles Treaty** (1919), Article 231. The American government did charge Germany for the costs of its part of the occupation army and the so-called *mixed claims*. These were claims by American citizens on Germany arising from damage to their property or rights as a consequence of the war, including the period of American neutrality. On might think of American passengers died at the sinking of the Lusitania. The notion 'mixed claims' is confusing: not the claims were mixed, but the commission that was to decide on the claims: it consisted of representatives from Germans and Americans and it was established in a separate agreement between the US and Germany, **FRUS** 1922, p. 262.

21 Of which (rounded) $300 million for Austria and $ 200 million for Hungary, based on data from **Popovics** (1925), p. 122 and **Strachan** (2004), p. 171 and an approximate exchange rate of 6.80 *marks* to the dollar. The debt pattern at the side of Central powers is more complicated if commercial credits with neutral countries are taken into account, such as the Netherlands, Sweden and Switzerland. These credits however are of a different nature than the inter-ally (and inter-government) debts, see for example **Popovics** (1925), pp. 125-128.

22 **Versailles Treaty** (1919), Article 261.

23 **ARST**, 1920, p. 348. The amount is in current dollars; advances have been corrected for (small) repayments. Other countries receiving credits were Serbia and (from July 1918) Czechoslovakia.

24 See previous note, ibid., pp. 330-337.

25 In 1920 France had much more effort to repay than Britain, because the exchange rate of the *franc* had entered a free-fall since autumn 1919. Payments had to be made in dollars that became more expensive by the day. To repay the debts, new loans had to be agreed, together with gold shipments both by France and Britain, **Wormell** (2000), pp. 463-465.

26 According to **Moulton & Pasvolsky** (1932), pp. 430-431, the amount was $ 11.7 billion. Loans to new countries such as Czechoslovakia, Yugoslavia, Hungary, Estonia, Latvia, Lithuania but also to Poland and Greece were a direct consequence of the war. They were different from previous loans to Britain, France and Italy in an *economic* sense: investment in reconstruction instead of purchase of armament. Financially however, the US government made no difference as the loans were all granted and approved by the *Liberty Bond Acts*. Therefore all these loans, war loans and post-war loans, are counted here and in the next chapters as American loans. Loans to non-European countries, notably Cuba, Liberia and Nicaragua and also those to Armenia and Russia, together $ 250 million, are left out in all figures presented here, except for one time in the amount of $ 11.7 billion. The loans to this latter group of countries were also treated differently by the United States government in the sense that there were different debt settlement agreements (or none at all).

27 **Moulton & Pasvolsky** (1932), p. 62.

28 Secretary of the Treasury Carter Glass, **ARST**, 1920, pp. 80-83.

29 **ARST**, 1926, pp. 67-69

30 **Gomes** (2010) has given a convenient review with the distance of 80 years. Economic and political context can also be found in **Balderston** (2002). A broad view on the reparations debate has been given by **Feldman** (2008). A key reference is the highly cited article of **Marks** (1969) published in the then new wave of interest in reparations; it refutes some

myths that possibly live on today in an analysis with a more political than economic approach. One of her much less known predecessors is **Borsky** (1942), writing in a more polemic style. In the literature on the First World War, **Ferguson** (1998) devotes a complete chapter to this subject, hauling Keynes over the coals in a personal manner, one of the first economists who gave attention to the subject of reparations.

31   **Versailles Treaty** (1919), Chapter VIII, Annex II, Article 12b: *'Germany's capacity to pay'*. Reparation payments had priority over payments (interest and principal) on domestic loans, while the tax burden in Germany should be proportionally as high in Germany as in victor countries.

32   Ibid., Articles 233-235.

33   The *Reparations Commission* consisted of representatives from the United States, Britain, France and Italy as permanent members; other countries such as Belgium had the right to vote on matters that concerned their particular interests.

34   Not contained in this amount were the foreign war debts of Belgium, estimated at 4 billion (gold) *marks*. It was understood that Germany had to pay these debts in any case.

35   It is very tempting to compare this amount with the French reparations of 1871. These latter were roughly 25% of the French GDP of the year 1817, whereas German reparations were roughly 330% of one year's German GDP in 1921, **Eichengreen** (1995), pp. 131-132, or 260% of the pre-war GDP, **Ritschl** (2005), p. 69. If one takes the more realistic amount of 50 billion *marks* (see next note) as a basis for calculation, it amounts to 83% of an average GDP over the years 1923-1931, **Occhino** *et al.* (2006), p. 5, or more than three times the burden of France in 1871. This kind of analysis however disregards the wealth position, among which the reparation France had to pay 'in kind', including the total production value and invested capital in Alsace-Lorraine lost by France in 1871 and by Germany in 1918/'19.

36   Technically, the 132 billion *marks* were split into 3 types of bonds to be issued by Germany, called 'A', 'B' and 'C'. The 'C' bonds to the amount of 82 billion *marks* were by far the largest, but also the most vague ones; **Marks** (1978), p. 237, calls them 'chimerical'. They were held by the *Reparations Commission* without bearing interest. The remaining 50 billion *marks* were split into 12 billion *marks* 'A' bonds and 38 billion *marks* 'B' bonds. The 'B' bonds were supposed to correspond more or less to the inter-ally debts, **Ritschl** (2005), p. 70.

37   **Lloyd George** (1932) p. 62; also **Gomes** (2010), pp. 68-70.

38   See for example **Marks** (1969), p. 364. Formally the 'C' bonds were still pending to be materialised sometime. For Germany they were a kind of built-in incentive to delay payments on the 'A' and 'B' bonds, because that would prevent the 'C' bonds from ever coming into the picture, **Furst** (1927), p. 113.

39   This sum, $ 11.9 billion, by the way, corresponds almost exactly to the debts of the allies to the United States at the end of 1922 when the US government had just started negotiations for settlements of these debts: $ 11.7 billion. The difference is that the reparations sum concerns the principal only (or at least understood to be so), whereas the debts sum includes arrears in interest payments. For conversion of currencies the pre-war exchange rate of 4.203 *marks* to the dollar has been used, since the reparations were expressed in *gold marks*, not the devalued *marks* of 1922.

40   **Bennett** (2006), pp. 285-286.

41   **Wunder** (2004), pp. 145-146.

42   **Gomes** (2010), pp. 65-66; also **Moulton & Pasvolsky** (1932), p. 152.

43   **FRUS**, 1919 nr. XIII, pp. 408-410; also **Borsky** (1942), p. 57.

44   The Reparations Commission valued these payments in the interim period at 7.9 billion (gold) *marks*. There was a large difference with the data Germany had presented, mainly due to the value of the deliveries in kind, estimated by Germany at 21 billion *marks* and at 5.7 billion *marks* by the Commission, **FRUS**, 1919, nr. XIII p. 439, see also note 23 on page 345.

45   During the period of occupation the allies are estimated to have extracted an amount of approximately 900 million (gold) *marks* from Germany, **Marks** (1978), p. 245, **Furst** (1927), p. 336, and **FRUS** 1919, XIII, p. 785. Meanwhile reparation payments to countries that were not involved in the Ruhr occupation partially continued until August 1923, **Gomes** (2010), p. 127.

46   The American position has been pointed out in detail in a letter to Lloyd George by the outgoing President Wilson the day after the elections of 2 November 1920 when he was defeated by Harding, **ARST** 1926, p. 72. United States representatives in international discussions received the instruction to deny explicitly and unambiguously any relation between debts to the United States and reparations; see for example the instruction to the American representative in the *Reparations Commission*, **ARST** 1920, p. 87.

47   **Moulton & Pasvolsky** (1932), pp. 101-103, also for amounts by country mentioned in this chapter.

48   The agreement with Britain was evidently less generous; in that case over 90% of the pre-Armistice debt remained due, ibid., p. 103.

49   'France has had generous treatment from the United States': Kellogg to his diplomatic and consular officers, 28 August 1926, in a comparison between British and French debt settlements, **FRUS** 1926, p. 105.

50   **Ahamed** (2010), pp. 256-258.

51   **Nouailhat** (1979), p. 408.

52   The Great Injustice, **Homberg** (1926), in particular pp. 55-56, where he fulminates against the statements of Secretary of the Treasury Houston (page 214). Houston had declared that 'This nation [US] has neither sought nor received substantial benefits from the war', **ARST**, 1926, p. 69. From the French perspective, the United States had kept a neutral position during three quarters of the war while playing a lucrative role of selling its products at the highest price to the fighting parties.

53   **The Economist** 24 April 1926, p. 819.

54   **USBUD** 1924-1930; **Moulton & Pasvolsky** (1932), pp. 482-485.

55   **ARST** 1929, p. 49; p. 303 ff. The French House of Representatives (*Assemblée Nationale*) voted the bill on 20/21 July 1929 with a narrow majority of 300-292; six days later, the French Senate (*Sénat*) agreed with 242-90, **Weill-Raynal** (1947), p. 491. The reluctance of French politicians to ratify the agreement and the threat posed by the deadline of the war supplies loan is apparent in many places in the diary of the *Banque de France* governor **Moreau** (1991).

56   Britain attributed these large debts to the decision taken during the war to direct the credits to Europe (partly) through London. The United States, on the other hand, maintained that it had lent to all countries; for the American-British controversy, see **Self** (2006), p. 34 ff.

57   The ratification of this Churchill-Caillaux Agreement was postponed for more than three years, much to the dismay of the British; it was finally ratified by the French parliament by show of hands immediately after the ratification of the Mellon-Bérenger Agreement, **Turner**

(1998), p. 258, **Weill-Raynal** (1947), p. 491. Nevertheless, in the meantime the French government punctually made the scheduled payments.

58   **Moulton & Pasvolsky** (1932), pp. 116, 124, 456. The amount had to be paid in pounds, without a gold clause. Calculated at the exchange rate of 1927 (the year of the initial payment), the total amount was almost exactly 100 billion *francs*.

59   Ibid., p. 123.

60   Ibid., pp. 118-119.

61   **Ahamed** (2010), pp. 197-199.

62   These were the essentials. Formally the commission was charged with the question if German budget equilibrium and stabilisation of the *mark*. These latter issues were clearly in line with the observations Houston had made a year before.

63   A comprehensive description of the plan and its backgrounds can be found in a special supplement to **The Economist** of 31 May 1924; see also **Gomes** (2010).

64   The amount could be adjusted on the basis of a highly complicated prosperity index including (among others) export, import, rail cargo, beer consumption and development of population, **The Economist** 31 May 1924, Supplement, p. 5.

65   One might think that the payments were used primarily for reparations, but this was not the case. All kinds of expenditure received priority, notably current management costs and the costs related to the occupation armies. Before the Dawes plan came into action, these costs were separately charged to Germany and not deducted from reparations. A rough calculation shows that roughly 2.0 million *marks* of the 2.5 million *marks* would be left for actual reparations payments; from the initial amount of 1.0 billion *marks*, only one half would be available for reparations proper.

66   This is the same condition that Germany had imposed on France in 1871, page 30.

67   Detailed inside information about the daily supervision activities can be found in the diary of Gijsbert Bruins, the man who was responsible for the German gold reserve, **Houwink ten Cate** (1989).

68   Germany's undisputed capacity to produce had been already formulated explicitly by McKenna addressing the American Bankers Association in 1922, **McKenna** (1922).

69   The total German gold stock would be sufficient for only six months of reparations payments according to the London scheme of 1921, **Moulton & Pasvolsky** (1932), p. 12.

70   **McAdoo** (1931), pp. 419-421; the value of the islands was not to be found in their economic potential but in taking over strategic positions. McAdoo derived the idea from a suggestion made in 1919 by Lord Rothermere, who was not afraid of strategic shifting with populations and relabeling areas anyway.

71   **The Economist** 18 October 1924, p. 600.

72   Again (see note 65), the actual reparation payments had the lowest priority in the annuity of 2.5 billion *marks*. The highest priority received interest and principal payments on the international loan, that is: private investors. Then followed management costs of the *Reparations Commission*, management costs of the Dawes plan, the Inter-allied Rhineland High Commission and the Military Commission of Control. After these came possible unpaid costs for the various European occupation armies and the American occupation army made before May 1921. Following in row were interest and capital payments on Belgian war debts and finally American mixed claims. What was left over, roughly 80%, was credited on the actual reparations bill, **Moulton & Pasvolsky** (1932), pp. 172-173.

73 **Glasemann** (1993), pp. 90-169. Roughly one third of the loans (apart from the Dawes and Young loans) were granted to public authorities and non-profit organisations. See also **Ahamed** (2010), p. 283.

74 **Euwe** (2010), p. 231.

75 **Schuker** (1985), p. 346, **Ritschl** (1999), p. 142.

76 **Schuker** (1985). The total influx of capital in Germany in the period 1919-1931 is estimated at 45 billion *marks*; as an annual average over this period this amounts to roughly 5.3% of the actual GDP; if corrected for reparation payments the rate is 3.3%, ibid., p. 369.

77 **The Economist** 18 October 1924, p. 600; ibid. 14 June 1930, p. 1317; **BIS** 1930, Annex X. Currencies of 1924 converted at the £/$ exchange rate of October 1924 (**The Economist** 24 January 1925, p. 133) and for other currencies at the annual average of 1924, **BMS** (1943); currencies of 1930 have been converted with official exchange rates from **BIS** 1931. Net proceeds are corrected for costs for the loans. The amounts in German *marks* have less significance because the proceeds of the loan were used largely to pay in non-German currency (Dawes loan: fully, Young loan 2/3).

78 **FRUS**, 1919, nr. 13, pp. 408-410; **The Economist** 21 June 1930, p. 1380.

79 **Ahamed** (2010), p. 327.

80 France saw its asset (the Rhineland occupation) decrease in value as already 9 of the 15 years had passed and cashing became urgent, **Marks** (1978), pp. 249-250 (another example of French linking of financial and political/strategic issues). Furthermore, its spirit became broken after the disastrous fall of the franc (-32%) in 1926, still apart from domestic political unrest; meanwhile Germany had learned that every new arrangement would bring a reduction of the burden.

81 Furthermore, there were some small corrections to the amount to be received by allied countries.

82 Comparable to the splitting of the total reparation bill into the 'A' + 'B' and 'C' bonds in the London scheme, page 339 note 36.

83 **Moulton & Pasvolsky** (1932), p. 206, pp. 471-472. This amount includes payments on the international Dawes loan, but not payments to the United States, for example for the occupation army, 60 million *marks*. This implies that in the literature both higher and lower amounts can be found: 612 million *marks* as the annual sum for the allies excluding the US and excluding the Dawes annuities, ibid., p. 206, or 660 million *marks*, **Gomes** (2010), p. 174 for the sum originally mentioned by the Commission, including the US, **Marks** (1978), p. 250. France was to receive the largest part of this unconditional part, roughly 500 million *marks*. Payments on the international Dawes loan were comprised in the unconditional part, which was set sufficiently low to be contained within the German *capacity to pay*.

84 **Pfleiderer** (2002), p. 185. This reference presents an extensive description of the negotiations of the Young Commission in Paris.

85 **The Economist** 15 February 1930, p. 351. If German payments to the United States that are apparently left out are taken into account, the total was 35 million *marks*. This amount is the present value of 59 annuities at a discount rate of 5.5%, the interest rate of the Young loan.

86 Starting with the realistic 50 billion *marks* of 1921 minus 18 billion *marks* paid before and during the Dawes scheme, the remainder is 32 billion *marks*. From the available data, however, it is unclear which part of the payments during the London and the Dawes

scheme should be considered as interest payments. If one assumes that interest payments were nil during the period 1919-1924 while under Dawes all interest due has been paid, there remains roughly an arrear amount of 9 billion *marks* of unpaid interest, making the total of interest and redemption payments approximately 40 billion *marks*. A present value of 35 billion *marks* then means a reduction of 11%. If however, all interest payments under the Dawes scheme still have to be paid, again roughly 9 billion *marks*, the reduction of the Young plan increases to 27%. **Gomes** (2010), p. 181, without giving additional details, mentions a reduction in present value of 'at least 20 per cent'.

87 **Moulton & Pasvolsky** (1932), pp. 194, 471. Incidentally, their assertion (p. 194) that there every year showed a surplus is correct only if *cumulative* amounts are taken; in individual years 1934 until 1941 there was a deficit of at most 2%.

88 Ibid., p. 193.

89 Ibid., pp. 471-473. See also **ARST** 1930, p. 334 ff.

90 At the issue price of 90 the effective yield was higher: 6.2%. In France the issue price was higher (98.25) because the bonds were tax exempt, **The Economist** 14 June 1930, p. 1418. German investors showed great interest for the loan: it was three times oversubscribed, possible as a consequence of foreign investors subscribing through German banks, **The Economist** 21 June 1930, p. 1386.

91 Without detailed information about individual subscriptions, it is impossible to conclude that bondholders in, for example Sweden or the Netherlands were actually citizens of these countries. It seems not unlikely that German investors used an indirect route via Stockholm or Amsterdam to invest (flight) capital in foreign currency, as it had happened with capital for German industry by constructions abroad, **James** (1984), p. 78. For the large share from France there are several explanations. In the first place, the country would receive the largest share of reparations, partly to be paid from the proceeds of the loan. Furthermore, the French government hoped that older French loans with high interest rates would be converted by this loan, and finally France had always advocated commercialisation of reparations, although this was only meaningful if the United States an Britain would have taken a large(r) share, **The Economist** 25 January 1930, p. 172.

92 **BIS**, 1931. The founding institutions and the first shareholders were the central banks from Belgium, Germany, Britain, France and Italy, a Japanese group of banks represented by the *Industrial Bank of Japan* and an American group in which *J.P. Morgan & Co.*, the *First National Bank of New York* and the *First National Bank of Chicago* participated. The *Federal Reserve* as such did not participate. The BIS was not involved in payments from Germany to the United States, which were settled directly between these countries.

93 The location of the conference was in the Dutch Senate's premises, not in The Hague Peace Palace as one might expect. A detailed day-to-day description including the tensions related to reparations can be found in **Pfleiderer** (2002), pp. 211-289.

94 Between the two sessions a couple of tricky issues had been resolved, such as the shares of the various countries in the total sum to be received from Germany and an agreement on shipping British coal to Italy. Almost in passing Austrian reparations were cancelled, **CMD** 3764; for details on other non-German reparations, see **Moulton & Pasvolsky** (1932), pp. 237-256.

95 These and other Dow Jones Index values are taken from **Williamson** (2017).

96 **Ezickson** (1938), p. 183. The man seen from the back is presumably German Finance Minister Paul Moldenhauer, **Salomon** (1978 [1931]), p. 23.

97 **RT** 427, p. 4412, shows the final vote: 265 in favour, 192 against, 3 abstentions and 6 invalid votes invalid. A result of 270-192, sometimes quoted in the literature, for example **Pfleiderer** (2002), p. 286, is based on the preliminary counting, **RT** 427, p. 4412, without correction for invalid votes.

98 *'Bis in die dritte Generation müßt ihr fronen!'*, the slogan of the National Committee for the German Referendum against the Young Plan and the War debt lie, *Reichsausschuß für das deutsche Volksbegehren gegen den Young-Plan und die Kriegsschuldlüge*, Berlin, October 1929.

99 **Pfleiderer** (2002), p. 195. Amounts mentioned in the literature vary lightly: **Clement** (2004), p. 34 mentions 115.2 billion *marks*; the sum of the annuities, including the amounts to be paid to the United States, are 114.6 billion *marks* according to **Moulton & Pasvolsky** (1932), pp. 471-473.

100 **Pfleiderer** (2002), pp. 281-282.

101 It is generally assumed that the referendum had a positive effect on the NSDAP's popularity, **Pfleiderer** (2002), 255, although a more sceptical view has also been put forward, **Jung** (1989).

102 There is some discussion about the shift between public and private creditors. **Ritschl** (1996), p. 193, attributes the panic at the German stock exchange and the pressure on the German *mark* in the spring of 1929 to the fear that in the Young plan reparations would be at the expense of private bondholders. **Balderston** (2002), p. 84, on the other hand states that the crisis was generated by the fear that the negotiations on the Young plan would fail, in which case Germany would not be able to meet its reparations obligations.

103 **Taylor**, A.J.P. (1991), *The Origins of the Second World War*, London, Penguin, p. 71, quoted by **Gomes** (2010), p. 221.

104 **Keynes** (1920), p. 240 ff.

Chapter 13 – The Financial Armistice of 1931

1 **BIS** 1931, Annex VIa, mentions 1,630 million *marks*, of which 250 million *marks* were a reservation. From the remaining 1,380 million *marks*, 130 million *marks* were allocated to interest and principal payments for the Dawes and Young loans. The amount of (rounded) 1.4 billion *marks* corresponds to $ 330 million (£ 73 million) at that time.

2 **ARST** 1931, pp. 358-359.

3 **Eichengreen** (1995), p. 258.

4 **Gomes** (2010), p. 202; **Euwe** (2012), p. 60; **Eichengreen** (1995), pp. 275-280; **Ahamed** (2010), p. 407. Although the banking position in Austria was rather different from that in Germany, the link between the countries as it was felt abroad was not unrealistic. In the spring of 1931 rumours about the intended customs union between both countries had appeared in the press, **The Economist** 28 March 1931, p. 659. For a compact account of the developments in Germany in 1931-1932, see also **Wertheimer** (1932).

5 In July 1931 the second largest German bank, the *Danat Bank* (*Darmstädter und National-bank*) went bankrupt. An additional remarkable phenomenon was that 'foreign' capital was not necessary 'non-German' capital. German citizens invested in German industry not only directly but also with short-term credits with a detour through Switzerland or the Netherlands, **James** (1984), p. 78.

6   **Brown** (1988), p. 251, p. 233; also: **Homer & Sylla** (2005), p. 513.

7   **Balderston** (2000), p. 79. Unemployment increased to 32% (of the number of members of labour unions) in December 1930 to 42% in December 1931, **HISTAT** (Petzina, D., *Arbeitslosigkeit in der Weimarer Republik*. GESIS Köln, Deutschland ZA8441 *Datenfile* Version 1.0.0).

8   **Gomes** (2010), p. 202. The first formal one in a series of similar standstill *(Stillhalte)* agreements took place on 17 September 1931, **BIS** 1932, p. 13; also: **Gomes** (2010), pp. 205-206; **Clement** (2010), p. 36, and **James** (1984), p. 82, mention an earlier standstill agreement in August 1931. See also The Economist 19 September 1931, p. 518, **Brown** (1988), p. 262 ff. Meanwhile foreign exchange trade had been regulated by 15 July 1931 and the *mark* was effectively inconvertible, The Economist 18 July 1931, p. 104.

9   **Eichengreen** (1995), pp. 260-261.

10   **Born** (1983), p. 228, quoted in **Gomes** (2010), p. 182.

11   **Ahamed** (2010), p. 407.

12   **ARST** 1931, pp. 359-361. France negotiated and received the (paper) promise that Germany would pay the unconditional part of the Young plan for one year, to be placed on a special account at the BIS in guaranteed German railroad bonds.

13   **ARST** 1932, p. 289.

14   The federal budget of 1932 was $ 1.9 billion (http://federal-budget.findthedata.org/l/34/1931). In the hypothetical case that all payments were shifted exactly one year, the United States would roughly lose one year's cumulated interest, about $ 8-10 million; in the individual agreements made after the moratorium, arrears were to be paid in a period of 10 years at a uniform interest rate of 4%.

15   The Economist 23 January 1932, supplement, p. 11: 9,500 million *marks*. The debt of allied governments to the US government was at that moment almost $ 12 billion, **ARST** 1931, p. 551: $ 11.6 billion as per 15 November 1931.

16   **Self** (2006), p. 201, **Gomes** (2010), p. 214. After the devaluation of the dollar, a few years later, this would be more or less restored.

17   **Gomes** (2010), p. 211, **Moulton & Pasvolsky** (1932), pp. 356-357.

18   **Frankfurther** (1961), p. 63.

19   According to **Clement** (2004), p. 47, Swedish bondholders would still be paid during the period May 1945-December 1945.

20   Ibid., p. 38 ff., with a detailed description of the unilateral German steps to reduce payments on the Dawes and Young loans since 1932, based on the BIS archives.

21   The Economist 2 July 1938, p. 32.

22   **Gomes** (2010), pp. 211-212; also **Moulton & Pasvolsky** (1932), p. 359; **Wormell** (2000), p. 609.

23   **Gomes** (2010), p. 212. This corresponds with **FRUS**, 1919, nr. 13, pp. 408-410. Data differ slightly in various sources. **Borsky** (1942), p. 61, mentions 21.2 (gold) *marks*, corrected for Dawes annuities. Germany assumed a considerably higher amount, about 33 billion (gold) *marks*, The Economist 32 January 1932, supplement, p. 4. The main difference is, that Germany incorporated more payments in kind (such as surrendered battleships) and/or at a higher value (for example non-military stores left at the fronts), **Holtfrerich** (1980), p. 144 ff., **Moulton & Pasvolsky** (1932), p. 262, **Borsky** (1942), p. 45.

24 Based on the present value of the various amounts paid over the years conform **FRUS** (1919) and an interest rate of 4.25% as (intended) in the inter-ally debts.

25 **Gomes** (2010), p. 212.

26 **ARST** 1933, pp. 27-28.

27 Letter from British ambassador Ronald Charles Lindsay to the American government, 4 June 1934. The other option was a deterioration of the exchange rate of Sterling, which could not be the intention of the Americans, as the ambassador pointed out, **ARST** 1934, pp. 227-230. It should be noted that *all* countries took protectionist measures during the 1930s, even Britain that had been a staunch advocate of free trade until the First World War.

28 13 April 1934, **ARST** 1934, p. 238. Token payments were not allowed too. During the Second World War, the Johnson Act was circumvented and Britain – still on default – received nevertheless financial support by the so-called lend-lease construction (p. 280, note a).

29 As compared to other nations, Britain certainly paid its share, as it had to pay 50% of all payments; the remaining 50% was to be paid by all other former allies together.

30 **ARST**, issues 1923-1976. Agreements made for the Second World War period are given in **USDSB** (1940), Volume III, no 76, pp. 501-502.

31 **ARST** 1950, p. 89.

32 **Mäkinen** (2001).

33 **ARST** 1934, p. 48.

34 **ARST** 1938, pp. 294-300.

35 **ARST** 1977, p. 164.

36 http://hungary.usembassy.gov/holy_crown.html.

37 **Eichengreen** (1988), p. 26.

38 The total includes the countries Belgium, Czechoslovakia, Estonia, Finland, France, Great Britain, Hungary, Italy, Latvia, Lithuania, Poland, Rumania and Yugoslavia; Greece received additional refunding loans and has been left out. The share has been calculated as the amounts paid cumulatively, divided by the sum of all annuities to be paid in 59 years, according to the original agreements (supplementary payment to compensate for the year of the Hoover moratorium have been ignored). A similar calculation based on present values evidently leads to higher percentages because early years contribute more to the present value. The picture of the outstanding commitments, however, would become less clear.

39 Calculated as the present value of all annuities forgone from 1932 until the scheduled dates of expiration (1984-1987, varying by country), using a uniform interest rate of 4.25% and based on payments done and settlements schemes, **ARST**, issues 1926-1937 and **Moulton & Pasvolsky** (1932), pp. 432-454, respectively. The total American loss was actually somewhat larger, since not all amounts due before 1932 had been paid. The table in **Ferguson** (1998), p. 419, which is based on **The Economist** 23 January 1932, Supplement, p. 7, gives a loss of £ 63.6 million, corresponding to the $ 240 million mentioned, but this is only the loss in the first (moratorium) year.

40 The average GDP of the United States over the (calendar) years 1931 and 1932 was $ 77 billion/year, **USBUD** 2016, Historical Tables, Table 1.2.

41 Payments calculated as the present value at the end of 1922 of the amounts actually paid from the fiscal year 1922/'23 onwards. Interest rate taken as 4.25% and based on data from **ARST**, issues 1933-1937 and **Moulton & Pasvolsky** (1932), pp. 482-485. The amount is

(rounded) $ 1.5 billion and the value of the debts has been taken as $ 12.0 billion, the value at the end of 1922, **Moulton & Pasvolsky** (1932), p. 101. This is exclusive the negligible debt of Greece, a country that had made special arrangements. The Russian debt to the US, $ 180 million in 1918 has been completely disregarded since no debt settlement had been made and the debt had to be written off in full.

42   See the extensive and interesting discussion 'How (not) to Pay for the War' in **Ferguson** (1998), p. 395 ff.

43   For example **Homberg** (1926), p. 64, and also **Petit** (1929), pp. 157-158.

44   A man like Hjalmer Schacht for example never ended to disseminate this view: '[therefore] Germany [...] is not morally committed to the Versailles Treaty', **Houwink ten Cate** (1989), p. 110.

Chapter 14 – Clearing domestic debris

1   Austria-Hungary is a story by itself with currency reforms and hyperinflation.

2   **Ritschl** (1996) has given a comparison of the way France, Germany and Britain dealt with high national debts in the light of international financial relations.

3   Ibid.

4   **Wormell** (2000), p. 731, p. 383 and **BOE3C**, based on **Mitchell**, (1988), *British Historical Statistics*, Cambridge, University Press. These figures are somewhat higher (but not fundamentally) than those mentioned by **Balderston** (1989), p. 227, which are derived from **Morgan** (1952), *Studies in British financial policy, 1914-1925*, London, Macmillan.

5   **Ferguson** (1998), p. 325, based on **Balderston** (1998) and **Fisk** (1924).

6   As a measure for the national debt the share has been taken of this debt in the GDP of the last pre-war year and the last year of the war, respectively. Because all amounts are nominal (in current pounds), this filters out the effect of inflation. During the First World War, this share increased by 400%: it quintupled. This increase is a dimensionless indicator as a real measure of the change in financial burden on the economy and can be compared between wars in different periods in history.

7   £ 360 million against £ 300 million, respectively, **Wormell** (2000), p. 383, and **BOE3C**. **Bogart** (1921), p. 394 compares the interest burden to pre-war civil expenditure and concludes that the former is twice as large as the latter.

8   £ 68 million of a budget of approximately £ 1,300 million, **Wormell** (2000), pp. 421, 425.

9   **BOEBR**.

10   **Wormell** (2000), p. 421, Figure 14.1 and p. 435, Table 14.4.

11   **Kirkaldy** (1921), p. 133.

12   On 20 September 1931 the Cabinet decided to postpone the convertibility of Sterling, definitely, as would proved to be afterwards, **The Economist** 26 September 1931, p. 554.

13   **The Economist** 2 July 1932, p. 1.

14   **Homer & Sylla** (2005), pp. 205, 206.

15   **Wormell** (2000), p. 608.

16   At that time, this amount represented roughly 5% of government expenditure, **The Economist** 2 April 1932, p. 722. Translated to today's situation it would be an *annual* cut in expenditure of £ 40 billion, **UKBUD** 2016, p. 6.

17   **Wormell** (2000), p. 622. Less than 8% of the amount outstanding was not converted by bondholders. They received the face value of their bonds in accordance with the conditions

of 1917 although they had purchased the bonds at the issue price of 95 (or at the actual market price in later years).

18   **Reinhart & Rogoff** (2009), p. 114.

19   **Grigg** (1948), p. 184, quoted in **Ahamed** (2010), pp. 234-235.

20   **Wormell** (2000), p. 618; **Train** (1985), p. 42.

21   Source of the photo: **Black & White**, London, 6 June 1908, p. 709.

22   Financial data for 1920 and 1921 based on realised expenditure, data for 1922 based on a revised budget. Budget data for 1923 are highly indicative due to the hyperinflation, **RT** 378, nr. 5903, pp. 4-8, 1st June 1923.

23   **RT** 382 nr. 218, 5 June 1924, p. 2.

24   If reparations are taken into account the deficit is obviously larger, but not excessively larger: expenditure would be 3.3 times revenues instead of 2.5 times. If only the years 1920-1922 are considered, the factor is 3.7 (in 1923 reparations were comparatively small), **RT** 378, nr. 5903, p. 8. As 'reparation payments' have been taken expenditure labelled 'implementation of the Peace Treaty' (*zur Ausführung des Friedensvertrags*).

25   For excessive capital gains, marginal tax rates were as high as 100% for a capital increase of over 100,000 *marks*, **RGBl.** 1919, Nr. 75, § 16. It would be interesting to find out how many people actually paid these rates.

26   For the effects, see also **Balderston** (2002), p. 7; **Holtfrerich** (1980), p. 300; **Witt** (1985), p. 69 ff. For the hostile relation between Erzberger and Helfferich, see **Williamson** (1971), *passim*.

27   **RGBl.** 1922, Nr. 53, Nr. 85.

28   There was a kind of sinking fund of 0.5% per annum, which implied that the redemption period could last some 200 years.

29   A highly cited review on the inflation period 1914-1923 has been given by **Holtfrerich** (1980). Detailed studies can be found in **Feldman** (1993), **Feldman** *et al.* (1984) and – with specific attention to the aftermath – in **Feldman & Müller-Luckner** (1985). A lively description has been given by **Fergusson** (1975) (Adam, not to be confused with Niall Ferguson).

30   The relation between inflation, reparations and the political climate in the Weimar Republic is less straightforward than is sometimes suggested. This relation is a popular subject for discussion. Some researchers claim that reparations are the ultimate cause of hyperinflation, for example **Eichengreen** (1995), p. 141, based on econometric analyses. This leaves the question whether causality can be derived from statistical correlation and without a carefully defined counterfactual for history as it has actually developed. Other authors, for example **Ferguson** (2001), p. 106, point out that one could very well imagine that domestic expenditure would have increased without reparations, in which case persistent budget deficits would inevitably have led to inflation. The scientific literature is rich on material that makes the necessary differentiations or, on the other hand, makes bold assertions. See for example **Holtfrerich** (1980), **Balderston** (1989 and 2002) and contributions by many authors in the volumes edited by **Feldman** *et al.* (1984) and **Feldman & Müller-Luckner** (1985); a practical overview of the discussion can be found in **Gomes** (2010), pp. 98-104.

31   **RT** 377, nr. 5791 and nr. 5822.

32   *Entwurf eines Gesetzes über die Berücksichtigung der Geldentwertung in den Steuergesetzen,* **RT** 377, nr. 5666, for example pp. 6471, 6474, 6477.

33   **RK**, *Weimarer Republik / Kabinette Stresemann I/II*, Nr. 42: *Das Reichsbank-Direktorium an den Reichskanzler*, dated 5 September 1923.

34   **Ahamed** (2010, p. 189) mentions a debt amount of 190 million new *reichsmarks*. It is unclear which debts have been taken into account in this calculation.

35   In the intermediate years bonds could have been used to pay taxes or to buy surplus army material. At the end of 1924, the outstanding debt of war loans was 51.3 billion *marks*, **RT** 400, nr. 805, p. 11. Until the end of September 1922, when the amount outstanding was 52.8 billion (old paper) *marks*, bondholders had used 25.2 billion *marks* for tax payments and 4.4 billion *marks* in the dump store. Meanwhile the government had bought bonds to an amount of 12.4 *marks* in the market in order to support the bond price, **RT** 376, nr. 5557 (*Anleihedenkschrift*), p. 3.

36   **RGBl.** 1925, Nr. 32, pp. 137-144.

37   This is a simplification. The actual schema was much more complicated. At first a bondholder received a bond of 2.5% of the value of the old war bond. For government bonds dated before 1ˢᵗ July 1920 this 2.5% bond would be redeemed fivefold, consequently at 12.5% of the face value of the original bond in new *reichsmarks*. Bonds dated after 1ˢᵗ July 1920 would be redeemed without this multiplication, hence at 2.5% of the original value. Apart from that, there was a graduated price scale assigning less drawing rights to large bondholders, meant to discourage (or punish) speculators. Afterwards, it is impossible to determine the average rate of payment to the entire population of bondholders, **Witt** (1985), p. 61. A complicating factor was that completely ruined people who had no other income could appeal to special social security services.

38   In the German *Reichstag* these speculators had been used (without much success) as an argument to differentiate in the conditions, **RT** 386 p. 3112. **Holtfrerich** (1980), pp. 326-327, mentions a fictitious example of a speculator who had bought German war loans in 1920 paying with dollars and at the then actual exchange rate. When his bonds were drawn for redemption in 1926 and the proceeds were converted into dollars again, profits of 50% in a 6-year period could be made.

39   Not only Germans suffered, but also foreigners who had given credit in *marks* (for speculative or other reasons). **Holtfrerich** (1977), p. 286, estimates the total loss outside Germany during the period 1919-1923 at 7-8 billion (gold) *marks*, roughly the same amount as Germany paid on reparations during that period.

40   The expression is from **Keynes** (1936), p. 376, though in the context of interest rates. It is quoted by **Blancheton** (2001), p. 84, as a reality in France.

41   Based on retail price index, **INSEE** 1966, p. 405; these data are reproduced in **Mitchell** (1980), *European Historical Statistics*, London, Macmillan, pp. 780-781; the inflation rates in **Ritschl** (1996), p. 186, and **Alesina** (1988), *The end of public debts*, in: Giavazzi & Spaventa, High public debt: the Italian experience, Cambridge University Press, p. 57, are based on the wholesale price index from INSEE, resulting in a somewhat different but globally equivalent picture.

42   The price of the bond, already as low as 70.80 at issue (illustration 9.2, page 121), had dropped below 12, a loss of 84%, **The Economist** 2 January 1926, p. 28. Meanwhile Dutch mobilisation loans had practically lost nothing over the years, *Algemeen Handelsblad* 8 January 1926, evening issue, p. 13, **KB.**

43   **Jèze & Truchy** (1927), p. 152. Data for 1917 and 1918 differ from data in **Knaus** (1923), p. 136, while those for 1919 also differ (considerably) from the data given by **Fisk** (1922), p. 186. It is difficult to compare them with the data in **Sauvy** (1984), part 3, p. 386.

44   *Décrets 5 septembre 1918* and *28 septembre 1920*.

45   **Vignat** (2001), p. 636, **Blancheton** (2001), p. 145 ff., p. 182 ff.

46   **Eichengreen** (1995), pp. 173-175; **Ritschl** (1996), p. 186.

47   **Blancheton** (2001), p. 207 ff.; **Sauvy** (1984), part 3, p. 394.

48   This stabilisation during 1926-1929 has been attributed to the constant influx of German reparations initiated by the Dawes scheme, that in their turn were financed by American credits to Germany, **Ritschl** (1996), pp. 188, 202.

49   **BMS** (1943), p. 670.

50   **Hautcœur** (2005), p. 187.

51   **Ahamed** (2010), pp. 256-257.

52   On 30 June 1920 the amount outstanding was $ 19.4 billion, **ARST** 1920, p. 429.

53   Ibid. p. 25.

54   Ibid. pp. 3-7.

55   The vast majority, three quarters, came from the fourth loan. The second and third loans were completely repaid, the first loan partially.

56   In the period 1920-1929 allied payments to the United States were $ 1.7 billion, **Moulton & Pasvolsky** (1932), pp. 482-482). The US government paid off an amount of $ 11.4 billion, **ARST** 1920, p. 429; **ARST** 1929, p. 453.

57   For example **Eichengreen** (1995), pp. 323-437. For a lively description of the day-to-day process of setting the gold value of the dollar, see **Ahamed** (2009), p. 472.

58   Joint Resolution 5 June 1933, **USSAL** 1934, vol. XLVIII, p. 112, reproduced in **ARST** 1933, p. 194.

59   Perry versus United States, U.S. Supreme Court, 294 U.S. 330, 18 February 1935.

60   **Reinhart & Rogoff** (2009), pp. 44, 113, classify this act of the United States government as a formal default.

61   **Reinhart & Rogoff** (2009) and the Hanke-Krus Hyperinflation table, http://en.wikipedia. org/wiki/File:The_Hanke_Krus_Hyperinflation_Table.pdf. Values for Austria calculated from **BMS** (1943), p. 663 and for Hungary based on the Stirling exchange rate, **The Economist** 24 January 1925. See also Annex, table A.1. Abandoning the Gold Standard has not been mentioned in the table, as it was common to all countries sooner or later.

Chapter 15 – Two Wars later

1   Data on the (non) settlement of the Dawes and Young loans have been derived from **Clement** (2004), pp. 47-48, unless stated otherwise. The operational difficulties in the settlement such as determining the amounts and legitimacy of claims in various countries can be followed from year to year in the BIS Annual Reports.

2   The considerations of the **London Agreement** starts with 'Desiring to remove obstacles to normal economic relations between the Federal Republic of Germany and other countries and thereby to make a contribution to the development of a prosperous community of nations', followed by 'important concessions' made by France, Britain and the United States 'on condition that a satisfactory and equitable settlement of Germany's pre-war external debts was achieved'. See also **Kaiser** (2013), p. 1.

3   The German Federal Republic already participated in the establishment of the European Coal and Steel Community in 1951.

4   On the moral aspect, see also **Buchheim** (1986), pp. 219-222. On restoring German credit in its various senses and the relation with the simultaneous Claims Conference in Wassenaar / The Hague, see **Schwartz** (1982), pp. 10 ff.

5   **Abs** (1991), pp. 56-63; **Kaiser** (2013), p. 4.

6   A detailed scientific overview of the conference, its preparations in 1951 and the proceedings, almost from day to day, can be found in the relatively recent work of **Rombeck-Jaschinski** (2005). The leader of the German delegation has given his account of the conference in several publications, **Abs** (1959), **Abs** (1991).

7   There was another old loan that cannot be related to the First World War, the so-called Kreuger (or 'match') loan. It had been concluded in 1929 by the Weimar Republic with the Swedish industrialist, entrepreneur and owner of match factories Ivar Kreuger (or rather with his holding company *Kreuger & Toll*), **RT** 439, Nr. 1572, Annex 4. Kreuger's imperium granted the loan in exchange for the monopoly of selling matches in Germany. It reflects the amazing world of the financial markets that the date of the agreement, 26 October 1929 fell precisely in the disastrous week at the New York stock exchange, between 'Black Thursday', 24 October and 'Black Tuesday', 29 October.

8   Actually, the arrangement was more complicated: bondholders received two types of new bonds, one for the principal of the original loans and one for capitalised arrears in interest payments. This was done because payments on principal of the loans had been suspended by Germany for all bondholders at the same moment in 1934, whereas interest payments had continued at various lower rates and for a period depending on the country of the bondholder (see box at page 243). The first bonds had an interest of 5% and 4.5% for the old Dawes and Young loans, respectively, **London Agreement**, Annex I, sub A, art. 1. For the American issues of the Dawes and Young loans, the interest rate was slightly higher by 0.5% point as a compensation for the cancellation of the gold clause, **Abs** (1991), pp. 166-172. A clear summary of the arrangements has been given by **Clement** (2004), pp. 47-48. Any gold clauses possibly left in original conditions for the loans were declared void, **London Agreement**, Article 12 and **Guinnane** (2004), pp. 28-30. Gold clauses were essentially replaced by a US dollar clause, **Glasemann** (1993), p. 29.

9   This amount is based on the total face value of the newly issued bonds, **BIS** 1970, pp. 180-181). A more detailed value is hard to determine because the bonds were issued over many years (starting in 1953) according to the date when bondholders registered, and in eight different currencies. **Abs** (1959), p. 42, mentions a sum of 1.61 billion *marks*, reasonably in agreement with BIS data: 1.64 billion *marks*, provided that they are calculated with 1930 exchange rates; if calculated with 1970 exchange rates it would be 1.43 billion *marks*.

10 **Rombeck-Jaschinski** (2005), p. 427.

11 **London Agreement**, Article 9 and **Rombeck-Jaschinski** (2005), pp. 352-353.

12 The word used was 'confirmed' (German: *bestätigt*); Germany had not 'assumed' the debts (*übernommen*), a subtle difference, ibid., p. 137.

13 Even if the lower interest rates of the new bonds were applied, it was still an amount of 475 million *marks*. As outstanding bonds are considered here the amounts mentioned for which a provision has been made after the 1953 conference (*'Regelungsbetrag'*) for the tranches

of the Dawes and Young bonds in various currencies, **Glasemann** (1993), pp. 90-168; currencies converted as per 1st July 1953, **The Economist** 4 July 1953, p. 61.

14 **London Agreement**, Annex I, sub A, art. 1(d) en 2(d). For the backgrounds, see also **Abs** (1991), pp. 179-183, **Guinnane** (2004), pp. 33-34 and **Clement** (2004), pp. 47-48.

15 A striking detail is that these certificates represented rights without being normal bonds. Technically they were warrants with an unspecified date ('reunification of Germany') and without formal quotation at the stock exchange. This had been done on purpose to prevent that a quotation of the certificates would act as a public indicator for a potential German unification, **Abs** (1991), p. 183. Nevertheless there have been temporarily quotations **Guinnane** (2004), p. 35.

16 The valuation of the certificates, incidentally, was a highly complicated operation with various conversion factors, since they had been issued in a multitude of currencies and denominations, **Glasemann** (1993), pp. 56-63.

17 **Clement** (2004), p. 48; the amount of 240 million *marks* mentioned by **Guinnane** (2004), p. 35, and based on **Glasemann** (1993), p. 53, includes the Kreuger loan and two smaller Prussian loans dating from 1926-'27.

18 **Finanzen** (2010), *Gesamtplan*, p. 12, author's underling.

19 See quote on page 273.

20 **Lauterpacht & Greenwood** (2007), pp. 563-564.

21 Obviously except from Finland's exemplary conduct, see the text box on page 246.

22 **ARST** 1953, p. 113.

23 Foreign Indebtedness to the United States, Hearing before the Subcommittee on International Finance and Resources (1978), Washington, 29 October 1973.

24 Ibid., p. 6. The amount comprises the mixed claims (see page 338, note 20), to the amount of $ 1.7 billion, **ARST** 1973, Appendix p. 298.

25 **USFCRS** 2009, pp. 32-34. Several requests by the author to the US Treasury have not led to more recent data becoming available.

26 At the end of 2016 the US national debt was $ 19,800 billion, http://www.usdebtclock.org/.

27 According to the source mentioned in the previous note, the US budget deficit was $ 590 billion at the end of 2016. An inter-ally debt of $ 40 billion and an interest rate of 2.5% would mean a reduction of the deficit in the order of 0.2 per cent.

28 https://www.gov.uk/government/news/chancellor-to-repay-the-nations-first-world-war-debt. The amount outstanding had been £ 1,940 million for many years.

Annex. What is the meaning of a sum of money of 1914-'18 a century later?

1 **BOE3C**.

2 GDP (nominal) data from IMF, http://data.imf.org/regular.aspx?key=60998112 (National accounts). £ 70 million was roughly $ 350 million in 1908.

3 **UKBUD** 2016, p. 5.

4 In 1908 the exchange rate was, roughly, $ 5 to £ 1.

5 https://www.nationalpriorities.org/campaigns/military-spending-united-states.

6 http://en.wikipedia.org/wiki/Young_Plan, for example, uses a factor of 14 (in dollars) for the conversion of German reparations, based on American *consumer price* indices; http://en.wikipedia.org/wiki/Dreadnought implicitly uses a factor of 97 for British battleships, derived from *retail price* indices from 1906 to 2015.

7   Although **Ahamed** (1010), p. 505 gives no references, it can be reconstructed as the (rounded) ratio of the US GDP of 2010 and 1931 (which is, incidentally, almost equal to the 1918 GDP).

8   For Britain, for example, there are the long-run time series of Feinstein, included in **BOE3C** (*Bank of England*).

9   For example **Burhop & Wolff** (2005) for a discussion on the German data.

10 **BMS** (1943), pp. 663-681; average values over the corresponding years; 1928 is taken as a final year, when various exchange rates had been temporarily stabilised (until 1931) after a range of crises and high volatilities.

11 **Eichengreen** (1995), p. 70.

12 **Hardach** (1987), p. 143. A correspondent in Russia once called the *rouble* market 'eccentric', and noted that 'banks here and in Stockholm have no fixed exchange', **The Economist** 17 October 1914, p. 637.

13 UK: **ONS** https: // www.ons.gov.uk/economy/gross domesticproductgdp/datasets/preli minaryestimateofgdp US: **USBUD** 2016, Historical Tables, Table 1.2 (estimate for 2015); exchange rate: Bank of England.

14 For the conversion to the reference year 1913, **Fisk** (1924), p. 350 uses wholesale price indices by country. These indices correspond reasonably well with the values given by **Hardach** (1987), p. 172, and for Germany with **Holtfrerich** (1980), p. 15. They are, however, different from the cost of living indices given by **Ferguson** (1998), p. 331, derived from (among others) **Maddison**. For Germany in particular, the cost of living index for 1918 is significantly higher than the wholesale price index (by a factor 1.5). For France, on the other hand, the reverse holds. It is evident, that the final result depends of the method used. The total amount ($ 215 billion in current dollars or $ 80 billion in 1913 dollars) remains beyond doubt in the same order of magnitude.

15 **Johnston & Williamson** (2017). Evidently, the comparison should be in *nominal* dollars.

16 http://costofwar.com, reference date 19 February 2017.

17 **Stiglitz & Bilmes** (2010).

Literature

Some remarks on sources

Recent literature and overviews

Apart from articles in scientific journals, the literature on financial and economic aspects of the First World War appeared in two waves: immediately after the war, with a continuation in the 1920s/1930s and a second wave in the last few decades. Among the most recent ones are the books by Hew Strachan, Niall Ferguson and Martin Horn. **Strachan** (2004) is a thorough reference work devoted to all belligerent parties and with a breath-taking density of information. It has been of great value for me. An interesting issue in this book is the financial relationship between Germany and the Ottoman Empire. It comprises an impressive list of references, but – very unfortunately – it ends abruptly in 1918. **Ferguson** (1998) is written in the language of a British/American perspective. It has a more personal and marked style than Strachan and contains views on the question 'to pay or not to pay'. Ferguson contributes his own calculations and presents interesting time series of bond prices. **Horn** (2002) deals in a detailed and balanced way with the financial side of the uneasy relationship between Britain and France during the war, whereas **Self** (2006) proceeds in the same manner regarding the 'unspecial' relationship between Britain and the United States after the war, when it came to paying debts; the relationship of the latter two powers during the war has been analysed and compactly summarised earlier by **Burk** (1985). For the francophone reader, the box of De la Gorce (1991) contains a balanced contribution by **Soutou** with a stronger focus on finance than his impressive *L'or et le sang*; the three volumes of **Sauvy** (1984), although they deal largely with the post-war period, also contain interesting data and **Nouailhat** (1979) deals with French-American relations during the war, including loans.

Other tertiary publications

The tertiary literature is largely the work of historians, a fact reflected in the presentation. Strachan's impressive work, for example, is written completely in text without a single table. Somewhat older, and for many years a frequently cited work, is the book by the economist **Hardach** (1973), written in a style of tacitian compactness; first published as a German *Taschenbuch*, it has been translated in the *Penguin* series.[a] A more recent economic – not primarily financial – study is **Broadberry & Harrison** (2005). German statistical data can be found in detail in **Roesler** (1987). **Zilch** (1987), written in the idiom of the former German Democratic Republic (DDR), contains much of the older German information, based on thorough research in archives.

Apart from these more comprehensive studies, specialised works are scattered all over the literature. An example is **Wormell** (2000), an impressively documented work of no less than 800 pages on the development and management of the British national debt from 1900 to 1932, conveniently covering the First World War. The relationship between the French government and the *Banque de France* is dealt with in **Blancheton** (2001) and **Vignat** (2001); the latter gives in her 3-volume PhD thesis all available details about the role played by governor Pallain. **Zilch** (1994) describes in detail the German issue of bank notes and coins in occupied Belgium and **Glasemann** (1993) contains a doubtless complete database of all public and private German loans issued abroad between 1924 and 1945, etc., etc.

The history of the inter-ally debt settlements has been described in **Moulton & Pasvolsky** (1932), an older work, but still of value. The role of the Gold Standard before, during and after the war, together with scientific arguments *pro* and *contra* can be found in **Eichengreen** (1995). Interesting details about the *dramatis personae* of the *haute finance* appear on the scene in **Ahamed** (2010) in an irresistibly compelling style. Unfortunately, works about individual central bankers are rare; Cunliffe, Pallain and Havenstein have not yet received the biographies that they undoubtedly deserve. Finance ministers are better off: biographies of Karl Helfferich and McKenna have been written by **Williamson** (1971) and **Farr** (2006), respectively. McAdoo has received attention from many biographers, ranging from the more hagiographic early work of **Synon** (1924) to the recent scientific publications of **Chase** (2008) and **Craig** (2013).

---

a   All page references in the present book refer to the English edition **Hardach** (1987).

Secondary sources

The secondary sources are part of the first wave of publications, dating from the period immediately after the war, sometimes even during the war. In virtually endless tables (*'The tables do not require extended comment'*[a]) economists, statisticians and bankers, rather than historians, tell the story of budgets, taxes, loans and debts on the basis of then available documents and data. **Kirkaldy** (1921) is a good example from the perspective of the London City and **Lotz** (1927) from the viewpoint of German national state finance, while **Knauss** (1923) compares the main European countries. American think tanks such as the *Carnegie Endowment for International Peace* and the *Brookings Institution* published rich sources of material; they are available in libraries and sometimes in antiquarian bookshops. **Jèze & Truchy** (1927), **Bogart** (1920, 1921) and Moulton & Pasvolsky, mentioned above, belong to this category of important secondary sources.[b] Separate mention should be made of **Pigou** (1916), who gave a century ago a clear treatise on the notion of costs, that is still worth reading today.

Different sources and common ancestors: a short observation on methodology

It appears that in many publications showing an overview of 'costs', the original source for conversion, exchange rates, etc. can be traced back to **Fisk** (1924), although this source is not always mentioned explicitly. **Hardach** (1987), for example, mentions as a source **Mendershausen** (1941), but Mendershausen derives his data from the original Fisk tables. **Ferguson** (1998), p. 322, mentions alongside with **Hardach** (1987) also **Fisk** (1922) as 'another estimate', whereas it is just an earlier version of the original data used and readjusted by Fisk in his later publication used by Hardach.

Another example is found in inter-ally debts where **Hardach** (1987), p. 148, gives as a source **Moulton & Pasvolsky** (1932), p 426, which can

---

a   **Fisk** (1924), p. 74.
b   It is remarkable that cultural differences between countries even left their traces in the structure of the early publications: **Lotz** (1927), writing about Germany, starts with financial legislation and the national budget, **Kilkardy** (1921) on Britain, characteristically opens his treatise with an analysis of the banking system, while the second part of **Jèze & Truchy** (1927) on France begins with a chapter about the normal revenues of the government. Even in the more recent **Gilbert** (1970), a general introduction on war finance is immediately followed by a chapter on the effect of the outbreak of the war on the American economy.

again be traced back to **Fisk** (1924), p. 345, apart from some corrections for gold transactions. Fisk himself, an employee of the *Bankers Trust Company*, declares that he requested the original sources, but he rarely mentions them in individual tables. In his methodological justification, Fisk explains that he consulted individual authorities to verify the data. It gives confidence that he crosschecked data, for example about the British-Canadian debts, where he received (considerably) different data from the British and the Canadian side. It is not always clear which choices Fisk has made in cases like this and which criteria he used. In some cases I could check his (unmentioned) sources and they were correct, for example his table of expenditure of European countries in the United States, his page 176 are one-to-one derived from **ARST** 1920, p. 338.

Certain French data in both **Strachan** (2004) and **Hardach** (1967) are derived from **Jèze & Truchy** (1927); British government expenditure data in **Broadberry & Howlett** (2005) have **Kirkaldy** (1921) as their source; German expenditure data in **Ferguson** (1998), p. 323, are from **Balderston** (1989), p. 225, which can be traced back via **Roesler** (1967) to German *Statistische Jahrbücher* from 1919 en later years, etc. Sources also differ in their firmness of presentation. For example **Jèze & Truchy** (1927), writing nine years after the war, are much more prudent than **Bogart** (1920) who wrote his first edition October 1919, when the ink of the Versailles Treaty was hardly dry and the pressure to publish data must have been high.[a]

Primary data

Finally, we have the primary sources. They are scattered in archives in all former belligerent countries, but the information has often been reproduced in secondary and tertiary literature, much to the benefit of the historian. Thanks to large-scale digitalisation efforts, an increasing

---

[a] Historians and economists sometimes appear to have completely distinct sources. Historian **Marks** (1978), for example, in her review paper on German reparations, describes Central and Eastern reparations as 'largely *terra incognita* to the historian'. Almost half a century earlier **Moulton & Pasvolsky** (1932) had devoted some 20 pages to this question – including the payment terms concluded at The Hague Conference – in their standard work on international debts, a reference not found in Marks. In the period 1919-1930 *The Economist* published several well-documented articles about non-German reparations and the Annual Reports of the **BIS** over the years 1931-1935 contain information about progress (and termination!) of reparations from Bulgaria, Hungary and Czechoslovakia.

amount of this material becomes available online. Examples are the minutes of the German *Reichstag* and British Parliament, the latter to be found under the name of the first printer, **Hansard**. The digital archive of **The Economist** is an almost inexhaustible source of information on (weekly!) bond prices, exchange rates and historical views from 1843 onwards. We conclude by mentioning the meanwhile digitally available (American) **Annual Reports of the Secretary of the Treasury**, a rich source not only of financial information, but also of diplomatic correspondence.

Nevertheless, with all modern wealth and convenience, the ultimate sensation for a researcher is to touch and hold an original document that has been lying safely in a vault for more than a century, waiting to be read, interpreted and quoted.

References

1. Public sources, series and data banks

ARST: *Annual Report of the Secretary of the Treasury* (up to and including 1980), Washington, Government Printing Office

BDFB: *Billets au porteur en circulation*, https://ibfi.banque-france.fr/file-admin/user_upload/banque_de_france/histoire/annhis/hb.w.22101.0000.txt

BDFCD: *Banque de France*, https://www.banque-france.fr/sites/default/files/arrete.pdf and https://ibfi.banque-france.fr/fileadmin/user_upload/banque_de_france/histoire/textes/arrete.pdf

BIS: *Annual Report*, Basel, Bank for International Settlements

BMS: Banking and Monetary Statistics, Washington, Federal Reserve Board

BOE3C: *Three Centuries of Macroeconomic Data*, London, Bank of England, http://www.bankofengland.co.uk/research/Documents/onebank/threecenturies_v2.3.xlsx

BOEBR: *Official Bank Rate History*, http://www.bankofengland.co.uk/statistics/documents/rates/baserate.xls

CCFE: *Committee on Currency and Foreign Exchanges after the War ('Cunliffe Committee'), First Interim Report, 15 August 1918*, Cd. 9182

CEPII: *Centre d'études prospectives et d'informations internationales* http://cepii.fr/francgraph/bdd/villa/mode.htm

CMD: *UK Command Paper*, London, HM Stationary Office, in partucular: Treaties Online, http://treaties.fco.gov.uk/treaties

ESFDB: *European State Finance Database*, http://www.esfdb.org/

Eurostat: http://ec.europa.eu/eurostat/web/government-finance-statistics/data/database

FRB: *Federal Reserve Bulletin*, Washington, Government Printing Office

FRUS: *Papers relating to the foreign relations of the United States*, Washington, Government Printing Office, in particular FRUS 1919: The Paris Peace Conference 1919, Volume XIII (published 1947)

HC: *Official reports of debates in Parliament* (Commons), London, http://hansard.millbanksystems.com/

HISTAT: *Zeitreihen zur Historischen Statistik*, Mannheim/Köln/Berlin, GESIS, http://www.gesis.org/histat/

INSEE: *Annuaire Statistique de la France*, in particular 1966: Résumé Rétrospectif, Paris, Institut National de la Statistique et des Études Économiques, http://gallica.bnf.fr/ark:/12148/bpt6k6424052p/f445.item

KB: *Digitised newspapers on line*, The Hague, Royal Library, http://www.delpher.nl/

KwBl. (1918), *Kriegswirtschaftliche Blätter*, Berlin, Reichsbank

London Gazette: *Official Public Record*, London, https://www.thegazetteco.uk/

ONS: Office for National Statistics, http://www.ons.gov.uk

PP: Parliamentary Papers, London, HM Stationary Office

RGBl.: *Reichsgesetzblatt*, Berlin

RK: *Akten der Reichskanzlei*, http://www.bundesarchiv.de/aktenreichskanzlei/1919-1933/0000/index.html

RT: *Verhandlungen des Reichstags*, Stenographic records and supplements, Berlin

UKBUD: *Budget*, London, HM Stationary Office

USBUD: *Budget,* Washington, Government Printing Office

USDSB: *Department of State Bulletin*, Washington, Government Printing Office

USFCRS: *U.S. Government Foreign Credit Exposure*, Washington (continuation of ARST over the years 1999-2009; also known as *Salmon Books*)

USMB: *US Office of Management and Budget*, Washington, www.whiteho use.gov/omb/budget/

USSAL: US Congress, *Statutes at Large of the United States of America*, Washington, Government Printing Office

2. Books and articles

Abs, H.J. (1959), *Zeitfragen der Geld- und Wirtschaftspolitik*, Frankurt/Main, Fritz Knapp.

Abs, H.J. (1991), *Entscheidungen*, Mainz, v. Hase & Koehler

Achterberg, E. (1969), *Havenstein, Rudolf Emil Albert*, in: Neue Deutsche Biographie 8 (1969), p. 137; http://www.deutsche-biographie.de/pnd116550 295.html

Ahamed, L. (2010), *Lords of Finance*, London, Windmill Books

Aldrich, N.W. (1908), *Entretien de M. Aldrich avec M. Georges Pallain, 26 septembre 1908*, Whitefish, Kessinger Publishing (reprint)

Aly, G., Chase, J. (transl.) (2006). *Hitler's beneficiaries: plunder, racial war, and the Nazi welfare state* [translation of: *Hitlers Volksstaat*], New York, Metropolitan Books / Henry Holt and Company

Andraos, J. (2000-2012), *Named things in chemical industry*, http://www.careerchem.com/NAMED/Industry.pdf

Angell, N. (1913), *The Great Illusion: Study of the Relation of Military Power to National Advantage*, New York / London, Putnam

Armeson, R.B. (1964), *Total Warfare and Compulsary Labor*, Den Haag, Martinus Nijhoff

Balderston, T. (1989), *War Finance and Inflation in Britain and Germany, 1914-1918*, The Economic History Review, New Series, Vol. 42, No. 2 (May 1989), pp. 222-244

Balderston, T. (2002), *Economics and Politics in the Weimar Republic*, Cambridge, University Press

Banque de France (1908), *Procès-verbal du Comité des Livres et Portefeuilles*, 2 décembre 1908

Banque de France (1914), *Procès-verbal du Conseil Général*, 1 août 1914

Banque de France (1980/1997) Cahier Anecdotique nr. 7: *La succursale de la Banque de France de Lille pendant la guerre de 1914-18*, Paris, Banque de France

Bastable, C.F. (1903 [first edition: 1897]), *Public Finance*. Third Edition, Revised and Enlarged, London / New York, Macmillan & Co. / The Macmillan Company

Bell, P.M.H. (1996), *France and Britain 1900-1940: Entente and Estrangement*, London / New York, Longman

Bendixen, F. (1919 [first edition: 1916]), *Währungspolitik und Geldtheorie im Licht des Weltkriegs*, 2nd edition, München / Leipzig, Dunker & Humblot

Bennett, G. (2006), *The Pepper Trader*, Jakarta / Singapore, Equinox

Blancheton, B. (2001), *Le Pape et l'Empereur. La Banque de France, la direction du Trésor et la politique monétaire de la France (1914-1928)*, Paris, Albin Michel

Bloch, J. [I.S.] (1936 [translation; original: 1899]), *The future of war in its technical economic and political relations*, Boston, Ginn & Company

Bogart, E.L. (1920 [first edition: 1919]), *Direct and Indirect Costs of the Great World War*, 2nd, revised, edition, New York, Oxford University Press

Bogart, E.L. (1921), *War Costs and their Financing*, New York, Appleton & Co.

Bonney, R.J. (2010), *The Apogee and Fall of the French Rentier Regime,* in: Cardoso, J.L & P. Lains (eds.), *Paying for the Liberal State: The Rise of Public Finance in Nineteenth-Century Europe.* Cambridge, University Press

Born, K.E. (1983), *International Banking in the 19th and 20th Centuries*, Leamington Spa, Berg; original: *Geld und Banken im 19. und 20. Jahrhundert*, 1977, Stuttgart, Alfred Kröner

Borsky, G. (1942), *The greatest swindle in the world*, London, The New Europe Publishing Co.

Brakman, S. & Ch. van Marrewijk (2007), *Transfers, Nontraded Goods, and Unemployment: An Analysis of the Keynes-Ohlin Debate*, History of Political Economy 39, pp. 141-143

Brand, R.H. (1921), *War and National Finance*, London, Edward Arnold & Co.

Brauer, J. & H. van Tuyll (2008), *Castles, battles & bombs; how economics explains military history*, Chicago, University Press

Breyer, S. (1973), *Battleships and Battlecruisers 1905-1970*, London, Macdonald and Jane's

Broadberry, S. & M. Harrison, eds. (2005), *The Economics of World War I*, Cambridge, University Press

Broadberry, S. & P. Howlett (2005), *The United Kingdom during World War I*, in: Broadberry, S. & M. Harrison, eds. (2005), *The Economics of World War I*, Cambridge, University Press

Broesamle, J.J. (1973), *William Gibbs McAdoo : a passion for change, 1863-1917*, Port Washington, Kennikat Press

Brown, B.B, (1988), *Monetary chaos in Europe. The end of an Era*, Beckenham, Croom Helm; re-issued 2010: Abingdon, Routledge

Brown, W.A. (1940), *The International Gold Standard Reinterpreted, 1914-1934*, New York, National Bureau of Economic Research

Bry, G. (1960), *Wages in Germany 1871-1945*, Princeton, University Press

Brucker, M. (2010), *Die Kriegswirtschaft Österreich-Ungarns im Ersten Weltkrieg. Rüstungsproduktion, Mannschafts- und Offiziersersatz, Transportsystem, Ernährungs- und Finanzwirtschaft sowie Kriegssozialismus*, Wien, Universität, thesis

Buchheim, C. (1986), *Das Londoner Schuldenabkommen*, in: Herbst, L. (1986), *Westdeutschland 1945-1955. Unterwerfung, Kontrolle, Integration*, München, Oldenbourg

Burhop, C. & G.B. Wolff (2002), *National Accounting and the Business Cycle in Germany 1851-1913*, unpublished preprint

Burhop, C. & G.B. Wolff (2005), *A Compromise Estimate of German Net National Product, 1851-1913, and its Implications for Growth and Business Cycles*, The Journal of Economic History, 65, nr. 3, pp. 613-657

Burk, K. (1985), Britain, *America and the Sinews of War 1914-1918*, Winchester (VS), Allen & Unwin

Burk, K. (2008), *Cunliffe, Walter, first Baron Cunliffe (1855-1920), merchant banker and governor of the Bank of England*, in: Oxford Dictionary of National Biography

Burkheiser, K. (1941), *Quellen und Methoden der Kriegsfinanzierung*, Finanzarchiv, Band 8, Heft 1, pp. 29-69

Capie, F. & A. Webber (1985), *A Monetary History of the United Kingdom, 1870-1982, Volume I: Data, Sources, Methods*, London, Routledge

Charbonnet, G. (1922), *La Politique financière de la France pendant la Guerre (Août 1914-Novembre 1920)*, Bordeaux, Imprimerie de l'Université, PhD thesis

Chase, P.M. (2008), *William Gibbs McAdoo: The last Progressive 1863-1941*, Los Angeles, University of Southern California, PhD thesis

Clark, C. (2012), *The Sleepwalkers. How Europe Went to War in 1914*, London, Penguin Books

Clark, J.M. (1931), *The Costs of the World War to the American People*, New Haven, Yale University Press

Clement, P. (2004), *'The touchstone of German credit': Nazi Germany and the service of the Dawes and Young Loans*, Financial History Review 11.1, pp. 33-50

Collins, D.N. (1973), *The Franco-Russian Alliance and Russian Railways, 1891-1914*, The Historical Journal, Vol. 16 nr. 4, pp. 777-788

Convention (1910), *Convention passée entre l'État et la Banque de France pour venir en aide aux sinistrés (du 18 mars 1910)*, in: BDFCD

Conventions (1911), *Conventions Passées entre le Trésor et la Banque de France (du 11 novembre 1911)*, in: BDFCD

Craig, D.B. (2013), *Progressives at war: William G. McAdoo and Newton D. Baker, 1863-1941*, Baltimore, John Hopkins Univerity Press

Dayer, R.A. (1976), *Strange Bedfellows: J.P. Morgan & Co., Whitehall, and the Wilson Administration During World War I*, Business History, Vol. 18, No. 2, pp. 127-151

Daunton, M. (2002), *Just Taxes; The Politics of Taxation in Britain, 1914-1979*, Cambridge, University Press

Décrets, in: BDFCD

Deist, W. (1970), *Militär und Innenpolitik im Weltkrieg 1914-1918*, Düsseldorf, Droste

Dennett, L. (1998), *A Sense of Security: 150 Years of Prudential*, Cambridge, Granta

Dietzel, H. (1912), *Kriegssteuer oder Kriegsanleihe?*, Tübingen, J.C.B. Mohr (Paul Siebeck)

Di Jorio, I., K.Oosterlinck, V. Pouillard (2012), *Advertising, Propaganda and War Finance; France and the US during WW I*, preliminary version, http://www.ebha.org/ebha2008/papers/diJorio-Oosterlink-Pouillard_ebha_2008.pdf

The Economist: *The Economist*, London, multiple issues

Edelstein, M. (2000), *War and the American economy in the Twentieth Century*, in: Engerman, S.L. & R.E. Gallman, eds., *The Cambridge Economic History of the United States*, Volume III, Cambridge, University Press

Eichengreen, B. (1988), *Resolving debt crises: an historical perspective*, National Bureau of Economic Research, Working Paper 2555, Cambridge MA

Eichengreen, B. (1995), *Golden Fetters*, New York / Oxford, Oxford Univerity Press

Einaudi, L.L. (2000), *From the Franc to the 'Europe': The Attempted Transformation of the Latin Monetary Union into a European Monetary Union, 1865-1873*, Economic History Review 53 (2000), pp. 284-308

Einzig, P. (1935), *World Finance 1914-1935.* New York, The Macmillan Company

Elwell, C.K. (2011), *Brief History of the Gold Standard in the United States*, Washington, Congressional Research Service,

Eurostat (2014), *Taxation trends in the European Union*, 2014 Edition, Luxembourg, Publications Office of the European Union

Euwe, J. (2010), *Financing Germany: Amsterdam's Role as an International Financial Centre, 1914-31*, in: Baubeau, P. & A. Ögren, eds. (2010), *Convergence and divergence of national financial systems: evidence from the gold standards, 1871-1971*, London, Pickering & Chatto

Ezickson, A.J. (1938), *Get That Picture! The Story of the News Cameraman*, New York, National Library Press

Farr M. (2005a), *Clann MacKenna's Edwardian Exile*, in: O'Neill, P., ed., *Exile and Homecoming: Papers from the Fifth Australian Conference of Celtic Studies*, University of Sydney: The Celtic Studies Foundation, pp. 207-224

Farr, M. (2005b), *'Squiff', 'Lliar George', and 'The McKennae'*, in: Toye, R. & J. Gottlieb (2005), *Making Reputations*, London, I.B. Tauris & Co.

Farr, M. (2008), *Reginald McKenna, Financier among Statesmen, 1863-1916*, London, Routledge

Feldman, G.D. (1966), *Army, Industry and Labor in Germany 1914-1918*, Princeton, University Press

Feldman, G.D, C.-L. Holtfrerich, G.A. Ritter, P.-C. Witt, eds. (1984), *Die Erfahrung der Inflation im internationalen Zusammenhang und Vergleich / The Experience of Inflation, international and comparative Studies*, Berlin, De Gruyter

Feldman, G.D. & E. Müller-Luckner, eds. (1985), *Die Nachwirkungen der Inflation auf die deutsche Geschichte, 1924-1933*, München, Oldenbourg

Feldman, G.D. (1993), *The Great Disorder*, New York, Oxford University Press

Feldman, G.D. (2008), *The Reparations Debate*, in: Fischer, C. & A. Sharp, eds., *After the Versailles Treaty*, Abingdon, Routledge

Feinstein, C. (1990), *New Estimates of Average Earnings in the United Kingdom, 1880-1913*, The Economic History Review, Vol. 43, No. 4

Ferguson, N. (1998), *The Pity of War*, London, Penguin Books

Fergusson, A. (1975), *When Money Dies, the Nightmare of the Weimar Collapse*, London, Kimber

Finances (1914), *Lettre du Ministre des Finances au Gouverneur de la Banque de France, relative aux avances de la Banque à l'Etat*, 18 septembre 1914, in: BDFCD

Finanzen (2010), *Bundeshaushaltplan 2010*, Berlin

Fisk, H.E. (1922), *French Public Finance in the Great War and Today*, New York / Paris, Bankers Trust Company

Fisk, H.E. (1924), *The Inter-Ally Debts. An Analysis of War and Post-War Public Finance 1914-1923*, New York / Paris, Bankers Trust Company

Flama (2009/2010), *De Wetgeving in het Etappengebied (West- en Oost-Vlaanderen) van het Vierde Duitse leger 1914*, Gent, thesis

Frankfurther, A. (1961), *In klinkende munt. Herinneringen van een bankier*, Amsterdam, De Brug/Djambatan

Frey, M. (1994), *Deutsche Finanzinteressen an den Vereinigten Staaten und den Niederlanden im Ersten Weltkrieg, Militärgeschichtliche Mitteilungen* 53, 327-353

Frey, M. (1998), *Der Erste Weltkrieg und die Niederlande*, Berlin, Akademie Verlag

Furst, G.A. (1927), *De Versailles aux Experts*, Nancy, Berger-Levrault

Fürstenberg, H. (1965), *Erinnerungen. Mein Weg als Bankier und Carl Fürstenbergs Altersjahre*, Wiesbaden, Rheinische Verlags-Anstalt.

Galbraith, J.K. (1961 [original: 1954]), *The Great Crash 1929*, Harmondsworth, Penguin Books.

Gay, E.W. (1926), *War Loans or Subsidies*, Foreign Affairs, Vol. 4, No. 3, pp. 394-405

Gere, J.A. & J. Sparrow, eds. (1981), *Geoffrey Madan's Notebooks*, Oxford, University Press

Gilbert, C. (1970), *American Financing of World War I*, Westport, Greenwood

Glasemann, H.-G. (1993), *Deutschlands Auslandsanleihen 1924-1945*, Wiesbaden, Gabler

Gomes, L. (2010), *German Reparations, 1919-1932, A Historical Survey*, Basingstoke, Palgrave Macmillan

Greenhalgh, E. (2009), *Victory through Coalition. Britain and France during the First World War*, Cambridge, University Press

Grigg, P.J. (1948), *Prejudice and Judgement*, London, Jonathan Cape

Guinnane, T.W. (2004), *Financial Vergangenheitsbewältigung: the London 1953 Debt Agreement*, New Haven, Yale University Economic Growth Center, discussion Paper 880, http://www.econ. yale.edu/growth_pdf/cdp880.pdf

Gumbel, E.J. (1954), *Statistical Theory of Extreme Values and some Practical Applications*, National Bureau of Standards Applied Mathematics Series, 33.

Guyot, Y. (1919), *Le Règlement des Comptes avec l'Allemagne*, Journal des Économistes, 6ᶜ Série, Tôme LXI, p. 3.

(the) Hague Conventions (1907), *Convention respecting the Laws and Customs of War on Land*, for example: http://avalon.law.yale.edu/20th_century/hague04.asp

Hamilton-Grace, R.S. (1910), *Finance and War*, London, Hugh Rees

Hardach, G. (1987 [translation; original: 1973]), *The First World War 1914-1918*, 1987, Harmondsworth, Penguin (original: *Geschichte der Weltwirtschaft im 20. Jahrhundert. Band 2. Der Erste Weltkrieg*, München, DTV

Harris, S. E. (1931), *Monetary Problems of the British Empire*, New York, The Macmillan Company

Harrow (1918), *Harrow Memorials of the Great War, Volume II*, Harrow, Philip Lee Warner

Hautcœur, P-C. (2005), *Was the Great War a watershed? The economics of World War I in France*, in: Broadberry, S. & M. Harrison, eds. (2005), *The Economics of World War I*, Cambridge, University Press

Helfferich, K. (1914 [4ᵗʰ edition; 1ˢᵗ 1913]), *Deutschlands Volkswohlstand 1888-1913*, Berlin, Georg Stilke

Helfferich, K. (1919), *Der Weltkrieg*, Berlin, Ullstein & Co.

Helfferich, K. (1923 [first edition: 1903]), *Das Geld*, Leipzig, Hirschfeld

Hiley, N. (1987) *Sir Hedley Le Bas and the Origins of Domestic Propaganda in Britain 1914-1917*, European Journal of Marketing, Vol. 21 No. 8, pp. 30-46

Höll, W., N. Kabay, A. SenGupta, M. Streat (2007), *Professor Fred Helfferich (editorial)*, Reactive & Functional Polymers 67, pp. 1419-1420

Holtfrerich, C.-L. (1977), *Internationale Verteilungsfolgen der deutschen Inflation*, Kyklos, vol. 30, Fasc. 2, pp. 271-292

Holtfrerich, C.-L. (1980), *Die deutsche Inflation 1914-1923*, Berlin / New York, Walter de Gruyter

Homberg, O. (1926), *La grande injustice (la question des dettes interalliées)*, Paris, Bernard Grasset

Homer, S. & R. Sylla (2005), *A History of Interest rates* [fourth edition], Hoboken, Wiley

Horn (2000), *A Private Bank at War: J.P. Morgan & Co. and France, 1914-1918*, The Business History Review, Vol. 74, No. 1, pp. 85-112

Horn, M. (2002), *Britain, France, and the Financing of the First World War*, Montreal, McGill-Queen University Press

Horn, M. & T. Imlay (2005), *France's Financial Preparations for the Two World Wars*, The International History Review, Vol. 27, No. 4 (December 2005), pp. 709-753

Houwink ten Cate, J.Th.M. (1989), *Bruins' Berlijnse besprekingen*, Den Haag, Nederlands Historisch Genootschap

Howe, A. (2010), Book Review of: *Reginald McKenna: Financier among Statesmen, 1863-1916*, by Martin Farr, English Historical Review cxxv. 515 (August 2010), pp. 1034-1035.

L'Illustration (1898), nr. 2863, 8 janvier 1899

Jeanneney, J.-M. & E. Barbier-Jeanneney (1985), *Les économies occidentales du XIX siècle à nos jours*, Paris, Presse de la Fondation nationale des sciences politiques

James, H. (1984), *The Causes of the German Banking Crisis of 1931*, The Economic History Review, Vol. 37, No. 1 (February 1984), pp. 68-87

Jèze, G. & H. Truchy (1927), *The War Finance of France*, New Haven, Yale University Press

Johnston, L. & S. H. Williamson (2017), *What Was the U.S. GDP Then?*, MeasuringWorth, http://www.measuringworth.org/usgdp/

Jung, O. (1989), *Plebiszitärer Durchbruch 1929? Zur Bedeutung von Volksbegehren und Volksentscheid gegen den Youngplan für die NSDAP*, Geschichte und Gesellschaft, pp. 489-510

Kaiser, J. (2013), *One Made it Out of the Debt Trap; Lessons from the London Debt Agreement of 1953 for current Debt Crises*, Berlin, Friedrich-Ebert-Stiftung

Kang, S.W. & H. Rockoff (2006), *Capitalizing patriotism: the Liberty Loans of World War I*, National Bureau of Economic Research, Working Paper 11919, http://www.nber.org/papers/w11919

Kautsky, B. (1931), *Reparationen und Rüstungen*, Wien / Leipzig, Hess & Co

Keegan (2000), *The First World War*, New York, Vintage Books

Keynes, J.M. (1920), *The Economic Consequences of the Peace*, London, Macmillan & Co.

Keynes, J.M. (1924 [1st edition: 1923]), *A Tract on Monetary Reform*, London, Macmillan & Co.

Keynes, J.M. (1936), *The general theory of employment, interest and money*, London, Macmillan & Co.

Keynes, J.M. (1971-'89): E. Scott Johnson, ed., *The Collected Writings of John Maynard Keynes*, London, Macmillan & Co.

Kindleberger, C.P. (1953), *International Economics*, Homewood, R.D. Irwin

Kindleberger, C.P. (1984), *A Financial History of Western Europe*, London, Allen & Unwin

Kirkaldy, A.W. (1921), *British Finance During and After the War*, London, Pitman & Sons

Klausinger, H. (1990), *The Early Use of the Term 'Veil of Money' in Schumpeter's Monetary Writings – A Comment on Patinkin and Steiger*, The Scandinavian Journal of Economics, 92, pp. 617-621

Klotz, L.-L. (1924), *De la Guerre à la Paix*, Paris, Payot

Knauss, R. (1923), *Die deutsche, englische und französiche Kriegsfinanzierung*, Berlin / Leipzig, Walter de Gruyter & Co.

Lachapelle, G. (1915), *Nos finances pendant la guerre*, Paris, Armand Colin

Langenhove, F. van (1927), *L'action du Gouvernement Belge en Matière Économique pendant la Guerre*, Paris / New Haven, Presses Universitaires de France / Yale University Press

Lasswell, H.D. (1938 [first edition: 1927]), *Propaganda Technique in the World War*, London, Kegan Paul, Trench, Trubner & Co.

Lathem, E.C., ed. (1960), *Meet Calvin Coolidge: The Man Behind the Myth*, Brattleboro, Stephan Green Press

Lauterpacht, E. & C.J. Greenwood (eds.) (2007), *International Law Reports* 129, Cambridge, University Press

LeBor, A. (2013), *Tower of Basel*, New York, PublicAffairs

Leroy-Beaulieu, P. P. (1874), *La dette publique de la France*, Revue des Deux Mondes, 1874, Tôme 6, 815

Lewandowski, L. (1923), *Comment L'Allemagne a su se faire payer; Lille sous l'occupation allemande*, Paris, Hachette

Lloyd George, D. (1932), *The truth about reparations and war-debts*, London, William Heinemann

Lloyd George, D. (1933), *War Memoirs 1915-1916*, Boston, Little, Brown and Company

Loi du 5 août 1914, in: BDFCD

London Agreement (1953), *Agreement on German External Debts*, London, 27 February 1953; CMD (1959), 626

Lotz, W. (1927), *Die deutsche Staatsfinanzwirtschaft im Kriege*, Stuttgart / New Haven, Deutsche Verlags-Anstalt / Yale University Press

Low, S. & L. C. Sanders (1907), *The history of England during the reign of Victoria (1837-1901)*, London, Longmans, Green & Co.

Maddison, A. (1982), *Phases of Capitalist Development*, Oxford, University Press

Mäkinen, I. (2001), *Finland Pays Its Debts and Gets Books in Return: ASLA Grants to the Finnish Academic Libraries, 1950-1967*, Libraries & Culture, vol. 36, no. 1, pp. 211-232

Marks, S. (1978), *The Myths of Reparations*, Central European History XI (1978) 3, 231-255

Martin, B.F. (1999), *France and the Après-guerre 1918-1924. Illusions and Disillusionment*, Baton Rouge, Louisiana State University Press

McAdoo, W.G. (1931), *Crowded Years. The Reminiscences of William G. McAdoo*, Boston / New York, Houghton Mifflin Company

McKenna, R. (1922), *Reparations and international debts*, Address at the Convention of the American Bankers Association, New York, Trust Company

McKenna, S. (1948), *Reginald McKenna 1863-1943*, London, Eyre & Spottiswoode

Mendershausen, H. (1941), *The Economics of War*, New York, Prentice-Hall

Mises, L. von (1974), *Planning for Freedom*, South Holland, Libertarian Press

Moreau, E. (1937), *Le relèvement financier et monétaire de la France (1926-1928). Souvenirs d'un gouverneur de la Banque de France*, Revue des Deux Mondes, Mars & Avril, pp. 53, 299, 550, 825

Moreau, E. (1954), *Souvenirs d'un gouverneur de la Banque de France, histoire de la stabilisation du franc, 1926-1928*, Paris, Génin; English translation by Stoller, S.D & T.C. Roberts (1991) as *The Golden Franc: Memoirs of a Governor of the Bank of France: The Stabilization of the Franc (1926-1928)*, Boulder, Westview

Morgan, E.V. (1952), *Studies in British Financial Policy, 1914-25,* London, Macmillan

Morley, J. (1903), *The Life of William Ewart Gladstone*, London / New York, Macmillan & Co. / Macmillan Co.

Moulton & Pasvolsky (1932), *War Debts and World Prosperity*. Washington, Brookings Institution

Münkler, H. (2013), *Der Große Krieg. Die Welt 1914 bis 1918*, Berlin, Rowolt

Nason, J.M. & S.P. Vahey (2007), *The McKenna Rule and UK World War Finance*, The American Economic Review, Vol. 97, No. 2, pp. 290-294

Nouailhat, Y.H. (1979), *France et États-Unis, août 1914-avril 1917*, Paris, Sorbonne

Occhino, F., K. Oosterlinck, E. N. White (2006), *How occupied France financed its own exploitation in World War II*, National Bureau of Economic Research, Working Paper 12137, http://www.nber.org/papers/w12137

Officer, L.H & S.H. Williamson (2014), *Five Ways to Compute the Relative Value of a UK Pound Amount, 1270 to Present*, https://www.measuringworth.com/ukcompare/

O'Farrell, H.H. (1913), *The Franco-German War Indemnity and its Economic Results*, Londen, Harrison & Sons

Parker, E.P. (1920), *Final Report of United States Liquidation Commission*, Washington, Government Printing Office

Parliamentary Papers (1911): *Declaration between the United Kingdom and France Respecting Egypt and Morocco*, London

Patat, J.-P., M. Lutfalla, R. Raymond (1986), *Histoire monétaire de la France au XXe siècle*, Paris, Economica

Petit, L. (1929), *Histoire des finances extérieures de la France pendant la guerre (1914-1918)*, Paris, Payot

Pfleiderer, D. (2002), *Deutschland und der Youngplan. Die Rolle der Reichsregierung, Reichsbank und Wirtschaft bei der Entstehung des Youngplans*, Stuttgart, PhD thesis

Pigou, A.C. (1916), *The Economy and Finance of the War*, London / Paris / Toronto, J.M. Dent & Sons

Pigou, A.C. (1941 [first edition: 1921]), *The Political Economy of War*, London /New York, The Macmillan Company

Pohl, M. (1978), *Gründerboom und Krise*, Bankhistorisches Archiv, Heft 4, pp. 20-59

Popovics, A. (1925), *Das Geldwesen im Kriege*, Wien / New Haven, Hölder-Pichler-Tempsky / Yale University Press

Ramon, G. (1929), *Histoire de la Banque de France d'après les sources originales*, Paris, Bernard Grasset

Ramstein, A. (1923), *Das Verhältnis der Notenbanken zur Kriegsfinanzierung in England, Frankreich, Deutschland und der Schweiz*, Bern, Paul Haupt

Redlich, J. (1925), *Österreichische Regierung und Verwaltung im Weltkriege*, Wien / New Haven, Hölder-Pichler-Tempsky / Yale University Press

Renauld, J. Ritter von (1901), *Die finanzielle Mobilmachung der deutschen Wehrkraft*, Leipzig, Duncker & Humblot

Reinhart, C.M. & K.S. Rogoff (2009), *This time is different: eight centuries of financial folly*, Princeton, University Press

Reinhart, C.M. & K.S. Rogoff (2011), *From Financial Crash to Debt Crisis*, American Economic Review 101, nr. 5, 1676-1706, Data Set https://www.aeaweb.org/articles?id=10.1257/aer.101.5.1676

Riesser, J. (1913 [first edition: 1909]), *Finanzielle Kriegsbereitschaft und Kriegführung*, 2nd edition, Jena, Gustav Fischer

Ritschl, A. (1996), *Sustainability of High Public Debt: What the Historical Record Shows*, Swedish Economic Policy Review 3, pp. 175-198

Ritschl, A. (1999) *Les Réparations Allemandes 1920-1933: une controverse Revue par la théorie des jeux*, Économie Internationale No. 78, 129-154

Ritschl, A. (2005), *Germany's economy at war, 1914-1918 and beyond*, in: Broadberry, S. & M. Harrison (2005), eds., *The Economics of World War I*, Cambridge, University Press

Ritschl, A. & M. Spoerer (1997), *Das Bruttosozialprodukt in Deutschland nach den amtlichen Volkseinkommens- und Sozialproduktsstatistiken 1901-1995*, Jahrbuch für Wirtschaftsgeschichte 1997/2, 27-54

Roberts, R. (2010), *The London financial Crisis of 1914*, in: Baubeau, P. & A. Ögren, eds., *Convergence and divergence of national financial systems: evidence from the gold standards 1871-1971*, London, Pickering & Chatto

Robineau, G. (1923), *Discours aux obsèques de Georges Pallain*, 16 mai 1923, Paris, Archives Banque de France

Rockoff, H. (2005), *Until it's over, over there: the United States economy in World War I*, in: Broadberry, S. & M. Harrison, eds. (2005), *The Economics of World War I*, Cambridge, University Press

Rockoff, H. (2012), *America's economic way of war*, Cambridge, University Press

Roesler, K. (1967), *Die Finanzpolitik des Deutschen Reiches im Ersten Weltkrieg*, Berlin, Duncker & Humblot

Rombeck-Jaschinski, U. (1995), *Schuld gegen Schulden? Die niederländischen Entschädigungsansprüche an die Bundesrepublik Deutschland 1950-1960*, in: Ackermann, V., B.-A. Rusinek, F. Wiesemann, *Anknüpfungen*, Essen, Klartext

Rombeck-Jaschinski, U. (2005), *Das Londoner Schuldenabkommen*, München, Oldenbourg

Salomon, E. (1978 [reprint from the original 1931]), *Berühmte Zeitgenossen in unbewachten Augenblicken*, München, Schirmer/Mosel; Maarssen, Schwartz

Saint Marc, M. (1983), *Histoire monétaire de la France : 1800-1980*, Paris, Presses Universitaires de France

Sauvy, A. (1984), *Histoire économique de la France entre les deux guerres*, (3 volumes), Paris, Economica (edited and highly restructured version by A. Hirsch of the 1965 edition of the same name, Paris, Fayard)

Schmidt, M.E. (1974), *Alexandre Ribot: odyssey of a liberal in the 3rd Republic*, The Hague, Martinus Nijhoff

Schmölders, G. (1968), *Geldpolitik*, Tübingen / Zürich, Mohr (Siebeck) / Polygraphischer Verlag

Schuker, S.A. (1985), *American 'Reparations' to Germany 1919-1933*, in: Feldman, G.D. & E. Müller-Luckner (1985), *Die Nachwirkungen der Inflation auf die deutsche Geschichte*, 1924-1933, München, Oldenbourg

Schwartz, H.-P. (1982), ed., *Die Wiederherstellung des deutschen Kredits*, Stuttgart, Belser

Self, R. (2006), *Britain, America and the War Debt Controversy. The economic diplomacy of an unspecial relationship, 1917-1941*, Abingdon, Routledge

Serrigny, B. (1909), *Les conséquences économiques et sociales de la prochaine guerre*, Paris, Giard & Brière

Sicsic, P. (1989), *Estimation du stock de monnaie metallique en France a la fin du XIXe siecle*, Revue économique, Vol. 40, pp. 709-736

Silber (2007), *When Washington Shut Down Wall Street*, Princeton, University Press

Smith, A. (1776), *An Inquiry into the Nature and Causes of the Wealth of Nations*. One of the many modern editions by Campbell, R.H. & A.S. Skinner, Oxford, Clarendon Press, 1976

Soutou, G.-H. (1989), *L'or et le sang*, Paris, Fayard

Soutou, G.-H. (1991), *Comment a été financée la guerre*, in: De La Gorce, P.M., *La Première Guerre Mondiale*, Paris, Flammarion

SPD (1891), *Protokoll über die Verhandlungen des Parteitages der Sozialdemokratischen Partei Deutschlands*, Berlin, Vorwärts

Spenkuch, H. (2003), *Die Protokolle des Preußischen Staatsministeriums 1817-1934/38*, Band 8/I, Hildesheim/Zürich/New York, Olms-Weidmann (series published by: Berlin-Brandenburgische Akademie der Wissenschaften, under supervision of J. Kocka & W. Neugebauer)

Steinmann-Bucher, A. (1909), *350 Milliarden Deutsches Volksvermögen*, Berlin, Otto Eisner

Stiglitz, J.E., A. Sen, J.-P. Fitoussi (2009), *Measurement of Economic Performance and Social Progress*, Paris, Insee, http://ec.europa.eu/eurostat/documents/ 118025/118123/Fitoussi+Commission+report

Stiglitz, J.E. & L.J. Bilnes (2010), http://www.washingtonpost.com/wp-dyn/content/article/2010/09/03/AR2010090302200.html

Strachan, H. (2004), *Financing the First World War*, Oxford, University Press

Sühl, K. (1988), *SPD und öffentlicher Dienst in der Weimarer Republik*, Berlin, Westdeutscher Verlag

Synon, M. (1924), *McAdoo. The man and his Times. A Panorama in Democracy*, Indianapolis, Bobbs-Merrill

Tooley, T.H. (2005), *Merchants of death revisited: armaments, bankers, and the First World War*, Journal of Libertarian Studies, Volume 19, no. 1, 37-78

Train, J. (1985), *Famous Financial Fiascos*, New York, Clarkson N. Potter

Tuchman, B.W. (1962), *The Guns of August*, London, Robinson

Turner, A. (1998), *The Cost of War. British Policy on French War Debts, 1918-1932*, Brighton, Sussex Academic Press

UN (2006), *Reports of international arbitral awards: Rosa Vollweiler (United States) vs. Germany,* Volume VIII, 8 March 1928, pp. 45-52, United Nations

US Department of Commerce (1976), *Historical Statistics of the United States*, Washington DC, quoted in: Cohn, R.L. (2010), *Immigration to the United States*, Economic History Association, http://eh.net/encyclopedia/immigration-to-the-united-states/

Versailles, Treaty of (1919), for example: http://avalon.law.yale.edu/subject_menus/versailles_menu.asp

Vignat, R. (2001), *La Banque de France et l'état: la politique de gouverneur Pallain*, Paris, Université de Paris X-Nanterre, PhD thesis

Wertheimer, M.S. (1932), *The Financial Crisis in Germany*, Foreign Policy Reports Vol. VII, No. 26, pp. 455-475

Wicksell, K. (1916), *Hinauf mit den Bankraten!*, Archiv für Sozialwissenschaft und Sozialpolitik, Band 41, pp. 745-757

Weill-Raynal, E. (1947), *Les Réparations allemandes et la France* (Tome III), Paris, Nouvelles Éditions Latines

Williamson, J.G. (1971), *Karl Helfferich; Economist, Financier, Politician*. Princeton, University Press

Williamson, S.H. (2017), *Daily Closing Value of the Dow Jones Average, 1885 to Present*, Measuring-Worth, http://www.measuringworth.com/DJA/

Wirtschaft und Statistik (1925), *Zahlen zur Geldentwertung in Deutschland 1914 bis 1923 (Sonderheft 1)*, Berlin, Statistisches Reichsamt

Wormell, J. (2000), *The Management of the National Debt of the United Kingdom, 1900-1932*, London, Routledge.

Wunder, G. (2004), *Karl Helfferich (1872-1924), der Vizekanzler aus Neustadt*, Pfälzer Heimat 55 (2004), Heft 4, pp. 141

Zilch, R. (1987), *Die Reichsbank und die finanzielle Kriegsvorbereitungen von 1907 bis 1914*, Berlin, Akademie-Verlag

Zilch, R. (1994), *Okkupation und Währung im Ersten Weltkrieg*, Goldbach, Keib

Index

Biographical index

Abs, Hermann Josef (1901-1994), banker (G) 351
Adenauer, Konrad Hermann Joseph (1876-1967), chancellor (G) 274
Aldrich, Nelson Wilmarth (1841-1915), senator (US) 39, 313
Asquith, Herbert Henry (1852-1928), prime minister (UK) 101, 104, 147, 258, 332

Baldwin, Stanley (1867-1947), prime minister (UK) 258
Beaverbrook, William Maxwell Aitken, Lord (1879-1964), politician (UK) 332
Bendixen, Friedrich (1864-1920), banker (G) 314
Bérenger, Henry (1867-1952), politician (F) 220, 340
Bethmann Hollweg, Theobald Theodor Friedrich Alfred von (1856-1921), chancellor (G) 83
Bismarck, Otto Eduard Leopold von Bismarck-Schönhausen (1815-1898), chancellor (G) 29, 30, 33
Bloch, Jan Gotlib (1836-1902), banker (PL) 75
Bonar Law, Andrew (1858-1923), prime minister (UK) 57, 106, 147, 148, 257, 258, 281, 318, 327, 328
Bradbury, John Swanwick, 1st Baron (1872-1950), public servant (UK) 146, 192
Bruins, Gijsbert Weyer Jan (1883-1948), economist (NL) 341
Bryan, William Jennings (1860-1925), politician (US) 169, 170

Caillaux, Joseph Marie Auguste (1863-1944), politician (F) 340
Cambon, Pierre Paul (1843-1924), diplomat (F) 332
Caprivi, Georg Leo Graf von Caprivi de Caprera de Montecuccoli (1831-1899), chancellor (G) 48
Carter, James Earl ('Jimmy'), (1924), president (US) 247
Caruso, Enrico (1873-1921), singer (I) 160
Chamberlain, Arthur Neville (1869-1940), prime minister (UK) 257, 281
Chamberlain, Joseph Austen (1863-1937), politician (UK) 224, 332
Chaplin, Charles Spencer (1889-1977), actor (UK) 159
Chéron, Henri (1867-1936), politician (F) 235
Churchill, Winston Leonard Spencer-Churchill (1874-1965), prime minister (UK) 102, 145, 165, 223, 258, 314, 340
Clausewitz, Carl Philipp Gottlieb von (1780-1831), general (G) 53
Cochery, Georges Charles Paul (1855-1914), politician (F) 38
Coolidge, John Calvin (1872-1933), president (US) 158, 165, 214, 224, 269
Cross, Doris Isabel (1909-2005), nurse (US) 330
Cunliffe, Walter (1855-1920), banker (UK) 55-57, 103, 130, 333, 356

Curtius, Julius (1877-1948), politician (G) 235

Dawes, Charles Gates (1865-1951), banker (US) 173, 224
Delbrück, Clemens Gottlieb Ernst (1856-1921), deputy chancellor (G) 127
Desart, Hamilton John Agmondesham Cuffe, 5th Earl of (1848-1934), barrister (IRL/UK) 54
Dietzel, Gottlob Heinrich Andreas (1857 1935), economist (G) 77, 313

Erhard, Ludwig Wilhelm (1897-1977), politician (G) 274
Erzberger, Matthias (1875-1921), politician (G) 82, 217, 259, 260, 348

Fairbanks, Douglas Elton Thomas Ullman (1883-1939), actor (US) 159
Faivre, Jules-Abel (1867-1945), artist (F) 140
Farrar, Geraldine (1882-1967), actress (US) 159
Furst, Gaston Adolphe (1885-1925), artilleryman (B) 216

Gambetta, Léon (1838-1882), prime minister (F) 38
Geibel, Emanuel (1815-1884), poet (G) 133
George V (1865-1936), monarch (UK) 56, 192
George, David Lloyd; see: Lloyd George, David
Gilbert, Seymour Parker (1892-1938), diplomat (US) 230
Gladstone, William Ewart (1809-1898), prime minister (UK) 102, 117, 271
Glass, Carter (1858-1946), politician (US) 338
Grenfell, Edward Charles (1870-1941), banker (UK) 173
Grey, Edward (1862-1933), politician (UK) 332

Hamilton-Grace, Raymond Sheffield (1881-1915), major (UK) 132
Harding, Warren Gamaliel (1865-1923), president (US) 84, 158, 165, 206, 214, 218, 269, 340
Havenstein, Rudolf Emil Albert (1857-1923), banker (G) 46, 81, 129, 130, 132, 133, 196, 216,
    262, 263, 325, 336, 356
Helfferich, Karl Theodor (1872-1924), politician (G) 47, 53, 68, 80-83, 85, 88, 89, 96, 108,
    131, 157, 180, 216, 217, 260, 274, 282, 317, 318, 348
Henderson, Arthur (1863-1935), politician (UK) 327
Hermes, Andreas (1878-1964), politician (G) 260
Hindenburg, Paul Ludwig Hans Anton von Beneckendorff und von (1847-1934), field marshal
    (G) 81, 274
Hitler, Adolf (1889-1945), chancellor (G) 217, 219, 236, 242, 243, 291
Holden, Edward Hopkinson (1848-1919), banker (UK) 323
Homberg, Octave Marie Joseph (1871-1918), banker (F) 340
Hoover, Herbert Clark (1874-1964), president (US) 210, 240, 241
Horner, Katharine Frances (1885-1976), (UK) 104
Houston, David Franklin (1866-1940), politician (US) 214, 340, 341
Hugo, Victor Marie (1802-1885), writer (F) 38

Jekyll, Herbert (1846-1932), colonel (UK) 104
Jekyll, Joseph (1663-1738), politician (UK) 320

Jekyll, Pamela Margaret (1889-1943), (UK) 104, 259
Joffre, Joseph Jacques Césaire (1852-1931), marshal (F) 39
Jolson, Al (Asa Youlson) (1886-1950), singer (US) 159
Jusserand, Jean Adrien Antoine Jules (1855-1932), diplomat (F) 333

Kautsky, Benedikt (1894-1960), economist (AU) 81
Kautsky, Karl Johann (1854-1938), philosopher (AU) 81
Kellogg, Frank Billings (1856-1937), politician (US) 220, 340
Keynes, John Maynard (1883-1946), economist (UK) 23, 84, 94, 101, 103, 138, 146, 180, 227,
    237, 265, 271, 286, 333, 339
Kitchener, Horatio Herbert, 1st Earl (1850-1916), field marshal (UK) 145, 314
Klotz, Louis-Lucien (1868-1930), politician (F) 37, 40, 140, 141, 333
Korsch, Karl (1886-1961), politician (G) 253
Kreuger, Ivar (1880-1932), entrepreneur (S) 351
Kühn, Hermann (1851-1937), politician (G) 82

Lafayette, Marie-Joseph Paul Yves Roch Gilbert du Motier, marquis de (1757-1834), major
    general (F) 183
Lamont, Thomas William, jr. (1870-1948), banker (US) 240
Law, Andrew Bonar; see: Bonar Law, Andrew
Le Bas, Hedley Francis (1868-1926), ad man (UK) 145
Lenin, Vladimir Iljitsj (Oeljanov) (1870-1924), revolutinary (R) 271
Léon, Maurice (1880-1952), lawyer (US) 331
Leroy-Beaulieu, Pierre Paul (1843-1916), economist (F) 140
Lindsay, Ronald Charles (1877-1945), diplomat (UK) 346
Liverpool, Robert Banks Jenkinson, Lord (1770-1828), prime minister (UK) 213
Lloyd George, David (1863-1945), prime minister (UK) 57, 90, 101-105, 122, 144, 171, 178,
    216, 314, 318, 320, 327, 332, 340
Lohr, Marie (née Löhr) (1890-1975), actress (AUS) 147
Loucheur, Louis Albert Joseph (1872-1931), politician (F) 235
Ludendorff, Erich Friedrich Wilhelm (1865-1937), general (G) 81

Malot, Hector-Henri (1830-1907), writer (F) 33
Mason, David Marshall (1865-1945), politician (UK) 117
McAdoo, William Gibbs (1863-1941), politician (US) 113-115, 145, 154-159, 184, 329, 333,
    341, 356
McKenna, Emma (née Hanby) (1823-1905), (UK) 104
McKenna, Reginald (1863-1943), politician (UK) 54, 102-106, 115, 122, 145-147, 157, 171,
    186, 258, 259, 314, 323, 332, 341, 356
McKenna, Stephen (1888-1967), writer (UK) 103
Mellon, Andrew William (1855-1937), politician (US) 220, 340
Mirabeau, Honoré Gabriel Riqueti, comte de (1749-1791), revolutinary (F) 38, 39
Mises, Ludwig Heinrich von (1881-1973), economist (AU) 18
Moldenhauer, Paul (1876-1947), politician (G) 344
Moreau, Émile (1868-1950), banker (F) 11, 340

Morgan, John Pierpont sr. (1837-1913), banker (US) 155
Morgan, John Pierpont jr. ('Jack') (1867-1943), banker (US) 167, 174, 331
Müffling, Annette von (née Anna von Siemens) (1886-1965), (G) 217

Napoléon Bonaparte (1769-1821), monarch (F) 37
Neymarck, Alfred (1848-1924), economist (F) 325
Norman, Montagu Collet (1871-1950), banker (UK) 38
Noulens, Joseph (1864-1944), politician (F) 135

Osborne, George Gideon Oliver (1971), politician (UK) 282

Pallain, Georges (1847-1923), banker (F) 35-40, 42, 53, 57, 130, 312, 313, 335, 356
Pershing, John Joseph (1860-1948), general (US) 239
Pickford, Mary (née Gladys Louise Smith) (1892-1979), actress (US) 159
Pigou, Arthur Cecil (1877-1959), economist (UK) 309, 357

Rathenau, Walther (1867-1922), politician (G) 217, 317
Reading, Rufus Daniel Isaacs, Lord (1860-1935), lawyer (UK) 320
Renauld, Joseph Ritter von Renauld, Edler von Kellenbach (1847-1913), colonel (G) 74
Ribot, Alexandre Félix Joseph (1842-1923), prime minister (F) 111, 134-136, 138, 140, 141,
    171, 177, 183, 195, 332
Ricardo, David (1772-1823), economist (UK) 318
Riesser, Jakob (1853-1932), economist (G) 43, 48
Robineau, Georges (1860-1927), banker (F) 35
Roosevelt, Franklin Delano (1882-1945), president (US) 158, 269
Rothermere, Harold Sidney Hamsworth, 1st Viscount (1868-1940), publisher (UK) 341
Rothschild, Alphonse (1827-1905) and Edouard Alphonse James (1868-1949), barons de,
    bankers (F) 38
Runciman, Walter (1870-1949), politician (UK) 314

Salomon, Erich Franz Emil (1886-1944), photographer (G) 235
Say, Jean-Baptiste (1767-1832), economist (F) 38
Say, Jean-Baptiste Léon (1826-1896), politician (F) 37
Schacht, Horace Greeley Hjalmar (1877-1970), banker (G) 216, 263, 264, 347
Schumpeter, Joseph Alois (1883-1950), economist (AU) 310
Siemens, Georg Johann von (1839-1901), banker (G) 217
Simon, John Allsebrook (1873-1954), politician (UK) 65
Smith, Adam (1723-1790), economist (UK) 99, 290

Talleyrand, Charles-Maurice de Talleyrand-Pérogiord (1754-1838), politician (F) 38
Tardieu, André Pierre Gabriel Amédée (1876-1945), politician (F) 235
Taylor, Alan John Percivale (1906-1990), historian (UK) 237
Thiers, Marie Joseph Louis Adolphe (1797-1877), prime minister (F) 29, 38

Warburg, Max Moritz (1867-1946), banker (G) 130

Wendel, François de (1874-1949), industrialist (F) 38

Wilhelm II (1859-1941), monarch (G) 29, 82, 83, 108, 129, 314

William III (1650-1702), monarch (UK) 13

Wilson, Eleanor Randolph (1889-1967), author (US) 157-159

Wilson, Thomas Woodrow (1856-1924), president (US) 61, 84, 155-158, 169, 170, 322, 340

Young, Owen D. (1874-1962), industrialist (US) 224

Subject index

Alsace and Lorraine 29, 34, 35, 339
Anglo-French loan 173, 175, 177, 181, 211, 212, 250, 255
Argentina 337
Armenia 338
Armistice 10, 23, 57, 70, 114, 122, 141, 147, 153, 157, 161, 182, 184, 189, 192, 193, 198, 203, 204, 207, 208, 211, 212, 217, 259, 266, 333, 335, 337, 340
Assemblée Nationale; see: France, parliament
assignats 268, 312
Australia 179
Austria 211, 213, 214, 239, 240, 338, 344, 347, 350
- reparations 343
Austria-Hungary 23, 67, 70, 75, 181, 211, 215, 253, 299, 316, 318, 331, 335
- bank notes circulation 187
- inflation 93, 94, 318, 347
- parliament 14, 85
- reparations 209
- war expenditure 72, 73
- war loans 161, 324, 330

Banca d'Italia 188
Bank for International Settlements (BIS) 230, 233
- history and organisation 343
- involved in reparations payments 242
- reparations payments 239, 242
- trustee for Dawes and Young loans 244, 275
bank notes circulation (see also individual countries) 92, 95, 188, 189, 198, 199, 261
Bank of England 37, 54, 103, 182, 188, 335, 336
- advances to the Treasury 149, 194, 195, 335
- bank rate 55, 150, 257, 336
- gold stock 36, 57, 173, 335
- history and organisation 13, 38, 56, 173
- independence 36, 55, 57, 60, 196, 197, 336
- lender of last resort 55, 103
- loans to France 170, 171
- notes issue 54, 191, 192, 196
- war loans 144, 257, 259, 327
- war preparation 55
Banque de France 11, 12, 30, 40, 172, 188, 332
- advances to the Treasury 31, 37, 39, 59, 135, 139, 143, 194, 195, 266, 312, 336
- bank rate 39, 53, 336
- gold stock 35-37, 41-43, 58, 59, 189, 312
- history and organisation 30, 35-40, 58
- independence 36, 40, 42, 55, 58, 59, 196, 267

- notes issue 30, 40, 42, 137, 188, 189, 195, 266, 267
- war loans 325
- war preparation 35, 37, 40-43, 49, 58, 59, 313
Bavaria 47, 81, 107
belga 299
Belgium 263
- Gold Standard 269, 310
- in Reparations Commission 218, 339
- loans from Britain 182, 185
- loans from the United States 178, 204, 247, 346
- National Bank 188, 343
- neutrality 165, 313
- occupation and occupation payments 21, 82, 95
- reparation claim on Germany 226, 228, 337
- war damage 203, 212
- war debts 208, 341
- war loans 323
belle époque 33, 60, 143
blockade 92, 109, 166-168
Brest-Litovsk 131
Brest-Litovsk, Treaty 133, 198, 319
Bretton Woods Conference 275
Bucharest, Treaty 319
Bulgaria 73, 209, 211, 215
Bundesrat; see: Germany, parliament

Canada 56, 173, 179, 185, 197
Cat and Mouse Act 102
censor 17, 89, 94, 195
central bank (see also 'Bank of England', etc.) 70, 78, 207
- bank rate 197
- gold stock 194
- independence 196-198
- involvement in war loans 85
- lender of last resort 55, 193
- monetary financing 77, 91, 187, 336
- notes issue 94, 198
- relationship with Treasury 91, 188
Central powers 165, 211, 215
Chile 96
Churchill-Caillaux Agreement 340
Communist Party of Germany (KPD) 253
confiscation 18, 95, 96
conscription 17, 18, 111, 131, 309
consols 85, 147

credit crisis
- 1866 103
- 1931 240, 256
credit rating 84, 85, 88, 89, 119, 138-140, 152, 164, 171, 172, 177, 181, 185, 317, 323, 324
Creditanstalt 213, 239
Cuba 338
currency conversion 24, 70, 299, 300, 312, 316, 326, 333
Czechoslovakia 204, 208, 338, 346

Danat Bank 344
Dawes Commission 224
Dawes loan 240, 342
- amount 227, 232, 342
- and reparations 227, 242
- BIS 233
- bondholders 227, 276, 278
- bonds 228
- conversion 275
- excluded from moratorium 241
- gold clause 243
- interest rate 123, 227, 244, 275, 277, 351
- issue and subscriptions 227-229
- payments 242, 243, 273, 277, 279, 342, 344, 345, 350, 352
Dawes plan 224-227, 229-231, 236, 237, 275, 341-343, 345, 350
debts
- inter-ally 210, 211, 214, 280, 338
- inter-ally and reparations 209, 210, 213, 220, 230, 231, 233, 234, 237, 238, 241, 251, 339, 340
- inter-ally and Second World War 280
- inter-ally between Central powers 211
- inter-ally, amount 185, 199, 208, 211, 281, 346
- inter-ally, annuities 231, 232
- inter-ally, cancellation 213, 223, 234
- inter-ally, default 245
- inter-ally, payments on interest and principal 221, 222, 240, 244-249, 268, 280, 281
- inter-ally, settlement 218-221, 223, 237, 238, 244, 248-250, 253, 273, 301, 340
- international connectedness 185, 207-210, 213, 220, 223, 281, 340
- Prussian 275, 277
- Second World War 273
- servicing 253, 254, 256
- short-term 32, 91-93, 108, 132, 140, 143, 150, 162, 207, 229, 240, 255, 256, 260, 268, 270, 314, 335
- token payments 245, 247, 249, 346
deflation 93, 199, 207
Deutsche Bank 82, 217

discount rate; see: Bank of England – bank rate, etc.

dump store (army surplus) 77, 97, 134, 204, 205, 220, 222, 349

economy
- agriculture 16, 47, 105, 331
- and finance 16, 309
- distribution of wealth 19, 85, 88, 98, 207, 256, 337
- economic systems 17, 33, 60, 99
- international development 33, 233, 239, 241
- macro-economic level 297
- national income and national wealth 18, 20, 21, 74, 113, 207, 299, 310, 317
- price index 297, 352, 353
- state-owned companies 79, 259
- veil of money 310
- war economy 66, 75
- war industry 17, 20, 78, 92, 105, 113, 119, 145, 193, 259

Entente Cordiale 54, 171, 314

Entente powers 73, 74, 165, 211, 284, 287, 288, 290

Estonia 204, 221, 338, 346

Eurobonds 271

European Central Bank (ECB) 263, 271

European Coal and Steel Community 351

exchange rate 57, 119, 172, 214, 226, 299, 300, 316, 336, 353
- dollar-pound 300, 332, 337, 346, 352
- French *franc* 185, 205, 222, 266, 267, 322, 326, 337, 338
- German *mark* 167, 225, 231, 326, 338, 349
- Italian *lira* 337
- pre-war 300, 316, 319, 332
- risk 121, 175, 206, 337
- Russian *rouble* 299, 353

Exchequer bonds, see: United Kingdom, National War Bonds

Federal Reserve System (FED) 37, 156, 233, 263, 313, 322, 343
- history and organisation 157, 188, 194
- notes issue 91, 193
- war loans 154

Finland 212, 219, 221, 245-247, 249, 280, 346, 352

First National Bank of Chicago 343

First National Bank of New York 343

floating debt (see also: debts, short-term) 92, 137, 149, 162

Fort Knox 247

France 75, 77, 84, 89, 95, 143
- bank notes circulation 40, 136, 137, 187, 189, 190, 198, 266, 267, 319, 334, 335
- *bons de la défense nationale* 47, 136, 137, 139, 140, 142, 143, 149, 152, 162, 193, 199, 319, 325-327

- borrowing abroad, contribution to war financing 185
- foreign assets 177
- gold reserve 35, 335
- in Reparations Commission 339
- inflation 93, 121, 136, 139, 197, 265-268, 270, 318
- loans from Britain 135, 171, 268
- loans from the United States 135, 222, 247, 268
- national debt and budget deficits 32, 34, 59, 143, 144, 266, 311
- *obligations de la défense nationale* 110, 137-139, 142, 162, 177
- parliament 14, 46, 86, 190, 220, 222, 250, 267, 340
- reparations claim on Germany 20, 206, 209, 213, 223, 228, 255, 266, 267, 270, 343
- spending by foreign troops 177
- tax and tax system 86, 110, 111, 115, 266, 267
- Third Republic 38, 141, 326
- war damage 203, 212
- war expenditure 72, 73, 100, 336
- war loans 134, 137-142, 149, 162-164, 195, 198, 266
Frankfurt, Treaty 29, 310
French revolution 110, 136, 268, 312

General Electric Company 224
General Society (Generale Maatschappij van België / Société Générale de Belgique) 188
German Democratic Republic (DDR) 273, 276, 279
German Federal Republic (BRD) 250, 273-277, 279, 351
German National People's Party (DNVP) 217
German unification
- 1871 43, 106
- 1990 213, 275-279, 352
German-Austrian customs union 213
German-Austrian monetary union 81
Germany 75, 89
- Act on redemption of public debt (*Gesetz über die Ablösung öffentlicher Anleihen*) 264
- bank notes circulation 49, 50, 187, 189, 190, 195, 196, 198, 264, 313, 319, 325, 335
- borrowing abroad 143, 165-167, 185
- credit rating 240, 242, 243, 259, 274
- *Darlehenskassen / Darlehenskassenscheine* 47-51, 136, 162, 187, 189, 193, 199, 264, 314, 319
- East Prussia 129, 276
- economic miracle (*Wirtschaftswunder*) 276
- federal states 73, 74, 86, 107, 108, 317
- forced loan (*Zwangsanleihe*) 260
- foreign asstets 176
- foreign investments in Germany 228
- Founder Epoch (*Gründerzeit*) 33
- gold reserve 172, 341

- inflation 49, 92, 94, 108, 121, 128, 134, 158, 195-198, 206, 207, 259-265, 270, 271, 318, 325, 336, 348
- levy for national defence (*Wehrbeitrag*) 85, 107
- loans to allies 211
- *Matrikularbeiträge* 108
- National Committee for the German Referendum against the Young Plan and the War debt lie 344
- national debt account (*Reichsschuldbuch*) 261, 262
- national debt and budget deficits 108, 134, 143, 259, 261, 264, 311
- National Debts Administration (*Reichsschuldenverwaltung*) 50, 314
- National Debts Committee (*Reichsschuldenkommission*) 167
- national railway company (*Reichsbahn*) 259
- parliament 14, 44, 46-48, 50, 59, 69, 80, 86, 96, 107-109, 120, 131, 217, 236, 253, 264, 314, 317, 318, 325, 349
- party truce (*Burgfrieden*) 86, 108
- *Reichskassenscheine* 50, 314
- *Reichsmark* 263, 264
- *Rentenmark* 263
- *Schatzanweisungen* 137, 335
- tax and tax system 80, 85, 86, 106-110, 115, 259
- War Acts 46, 50, 51, 108, 189, 196
- war credits 46
- war expenditure 72, 73, 96, 100
- war loans 89, 93, 109, 126-128, 130-134, 140, 144, 146, 149, 161-164, 198, 323
gold 30, 31, 44, 57, 156, 166, 171, 172, 187, 189, 225, 245, 269, 313, 314, 319, 323, 338
- as collateral 172, 173, 178, 181
- British reserve 57, 173
- convertibility of bank notes 41, 42, 46, 54, 55, 91, 171, 188, 315, 335
- French reserve 35, 58, 172
- gold surrender campaign 20, 80, 189
- Russian reserve 181
- shipments from France to Britain 172, 332, 333
gold backing (bank notes)
- Britain 192, 335
- France 189, 191, 312, 331
- Germany 50, 189, 198, 314
gold clause 158, 243, 268-270, 314, 341, 351
Gold Standard 21, 93, 299, 310, 316, 350
- Britain 54, 55, 188, 241, 249, 257, 258, 270, 310, 315
- France 42, 171, 315, 331
- Germany 25
- United States 156, 269, 315
Greece 182, 221, 338, 346, 347

the Hague Conventions 40, 95, 96, 319
the Hague Conference on the Final Liquidation of the War 233-236
the Hague (Wassenaar) Claims Conference 274, 351
Hindenburg programme 18
Hoover moratorium 211, 222, 240, 241, 245-251, 256, 280, 346
HSBC 258, 335
Hudson & Manhattan Railroad Company 155
Hudson tunnels 155
Hungary 209, 211, 246, 247, 338, 346, 347, 350

import duties 107, 112, 113, 156, 205, 250
Indian subcontinent 179
Industrial Bank of Japan 343
inflation 92-94, 104, 120, 139, 162, 194, 198, 199, 253
-   Austria-Hungary 93, 94, 318, 347
-   Britain 93, 104-106, 119, 145, 146, 148, 195, 197, 255, 329
-   France 93, 121, 136, 139, 197, 265-268, 270, 318
-   Germany 49, 92, 94, 108, 121, 128, 134, 158, 195-198, 206, 207, 259-265, 270, 271, 318, 325, 336, 348
-   Germany 1870s 33, 311
-   hyperinflation 21, 94, 121, 196, 198, 206, 240, 259-264, 270, 271, 299, 347, 348
-   suppressed inflation 92, 193
-   taxation on capital 94, 336
-   United States 153
institutional investors 83, 118, 128, 129, 133, 144, 150, 162, 175
Inter-allied Rhineland High Commission 341
International Monetary Fund (IMF) 246, 275
Ireland 73, 163, 192, 255, 311, 318
Iron Curtain 247
Italy 34, 55, 67, 68, 75, 80, 84, 178, 179, 218, 226, 228, 343, 346
-   emigration to US 311
-   in Reparations Commission 339
-   international loans 23, 207-209, 211, 212, 221, 223, 337
-   loans from Britain 181, 182, 185
-   national debt and budget deficits 311
-   war expenditure 72, 73
-   war loans 161

J.P. Morgan & Co 170, 172-174, 178, 184, 227, 240, 332-334, 343
Japan 67, 343
Jekyll Island 313, 320
Johnson Act 245, 280, 346

Kaiserschlacht (Operation Michael) 133
Kreuger loan 351, 352

krone 70, 94, 299

Latin monetary union 21, 310

Latvia 204, 221, 338, 346

Lausanne conference and Lausanne Agreement 241, 242, 244, 273, 279

Lausanne, Treaty 209

legal tender 42, 45, 48, 91, 130, 153, 188, 192, 196, 325, 334

lend-lease construction 280, 346

Liberia 338

Liberty Loans; see: United States, war loans

Lithuania 204, 221, 338, 346

Liverpool 213

loans (see also 'war loans' and 'loans, international')
-   source for war financing 65, 77, 80, 83-86, 89, 97, 100, 117, 161, 165

loans, international from allies 73, 77, 83, 84, 97, 184, 185, 280
-   Belgium 184, 207, 208, 211, 212, 337, 339
-   Britain 184, 186, 207, 208, 211, 212, 219, 245, 338
-   France 135, 139, 171, 183, 184, 186, 206-208, 211-213, 219, 221, 223, 332, 338
-   interest rate 171, 183, 184, 206, 212, 219, 222, 223, 345
-   Italy 184, 207-209, 211-213, 221, 333, 337, 338
-   payments on interest and principal 212, 214, 218-220, 239, 241, 247, 346
-   Russia 184, 208, 211, 338

loans, international in private market 77, 83, 97, 180, 184, 185, 226
-   Britain 168, 172-175, 177-180, 184-186, 211, 333
-   collateral 83, 88, 175-179, 182, 185, 186
-   France 168-170, 173-175, 177-179, 186, 211
-   Germany 165, 166, 168
-   interest rate 173, 175, 178, 179, 182, 250

London Agreement on German External Debts 273, 275, 276, 279

London German Debt Conference 273-275, 278, 280

London, City & Midland Bank 258, 259

looting 95

Lusitania 170, 338

Luxemburg 323

Marne, battle 127, 142

Marshall Plan 273

Mefo-bills 90

Mellon-Bérenger Agreement 220, 222, 340

military commanders 14, 22, 58, 120
-   Britain 14
-   France 35, 39
-   Germany 14, 18, 40, 68, 81, 134, 180
-   United States 239

Military Commission of Control 341

mixed claims 338, 341, 352

mobilisation costs and mobilisation measures 22, 39, 40, 44, 48, 58, 91
monetary financing 15, 80, 91, 92, 94, 97, 165, 187, 197, 198, 204
- Britain 179, 195
- France 140, 198, 266, 336
- Germany 59, 109, 132, 198, 206
- United States 114, 336
moral pressure 17, 117, 118, 125, 131
moratorium 135
Morgan Grenfell 173, 332
Moscow, Treaty; see: Two-plus-four Treaty

National City Bank 169, 170
National Socialist German Workers' Party (Nazi Party, NSDAP) 236, 242, 344
Nazi regime 90, 217, 242-244, 274, 278
Netherlands 12, 71, 165, 166, 177, 185, 232, 263, 266, 269, 310, 323, 331, 338, 343, 345
Neuilly-sur-Seine, Treaty 209
neutral countries 21, 71, 119, 120, 132, 165, 166, 185, 232, 233, 300, 323, 338
New York Stock Exchange 156, 229, 233, 234, 268, 269, 315, 351
New Zealand 179
Nicaragua 338

Österreichisch-ungarische Bank 188
Ottoman Empire 73, 96, 181, 209, 211, 215, 253, 319
Overend, Gurney & Company 103

Panama Canal 59
Paris Peace Conference 212
patriotism 31, 89, 118, 125-127, 129, 133, 141, 159, 166, 189, 195, 257, 270, 323
payment ethics 249, 250, 270
Peace Palace 343
Poland 205, 208, 338, 346
printing press (bank notes); see: monetary financing
propaganda 94
Prudential Assurance Company 175
Prussia 47, 48, 107, 310, 314
Prussian National Bank 130

Reichsbank 47, 81, 82, 129, 166, 188, 216, 240, 315, 335, 336
- advances to the Treasury 49, 140, 194, 195
- and Darlehenskassen 49, 50
- and reparations 225, 230, 232, 236
- and war loans 126, 127, 129
- bank rate 240, 336
- gold stock 37, 43, 50, 172, 189, 240, 341
- history and organisation 43, 46, 130, 263, 313

- independence 55, 130, 196, 336
- notes issue 48, 130, 187, 189, 195, 260, 313
- War Economy Papers (*Kriegswirtschaftliche Blätter*) 336
- war preparation 43-45, 59, 130
Reichstag; see: Germany, parliament
rentier 139, 143, 177, 265, 326
reparations 33, 82, 84, 95-97, 198, 209, 225
- Agent General 230, 232
- as a source for war financing 18, 77, 96
- Austria 209, 343
- Bulgaria 209
- commercialisation 32, 227
- Franco-Prussian War 29-35, 44, 59, 215, 227, 323, 339, 341
- Germany 51, 209, 214-216, 218, 223, 224, 242, 244, 261, 275, 278-280, 317, 319, 338, 339, 343, 348, 352
- Germany, amount 57, 210, 214-218, 224, 230, 231, 236, 242, 243, 260, 261, 266, 339, 342-344
- Germany, and inter-ally debts 199, 209, 210, 213, 220, 223, 231, 233, 234, 237, 238, 241, 251, 253, 255, 281, 340
- Germany, cancellation provision 215
- Germany, capacity to pay 215, 218, 224, 225, 235, 249, 339, 342
- Germany, commercialisation 237, 317
- Germany, payments 209, 222, 226-229, 232, 233, 240, 244, 259, 341-344, 348-350
- Germany, reduction 210, 223, 224, 230, 231, 234, 236
- Germany, Second World War 275, 276, 279
- Germany, termination 242, 244, 249, 273, 278
- Hungary 209
- in cash 218, 226, 236, 244
- in gold 226, 341
- in kind 218, 226, 236, 244
- London Agreement / scheme 217, 218, 224, 225
- Ottoman Empire 209
- Reparations Commission 215, 216, 218, 230, 233, 339-341
- Rumania 319
- Russia 198, 319
- Transfer Committee 225, 230, 232
Rhineland occupation 236, 342
roaring twenties 256, 268, 269
Rothschild (bank) 171, 335
rouble 299, 353
Royal Bank of Scotland 125
Ruhr occupation 218, 223, 224, 230, 263, 267, 340
Rumania 208, 209, 223, 346
Russia 23, 55, 67, 68, 75, 77, 93, 143, 174, 216, 237, 253, 316, 335
- bank notes circulation 187

- borrowing abroad 171, 178, 181
- February Revolution 132, 133
- gold reserve 36, 312
- loans from Britain 180-182, 208, 333
- loans from France 181
- mobilisation 142
- October Revolution 142
- parliament 14, 85
- pre-war bonds 142
- railways 35, 59, 142, 177
- reparations imposed by Germany 198
- state monopoly 80
- tax and tax system 80
- war expenditure 72, 73
- war loans 161
- war preparation 80

Saint-Germain-en-Laye, Treaty 209
Sarajevo 55, 135
Saxony 107
Scandinavia 71, 165, 166, 177, 311
schilling 299
Schlieffen Plan 313
Scotland 163, 192, 318
Sénat; see: France, parliament
Senate; see: United States, parliament
Serbia 182, 299, 338
Sèvres, Treaty 209
Silesia 276
sinking fund 87, 123, 164, 268, 348
Social Democratic Party of Germany (SPD) 107, 321
Somme, battle 132, 148, 178, 331
South Africa 179
Soviet Union 274
Spanish flu 65, 160, 203
standstill agreements 240, 345
stock exchange crash
- Germany 1873 33, 311
- Wall Street 1929 229, 233, 234, 268, 269, 351
submarine war 132, 151, 154, 180
Suez Canal 59
Sweden 232, 323, 338, 343
Switzerland 71, 165, 166, 177, 243, 266, 323, 338, 344

tariff; see: import duties

tax
- as collateral 80
- evasion 87
- exemption (see also 'war loans') 113, 137
- in occupied territories 95, 97
- income tax 60, 78, 85, 86, 101, 104-106, 108, 110-115, 124, 156, 158, 259, 322
- indirect 86, 101, 104, 106-108, 110, 112, 113, 115
- inflation 94, 97, 197, 198, 336
- inheritance tax 104, 125, 152
- on luxury goods 20, 86, 101, 104, 106
- property tax 78, 86, 101, 108
- reallocation effects 88
- source for war financing 65, 77, 79, 85, 97, 99, 105, 106, 114, 115, 165, 213
- turnover tax 86
- war profits and excess profits 101, 105, 106, 109, 111, 113-115, 193, 204, 259, 266
taxpayer 60, 78, 88, 142, 184, 221, 223, 249, 256, 270, 281, 282, 318, 321
transfer problem 225-227, 232, 245, 246, 276
treasury bills and treasury notes 91, 97, 162, 207
- Britain 149-151, 255, 315, 328
- France 136, 137, 139, 140, 142, 143, 149, 152, 162, 169, 171, 193, 199, 319, 325-327
- Germany 128, 132, 264, 326
- United States 154
Trianon, Treaty 209
Turkey 211, 215
Two-plus-four Treaty 273, 279, 280

Ukraine 237
UN Security Council 246
United Kingdom 77, 84, 89
- Admiralty 102, 105, 314
- bank notes circulation 105, 191, 192, 198, 319, 335
- Board of Trade 314
- borrowing abroad, contribution to war financing 185
- British Expeditionary Force (BEF) 170, 309
- Cabinet Committee on the co-ordination of military and financial effort 332
- Committee of Imperial Defence (CID) 54
- Commonwealth 23, 73, 208, 245, 334, 337
- credit rating 245, 249, 254, 255, 270
- Currency and Bank Notes Act 335
- currency notes 191, 192, 199, 335
- Desart Committee 54
- financial war preparation 192
- foreign assets 175, 176, 179, 185, 186
- gold reserve 197, 312

- Gold Standard 310
- in Reparations Commission 339
- inflation 93, 104-106, 119, 145, 146, 148, 195, 197, 255, 329
- loans from the United States 245
- loans to allies 223, 280
- loans to France 171, 179, 185, 207, 208, 332
- loans to Russia 185
- Ministry of Munitions 101, 314
- national debt and budget deficits 143, 144, 254-256, 311, 347
- National War Bonds 149, 152, 162
- parliament 14, 54, 87, 117, 122, 145, 175, 176, 318, 323, 327, 328, 332
- Post Office Savings Bank 144, 146
- reparations claim on Germany 20, 255
- Royal Navy 100, 309
- spending by troops abroad 177
- tax and tax system 86, 99, 102, 105, 106, 115, 255
- Treasury Bills 149-151, 315
- war expenditure 73, 99, 100, 106, 114, 115
- War Expenditure Certificates 328
- war loans 138, 143-151, 152, 161-164, 204, 281, 328
- War Office 314
- War Savings Committees 148
- ways & means advances 149, 335
United States 165, 180
- bank notes circulation 156, 160, 188, 191
- Certificates of Indebtedness 154, 162
- credit rating 270
- entry into the First World War 112, 132, 143, 151, 153, 179-182, 185, 186, 193
- Federal Land Bank 157
- Federal Reserve Act 156
- immigration 33, 311
- in Reparations Commission 339
- inflation 153
- isolationism 214, 274
- Liberty Bond Acts 338
- loans to allies 154, 181, 204, 206-209, 212, 222, 249, 338
- loans to allies, amount 182, 184, 204, 211, 212, 280
- loans to allies, conditions 181, 183, 206, 213, 218
- loans to allies, repayment 221, 244, 246
- national debt and budget deficits 281, 311, 352
- National Women's Liberty Loan Committee 159
- neutrality 61, 112, 113, 115, 153, 166, 168, 169, 179, 193, 338, 340
- parliament 46, 112, 114, 156, 182, 183, 213, 219, 221, 241, 245, 246, 269, 281
- private capital market 166, 168-170, 173, 175, 178, 179, 185
- spending by troops abroad 177

- Supreme Court 112, 269
- tax and tax system 86, 99, 112-115, 269
- Trading with the enemy Act 315
- war expenditure 72, 73, 100, 115, 203
- war loans 153, 154, 157, 159-163, 184, 204, 221, 249, 268, 269, 297
- War Revenue Act 114, 330
- World War Foreign Debt Commission 219

Verdun, battle 132, 178, 331
Versailles, Treaty 29, 32, 57, 143, 162, 204, 209-215, 218, 227, 233, 236, 237, 242, 279, 280, ...
    338, 339, 347
Victory Loan; see: United Kingdom, war loans
Victory Liberty Loan; see: United States, war loans
Vittorio Veneto, battle 70

Wales 103
War
- Boer War 60, 153, 320
- Civil War (US) 112, 153, 158
- Cold War 24, 273, 274, 279, 281
- Crimean War 60, 117, 271
- Franco-Prussian War 29, 32-35, 43, 48, 133, 153, 215, 318
- Napoleonic wars 54, 96, 101, 213
- Nine Years' War 13
- Second World War 24, 39, 57, 90, 219, 243, 246, 247, 250, 251, 273, 276, 279-281, 319,
    337, 346
- War of Independence (US) 183, 320
war chest 43, 44, 59, 74, 77, 313
war credits 68
war expenditure 71, 75, 99, 203, 297, 301, 309
- after Armistice 204
- allocation 15, 67, 68
- and war costs 15, 16, 18, 19, 177
- as a share of GDP 15, 72, 75
- concept 65, 66
- data 68-70
- defining 66, 74
- interpretation 72
- mobilisation 44
- money costs 15, 65, 70, 71, 73
- pre-war budgets 14
- pre-war estimates 74, 75
war guilt issue 9, 29, 207, 210
war loans (domestic) 83, 97, 161, 162, 197
- amount and term 122-124, 128, 264, 268, 349

- and collateral 84, 136, 193, 325
- appeal factors 117, 124, 134, 138, 140, 142, 152, 153, 159, 261, 262
- as a referendum 89, 90
- Austria-Hungary 324
- Britain 122-125, 138, 143-152, 162-164, 204, 281
- conversion 124
- conversion, Britain 146-148, 153, 255-258, 270, 281, 328, 347
- conversion, France 138, 143
- conversion, Germany 264
- conversion, United States 154, 159, 161, 268, 270, 329
- denominations 126, 144, 146, 262
- France 119, 121, 123, 125, 134, 137-142, 149, 162-164, 195, 198, 266, 330
- Germany 93, 120-128, 130-134, 140, 146, 149, 162-164, 198, 264, 330
- interest rate 118-120, 122, 124, 127, 163, 323
- interest rate, Britain 144, 146, 148-152, 255- 257, 281, 315, 327, 328
- interest rate, France 119, 121, 135, 136, 138-141, 323, 326, 343
- interest rate, Germany 126-129, 163
- interest rate, United States 153, 154, 159, 160, 212, 329, 333
- issue price 119-121, 124, 128, 131, 138, 139, 141, 144, 149, 323, 328, 348
- Italy 330
- payments on interest and principal 19, 87, 88, 115, 118, 119, 121, 164, 207, 271, 323
- payments on interest and principal, Britain 148, 152, 153, 255, 256, 270, 281, 282
- payments on interest and principal, France 111, 266
- payments on interest and principal, Germany 109, 134
- payments on interest and principal, United States 158, 184, 268
- perpetual 87, 123, 139, 163, 257, 281
- propaganda 83, 117, 126, 127, 131, 133, 139-141, 145-148, 153, 159, 161, 323
- pros and cons 85-89
- small savers 124, 128, 129, 131, 135, 144-146, 148, 160, 162, 262
- source for war financing 77, 117, 161, 165
- subscriptions 18, 21, 89, 90, 118, 122, 124-126, 162, 325
- subscriptions, Britain 144, 146, 147, 152, 327
- subscriptions, France 325
- subscriptions, Germany 129, 131, 133
- subscriptions, United States 154, 159, 160, 329, 330
- tax exemption 110, 124, 138, 143, 148, 159, 161, 163, 328, 329
- United States 123-125, 153, 154, 157, 159, 160, 162, 163, 204, 212, 249, 268, 269, 297, 330
war profits 20, 88, 109, 111, 115, 119, 148, 162
war ships 13, 66, 67, 96, 100, 102, 144, 298, 315, 345, 352
Weimar Republic 83, 216, 242, 261, 348, 351
World Bank 246, 275

Young loan 240, 342
- amount 232, 342
- and reparations 242

- BIS 233
- bondholders 276, 278
- bonds 228
- conversion 275
- excluded from moraorium 241
- gold clause 243
- interest rate 232, 275, 277, 342, 351
- issue and subscriptions 229, 232, 235, 343
- payments 242, 273, 277, 279, 344, 345, 350, 352
Young plan 224, 230-233, 235, 236, 239, 343-345
Yugoslavia 204, 212, 223, 338, 346

Zimmermann & Forshay 167

List of illustrations

1.1 Phases in the military/political development of the First World War and its financial counterpart 22

2.1 France's already relatively high national debt increased rapidly after the Franco-Prussian War 32

3.1 The *Banque de France* systematically built up her gold reserve; it was permanently far ahead of the German Reichsbank in a kind of financial arms race 37

3.2 The Blue Circular: 'act with calmness, alertness, initiative and determination; ...and cease issuing gold immediately!' 41

4.1 Examples of the scientific discussion in Germany about war financing before the Great War 45

4.2 *Darlehenskassenschein*, a source of paper money. The note bears the date 5 August 1914, one day after the German Parliament voted on the Act introducing the notes, an indication of a thorough preparation 48

5.1 Financial and military mobilisation measures 58

6.1 There are several ways to express the total money costs of the First World War. In 1913 prices, the sum was roughly $ 80 billion 71

6.2 The United States and Britain paid almost half of the total money cost of the war, as measured in 1913 dollars [in brackets $ amounts per capita] 73

6.3 Only a few pre-war estimations approximated the real expenditure 74

7.1 The principal war financing mechanisms in a simplified picture 79

7.2 Massive subscriptions to war loans meant massive popular support; to the boys in the trenches: you too, subscribe, please! 90

7.3 In 1916 German war finance went out of control. Short-term debts (depicted in the illustration) increased rapidly and the semi-annual war loans were less and less sufficient to reduce it 93

8.1 The major part of war expenditure in the First World War was financed with loans, not from taxes 100

9.1 Posters for war loans: patriotism, moral pressure and investment 118

9.2 Cultural differences in war loan conditions 121

9.3 Revenues from German war loans reflect ups and downs at the military theatres; the trend is upwards if measured in marks, but corrected for inflation the trend is unmistakably downwards from September 1915 133

9.4 Movie star Marie Lohr buys a War Bond at a 'Bank Tank' placed in Trafalgar Square as part of a propaganda campaign, March 1918 147

9.5 The turning point in the interest rate on 3 months British Treasury bills: the Americans are coming! 151

9.6 Fund raising American style: star tenor Enrico Caruso raises $ 2.2 million for the third Liberty Loan in a night at the opera with the assistance of the French Tricolour and a group of French 'Blue Devils' from the trenches 160

9.7 Almost half of the money from large domestic war loans was raised in Britain and the United States; nominal values in own currency [in brackets indicative amounts in billions of 1913 dollars] 161

9.8   Practically all countries used long-term and short-term loans parallel to each other; the illustration presents comparable types of loans by country; banknotes have been included as additional information only 163

10.1   British advances from J.P. Morgan & Co. increased at an average speed of $ 25 million per month from May 1916 until finally the American government itself acted as the main war creditor (April 1917) 174

10.2   During 1916 and early 1917 the British government borrowed extensively in the American private capital market against high interest rates and with securities as collateral 179

10.3   Britain and France used United States government credits to buy food, ammunition and clothing; figures in million dollars 183

10.4   American entry into the war was a turning point for France and Britain in their possibilities to borrow abroad 186

11.1   In Germany, an abundance of paper money drove out coins from circulation 190

11.2   In France, the amount of banknotes grew considerably as well 190

11.3   In Britain, currency notes added considerably to the notes in circulation 191

11.4   In the United States, FED notes in circulation multiplied 191

12.1   When hostilities ended, money flows went on; American expenditure for the war peaked in December 1918, after the Armistice 204

12.2   At the end of the war a complex system of inter-ally debts had been built up; this would only grow in the following years by reconstruction and relief loans 208

12.3   The two mutually affecting issues: the inter-ally debts and German reparations 210

12.4   While Britain started paying off its debt to the United States, France applied all sorts of arguments to wriggle out 221

12.5   Dawes and Young bonds 228

12.6   Private investors in many countries subscribed to the international loans in 1924 and 1930, by which Germany paid part of its reparations 229

12.7   Successive reparation schemes became more and more specific, while the amounts decreased 234

12.8   Exhausted politicians in the early morning hours at the Hague Conference on the Young plan, January 1930 235

12.9   A short chronology of events in international debt reduction after the First World War, part I: 1918-1930 238

13.1   From July 1931 on, repayments of European allies on their war debts to the United States stuck at 7.5% of the agreed amount 248

13.2   Timetable of developments in the debt problem after the Hoover moratorium until the Second World War 252

14.1   During the First World War Britain's public debt increased more than in any other recent war 254

14.2   Inflation in France was generally high in the 1920s, often in double digits 265

14.3   Immediately after the war, the French franc depreciated quickly; subsequently in the period 1920-1920 the exchange rate fell once more with over 50% 267

14.4   All belligerent countries failed to some extent in meeting their domestic war debt obligations; some countries failed completely 271

15.1 After the London Debt Conference of 1953, bondholders of the original 1924 Dawes and 1930 Young loans received a claim to compensate for unpaid interest by the Nazi regime; the claim could be cashed 'in the event of the reunification of Germany' 278

15.2 In 2010, Germany made the final payments on the loans related to the First World War: nearly € 70 million, an amount negligible as compared to the actual debt burden 278

A.1 Exchange rates for some currencies 299